D0706867

Crisis
Intervention
and
Time-Limited
Cognitive
Treatment

Crisis Intervention and Time-Limited Cognitive Treatment

Albert R. Roberts
Editor

SAGE Publications
International Educational and Professional Publisher
Thousand Oaks   London   New Delhi

For information address:

 SAGE Publications, Inc.
2455 Teller Road
Thousand Oaks, California 91320
E-mail: order@sagepub.com

SAGE Publications Ltd.
6 Bonhill Street
London EC2A 4PU
United Kingdom

SAGE Publications India Pvt. Ltd.
M-32 Market
Greater Kailash I
New Delhi 110 048 India

Printed in the United States of America

Library of Congress Cataloging-in-Publication Data

Roberts, Albert R.
    Crisis intervention and time-limited cognitive treatment / Albert
  R. Roberts, editor
      p. cm.
    Includes bibliographical references.
    ISBN 0-8039-5629-0. — ISBN 0-8039-5630-4 (pbk.)
    1. Crisis intervention (Psychiatry) 2. Brief psychotherapy.
3. Cognitive therapy. I. Title.
RC480.6.R63 1995
616.89′14—dc20   95-4420

This book is printed on acid-free paper.

95 96 97 98 99 10 9 8 7 6 5 4 3 2 1

Sage Production Editor: Diane S. Foster

DISCARD

Brief Contents

Detailed Contents

PART III: Crisis Intervention With Diverse Client Groups

Acknowledgments

First and foremost, I would like to thank all of the authors who wrote original chapters for this book. They deserve my sincere gratitude.

To Sophia Dziegielewski, one ot the most diligent and brilliant co-authors with whom I have ever collaborated, I extend my deepest appreciation.

I appreciate the support and encouragement of C. Terry Hendrix, Senior Editor. I also thank him for engaging me in a provocative dialogue about the life-saving nature of 24-hour crisis hotlines.

I am also grateful to Diane Foster, the Senior Production Editor who skillfully and patiently guided all our efforts. As a result of her friendly reminders, meticulous care for detail, and expert assistance, this book was produced on schedule.

Finally, special acknowledgment goes to Lenny Friedman and his marketing staff for their intensive promotional efforts.

PART I

Overview

Foundation Skills and Applications of Crisis Intervention and Cognitive Therapy

ALBERT R. ROBERTS

SOPHIA F. DZIEGIELEWSKI

DOMESTIC VIOLENCE

A case that has raised almost immediate and unprecedented attention to the scene of domestic violence as probability for the outcome of homicide is the case of O. J. Simpson and Nicole Brown Simpson. This case has brought America's attention to the already proclaimed probability that domestic violence has no boundaries based on age, race, income, and social status. It continues to permeate the mesh of our society, and can and does happen in the wealthiest of families. Excerpts of a terrified Nicole Brown Simpson and her 911 telephone calls begging for help echo in our minds, and a distraught O. J. Simpson, the accused killer of his wife Nicole, reportedly holding a gun to his head in a car chase on national television, remind us of the seriousness and intensity of the aftereffects that can surround this type of relationship. To further highlight the intensity, in this battering relationship as in so many others that surround domestic violence, O. J. Simpson in his 1995 book

3

(with Schiller) titled *I Want to Tell You* refers to his relationship with his wife as so important that he could consider dying in her place. As stated by Dziegielewski and Roberts in Chapter 4, *"Many times the stalker is consumed with . . . intense feelings of anger and fear about the uncontrollable desire felt toward the victim."*

In this case, determination of the guilt of O. J. Simpson remains up to the jury. Currently, the only thing that remains questionable from a legal standpoint is who committed the violent murders of Nicole and her male friend, Ronald Goldman. Now, based on the typology of the profile provided by Roberts and Dziegielewski in Chapter 4, could O. J. Simpson possibly fit the profile of the *domestic violence stalker* described there? And, if so, could a form of crisis intervention and time-limited treatment have helped to address this situation before any violence erupted? Unfortunately, at this late date, only the jury can officially decide the fate of O. J. Simpson. Yet, few people seem to be focusing their attention on how early and strategically placed therapeutic intervention could have altered and possibly prevented this pattern of violent abuse.

SURVIVORS OF RAPE

Tennessee law has had a "rape by fraud" clause listed in the state's criminal statutes since 1989 (Schmitt, 1995). This clause was included to convict men who pretend to be their victim's husbands or unscrupulous professionals who convince their patients that having a sexual relationship is treatment. In this statute, it is stated that rape is unlawful sexual penetration accompanied by any one of the following circumstances: (a) Force or coercion is used to accomplish the act; (b) the defendant knows or has reason to know that the victim is mentally defective, mentally incapacitated, or physically helpless; or (c) the sexual penetration is accomplished by fraud (Schmitt, 1995). According to Schmitt (1995), however, legal experts have been able to find few cases of this law being used in the case of fraud.

Recently, in the state of Tennessee, there has been a stir of controversy surrounding the case of Raymond Mitchell III, also known as "Fantasy Man." Fantasy Man is known to have called numerous women during the late night whispering words of seduction to the sleepy women and convincing them that he is a love interest of theirs, generally a boyfriend or someone the woman is dating. He then tries to convince the woman to allow him to come over and enact a fantasy lovemaking scene. The fantasy he describes is to make love to the woman while she is blindfolded and waiting for him in the dark. He tells his female victim that as part of the fantasy, she must pretend he is a stranger and that no words are to be spoken. He further instructs the woman not to discuss what happened during their fantasy time together unless he (Fantasy Man) mentions it first. After the sexual fantasy has been completed, he simply leaves the woman's home. If upon a second call the woman does not seem to suspect the fraud, he again entices her into another similar fantasy experience.

Fantasy Man, a married man with two children, openly admits that he has been calling women and trying to talk them into having sex acts since the 1970s. In his defense, however, he states that the acts Fantasy Man commits are consensual and there is no pretense of his being anyone other than a mystery man on the telephone. In 1989, however, Fantasy Man was charged with calling a coworker and pretending to be a man she had dated earlier in the week. The woman, however, recognized, when he drove up, that Mitchell was not the man she had dated the week before. While he knocked on her door for entry, she telephoned police. Charges were filed and Fantasy Man was indicted on a charge of attempted rape and received 2 years probation. Since then, seven women have reported to police that they have received calls late at night from a man pretending to be their boyfriend and trying to involve them in sex acts. Three other women have reported actually having sex with the man and not realizing until either during or after intercourse that the man was a fraud. Mitchell has admitted calling all 10 of these women—but denies tricking any of them.

The most recent case is that of a 26-year-old women who had sexual relations with Fantasy Man just one time. She states that she was tricked into believing he was a love interest but that soon after he touched her she knew it was not her lover. She stated that she did not resist because she feared for her life. After talking with a friend, she called the police. The victim in this scenario, like that in many other cases of rape, asked herself why she allowed this to happen and regretted not doing something differently to have prevented it (Schmitt, 1995, p. 10A).

The courts must now decide whether or not this is rape. Does it meet the criteria for the current statute definition? It is important to note, however, that no matter what the outcome, the victim believes it was *rape,* and she will need help to deal with the aftermath of this traumatic event. Chapter 5 of this book, by Patricia Resick and Mindy Mechanic, will discuss how professionals can assist victims of these crimes of violence to deal with this trauma.

The case of Nicole Brown Simpson and that of the alleged victims of Fantasy Man are used to portray current traumatic events in our society that can cause acute psychological crisis or life-threatening events. The primary purpose of this book is to integrate and present the latest information about crisis intervention and time-limited cognitive treatment strategies applied to persons in acute psychological crisis or life-threatening situations. The two major reasons for stressing this type of treatment focus are (a) the practice requirements and limitations that therapists are encountering in the practice setting and (b) the need to find the best way to satisfy (as quickly as possible) the individual needs and requirements of the traumatized client.

In regard to the practice setting, a growing number of therapists and counselors are being forced to use similar theoretical orientations and techniques. The primary reason for this trend toward conformity is increasing limitations placed by health insurance providers on the number of reimbursable sessions per client with particular diagnoses. Many times, specific goals and treatment plans will be required for direct reimbursement from third-party payers. Therefore, professional counselors are being forced not only to be consistent in their treatment modalities but to do their best to resolve their client's problems in the shortest amount of time possible (Wells, 1994).

The second area to be addressed in this book, and probably the most important of the two, is how to best satisfy (as quickly as possible) the individual needs and requirements of the traumatized client. Millions of individuals throughout the world are traumatized and subsequently victimized by rapists, terrorists, or murderers, and/or required to cope with such problems as AIDS, depression, heart attacks, the death of a loved one, natural disasters, and unemployment. Unfortunately, the vast majority of the millions of people whose lives are affected by hazardous and traumatizing events leave them doubly vulnerable to crisis reactions.

It is important to note that many individuals in our society still may either deny the fact that they have a serious mental health problem or avoid contacting a clinician. Unfortunately, this hesitancy means that professional help is often sought only after the problems have escalated into a full-blown crisis. Therefore, this book has been developed to fill the knowledge gap created by the everyday requirements of the practice environment and to determine the best way to satisfy the needs of the traumatized client. Each of the chapters in this book was written to provide in-depth information on the latest applications of crisis intervention and the time-limited cognitive treatment approach.

In this book, the short-term effects and impact of crisis events, as well as recent applications of crisis intervention and time-limited cognitive therapy, are examined. In recent years, as supported in the case examples depicted in this book, we have seen an extraordinary increase in attention to acute psychological and situational crisis. Today, due to practice limitations and the emphasis on efficiency and effectiveness, models employing either cognitive or cognitive-behavioral techniques are viewed as essential modes of treatment used by many mental health professionals in the United States and Canada. There appears to be a growing awareness of the need for a review of the principles and techniques of brief clinical intervention with survivors of crisis events. Both crisis intervention and cognitive treatment strategies have been found to be successful with survivors of rape, woman battering, community disasters, or attempted murder, as well as the millions of people suffering from depression, domestic abuse, unemployment, or life-threatening illness.

THE FOUNDATION OF CRISIS INTERVENTION AND TIME-LIMITED COGNITIVE THERAPY

Crisis Theory: The Beginning

Although the emergence of a cohesive theory of crisis management did not develop until the 20th century, crisis intervention theory can be traced to its roots in and elements from antiquity. In ancient Greece, the word for *crisis* came from two root words, one meaning "decision," and the other meaning "turning point." Likewise, in the Chinese language, there are two Chinese symbols in the ideograph for crisis. One represents danger and the other represents opportunity. Implicit in these definitions is the historical and universal message that crisis can bring breakthrough—as well as breakdown. Although crisis can contain the seeds of growth and impetus for change, the strong emo- tions generated can also bring about strong dysfunctional reactions.

In viewing the acquisition of crisis skills as normal social develop- ment, Eric Erikson postulated that all human beings will experience normal and maturational crises over the course of their lives. He as- serted that an individual's ability to solve the key psychosocial crises in his eight-stage developmental model could influence the individual's future ability to master maturational crisis in subsequent stages. Moreover, he offered the idea that crisis and major life transitions were similar in composition; however, the variation in degree and intensity remain the stuff of which life is made (Erikson, 1950).

Over the years, there have been numerous mental health profes- sionals that have made contributions in regard to the development of present-day crisis theory. For example, military psychiatrists in World War II learned that soldiers suffering from "combat neurosis" who were given prompt treatment and had support from their buddies and supe- riors were more resilient and could return to combat (Golan, 1972). This was further exemplified in examining the effects on American soldiers who returned from Vietnam. Based on these events related to combat stress, the Army implemented a plan in the Saudi conflict that put social work professionals near the forefront of the fighting at the Battalion Aid stations. There, these professionals could provide immediate support and reassurance, assisting the soldiers to quickly recover from the trauma of battle and return to the fighting area.

Generally, however, the mental health practitioner most often re- ferred to as a pioneer in crisis theory is Eric Lindemann, who not only gave mental health treatment a new understanding of crisis but also pioneered a systematic approach to treating it. Among his contributions was his initial and classic study of bereavement. It focused on family members after a fire in Boston in which nearly 500 people perished. He and his team of professionals worked intently with the 101 survivors as well as bereaved family members. It is this work and his resulting report on the psychological symptoms of the survivors that became the corner- stone for subsequent theorizing on the grief process, particularly on how individuals accept and resolve loss (Lindemann, 1944; Roberts, 1990a).

Based on these observations of the acute and delayed reactions of survivors and the unresolved grief among the relatives, Lindemann

(1944) asserted that acute grief was a natural and necessary reaction to a significant loss. He characterized loss generally as brief, acute, and with identifiable onset. But he found that the duration, severity, and resolution of the bereavement process depended on the extent to which each survivor or relative could complete a series of phases. He named this continuum "grief work." It consisted of a mourning period, or emancipation from bondage to the deceased; an eventual acceptance of the loss, or a readjustment to the environment in which the deceased is missing; and, later, a period when the survivor is able to form new relationships (Dixon, 1979). Perhaps most important, this study caused him to conclude that "a crisis in and of itself is not normal or pathological but that the inattention to or delay of the normal process of grief work might have a negative or psychopathological outcome" (Roberts, 1991b, p. 5).

A second psychiatrist from the Harvard School of Public Health and a close associate of Lindemann was Gerald Caplan. His interest in crisis intervention evolved from his work with immigrant mothers and children in Israel after World War II. Caplan built on Lindemann's constructs of grief and loss and extended them to the larger category of universal human reactions and traumatic events. In Caplan's purview, *crisis* refers to one's emotional reaction and not to the situation itself (Ewing, 1978). Although crisis is naturally an individual matter, he identifies an accidental precipitant, such as the loss of a loved one, as universally crisis provoking. In agreement with Lindemann, he stated that crisis is not, in itself, a pathological state, but a struggle for adjustment and adaptation in the face of problems that are, for a time, unsolvable (Ewing, 1978). He did state, however, that an examination of the history of psychiatric patients shows that, during certain of these crisis periods, these individuals seemed to have dealt with their problems in a maladjusted manner and to have emerged less healthy than they had been before the crisis (Whitlock, 1978). It is important to note that this may have contributed to today's recognition that persons in crisis will frequently restore equilibrium—whether it is a healthy balance or not.

Defining Crisis and Crisis Intervention in Treatment

The term *crisis* has been defined as a temporary state of upset and disequilibrium, characterized chiefly by an individual's inability to cope with a particular situation using customary methods of problem solving and by the potential for positive or negative outcome (Roberts, 1990a). According to Burgess and Baldwin (1981), "When the individual experiences an emotionally hazardous situation and is unable to effectively utilize previously learned coping behaviors . . . then an emotional crisis may ensue" (p. 26). This is further supported by Roberts (1990a), who stated that a person in a crisis state has experienced a hazardous or threatening event, is in a vulnerable state, has failed to cope and lessen the stress through customary coping methods, and thus enters into a state of disequilibrium.

It is important to note, however, that any definition of the term *crisis* must remain somewhat subjective because what precipitates a crisis state in one individual might not generate such a response in another (Roberts, 1990a). A state of crisis occurs when an individual perceives an event as a threat to need fulfillment, safety, or meaningful existence. In other words, the term *crisis* usually refers to a person's perception or feelings of fear, shock, and distress about the disruption rather than the disruption itself (Roberts, 1990a). This leads to the premise that underlies crisis intervention. Through the techniques used in crisis intervention, the crisis situation can eventually be reformulated within the context of growth—ultimately reaching a healthy resolution where the individual can emerge with greater strength, self-trust, and sense of freedom than before the crisis event occurred (Burgess & Baldwin, 1981).

According to Golan (1972), when providing intervention, the onset of crisis situations can be identified as having several predictable characteristics. First, the formation of a subjectively defined or precipitant tied to a hazardous event can develop. Second, this can result in severe upset or disequilibrium in which previous methods of problem solving break down and the active crisis or debilitating emotional response can occur. During this phase, however, the potential for hope and expectancy emerge. Third, it is useful to note that the development of a potential link between crisis and other unresolved conflicts may begin to surface. Fourth, this results in the opportunity for the specified intervention to break the linkage between this crisis and other unresolved crises, and instead implement new coping methods. Finally, the individual who enters into a crisis state will be restored to some type of homeostasis, and some form of resolution of the problem will result within 4 to 6 weeks (Golan, 1972; Roberts, 1990a). This makes the immediate and short-term nature of the intervention essential.

Crisis intervention theory and practice were designed to address the exact characteristics of the crisis situation. It is a dynamic form of treatment that focuses on a wide range of phenomena that affect an individual's, family's, or group's equilibrium. Although it includes elements specific to its own model, it has been referred to and used as an essentially eclectic approach (Fischer, 1978).

Crisis intervention addresses itself to acute problem situations and often has universal applications. Its purpose is always to help the individual discover an adaptive means of coping with a particular crisis. Time is always crucial. As will be highlighted in this book, it has been used in a wide range of primary and secondary settings and with many different individuals and groups. Settings include crisis intervention units, schools, mental health centers, rape crisis and sexual assault treatment centers, and hospital emergency rooms. Populations that are served include potential suicide victims, natural disaster survivors, rape survivors, the unemployed, and the terminally ill.

The Importance of Time-Limited Treatment

A second characteristic of crisis intervention is that it is a form of short-term treatment (Wells, 1994). The time-limited nature of crisis intervention is important because the state of crisis is by its nature self-limiting (Dziegielewski & Resnick, in press; Roberts, 1990a). Time-limited intervention is intended to accomplish a set of therapeutic objectives with a sharply limited time frame and its effectiveness appears to be indistinguishable from that of long-term treatment (Bloom, 1992). According to Parad et al. (1990), using minimum therapeutic intervention during the brief crisis period can often produce maximum therapeutic effect. These authors suggest the use of supportive social resources and focused treatment techniques to facilitate therapeutic effectiveness (Parad et al., 1990).

The Role of Time-Limited Cognitive Intervention

In the early 1970s, the importance of applied behavioral analysis and the power of reinforcement in influencing human behavior was explored (Skinner, 1953). Many theorists believed that this explanation alone was not enough, however, and that human beings acted or reacted based on an analysis of the situation and the thought patterns that motivated them. In cognitive therapy, the important role of the thought process and how individual emotions are influenced by cognitive processes and structures is highlighted. When exploring the roots of cognitive therapy, the work of Aaron Beck (1991) is often described. Dr. Beck and his colleagues postulated how to use this form of therapy in addressing numerous mental health problems (Beck & Emery with Greenberg, 1985; Beck, Freeman, & Associates, 1990; Beck, Rush, Shaw, & Emery, 1979; Beck, Wright, Newman, & Liese, 1993). In this book, the authors in each chapter have applied some form of intervention using cognitive therapy in regard to specific time-limited crisis intervention techniques. According to Beck et al. (1990), all individuals form *schemas*. As children enter into the social world, they are presented with events that create the basis for the development of their early childhood experiences. These experiences are transformed into what an individual believes to be true within certain limits or conditions. The *schema* that develops is referred to as the cognitive structure that organizes experience and behavior (Beck et al., 1990). Schemas involve the way individuals view certain aspects of their lives including relationship elements such as adequacy and the ability of others to love them. Once these schemas have been formulated as part of normal development, the individual progressing in the normal life process will be exposed to critical incidents. These critical incidents will be interpreted and thus reacted to by the individual. This reaction will be based on the basic and conditional beliefs that the individual has developed and incorporated into his or her schemas. The schema that one subscribes to will have a profound effect on the behaviors and emotions that are exhibited.

The literature supports the concept that individuals develop different styles or patterns of information processing based on their life experiences, and these schemas may influence an individual's reaction, resulting in cognitive distortion when interpreting a current situation or event (Beck et al., 1979; Burns, 1980). Beck et al. (1979) discussed the types of systematic errors that can lead to emotional distress. The first systematic error identified was termed *arbitrary inferences*. Here an individual may reach conclusions that are not based on accurate supporting evidence. For example, in the case of domestic violence, a woman might conclude, "Father hit mother and they loved each other, therefore, my husband hits me because he wants to show how much he loves me."

The second type of systematic error was termed *selective abstractions*. Here an individual focuses on one or more details in a situation that are taken out of context while seeming to ignore the more pronounced features of the incident or situation. For example, in a rape situation, a woman might tell herself, knowing that the man who assaulted her also had a previous record of assault on elderly women, "If my dress was not so short, I could have avoided this situation happening to me." The length of her dress may or may not have attracted attention to herself; however, the woman seemingly ignores that this has happened to other women who may not have been wearing skirts at all.

The third cognitive distortion that results in systematic error in thinking is the process of *overgeneralization*. When committing this type of error, the individual draws a global generalization from a single and possibly isolated incident. For example, the unemployed worker may say to him- or herself, "Because I am unemployed and cannot find a job, I will also become a failure at other aspects of my life such as my marriage, parenthood, and so on."

The fourth type of systematic error is termed *magnification and minimization*. Here the individual distorts the reality of what has happened, inappropriately representing the magnitude of what has actually transpired. For example, in the case of stalking, the erotomaniac stalker may magnify a situation that has transpired, seeing the victim as in love with him or her because the victim said hello or smiled. In minimization, the victim of the stalker might not take seriously the acts of the stalker, stating: "It is just a crush and he or she will just give up."

In *personalization*, an individual relates external events to him- or herself with no basis for such connections to be made. For example, in the case of alcohol abuse, a woman married to an alcoholic might tell herself, "If I only loved him more, maybe he would not have felt so insecure that he was forced to drink."

The final systematic error in thinking is defined as *absolutist, dichotomous thinking*. Here the individual seems to perceive experiences in an intense manner. This person may tend to polarize thoughts and reactions. For example, in the case of the stalker, "If I do something wrong, no matter how small, the person I love will hate me."

Based on an individual's early childhood experience, schemas are formed that reflect the basic and conditional beliefs an individual has. These schemas provide the framework in which an individual will react to the critical events in his or her life. A traumatic incident clearly can constitute the occurrence of a critical event. The way an individual perceives this event remains subjective (Roberts, 1990a), and building on the basic premise of cognitive therapy, an individual's perceptions may or may not be problematic. Therefore, understanding the schema a person subscribes to is essential. Individuals can and do distort reality based on how it is perceived, and these cognitive distortions can result in negative feelings, maladaptive behaviors, and, if carried to the extreme, psychopathology (Liese, 1994).

Goals of Cognitive Treatment in Crisis Intervention

When dealing with a client who has experienced trauma, it is important to establish the goals and behavioral objectives of the treatment strategy. Simply stated, a goal constitutes what you and the client want to accomplish, and the behavioral objectives state exactly what you plan to do to address the identified goal(s). It is important to note, however, that many professionals do not make the fine distinction between *goals* and *objectives* and often use the terms interchangeably.

Cormier and Cormier (1991) stress the importance of clearly defined goals in direct practice. They see goals as providing direction and structure for the professional practice of intervention. This is particularly important when dealing with individuals in the crisis situation, because often these individuals feel the distress and the desire for change but lack the ability to establish direction for their efforts.

Goals also permit the practitioner to establish whether he or she has the skills and/or desire to work with the client (Cormier & Cormier, 1991). It is important in time-limited crisis intervention to be sure that the individual will be able to secure the services that are needed and, in turn, to ensure that the therapist is able to help the client focus in on change efforts that will allow the client to return to a previous level of functioning. The goals and behavioral objectives chosen also help to outline the needed intervention and the particular practice strategies and techniques that will be needed. Finally, goal setting is a crucial element in measuring the effectiveness of treatment because it can provide the standards against which progress is measured (Brower & Nurius, 1993).

Brower and Nurius (1993) suggest two key characteristics that need to be present when designing effective intervention goals. First, goals need to be specific, clear, verifiable, and measurable. This remains consistent with crisis intervention, where the established goals need to be as concrete and behavior specific as possible. The objectives therefore should be designed to further quantify the goals. For example, if an individual is suffering from a grief reaction, the therapist would want the goals and objectives to be specific to what will help to restore equilibrium.

A second major point made by Brower and Nurius (1993) reminds us of the importance of the established goals being mutually agreed upon by both the helping professional and the client. This may seem difficult at times in crisis intervention when the helping professional may be required to take on an extremely active role to help the client. This role, however, should always be one of facilitation, in which the client is helped to achieve what he or she has deemed essential to regain an enhanced homeostatic balance. Clients must also contribute so as to determine whether the goals and objectives sought are consistent with their own culture and values. It is up to the therapist to help clients structure and establish the intervention strategy; however, emphasis on mutuality is central to the development of goals and objectives.

In the actual designing of the intervention format, the role of the helping professional is essential in ensuring that the problem that needs to be dealt with is addressed. Goals should always be stated positively and realistically so that motivation for completion will be increased (Brower & Nurius, 1993). It is also essential, in order to establish the effectiveness of what is being done, that the goals (particularly the objectives) be stated in as concrete and functional terms as possible. In setting the appropriate goals in the crisis intervention setting, the focus is not on process but on the outcome that is desired.

Crisis Intervention and Treatment Strategies

We now know that acute crisis events can be identified, controlled, and lessened. Successful resolution can be achieved when clinicians apply the established crisis intervention and cognitive therapy models to persons in emotional crisis. To a greater extent, in recent years, we have been able to document the positive outcomes of therapeutically working through an individual or group crisis. Most mental health practitioners now agree in recognizing crisis as an opportunity for change.

Stages of crisis intervention

Generally, in the application of a crisis intervention approach, the first stage involves assessment to identify the triggering or precipitating event, or particular problem that started the chain of events leading to a crisis state. The second stage involves helping the person in crisis to prioritize his or her concerns. The first and second stages of treatment often lead to what is referred to as the middle phase of treatment. In this middle phase, the crisis intervention approach should focus on encouraging the person in crisis to talk to the counselor about the event, understand and conceptualize the meaning of the event, and integrate the cognitive, affective, and behavioral components of the crisis (e.g., case examples and implementation strategies are discussed in Chapters 4 through 10). The third stage of treatment, which generally ends the middle phase, consists of helping the person in crisis to problem-solve and find effective coping methods.

In the middle phase of treatment, therapists are encouraged to view a psychological crisis as both danger and opportunity. Generally, when an individual is in this crisis phase, he or she is open to the future and has heightened motivation to try new coping methods. It is important to remember that the outcome of a crisis is either a change for the better or a change for the worse. Although uncomfortable, this active crisis state provides an important turning point. A critical question is this: What makes one crisis event result in growth or positive change and another result in harmful psychological problems? Certain types of crisis events have extremely high potential for precipitating a crisis state in an individual, such as being raped or being diagnosed HIV-positive. It is important to note, however, that the outcome of a crisis can rely heavily on an individual's personal resources, problem-solving skills, and adaptability in withstanding sudden intensely stressful life events. In addition, one's social support network is critical in negotiating an adaptive turning point. Crisis resolution is often facilitated if the individual in crisis has a significant other who can provide support and reassurance in a nonjudgmental way. As the mental health professional works with the individual in crisis, these issues must be addressed and support systems identified.

In conclusion, in the final stage of treatment, whether the client is seen in person or counseled on the phone (as a hotline caller), the client needs to be prepared to deal with recurring problems stemming from the original crisis event. For example, violent crime victims may experience flashbacks or intrusive thoughts about the victimization 1 month and/or 1 year after being mugged and raped (see Chapter 5 by Resick and Mechanic). It becomes essential to prepare the victim for common reactions such as being terrified over a loud piercing noise or cringing at the sound of a screaming actor or actress on the television. In the final session, it is also useful to help the violent crime victim decide on the best person to turn to for support in dealing with delayed or post-traumatic reactions if they should develop, even if at the current time they have not occurred. The working through of the actual traumatic event and integrating oneself was the primary goal in the middle phase of the crisis intervention strategy; but now, in the final phase of treatment, emphasis is placed on the ability of an individual to adapt and/or restore him- or herself to a balanced state—preferably one that exhibits restored levels of confidence and coping.

In the application of crisis intervention, it is important to note that psychological trauma can be understood as an "affliction of the powerless" (Herman, 1992, p. 33). Threat to life and bodily integrity overwhelms normal adaptive capabilities, producing extensive symptomatology. Adopting a pathological view of symptomatology is not helpful; it is more beneficial when clients can comprehend their symptoms as signs of strength. Symptoms that are understood as coping techniques developed by the survivor to adapt to a toxic environment can enhance self-esteem (Dziegielewski & Resnick, in press). Focusing away from the term *victim* and reenforcing the term *survivor* may help in building self-esteem and making the client feel as though he or she is a winner rather than a loser (Dziegielewski & Resnick, in press).

APPLICATION OF ROBERTS'S
SEVEN-STAGE CRISIS INTERVENTION MODEL

Effective intervention with trauma survivors in crisis requires a careful assessment of individual, family, and environmental factors. A crisis by definition is short term and overwhelming. According to Roberts (1990a), a crisis can be described as an emotionally distressing change. The crisis can cause a disruption of an individual's normal and stable state in which the usual methods of coping and problem solving do not work.

Roberts (1991b) describes seven stages of working through crisis: (a) assessing lethality and safety needs, (b) establishing rapport and communication, (c) identifying the major problems, (d) dealing with feelings and providing support, (e) exploring possible alternatives, (f) formulating an action plan, and (g) providing follow-up. Roberts's seven-stage model applies to a broad range of crises and is often used as the framework for time-limited cognitive treatment throughout the book.

To enhance the application of this crisis intervention model to practice, the therapeutic environment is characterized by the following: (a) a here-and-now orientation, (b) a time-limited course (typically 6 to 12 sessions), (c) a view of the adult survivor's behavior as an understandable (rather than a pathological) reaction to stress, (d) the assumption by the mental health worker of an active and directive role, and (e) the overall strategy to increase the individual's remobilization and return to the previous level of functioning (Dziegielewski & Resnick, in press).

Stage 1: Assessing Lethality

There are many hazardous events that can initiate a traumatic response. Listed below are some of the hazardous events or circumstances that can be linked to the recognition or reliving of traumatic events. These events have the likelihood of triggering anxious responses from clients so that they seek help, even if the traumatic event is not immediately identified as the crisis issue: (a) growing public awareness of the prevalence of the traumatic event or similar traumatic events, (b) the acknowledgment by a loved one or someone that the client respects that he or she has also been a victim, (c) a seemingly unrelated act of violence being committed on them or someone they love such as rape and/or sexual assault, (d) the changing of family or relationship support issues, and (e) the sights, sounds, or smells that trigger events from the clients' past (these can be highly specific to individuals and the trauma experienced).

Immediate danger. With the number of suicides on the rise, intervention requires careful assessment of suicidal ideation and the potential for initial and subsequent hospitalization and/or medication. Questions to elicit pervasive symptomatology should be asked (e.g., depression, suicidal ideation, anxiety, eating disorders, somatic complaints, sleep disorders, sexual dysfunction, instances of promiscuity, substance abuse, psychological numbing, self-mutilation, flashbacks, and panic attacks). Based on age and the circumstances in which the trauma was experienced, the client's living situation should be assessed to assure that the client is not still in danger and an adequate support system does exist. Several structured and goal-oriented sessions may be needed to help the client move past the traumatic event, generating an understanding that what happened in regard to the traumatic event may have been beyond his or her control.

In these initial sessions of therapy (sessions 1-3), the goal of the therapeutic intervention is recognizing the hazardous event and acknowledging what has actually happened. For some reason (based on the triggering catalyst), the survivor of trauma is currently being subjected to periods of stress that disturb his or her sense of equilibrium. (It is assumed that the individual wants to maintain homeostatic balance, and physically and emotionally the body will seek to regain equilibrium.) Often, as stated earlier, the survivor may not present with the actual crisis event, and the mental health counselor may have to help the survivor get to the root of the problem (i.e., the real reason for the visit). During these initial sessions, the survivor becomes aware and acknowledges the fact that the trauma has occurred; once this happens, the survivor enters into a vulnerable state. The impact of this event disturbs the survivor, and traditional problem-solving and coping methods are attempted. When these do not work, tension and anxiety continue to rise and the individual becomes unable to function effectively. In the initial sessions, assessment of both past and present coping behaviors of the survivor are important; however, the focus of intervention clearly must remain in the "here and now." The mental health worker must attempt to stay away from past issues or unresolved issues unless they relate directly to the handling of the traumatic event.

Stage 2: Establishing Rapport and Communication

Many times, survivors of trauma feel as though they have been abandoned by family and friends, or that they are being punished for something they did or did not do. These unrealistic interpretations may result in feelings of overwhelming guilt. It is possible that the capacity for trust has been damaged and this may be reflected in negative self-image and poor self-esteem. A low self-image and poor self-esteem may increase the individuals' fear of further victimization. Many times, survivors of trauma question their own vulnerability and know that revictimization remains a possibility. This makes the role of the counselor in establishing rapport with the client essential.

Whenever possible, the mental health professional should proceed slowly and try to let the survivor set the pace of treatment. Let the client lead because he or she may have a history of being coerced, and forcing confrontation on issues may not be helpful. Allowing the client to set the pace creates a trusting atmosphere that gives the message: "The event has ended, you have survived, and you will not be hurt here." Survivors often need to be reminded that their symptoms are a healthy response to an unhealthy environment (Dziegielewski & Resnick, in press). They need to recognize that they have survived heinous circumstances and continue to live and cope. Trauma survivors may require a positive future orientation, with an understanding that they can overcome current problems and arrive at a happy, satisfactory tomorrow (Dolan, 1991). Hope that change can occur is crucial to the survivor's well-being.

Perhaps more than anything else, throughout each of the sessions, these clients need unconditional support, positive regard, and concern. These factors are especially crucial to the working relationship given that a history of lack of support, "blaming," and breach of loyalty are common. The therapeutic relationship is seen as a vehicle for continued growth, development of coping skills, and the ability to move beyond the abuse (Briere, 1992).

Stage 3: Identifying the Major Problems

Once the major problems relevant to the particular event are identified and addressed, the concept of support remains essential. Group participation has been effective as well as journal writing, relaxation techniques, physical exercise, and development of an understanding that the victim needs to be good to him- or herself at this time.

In these next few sessions (sessions 3-6), the mental health worker needs to assume a very active role. First, the major problems to be dealt with and addressed must be identified. These problems must be viewed in terms of how they have affected the survivor's behavior. The effects and consequences of this type of trauma are discussed. Here, the precipitating factor, especially if the event was in the past, must be clearly identified. Complete acknowledgment of the event can push the person into a state of active crisis marked by disequilibrium, disorganization, and immobility (e.g., the last straw). Once the survivor enters full acknowledgment, new energy for problem solving will be generated. This challenge stimulates a moderate degree of anxiety plus a kindling of hope and expectation. This actual state of disequilibrium can last four to eight weekly sessions or until some type of adaptive or maladaptive solution is found.

Stage 4: Dealing With Feelings and Providing Support

The energy generated from the survivor's personal feelings, experiences, and perceptions steer the therapeutic process (Briere, 1992). It is critical that the therapist demonstrate empathy and an anchored understanding of the survivors' world. Their symptoms are seen as functional, and as a means of avoiding abuse and pain. Even severe symptoms such as dissociative reactions should be viewed as a constructive method of removing oneself from a harmful situation and exploring alternative coping mechanisms. Survivors' experiences should be normalized so they can recognize that being a victim is not their fault. In this stage (sessions 6-8), the survivor begins to reintegrate. The survivor gradually begins to become ready to reach a new state of equilibrium. Each particular crisis situation (i.e., incest, rape, and so on, including type and duration) may follow a sequence of stages that can generally be predicted and mapped out. One positive result from generating the crisis state in stage three is that in treatment, after reaching active crisis, survivors seem particularly amenable to help.

Once the crisis situation has been reached, distorted ideas and perceptions regarding what has happened need to be corrected and information updated so that the client can better understand what he or she has experienced. Victims eventually need to confront their pain and anger so that they can develop better strategies for coping. Increased awareness helps the survivor to face and experience contradicting emotions (anger/love, fear/rage, dampening emotion/intensifying emotion) without the conditioned response of escape (Briere, 1992). Throughout this process, there must be recognition of the client's continued courage in facing and dealing with these issues.

Stage 5: Exploring Possible Alternatives

Moving forward requires traveling through a mourning process (generally in sessions 8-10). Sadness and grief at the loss need to be experienced. Grief expressions surrounding betrayal and lack of protection permit the victim to be open to an entire spectrum of feelings that have been numbed. Now, acceptance, letting go, and making peace with the past begins.

Stage 6: Formulating an Action Plan

Here, the mental health worker must be very active in helping the survivor to establish how the goals of the therapeutic intervention will be completed. Practice, modeling, and other techniques such as behavioral rehearsal, role-playing, and writing down one's feelings as well as an action plan become essential in intervention planning. Often, survivors come to the realization that they are not at fault or to blame. The doubt and shame regarding what their role was and what part they played become more clear, and the self-fault less pronounced. Survivors begin to acknowledge that they did not have the power to help themselves or to change things. Often, however, these realizations are coupled with anger at the feelings of being helpless to control what has happened to them. The role of the mental health professional becomes essential here in helping clients to look at the long range consequences of acting on their anger and in planning an appropriate course of action. The main goal of these last few sessions (sessions 10-12) is to help the individual reintegrate the information learned and processed into a homeostatic balance that allows him or her to function adequately once again. Referrals for additional therapy should be considered and discussed at this time (i.e., additional individual therapy, group therapy, couples therapy, family therapy).

Stage 7: Follow-Up Measures

This area is very important for intervention in general, but one that is almost always forgotten. In the successful therapeutic exchange, significant changes have been made for the survivor in regard to his or her previous level of functioning and coping. Measures to determine whether these results have remained consistent are essential. Often, follow-up can be as simple as a phone call to discuss how things are going. Follow-up within 1 month of termination of the sessions is important.

Other measures of follow-up are available but require more advanced planning. A pretest/posttest design can be added to the design simply by using a standardized scale at the beginning of treatment and then later, at the end. Scales to measure depression, trauma, and so on are readily available. See Corcoran and Fischer (1994) for a thorough listing of measurement scales that can be used in the behavioral sciences.

Finally, it is important to realize that at follow-up many survivors may now realize that they want additional therapeutic help. After they have adapted to the crisis and have learned to function and cope, they may find that they want more. After all, returning survivors to a previous state of equilibrium is the primary purpose for the application of this brief crisis intervention therapy. If the client does want more, the mental health worker should be prepared to help the client become aware of the options for continued therapy and emotional growth by giving the appropriate referrals. Referrals for group therapy with other survivors of similar trauma, individual-growth-directed therapy, couples therapy that is to include a significant other, and/or family therapy should be considered.

FUTURE DIRECTIONS

Violent crime, domestic violence, AIDS, unemployment, depression, and suicide are six of the most serious problems facing our nation today. In the United States, there are over 6 million violent crime victimization attempts reported each year by the Bureau of Justice Statistics (1992), and one in five Americans of typical working age (18-65) were unemployed sometime during 1991 (Pomice, Black, Collins, & Newman, 1992).

As of July 1993, there were 194,000 AIDS-related deaths and 315,000 new reported cases for the first 6 months of 1993 (Centers for Disease Control, 1993). The World Health Organization estimates that there will be 40 million cases of AIDS throughout the world by the end of the decade, and, as of 1991, we had 1.5 million documented cases of AIDS in the United States (Treatment Team, 1991).

Over 30,000 suicides take place each year in the United States. In addition, there are between 150,000 and 200,000 suicide attempts each year. According to the latest epidemiological Catchment Area study, over 15.1 million people suffer from affective disorders—bipolar, unipolar, major depression, and dysthymia (Manderscheid, Rae, Narrow, Locke, & Reiger, 1993; Narrow, Reiger, Rae, Manderscheid, & Locke, 1993; Reiger et al., 1993). Finally, a total annual prevalence rate of 15.05 million cases of alcoholism and chemical dependency have also been reported (Manderscheid et al., 1993; Reiger et al., 1993).

As depressing as these numbers may sound, learning to live and deal with crisis situations and events is a necessity for the 1990s. Many times, changes in social policy are postulated as a means to address change in the current structure. Three policy change strategies that have been proposed for resolving this are as follows: (a) There could be a resolution to pass legislation that would create jobs for everyone (e.g., welfare mothers, high school dropouts, unemployed college graduates); (b) there could be a resolution to spend more money (at least $300 billion a year) to thoroughly research and find cures for cancer, AIDS, and other deadly diseases; and (c) there could be a resolution that all convicted terrorists, rapists, armed robbers, and murderers are exiled to a newly created Devil's Island—with no means of escape. Obviously, none of these radical resolutions would work. We do, however, contend that an important partial solution is currently gaining slow but steady momentum throughout the nation. We believe that a large part of the mental health problems that affect our country could be lessened or, better yet, eliminated through increased mental health treatment for all Americans. Unfortunately, to finance such a plan, insurance reimbursement must be pursued. It is true that as the number of people suffering from anxiety and depressive disorders, self-destructive acts, and life-threatening illnesses has steadily risen, so has the need for counselors, social workers, and psychologists.

Talk about universal health care coverage (similar to that in England) and a single-payer reimbursement system (similar to the one in Canada) still echoes luminously in the background of our managed-care environment. The proposal submitted by the National Association of Social Workers entailing a single-payer health care delivery system that includes benefits for mental health and long-term care remains unheeded, as do the other proposals with it (Gorin & Moniz, 1992; Ross, 1992). These plans offered much promise for the future; unfortunately, the implementation of either a single-payer system or one of universal health care coverage continues to lie dormant. The reality of the "managed care" environment over the originally proposed single-payer system remains intact. Realistically speaking, it will probably take at least another decade before comprehensive universal national health insurance is passed and funded in the United States.

In the meantime, crisis interventions and time-limited cognitive therapy lasting from 1 to 20 sessions offer the most promise for meeting the urgent psychosocial and crisis-related needs of persons in distress. Based on the crisis situations that exist in our current environment, clients need the help and assistance that can only be given by competent professionals, and professionals need to have the tools to provide this much needed service. This book has been written in hopes of providing just that. We strive to provide an overview of crisis that highlights the importance of using time-limited cognitive approaches in dealing with these inevitable crisis events and situations.

OVERVIEW OF THE BOOK

Each chapter documents the theme that a crisis situation provides an opportunity, a challenge, and a sudden turning point when the client is willing to make one more attempt to regain equilibrium and begin recovery. The ability to stay calm and self-assured, to be an active listener, empathic and nonjudgmental, accepting and focused, and aware of options and alternative coping methods for crisis callers is not inherited. The knowledge base and skills of crisis intervention come from education, training, and experience. This book is intended to facilitate graduate students' and therapists' acquisition of time-limited treatment concepts and skills. Acute crisis events, clinical issues, crisis intervention, and short-term treatment approaches are examined through current and detailed case illustrations.

Part I of the book provides a national perspective on the functions of crisis intervention and cognitive therapy with depressed individuals, suicide attempters, individuals with life-threatening illnesses, battered women, sexual assault survivors, unemployed persons, and survivors of disasters. The introductory chapter by Albert Roberts and Sophia Dziegielewski is designed to provide not only an overview of the book but also an overview of the use and strategy of time-limited cognitive therapy. The second chapter by Bruce Liese invites the reader to integrate crisis theory, crisis intervention, and the need and use for triage in the mental health treatment and medical environment. The third chapter, by Albert Roberts, is designed to provide the reader with a description and overview of the structure and functions of 107 crisis intervention units and centers throughout the United States.

Part II of the book provides a national perspective on the practice of crisis intervention with high-risk groups, including stalking victims, sexual assault survivors, and groups in hostage situations. This part provides specially designed chapters on the application of both individual and group crisis intervention approaches as well as time-limited modalities used at women's centers, rape crisis programs, battered women's shelters, criminal justice settings, and by independent private practitioners.

Chapter 4 on stalking, by Sophia Dziegielewski and Albert Roberts, presents a typology for the identification of stalking victims complete with case scenarios. Legal issues and the application of crisis treatment with this population are explored. Chapter 5 on assisting the victims of rape, by Patricia Resick and Mindy Mechanic, deals with the issues of crisis management and cognitive processing therapy provided for sexual assault survivors. Chapter 6 on victims of hostage situations, by Thomas Strentz, stresses the importance of realizing the stress and danger the hostage is exposed to, and examines survival strategies.

Part III of this book focuses on crisis intervention strategies with diverse client groups ranging from survivors of community disasters and mass murders to persons with AIDS. Chapter 7 by Marlene Young explains the crucial role of crisis response teams and how these teams participate in issue identification and provide treatment and support to the survivors. Chapter 8 by Ann Abbott deals with strategies for dealing with clients who are experiencing the impact of unemployment. She explores the unemployment literature and the dynamics that surround individuals who find themselves in this situation, and provides a framework formulating a time-limited practice strategy to assist these clients. Chapter 9 by Elaine Congress deals with the crisis situations that particularly affect the lives of women. Identification of and treatment for problems such as AIDS and depression are highlighted. Chapter 10 by Grace Christ, Rosemary Moynihan, and Les Gallo-Silver deals with a crisis that has reached pandemic proportions and will at some point either directly or indirectly affect every human being on this earth. Treatment strategies and issues for the patients infected with AIDS and their families are presented.

The last part of the book, Part IV, contains two chapters on crisis lines and 24-hour hotlines. The first chapter in this part, Chapter 11 by Judith Waters and Eric Finn, focuses on how best to handle telephone crises addressing callers who are identified as cocaine abusers, suicide attempters, people with other medical emergencies, and persons who have been diagnosed as HIV-positive. Chapter 12, by Anne Horton, identifies 10 of the most common sexual problems that callers present. The book ends with the Appendix, which provides the reader with a national directory of crisis hotlines.

I am pleased to announce that, since 1990, several volumes have been published on crisis intervention; other books have been published on brief treatment strategies. This, however, is the first up-to-date volume presenting a wealth of information on 24-hour crisis hotlines, crisis intervention units, as well as the cognitive therapy approaches used by Ph.D., Psy.D., D.S.W., and M.D. therapists; licensed clinical social workers (L.C.S.W.s); behavioral clinicians (M.A.s or M.Ed.s); and trained crisis intervenors (B.A. level).

Integrating Crisis Intervention, Cognitive Therapy, and Triage

BRUCE S. LIESE

Crises yield rich opportunities to reach new heights and higher levels of functioning if they are encountered fully and if all available resources are drawn upon to resolve them. On the other hand, if crises are avoided or handled inappropriately, they may lead to depths of depression never before experienced.

Robert R. Carkhuff (1969, p. 71)

In his classic work over 25 years ago, Carkhuff (1969) discussed the role of crises in counseling and psychotherapy. He explained that crises tended to motivate individuals to seek mental health services, potentially resulting in personal changes and growth: "While crises or the anticipation of crises lead the individual to seek help, they also provide the potential vehicle within the helping process that will enable him to go on to function at higher, self-sustaining levels" (p. 70).

Since Carkhuff's work, multiple texts have appeared that have addressed crisis intervention (e.g., Aguilera & Messick, 1982; Dattilio & Freeman, 1994; Greenstone & Leviton, 1993; Hoff, 1989; Janosik, 1984; Kliman, 1978; Roberts, 1990b, 1991a; Rosenbluh, 1986). The purpose of this chapter is to expand on this work by applying the concepts of cognitive therapy and triage to crisis intervention. In the next section, crisis and crisis intervention are defined. A brief overview of cognitive therapy (CT) is provided. Next, CT is woven into Roberts's crisis intervention steps. And, finally, "triage" is offered as a decision-making strategy for crisis intervention. Triage involves the evaluation of individuals in crisis to make decisions about their treatment.

DEFINING CRISIS
AND CRISIS INTERVENTION

Roberts (1990b) describes a crisis as an emotionally distressing change or a "turning point in a person's life" (p. 8). He also characterizes a crisis as "a period of psychological disequilibrium" (Roberts, 1991a, p. 4). Numerous circumstances can trigger crises, including psychiatric, medical, legal, career, and family problems. All individuals are potentially vulnerable to crises and most adults have experienced crises in their lives. The following case examples illustrate several individuals in crisis.

Tim was 34 years old and married with three children when he lost his job as an electrician. His family had relied on him exclusively for financial support. In response to unemployment, Tim lost confidence in himself. He became tense, nervous, and worried. Eventually, he reported that he had become "too uptight to even look for a job."

Jack was a 59-year-old businessman when he suffered a massive heart attack. Though Jack's doctors strongly encouraged him to participate in extensive cardiac rehabilitation, Jack argued that he "couldn't afford to do so." He prematurely returned to work, risking his life and ignoring the advice of friends, family members, and physicians.

Marcia was a 21-year-old college student who had suffered from chronic depression as a teenager. While walking home from college classes one day, she was attacked and raped by a stranger. In response to this event, she became despondent, withdrawn, and isolated. Her crisis was only discovered when a faculty member noticed that Marcia was not attending classes.

These are just a few case examples of commonly occurring crises. Each represents an individual's experience of disequilibrium (i.e., disruption) in his or her life.

Crisis intervention is defined as any therapeutic strategy that helps an individual to cope (i.e., adapt effectively) in a crisis. Crisis interventions vary widely in their duration. An individual in a minor crisis might require only a brief encounter (i.e., 30 minutes) with a crisis worker. In a more complicated crisis, however, an individual may require hours across multiple sessions just to establish a therapeutic relationship and define a central problem. Roberts (1990b), from his review of the crisis intervention literature, has developed a seven-step approach for helping individuals in crisis. The following is a summary of Roberts's seven steps:

1. Rapidly establish the relationship.
2. Examine the dimensions of the problem.
3. Encourage exploration of feelings and emotions.
4. Explore and assess past coping attempts.
5. Explore alternatives and specific solutions.
6. Restore cognitive functioning through implementation of an action plan.
7. Follow up.

Roberts's (1990b) steps provide an excellent structure for crisis intervention, with emphasis on establishment of the therapeutic relationship and problem definition. In this chapter, cognitive therapy (CT) and triage are integrated with Roberts's structure and model.

COGNITIVE THERAPY

The choice of cognitive therapy for crisis intervention is based on its successful application to a wide variety of clinical problems, including depression (Beck et al., 1979), anxiety (Beck et al., 1985), marital problems (Beck, 1988), personality disorders (Beck et al., 1990), and substance abuse (Beck et al., 1993; Liese, 1994). Recently, Liese and his colleagues have applied cognitive therapy to the crises associated with life-threatening illnesses (Liese, 1993; Liese & Larson, 1995) and substance abuse (Liese, 1994). Dattilio and Freeman (1994) have devoted an entire text to cognitive-behavioral strategies in crisis intervention.

Cognitive therapy, developed by Dr. Aaron T. Beck, provides a comprehensive psychological theory and specific methods for helping individuals with psychological and behavioral problems. Cognitive therapy is based on the premise that individuals' behaviors, feelings, and physiological responses are mediated by cognitive processes, including basic beliefs and automatic thoughts (Beck et al., 1979, 1985, 1990, 1993). For example, individuals experiencing depression are likely to hold such basic beliefs as "I am unlovable" or "I am inadequate" (Liese, 1993, 1994). These beliefs, which develop early in life, tend to be activated by critical incidents. Thus, when Marcia (from the above example) was raped (a critical incident), she experienced a major depressive episode. Marcia's critical incident activated such latent beliefs as "I'm basically stupid" and "I deserve to be punished." Another person might have responded to the same critical incident with anger and outrage rather than depression. Feelings of anger might have corresponded with the beliefs that "I was unjustly violated!" or "He had no right to do that to me!"

Jack, from the above example, held the conditional belief that his worth was based on his ability to earn a high income. Conditional beliefs take the form: "If I _____, then _____." Consequently, Jack's heart attack served as a critical incident that activated his conditional belief: "If I don't provide for my family, I am a failure." This belief contributed to his emotional crisis and related maladaptive behaviors (e.g., his premature return to work).

Unemployment was the critical incident that activated one of Tim's beliefs about his inadequacy: "I can't do anything right." He predicted that he would ultimately fail: "No one will want to hire me!" As a result, he experienced tension, nervousness, anxiety, and avoidance. Some individuals in similar circumstances but with more positive basic beliefs might have experienced unemployment as an opportunity to make some positive changes in their lives.

Freeman and Dattilio (1994) describe eight features of cognitive therapy that make it "ideal for crisis intervention" (p. 5). Specifically, cognitive therapy is

1. *active* (both therapist and patient take a participatory role in the intervention process);
2. *directive* (the therapist sometimes acts as a resource, a case manager, and an advocate for the patient);
3. *structured* (the therapist remains focused on the patient's agenda);
4. *short term* (time is used in an efficient manner);

5. *collaborative* (the therapist and patient are expected to work as a "team");
6. *dynamic* (the therapist promotes the patient's self-disclosure and self-understanding);
7. *psychoeducational* (the process is focused on skill-building); and
8. *social/interpersonal* (the therapist is attentive to the patient's relationships).

In addition to these features, there are many others that make cognitive therapy extremely appropriate for crisis intervention. First, CT has been applied successfully to numerous clinical problems (e.g., depression, anxiety, substance abuse, marital problems, family problems, and severe psychiatric disorders). Second, CT is time-efficient, with each CT session highly structured and focused. And, third, CT provides practical and useful strategies for conceptualizing and treating complex emotional problems. In the next sections, CT is described in more detail.

Cognitive therapy is composed of five components (Liese, 1994): a collaborative therapeutic relationship, an accurate case conceptualization, therapeutic structure, socialization of the patient (i.e., education), and cognitive-behavioral techniques. These components are introduced in this section and they are further discussed later in this chapter.

The Collaborative Therapeutic Relationship

Collaborative therapeutic relationships are essential to effective crisis intervention. Collaboration occurs when therapists and patients *share responsibility* for crisis definition and resolution. Because individuals in crisis experience heightened levels of vulnerability and dependency, effective therapists encourage them to take significant responsibility for resolving their own crises. In contrast, some clinicians are tempted to take charge or rescue individuals in crisis. These clinicians may offer simple solutions to complex problems or they may give superficial reassurances such as the following: "Things will turn out OK" or "Everything happens for a reason." When such shortcuts are offered, individuals in crisis are unlikely to feel validated and they may not experience ownership of their problems or the solutions to their problems. As a result, they may be more vulnerable to premature dropout, relapse, or the development of maladaptive dependencies on therapists.

Even in their early formulations of cognitive therapy, Beck and his colleagues highlighted the importance of the collaborative therapeutic relationship. They emphasized the importance of warmth, accurate empathy, and genuineness in the therapeutic relationship and they related these characteristics to the development of a "milieu in which the specific cognitive change techniques can be applied most effectively" (Beck et al., 1979, p. 46).

Safran and Segal (1990) move beyond the concepts of empathy and collaboration to explore the complexity of the interpersonal therapeutic relationship. Their work is reviewed in detail here because of its high degree of relevance to the process of crisis intervention. These authors advise therapists to use the interpersonal context of cognitive therapy to identify and explore patients' "core cognitive processes," which are basic beliefs associated with individuals' interpersonal schemas. For example, the core cognitive processes triggered by Jack's heart attack may have been beliefs about his adequacy as a provider to his family.

The authors also recommend that therapists function as participant-observers in the therapist-patient interaction, allowing themselves to "feel the patient's interpersonal pull" (Safran & Segal, 1990, p. 80). The term *interpersonal pull* refers to patients' tendencies to elicit cognitive, emotional, and behavioral reactions from others (and therapists). Crises tend to *magnify* individuals' usual coping strategies and consequently the interpersonal pull from these individuals is likely to be intensified. An astute clinician uses a crisis as an opportunity to identify and evaluate the core cognitive processes associated with the interpersonal pull. For example, one of Marcia's core cognitive processes has always been mistrust of others, resulting in her extreme cautiousness in relationships. The crisis of rape magnified Marcia's cautiousness to a level of near-paranoia and she coped by withdrawing from all others. Her therapist experienced Marcia's coping strategy as others did: He was tempted, or pulled, to her rescue. He resisted the urge to do so, however, realizing that there were no quick or simple solutions to her problems or to her emotional pain.

Safran and Segal (1990) use the term *interpersonal markers* to describe therapists' emotional and behavioral responses to patients' subtle and overt interpersonal behaviors. Similar to feelings of countertransference, interpersonal markers may include therapist boredom, anger, confusion, and frustration as well as behaviors such as lateness for sessions, sarcasm toward the patient, and early termination of sessions. In the context of crisis intervention, interpersonal markers may provide the therapist with valuable data about the patient. For example, a therapist working with Jack might feel bored (the interpersonal marker). Thus, boredom might alert Jack's therapist to Jack's characteristic tendency toward minimizing his feelings.

The authors further point out that therapists become hooked into patients' maladaptive interpersonal processes. They advise therapists to accurately appraise their own feelings, beliefs, and behaviors to avoid being driven by such inner processes. In working with Marcia, for example, the therapist might feel pity or helplessness toward her. Such feelings are likely to render the therapist ineffective unless they are managed well. Disengagement from emotional hooks begins when therapists understand their own issues and idiosyncrasies that are triggered by patients' interpersonal strategies.

Safran and Segal (1990) emphasize the importance of accurate empathy in cognitive therapy. They point out that "empathy and cognitive exploration are . . . *completely interdependent*" (p. 85). Thus, empathy and cognitive exploration cannot exist without each other. Empathy facilitates the untangling of complex and confusing thoughts, feelings, and behaviors so as to help patients regain objectivity and control. For example, the clinician who empathizes with Jack's desire to return to work is more likely to help Jack than the clinician who is incredulous about his life-threatening behavior.

It is essential to distinguish between *empathy* (which is adaptive) and *sympathy* (which is less adaptive) in providing crisis intervention. Empathy is defined as an accurate understanding of individuals' thoughts, feelings, and behaviors. In contrast, sympathy involves actually experiencing patients' feelings (e.g., sadness, helplessness, pity, rage). Sympathy may be problematic because it usually reflects a loss of objectivity in the therapist. For example, a sympathetic therapist working with Marcia might begin to feel despair (reflecting Marcia's despair) when he or she begins to believe Marcia's helpless, hopeless thoughts. It is not necessary to sympathize with patients to care about them. Instead, a crisis worker or therapist might care deeply about, and empathize with, individuals in crisis without experiencing sympathy for them. (Perhaps burnout in crisis workers is related to excessive levels of sympathy. If so, it would seem that an antidote to burnout might be rigorous training in accurate empathy.)

Safran and Segal (1990) advise the therapist to carefully explore "ruptures" in the therapeutic relationship. According to Safran, Crocker, McMain, and Murray (1990): "An alliance rupture consists of an impairment or fluctuation in the quality of the alliance between the therapist and client" (p. 154). Jack, for example, might become impatient or angry with the therapist who does not provide immediate, practical answers to his problems. Such disruptions provide opportunities for therapeutic understanding and growth. To heal therapeutic alliance ruptures, the therapist is encouraged to explore patients' immediate thoughts and feelings in highly supportive, empathic ways (Safran et al., 1990).

Finally, Safran and Segal (1990) emphasize the importance of understanding patients' interpersonal schemas, especially as they are manifested in maladaptive cognitive-interpersonal cycles. For example, Tim's interpersonal schemas might include the following: "Relationships are meant to be only functional and practical" and "It's wrong to ask for sympathy or nurturance from others." As a result, Tim might take little initiative to elicit support or nurturance from his family, even in a crisis. His lack of initiative would further contribute to his belief that relationships are not nurturant, leading to an increasingly vicious cognitive-interpersonal cycle. In this example, the most effective strategy of the crisis worker might be to identify the vicious cycle and share it directly with the individual in crisis in an empathic and caring manner.

Case Conceptualization

The case conceptualization involves the collection and integration of data about the patient's past and present psychological (i.e., cognitive, behavioral, and affective) functioning. The case conceptualization has received increasing attention over the past few years (e.g., Beck et al., 1990, 1993; Persons, 1989; Young, 1994; Young & Lindemann, 1992), especially as CT has been applied to the treatment of severe and chronic mental disorders.

The case conceptualization consists of several important steps (Beck et al., 1993):

1. collection of important background information,
2. establishment of psychiatric diagnoses,
3. summary of the individual's presenting problem and current functioning,

4. construction of a developmental profile,
5. construction of a cognitive profile,
6. summary and integration.

The fourth edition of the *Diagnostic and Statistical Manual of Mental Disorders* (*DSM-IV*; American Psychiatric Association, 1994) provides a multiaxial system of psychiatric diagnosis. Two axes in particular, Axes I and II, are essential to the case conceptualization. Axis I is used to diagnose acute psychiatric syndromes (i.e., mental disturbances such as schizophrenia, affective disorders, anxiety disorders, adjustment disorder, post-traumatic stress disorder). Personality disorders (e.g., dependent, avoidant, borderline, antisocial, obsessive-compulsive) are diagnosed on Axis II. Personality disorders are defined as inflexible and maladaptive patterns of functioning that are chronic and long-standing, causing impairment or subjective distress.

It is important to carefully assess the presence of psychiatric disorders to accurately understand and treat individuals in crisis. As mentioned previously, some degree of emotional distress is inevitable for individuals in crisis. Psychiatric diagnostic criteria enable the clinician to distinguish between normal and pathological responses to stress. Careful consideration of diagnostic criteria is useful in determining whether individuals have had psychiatric disorders prior to their crises. Those who have received treatment for psychiatric problems in the past may be able to describe what they need from the crisis worker (e.g., moral support, "just someone to listen," advice). Individuals with severe preexisting psychiatric disorders (e.g., schizophrenia) may need more intensive treatment (e.g., medication) in a crisis.

Returning to the case examples above, Marcia's history and current functioning are consistent with a diagnosis of post-traumatic stress disorder (PTSD). Specifically, she experienced a terrifying life-threatening event (i.e., rape), resulting in vivid, recurrent, intrusive memories and dreams about the experience. Since the occurrence of the event, she has experienced anxiety, depression, withdrawal, sleep difficulties, and problems with concentration. Prior to Marcia's crisis, she had experienced major depressive episodes characterized by these same symptoms. A careful review of Jack's mental status revealed no current or prior Axis I disorder. It became apparent, however, that his obsessive-compulsive personality features had been present since early adulthood (e.g., perfectionism, preoccupation with details and rules, rigidity, stubborn-ness, and reluctance to become emotionally vulnerable).

The developmental profile involves the collection of data about an individual's history (e.g., family, social, vocational, economic) as it relates to his or her current psychological status. An excellent format for phrasing developmental questions is: "What messages have you received from others about yourself?" The reason for asking about "messages" is that such messages substantially contribute to individuals' current thought processes. Thus, if a person in crisis appears to blame himself excessive-ly for the occurrence of a crisis or for his or her reaction to a crisis, the clinician might ask: "Were you typically blamed for problems when you were growing up?" If the individual seems clinically depressed, the clinician might ask: "What messages did you receive about your self-worth as a child?"

The cognitive profile involves the collection of data about the in-dividual's cognitive, behavioral, and affective patterns. To accomplish the cognitive profile, the clinician is encouraged to ask such questions as the following: "What are your thoughts about yourself, generally?" "How would you describe your self-esteem, currently?" "What types of situations (i.e., critical incidents) tend to make you feel upset?" "When you are upset, how do you cope (i.e., react behaviorally)?"

Over the past few years, increasing attention has been paid to the role of schemas in the development and maintenance of mental disorders (e.g., Young, 1994; Young & Lindemann, 1992). Schemas are defined as cognitive structures that develop early in life and guide other psychologi-cal processes later in life. Horowitz (1994) underscores three important points about schemas: (a) They comprise mental representations, (b) their elements are interrelated, and (c) their elements function as a unit.

Two important schema domains are "adequacy" and "lovability." Individuals' adequacy and lovability schemas determine how they respond to life's challenges and problems, and therefore schemas are particularly important in the context of crisis intervention. It is hypothesized that positive schemas ("I am lovable and adequate") will reduce the negative magnitude of a crisis while negative schemas ("I am unlovable and inadequate") will increase the negative magnitude of a crisis.

According to Young (1994), there are three major schema processes: schema maintenance, schema avoidance, and schema compensation. In general, schemas are relatively stable; individuals tend to maintain both negative and positive schemas for much of their lives. When schemas are particularly negative and maladaptive (e.g., "I am unlovable" or "I am inadequate"), individuals strive to avoid them because such schemas trigger emotional distress. It is hypothesized that some individuals cope with maladaptive schemas by engaging in the process of schema compensation. Schema compensation, or compensatory strategies, involves the use of a variety of strategies (e.g., substance abuse and chronic avoidance) to cope with the emotional pain caused by maladaptive schemas. Unfortunately, compensatory strategies may ultimately cause more pain than they resolve. Two of the most salient features of crises are that they activate previously avoided negative schemas, and they threaten individuals' usual compensatory strategies. To a large degree, the activation of previously avoided schemas and the breakdown of compensatory strategies contribute to the emotional pain of a crisis.

For example, Jack has always held the maladaptive schema: "I am inadequate." He has *maintained* this schema by working in an extraordinarily competitive environment and by marrying an extremely demanding woman. He has *avoided* this schema by working 18 hours per day, 7 days per week. And he has *compensated* for this schema by climbing to the top of the corporate ladder, drinking heavily, and smoking two packs of cigarettes per day. Upon suffering a heart attack, Jack was unable to work and his doctor insisted that he quit smoking, putting a sudden halt to Jack's most salient compensatory strategies.

To identify maladaptive schemas, the clinician is encouraged to ask specifically about individuals' lifelong beliefs about their adequacy and lovability. The following questions are designed to facilitate the case conceptualization:

(1) Background information.
- Tell me about yourself and your current living situation (your age, marital status, job, home life).

(2) Psychiatric diagnoses.
- Have you ever had any emotional problems? For example, have you ever had any problems with depression, anxiety, drugs, or alcohol? If so, tell me about these problems.
- Have you ever had any significant problems getting along with others?

- Have other people (such as family or friends) ever been concerned about how you cope or have they ever suggested that you seek professional counseling?
- Have you ever sought counseling for emotional problems or been hospitalized?

(3) Presenting problem and current functioning.
- What are the problems/concerns troubling you today?
- How are you coping with these problems currently? For example, are you able to eat, sleep, concentrate, and fulfill your daily responsibilities?
- How do you cope generally (at school, work, in your relationships)?

(4) Developmental profile.
- How would you describe your early life or childhood?
- How have you gotten along with other people in the past?
- What significant medical or psychiatric problems have you experienced in your life?
- Tell me about your work/school history.
- How do you get along with other people generally?
- Tell me about any significant events or traumas you have experienced in your life. For example, have you ever been abused in any way, including verbally, physically, or sexually? If so, please tell me about these experiences.

(5) Cognitive profile.
- What are some typical situations that cause you problems?
- When you find yourself in difficult situations, what are your typical automatic thoughts, feelings, and behaviors in these situations?
- How do you generally see yourself? For example, do you generally see yourself as lovable? adequate?
- What are your conditional beliefs? For example, what would it mean to you if you _____ (e.g., couldn't work)?
- What rules, like "shoulds" and "musts," do you try to follow in your life?

Upon ascertaining a diagnosis, developmental profile, and cognitive profile, the clinician can begin to integrate this information and develop a greater understanding of the individual's current functioning. The clinician is encouraged to summarize the case conceptualization with the individual in crisis to provide the person with a greater understanding of his or her functioning. The following summary, made by the clinician to Tim (from the example above), is presented to illustrate this process:

Tim, we've been talking for the past hour and I'd like to share my impressions. First, you're certainly depressed right now. Your depression doesn't seem exclusively due to your unemployment, however. It seems that you've been somewhat self-critical most of your life. In your childhood you often heard your father calling you "lazy" and "stupid." These messages have had a long-term impact. Now your unemployment reinforces your negative view of yourself. It gives you a reason to call yourself "lazy" and "stupid." What do you think of this assessment?

By sharing this formulation with Tim, the clinician conveys accurate empathy while also testing some of his or her hypotheses. As a result, Tim has a somewhat more comprehensive and integrated view of his own emotional distress. He responds:

I hadn't really thought about myself that way before. I just thought "I could never really do enough." Now that you mention it, my wife says I'm kind'a hard on myself. Maybe I oughta just chill out.

The development of an accurate case conceptualization may appear deceptively simple when, in fact, it is a profoundly complex and challenging process. The crisis worker is encouraged to take the time and effort necessary to formulate an accurate case conceptualization despite temptations to launch into (often premature) behavior change strategies.

Therapeutic Structure

Among the most distinctive features of CT is its structure. The structure of CT manifests itself in numerous ways. Perhaps most important, each standard CT session follows a specific pattern (Beck et al., 1993):

1. agenda setting,
2. mood check,
3. bridge from last session,
4. discussion of today's agenda items,
5. capsule summaries,
6. homework assignments,
7. feedback from the patient about the session.

Compared with typical psychotherapy, the parameters of crisis intervention (e.g., number and length of visits) may vary widely. Nonetheless, crisis intervention sessions will be enhanced by applying the above structure. Initially, the clinician establishes an *agenda* by asking: "What problem or problems would you like to discuss right now?" After an agenda is generated, the clinician inquires about the individual's *mood*. If the clinician and the individual in crisis have previously met, the clinician *bridges* (i.e., reviews) from their last meeting. Next, they *discuss agenda items* using a method known as guided discovery. Guided discovery involves the clinician's probing (with open-ended questions) about issues important and relevant to the individual in crisis. At various points throughout the session, the clinician provides *capsule summaries* to the individual in crisis. These summaries are intended to reflect what has been discussed thus far, in a way that is meaningful to the individual. For example, upon hearing about Jack's crisis, the clinician might summarize with emphasis on Jack's dichotomous (i.e., all-or-none) thinking. Later in the session, the clinician suggests *homework* that is an extension of their present discussion. Homework facilitates continued benefit to this patient after the session has ended. At the end of each session, the clinician asks the individual to provide *feedback* about the session. (In fact, the clinician is encouraged to ask for feedback several times during the session.) Such feedback enables the clinician and individual to assess the impact of the visit.

Socialization of the Patient

To conduct maximally effective cognitive therapy, therapists are encouraged to socialize their patients to the cognitive therapy models most appropriate to their problems (e.g., depression, anxiety, substance abuse). The socialization process involves educating patients about the interplay between their thoughts, feelings, and behaviors. In a crisis, individuals are taught to see their thought processes as essential to how they cope. Consider the following example in which Marcia's therapist provides some socialization to CT:

Th: How do you feel today?
M: Very sad.

Th: What are the thoughts running through your head?

M: I'm really screwed up.

Th: How did you reach that conclusion?

M: I just know it's true.

Th: What do you mean by "screwed up"?

M: You know, I'm not worth a damn.

Th: Marcia, given your negative thoughts about yourself, I can certainly understand how you'd feel very sad. It sounds like you label yourself and overgeneralize about your weaknesses. That type of thinking would naturally lead most people to feel emotionally upset.

In this example, the therapist has only just begun to socialize the patient to the CT model. Depending on how the patient responds to this intervention, the therapist may or may not proceed with a complete explanation about cognitive distortions. (Cognitive distortions are systematic errors in thinking that perpetuate emotional distress.) Too often, therapists begin to socialize patients too early in the therapy process, for example, by introducing a list of cognitive distortions in the first session.

Cognitive and Behavioral Techniques

There are hundreds of cognitive and behavioral techniques associated with CT (for numerous examples, see McMullin, 1986). Mahoney (1991) defines techniques as "meaningful rituals of communication, human relatedness, awareness and social influence" (p. 253). He warns against "technolatry," however (i.e., technique worship). According to Mahoney and numerous others, it is not merely what technique is used but also *how* the technique is applied. To be maximally effective, all CT techniques require the skillful application of guided discovery. In guided discovery, the clinician asks numerous open-ended questions and provides empathic, accurate, meaningful capsule summaries. These responses enable patients to understand their lives and problems in a more objective, adaptive manner. The process of guided discovery, so central to good cognitive therapy, may be limited by therapists' tendencies toward giving advice, making premature recommendations, and offering reassurances to the person in crisis.

Perhaps the most important and common cognitive strategy is the three-question technique, in which the clinician asks a series of three open-ended questions that help individuals to be more objective about their problems and crises. The three questions, applied to any maladaptive belief, are as follows: (a) What is your evidence for that belief? (b) How else could you explain that belief? (c) What are the implications if your belief is true? For example, in using the three-question technique with Tim, the clinician might ask: "What is your evidence for your belief that you won't get a job?" "How else might you look at the job search process?" "What are the implications, if your belief is true?" In other words, what does it say about you as a person if you don't get a job for some time? For much more on cognitive and behavioral techniques, see the texts by Beck and his colleagues (1979, 1985, 1990, 1993) and McMullin (1986).

INTEGRATION OF CRISIS
INTERVENTION AND COGNITIVE THERAPY

In this section, Roberts's seven steps of crisis intervention are discussed, with emphasis on the relevant principles and techniques of cognitive therapy.

(1) Rapidly establish the relationship. Individuals in crisis are likely to be emotionally *vulnerable.* As a result of being in a state of disequilibrium, an individual might be easily hurt by the actions or responses of others. In this heightened state of emotional vulnerability, an individual in crisis might become uncharacteristically more or less *receptive* to psychological interventions, depending on the crisis and the individual's personality.

Tim (from the example above) became profoundly disappointed in himself after becoming unemployed. Prior to this crisis, Tim was typically private about his thoughts and feelings (i.e., he rarely disclosed personal information to anyone). As he became increasingly disappointed in himself, he became more willing to be open with others about his feelings. In contrast, Marcia became more isolated and withdrawn from others after she was raped. Her crisis resulted in heightened emotional vulnerability and, in response, she became less receptive to psychological interventions. Finally, Jack maintained his typical pattern of denying negative feelings (especially fear or depression) after his heart attack.

Clinicians providing crisis intervention are encouraged to make and rapidly establish an *appropriate* level of psychological contact. As implied earlier, appropriateness varies from person to person and from crisis to crisis. Thus, the clinician is encouraged to be aware of individuals' levels of vulnerability and receptivity to the therapeutic relationship. This awareness can best be facilitated by a collaborative therapeutic environment where the therapist carefully listens to, and empathizes with, the patient.

(2) Examine the dimensions of the problem. There are many dimensions to emotional problems. In crises, the dimensions of adaptive functioning (or, conversely, impairment) are particularly important. As previously discussed, CT provides a comprehensive method for conceptualizing individuals, which involves examining the past, present, cognitive, affective, and behavioral dimensions of a problem or crisis. Thus, the cognitive case conceptualization can serve as an excellent tool for examining the dimensions of a problem.

In crisis intervention, it is essential to evaluate potential lethality (i.e., suicide or homicide) or harm to self or others (Gilliland & James, 1993; Hoff, 1989; Roberts, 1991a). Clark and Fawcett (1992) describe suicide as a "major public health problem" (p. 16). They report that suicide is the eighth leading cause of death in the United States, accounting for 1.4% of all deaths (over 30,000 in 1989). In reviewing the risk factors, these authors emphasize the following psychiatric predictors of suicide: depression, alcoholism, and schizophrenia. In their excellent review of the research on suicides, Clark and Fawcett (1992) find that 57% to 86% of completed suicides occur in depressed and alcoholic persons. They suggest a 10-step process for detecting and gauging suicidal ideation:

1. Listen to the individual's conceptualization of his or her problem.
2. Pinpoint dysphoric affects (sadness, apathy, loss of interest in life, irritability, anxiety, and so on).
3. Evaluate hopelessness (which is highly predictive of suicide).
4. Probe for morbid thoughts.
5. Evaluate the degree to which thoughts are active (rather than passive).
6. Check for consideration of specific methods of suicide.

7. Inquire about the actual likelihood of suicide.
8. Assess all suicidal plans: How often considered? mentally rehearsed? any actions taken?
9. Probe for homicidal thoughts.
10. Interview other family members (based on Clark & Fawcett, 1992, p. 25).

Later in this chapter, a standardized instrument for assessing lethality, the Crisis Triage Rating Scale, is reviewed (see Appendix 2.A; Bengelsdorf, Levy, Emerson, & Barile, 1984). This scale provides a method for quantifying three important variables regarding potential harm to self or others: dangerousness, support system, and ability to cooperate.

(3) Encourage exploration of feelings and emotions. Individuals' emotions serve as thermostats, reflecting the individuals' coping processes, or adaptation to problems. Extreme emotional responses (e.g., lability or numbness) may be "normal" during crises; when sustained, however, such states may indicate maladaptive coping.

According to cognitive therapy, emotions are mediated by cognitive processes. For example, depressed moods can be linked to individuals' distorted negative beliefs about themselves (e.g., "I am inadequate"), their personal worlds (e.g., "People can't be trusted"), or their futures (e.g., "Things are bound to get worse"). Beck et al. (1979) referred to these three domains of beliefs as the "cognitive triad." Similarly, anxious moods may be related to perceptions of threat, harm, or vulnerability (e.g., "I will fail.")

To illustrate the relationships between cognitive processes and emotions, again consider the examples from above. Tim felt *anxiety* as a result of thinking: "I won't find another job." He felt *sadness* as a result of thinking: "I'm not good enough to compete." Jack felt *restless* as a result of thinking: "If I give in to this illness, I will be less of a man." Marcia felt *despair* as a result of her thought: "I am destined to a life of suffering and pain."

Clinicians working with individuals in crisis are most effective when they are attentive and responsive to individuals' verbal and nonverbal cues relating to emotions and underlying cognitive processes. Several active listening skills are particularly useful for monitoring emotions and corresponding thoughts, including open-ended questions, reflections, silences, and capsule summaries. *Open-ended questions* elicit information about the form and content of, as well as relationships between, thoughts, feelings, and behaviors. The following are examples of open-ended questions: "How do you feel?" "What do you think?" "What is your reaction to that?" *Reflections* involve feedback to the individual regarding his or her thoughts, feelings, or behaviors. The following are examples of reflection: "That seems to really make you angry." "You look very discouraged right now." "You sound somewhat hopeless." Silence is defined as any pause in the conversation lasting more than 10 seconds. Individuals in crisis may derive substantial benefit from silences for two reasons. First, silences allow individuals to scrutinize their thoughts, feelings, and behaviors. Second, appropriately timed silences convey that the listener is comfortable with, and accepts, the thoughts and feelings of the individual in crisis. *Capsule summaries* are essential to the active listening process. A capsule summary is the cumulative reflection of what has been said by an individual. The following is an example of such a summary:

> Jack, we have been talking about your heart attack and its effect on your life. You've experienced many different emotions since your heart attack. At first, you were very frightened, but eventually you felt numb about it. Now you seem determined to override your feelings and just get on with your life.

(4) Explore and assess past coping attempts. The evaluation of an individual's precrisis functioning is an essential part of the intervention process. Such an evaluation provides the clinician with clues for understanding the individual's current coping strategies. An examination of past coping strategies may also uncover psychiatric problems that might bear on an individual's current crisis. In cognitive therapy, the case conceptualization is the vehicle for assessing past coping attempts. Specifically, the clinician learns about past coping attempts by establishing a psychiatric diagnosis and developmental profile.

The skills necessary for exploring and assessing past coping attempts were presented in an earlier section (see step 3, "Encourage Exploration of Feelings and Emotions," above). They included open-ended questions, reflections, silences, and capsule summaries. The following are examples of open-ended questions regarding past coping attempts: "How have you coped with problems in the past?" "To what extent have you had similar crises in the past?" "How would you describe your style of coping with problems?"

(5) Explore alternatives and specific solutions. As an extension of the last step, individuals in crisis are actively encouraged to consider alternatives and solutions to their problems. For example, after being asked about past coping strategies, an individual in crisis might be asked: "How well might that strategy work in this situation?" As a follow-up, he or she might be asked: "What other solutions do you see?" In this chapter, the use of triage is encouraged for persons in crisis. Triage involves the process of evaluating crises, coping skills, and available resources to make decisions about follow-up treatment. This process is discussed more fully later in this chapter.

(6) Restore cognitive functioning through implementation of an action plan. When individuals in crisis have followed triage as planned, they should begin to experience a restoration of psychological functioning. For example, Marcia's action plan involves the pursuit of intensive psychotherapy. As a result of receiving excellent therapy, she experiences an improvement in her overall functioning.

(7) Follow up. It is suggested that the clinician establish a plan for contacting the individual at a later date to follow up on the initial intervention. Especially in cases where there is some question about potential lethality, the clinician has a moral and possibly legal responsibility to provide follow-up.

CUSTOMIZING CRISIS
INTERVENTION STRATEGIES

Although there are many commonalties among crisis interventions, specific strategies will vary as a function of the unique individual in crisis, the nature of the crisis, and the skills and abilities of the clinician providing crisis intervention. Numerous factors may be considered in formulating the crisis intervention plan. The most obvious source of data for customizing the intervention is the case conceptualization. For example, individuals found to have severe, long-standing, pervasive, debilitating psychiatric disorders may be stabilized while efforts are made to locate comprehensive care. On the other hand, individuals found to have minimal or no psychopathology might be seen only briefly by a crisis intervention worker.

To illustrate this point, we return to the case examples presented above. Jack, who refused to engage in cardiac rehabilitation, is likely to reject professional counseling. As an alternative, he might be encouraged to discuss his stress with his family physician. Tim might be receptive to counseling or psychotherapy to get relief from his current symptoms. Marcia would probably require intensive psychotherapy and possibly medication to facilitate her recovery.

A major goal of this chapter has been to present methods for evaluating (i.e., conceptualizing) individuals who are in crisis so as to make appropriate decisions regarding the most suitable intervention. This process, called "triage," is discussed in detail in the next section of this chapter.

TRIAGE

The term *triage* has been used extensively in medicine to refer to the process of assigning patients to appropriate treatments depending on their medical conditions and available medical resources. At least one textbook (Rund & Rausch, 1981) and hundreds of articles have addressed the process of medical triage. Relatively few publications, however, have addressed psychiatric triage. In fact, Rund and Rausch (1981), in their text on triage, offer no protocols for psychiatric triage. In their article on psychiatric triage, Boren and Zeman (1985) explain that physicians and emergency room personnel "do not view the psychiatric patient or his presenting dilemma as a 'real emergency' as they do a patient with severe chest pain or an acute abdomen" (p. 570).

Few, if any, references to triage can be found in the current crisis intervention literature, despite the fact that the concept of triage has been so salient in medicine. Given that individuals who experience crises are a heterogeneous group with varying problems, needs, resources, and coping skills, it seems obvious that some method of matching patients to treatments (i.e., triage) would be extremely useful.

As mentioned earlier, *triage* is defined as the process of assigning patients to appropriate treatments depending on their medical conditions and available resources (Estrada, 1981; Mezza, 1992; Rowe, 1992; Rund & Rausch, 1981). Triage as a medical phenomenon was first used by the military to meet the needs of servicemen wounded in action. The process of triage results in the assignment of injured and sick patients to various treatment levels ranging from "nonemergent" (no care required) to "emergent" (immediate care required).

When an individual experiences an emotional crisis, triage is an appropriate process for determining treatment. Several authors (e.g., Bengelsdorf et al., 1984; Pollun & Labbage, 1992; Rotheram-Borus & Bradley, 1991; Schneider-Braus, 1987; Turner & Turner, 1991) have addressed the issue of psychiatric triage, though most are concerned primarily with lethality (i.e., harm to self or others). Bengelsdorf et al. (1984) developed a useful instrument, the Crisis Triage Rating Scale (CTRS; see Appendix 2.A), for assessing lethality risk in psychiatric patients. The CTRS has been validated by Turner and Turner (1991).

Triage with the CTRS generally results in one of two dispositions: emergency inpatient hospitalization or discharge to outpatient treatment. The clinician using the CTRS evaluates three important areas of functioning (see Appendix 2.A): dangerousness, support system, and ability to cooperate. Each of these areas is rated by the clinician from "1" (highest risk) to "5" (lowest risk), and the three individual ratings are added together for a total score. Individuals who score less than or equal to 9 on the CTRS are recommended for inpatient hospitalization; individuals who receive scores greater than 9 are discharged to outpatient treatment (Bengelsdorf et al., 1984; Turner & Turner, 1991).

To illustrate the use of the CTRS, consider the three cases presented earlier.

Tim has fleeting suicidal thoughts but he clearly wishes to live (dangerousness score = 4). His wife wishes to be supportive but she currently feels overwhelmed (support system score = 4). Tim wants to get help but he is ambivalent about pursuing counseling (cooperativeness score = 4). Tim's total score equals 12; he does not require inpatient hospitalization.

Jack has no history of suicidal ideation (dangerousness score = 5). He has family and friends who are supportive (support system score = 5). He is skeptical about receiving professional help (cooperativeness score = 4). Jack's total score equals 14; he does not require inpatient hospitalization.

Marcia has a past and present history of ambivalence about suicide and has made some ineffective gestures in the past (dangerousness score = 3). Her support system is quite limited, because she has few friends and her family is quite dysfunctional (support system score = 2). She passively accepts intervention maneuvers (cooperativeness score = 3). Marcia's total score equals 8; inpatient hospitalization is advised.

Although the CTRS is useful for determining lethality in a crisis, it does not discriminate between more subtle, yet important psychological variables. Hence, the CTRS may be used in conjunction with the cognitive case conceptualization.

Currently, the CTRS results in one of two potential recommendations: inpatient or outpatient treatment. In this chapter, we expand the options from the two recommended by Bengelsdorf et al. (1984). The following are the three recommended triage options:

(1) Emergency psychiatric treatment. This level of triage is necessary when individuals experience severe acute psychiatric symptoms with substantial impairment or potential lethality (e.g., depression with suicidal ideation, psychoses, mania; CTRS scores lower than or equal to 9). These individuals have current views of themselves, their personal worlds, or their futures that are severely distorted (e.g., extremely global and negative). Such individuals typically meet psychiatric diagnostic criteria for acute mental disorders. Initial treatment typically involves hospitalization and protection from self-harm or harm to others. This may be achieved by psychopharmacotherapy, isolation, or simple observation.

(2) Outpatient counseling/psychotherapy. This level of triage occurs when an individual experiences acute psychiatric symptoms with some impairment and no current potential lethality (e.g., depression, anxiety, adjustment disorder; CTRS scores greater than 9). At this level of triage, the clinician recommends traditional outpatient psychological counseling. After the individual in crisis is seen initially for assessment and intervention, he or she is referred for psychotherapy. There are many

options across outpatient psychotherapy settings. These options vary by therapist style, orientation, specialty, education, and emphasis. (Naturally, my bias is to refer individuals to a setting where they will receive cognitive therapy!)

Outpatient psychotherapy may be short term (e.g., 10-15 weekly sessions) or it may be long term (several sessions per week for many years) depending on the therapeutic modality and severity of the patient's problems. Traditionally, the cognitive and behavioral therapies have been short term while the psychodynamic therapies (e.g., psychoanalysis) have been long term.

(3) Basic emotional support, validation, and education. At this level of triage, an individual's reaction to a crisis can be considered "normal" under the circumstances, without substantial impairment or potential lethality. No immediate referral is made at the end of the crisis intervention, because the individual shows no signs of long-term impairment. Individuals who fall into this group may receive a high degree of comfort and satisfaction from a relatively brief crisis intervention effort.

SUMMARY AND INTEGRATION

In this chapter, the basic principles and techniques of cognitive therapy and triage have been applied to crisis intervention. Several case examples have been provided to illustrate this process. It has been argued that cognitive therapy and triage should naturally be components of crisis intervention, and specific cognitive therapy and triage techniques were introduced for crisis intervention.

Crisis intervention is an extremely challenging endeavor. Crises manifest themselves in all shapes, sizes, and colors. Similarly, there is wide variability across crisis workers. The main goal of this chapter has been to provide a well-validated psychological model and strategies for dealing with crises. Emphasis has been placed on the collaborative therapeutic relationship, case conceptualization, structure, socialization, and techniques of therapy. The CTRS was also presented as a strategy for conceptualizing individuals in crisis.

Appendix 2.A

Crisis Triage Rating Scale

Instructions: score 1 to 5 in each category using descriptive statements as guidelines.

A. Dangerousness (circle number)

1. Expresses or hallucinates suicidal/homicidal ideas or has made serious attempt in present illness. Unpredictably impulsive/violent.
2. Same as 1, but ideas or behavior are to some degree egodystonic or history of violent or impulsive behavior but no current signs.
3. Expresses suicidal/homicidal ideas with ambivalence or has made only ineffective gestures. Questionable impulse control.
4. Some suicidal/homicidal ideation or behavior, or history of same, but clearly wishes and is able to control behavior.
5. No suicidal/homicidal ideation or behavior. No history of violent/impulsive behavior.

B. Support system (circle number)

1. No family, friends, or others. Agencies cannot provide immediate support needed.
2. Some support might be mobilized but its effectiveness will be limited.
3. Support system potentially available but significant difficulties exist in mobilizing it.

4. Interested family, friends, or others but some question exists of ability or willingness to help.
5. Interested family, friends, or others able and willing to provide support needed.

C. Ability to cooperate (circle number)

1. Unable to cooperate or actively refuses.
2. Shows little interest in or comprehension of efforts to be made in his behalf.
3. Passively accepts intervention maneuvers.
4. Wants to get help but is ambivalent or motivation is not strong.
5. Actively seeks outpatient treatment, willing and able to cooperate.

Total score: _____

Disposition:

SOURCE: Bengelsdorf et al. (1984).

Crisis Intervention Units and Centers in the United States

A National Survey

ALBERT R. ROBERTS

Each year, millions of people experience crisis-inducing stressful events. Unable to afford the high cost of psychotherapy, many individuals in crisis never see a social worker, clinical psychologist, or psychiatrist in private practice. They must find some other method of obtaining immediate professional help. Consequently, over 1.5 million persons in acute crisis annually seek help from a crisis center or hotline in their community. Whether the person in crisis is suffering from depression, a suicide attempt, substance abuse, marital problems, or homelessness, trained volunteers and professional staff are available 24 hours a day to respond to callers in crisis.

Throughout the nation, a growing number of such crisis intervention programs have been developed to respond to callers in crisis quickly and effectively. This national survey was conducted to determine the

NOTE: Adapted from *Contemporary Perspectives in Crisis Intervention and Prevention*, edited by A. R. Roberts (Englewood Cliffs, NJ: Prentice Hall, 1991), by permission of the editor and author.

objectives, priorities, funding sources, staffing patterns, and types of services provided by crisis intervention programs.

Over the years, the number and types of crisis intervention programs have varied. As the number and types of federal and state grants and contracts have changed, so have the objectives and the number of crisis intervention programs. In the late 1960s, when suicide prevention hotlines were rapidly expanding, crisis intervention activities were limited for the most part to persons contemplating suicide. By the mid-1970s, as a result of federal funding through the Community Mental Health Centers Act, over 700 local community mental health centers had been opened, each with a crisis intervention unit.

As public pressure mounts to provide adequate and accessible crisis services to all citizens, it is important to know about the extent of crisis intervention programs within health and hospital settings, mental health centers, and suicide prevention agencies. Crisis intervention practices and programs have come a long way in the past 25 years. In 1966, there were only 28 suicide prevention centers in the United States (Roberts, 1970). Two years later, there were 63 (Haughton, 1968). By 1989, there were more than 225 suicide prevention centers listed in the directory of the American Association of Suicidology.

This chapter is about the work of crisis centers. It focuses on the organizational structure and functions of crisis intervention units, centers, and hotlines nationwide and presents the major findings of a national survey of crisis units and centers. This survey provides data on the major priorities, components, and problems of crisis centers. Data were gathered on the following topics:

- Objectives of the crisis centers and programs
- Types of services provided
- Callers' most frequent presenting problem
- Agencies or programs to which clients are frequently referred
- Organizational issues (e.g., total number of persons served annually, annual budgets, funding sources, staffing patterns)

Program development in crisis intervention and preventive risk reduction strategies have increased considerably since the start of the 1970s.

HISTORICAL BACKGROUND

The origin of crisis intervention services in the United States can be traced to the opening of a suicide prevention program in New York City in 1906, known as the National Save-a-Life League. The league was started by Reverend Harry M. Warren Jr., an ordained minister and pastoral counselor keenly interested in helping individuals who were contemplating suicide. The New York City program continued its suicide prevention activities throughout the major nationwide expansion of such programs between 1965 and 1972, but it remained a very small program with two to four full-time staff members and a strong reliance on trained volunteers and student interns from local social work education and psychology programs.

A second early influence on the history of the suicide prevention movement was Louis I. Dublin, a life insurance actuary and statistician, public health reformer, and demographer. In 1933, Dublin published his seminal book, *To Be or Not to Be*, in which he attempted to awaken and stimulate society's awareness of the problem of suicide. Three decades later, Dublin (1963) took county and state health department officials to task for neglect and apathy toward the problems of suicide—a preventable cause of death. (After his retirement in 1970, Dublin was hailed as the "pioneer of suicidology.")

During the 1950s, clinical psychologists Norman Farberow and Edwin S. Shneidman came upon several hundred authentic suicide notes in the files of the Los Angeles County medical examiner. They used these in the first of what became many retrospective analyses of the psychological processes of individuals about to take their own lives. The researchers revealed states of ambivalence and clues to eventual self-destruction. As a result of these early "psychological autopsies," these two suicidologists became convinced that suicide could be prevented and many lives could be saved (Farberow & Shneidman, 1965).

Farberow and Shneidman received two multiyear demonstration grants from the National Institute of Mental Health (NIMH). The first award, in 1958, was a 5-year grant that enabled the Los Angeles Suicide Prevention Center (LASPC) to become fully operational. The second grant was for a period of 7 years (1963-1969). Between 1958 and 1965, the LASPC staff developed the concepts, procedures, training manuals, and empirical data that constituted the foundation and technology of the suicide prevention movement. New programs throughout the United States were developed based on the following contributions by the LASPC:

1. The 24-hour telephone intervention service
2. Telephone method of determining lethality, establishing rapport and communication, and formulating an action plan
3. Training of volunteer housewives for telephone crisis duty
4. Semiannual training institutes for new staff members at suicide prevention and crisis intervention services all over the United States (including social work interns, clinical psychology interns, medical students, and psychiatric residents)
5. A 1-year residence program for research fellows of the Center for the Scientific Study of Suicide

By the last half of the 1960s, the suicide prevention movement had made significant strides. In December 1966, the NIMH set up the now defunct Center for Studies of Suicide Prevention. The center was the first large scale effort by the federal government to plan and fund research and demonstration projects on suicide prevention.

The goals of suicide prevention agencies have not changed much in the ensuing decades. The primary goal of these agencies has been the immediate and long-term deterrence of suicide. The selection, evaluation, referral, and crisis intervention activities of suicide prevention agencies are conducted with the goal in mind (Roberts, 1975).

Another important development parallel to the emergence and growth of suicide prevention and 24-hour crisis services was the Community Mental Health Centers (CMHC) Act of 1963, which mandated five essential services for all of these centers that were federally funded. Among the most important developments as a result of this legislation were 24-hour crisis intervention and emergency services. The primary emphasis of the community mental health movement was to return mental health services to community settings rather than restricting care to large state mental institutions.

Additional emphasis was placed on early intervention to prevent problems and crisis events from developing into serious psychopathology. Thus, 24-hour crisis intervention and emergency services were viewed as a major component by a number of the newly built CMHCs.

Currently, several hundred 24-hour crisis intervention units are in operation. Over 700 of them serve as a major component of CMHCs, providing early intervention and crisis stabilization not only for suicidal callers but also for substance abusers, crime victims, and people suffering from psychiatric emergencies (Roberts, 1990b).

THE SURVEY

Purpose

The purpose of the national survey of crisis intervention units and centers was to systematically collect and analyze data on the structure, functions, and services provided by these centers. I wanted to learn more about the specific services provided by these centers, their objectives, availability, initial procedures with crisis callers, referral policy, funding sources, and staffing patterns. The survey provides a national perspective on 107 crisis intervention centers located in the 10 major geographic regions of the United States.

Methodology

A membership list of 225 crisis centers and programs was obtained from the American Association of Suicidology (AAS). A detailed five-page questionnaire was developed, pretested, revised, and mailed to each of the centers in November 1987. The questionnaire was sent with two cover letters: one letter introduced the survey and the other one, written by Julie Pearlman, executive director of the AAS, cited the importance of the survey. A follow-up letter and another copy of the questionnaire were sent to all nonrespondents in early February 1988. By May of that year, completed questionnaires had been received from 107, or 47.5%, of the centers.

The respondents were from 37 states, representing the 10 major geographic regions of the nation. Some states were adequately represented by the responding programs; others were underrepresented. The states with the largest number of responding crisis centers were California (10), Florida (7), New Hampshire (6), Ohio (6), Illinois (5), and

Michigan (5). The following 12 states and the District of Columbia had no respondents: Hawaii, Idaho, Indiana, Mississippi, Montana, Nebraska, New Jersey, New Mexico, South Dakota, Vermont, West Virginia, and Wyoming.

The two regions of the United States with the largest number of responding crisis centers were the Great Lakes states (21 respondents) and the southern states (17 respondents). The Great Lakes states consist of Illinois (5), Indiana (0), Michigan (1), Minnesota (1), Ohio (6), and Wisconsin (4). The southern states consist of Alabama (1), Florida (7), Georgia (1), Kentucky (3), Mississippi (0), North Carolina (1), South Carolina (2), and Tennessee (2).

Results

Objectives and Purposes of Crisis Centers

The overwhelming majority of the 107 respondents indicated that they have four or more objectives. The most frequently mentioned objectives were these:

Suicide prevention (99 responses)
Crisis intervention (96)
Referral (93)
Community education (87)

Additional objectives, identified by one fifth to almost one third of the programs, were these:

Acute psychiatric emergencies (33)
Family violence intervention (27)
Rape crisis work (24)

The listed objective with the smallest number of responses was forensic services to the local jail (14 responses).

The data indicate that crisis centers and units provide not only crisis intervention services (tertiary prevention) to facilitate resolution of acute crisis episodes but also primary and secondary prevention activities.

Availability of Crisis Services

All of the respondents indicated that they provide telephone crisis intervention services, and 9 out of 10 indicated that their services were available on a 24-hour-a-day basis. Thus, most of the crisis services are able to provide help quickly to persons at risk of suicide or experiencing acute crisis episodes. In addition to the crisis hotline, 59 programs offer direct, face-to-face services, and 35 programs provide outreach services.

The Year Crisis Services Were Established

One half of the programs were established between 1968 and 1972. The peak year was 1970, when 15 of the crisis services became operational. Prior to 1968, only 12 respondents were in operation. Over one third (37 programs) were established between 1974 and 1987. Although human service programs were buffeted by budget woes throughout the 1980s (which has been referred to as the decade of scarcity because of federal, state, and local budget cuts), close to one fourth (25) of the crisis services were established between 1980 and 1987. Of these 25 programs, however, 10 were established in 1980 and 1981, before the most severe budget slashing took place.

Physical Setting

The sponsorship and autonomy of a crisis service plays a significant role in determining its location. Being located in or near a hospital or a community mental health center increases the accessibility of a crisis service and the likelihood of drop-ins and face-to-face contact with callers. In other cases, suicide prevention crisis services, with only limited staff and telephone services, keep their location unknown to the general public to protect the anonymity of callers and to discourage drop-ins.

Slightly over one third (37, or 34.9%) of the 106 programs that responded to this question indicated that they are autonomous and housed in a building separate from the hospital or community mental health center. Of this group, 12 are housed in a building located near a hospital, while 23 are located more than 10 blocks from a hospital. One quarter of the respondents (27, or 25.4%) indicated that they are housed in a building with other social services, and another quarter (26, or 24.5%)

Figure 3.1.
SOURCE: Carole Roberts; used by permission.

indicated that their services are located in a freestanding community mental health center.

Only 12 services (11%) indicated that they are located in a hospital. Of those, 5 stated that they deliver only part of their services there; they also have facilities outside the hospital. For example, one program provides prehospital screening at the hospital, operates a sexual abuse program and a crisis shelter at a second location, and offers other services at a third location. Another operates from a community mental health center during business hours but provides services after hours and on weekends from a hospital setting. There were 10 responses in the "other" category, including being housed in an office building, a county jail, a church, or a mobile unit. Two respondents stated that their location is kept confidential.

Informing the Community

The agencies were asked to identify the three most frequently used methods of informing the community of their services. Some identified more than three, resulting in 352 responses. The seven most frequently cited methods were public information talks, often mentioned in conjunction with a speaker's bureau (52 respondents); newspaper ads and articles (47); public service announcements (42); radio announcements (30); television appearances (29); brochures and fliers (40); and telephone directory listings and ads (23). The least frequently mentioned methods were billboards (2), annual reports (1), and bumper stickers (1).

Presenting Problems

Of the respondents, 64 provided estimates of the percentage of their clients (totaling 578,793 served during 1986-1987) who had specific presenting problems. The five most frequently cited presenting problems are as follows (see Table 3.1):

Depression (19.3%)
Substance abuse (14.6%)
Suicide attempt (12.4%)
Marital maladjustment (8.6%)
Behavioral crisis (7.9%)

TABLE 3.1 Most Frequent Presenting Problems

Problem	Frequency	Percentage of Clients
Depression	111,709	19.3
Substance abuse	84,946	14.6
Suicide attempt	72,250	12.4
Marital maladjustment	49,504	8.6
Behavioral crisis	45,716	7.9
Homelessness	35,656	6.2
Problems of sexuality	25,530	4.4
Psychiatric emergency	23,633	4.0
Woman abuse	19,948	3.4
Child abuse	15,694	2.7
Rape trauma victims	4,738	0.8
Victims of violent crime	3,102	0.5
Vehicular accident victims	958	0.2
Other	85,409	14.7

NOTE: This is based on a total of 578,793 clients.

Nearly one fifth of the persons contacting crisis services during the 1986-1987 fiscal year did so because of depression. Persons suffering from clinical depression often are unable to function in everyday life. This mood disturbance can interfere with a person's ability to think, concentrate, and function adaptively. Some depressed people are at a high distress and discomfort level and as a result are willing to call a hotline or crisis line in the hope that they can be helped.

Staff Training

A distressed person experiencing an acute crisis episode is in no position to assess the qualifications of the crisis intervenors answering their calls to hotlines and crisis lines. In the life-threatening situations often encountered by volunteer hotline workers, however, it matters greatly whether the volunteer staffers have been adequately trained and whether the crisis center's director has the appropriate professional credentials.

Nearly all of the responding crisis services indicated that they provide both orientation and in-service training for their staff. Only one program administrator indicated that training is not provided. There

TABLE 3.2 Agencies to Which Callers Are Most Frequently Referred

Agency	Ranking 1	Ranking 2	3	Total Ranked Responses
Outpatient mental health	59	12	2	73
Substance abuse treatment	4	27	35	66
Family service agency	11	16	11	38
Inpatient mental health	4	12	6	22
Private practice	1	7	10	18
Women's shelter	6	4	7	17
Salvation Army	0	1	6	7
Child guidance clinic	0	2	4	6
Women's center	0	1	4	5
Child sexual abuse program	0	1	1	2
Community support program	1	0	0	1

NOTE: This is based on a total of 86 services.

was, however, enormous variation in the type and length of the training. The number of training hours for new staffers and volunteers ranged from a low of 2 hours to a high of 112 hours, with an average of 38. The type and frequency of in-service training also varied greatly, with almost half (47%) of the programs stating that they provide in-service training once a month. The length of the training sessions ranged from a low of 1 hour to a high of 10 hours.

Two thirds (67%) of the crisis center directors had a master's degree in social work, psychology, guidance and counseling, or education. A bachelor's was the highest degree for one quarter of the directors. Only 6% had a Ph.D. in psychology.

Agencies to Which Clients Are Most Frequently Referred

Respondents were asked to identify, in rank order, the types of agencies to which they most frequently refer their clients (see Table 3.2). The overwhelming majority of respondents to this question (73, or 84.8%) stated that the most frequent referral is to outpatient mental health services. The referral agencies with the second and third highest frequency are substance abuse treatment facilities (66, or 76.7%) and family service agencies (38, or 44.2%).

Organizational Issues

The survey results provided information on a number of organizational issues, including staffing patterns, the use of volunteers, and the range and size of crisis center budgets and the variety of sources used to fund them.

Budget. The annual budgets for the 1987-1988 fiscal year ranged from a low of $5,800 to a high of $5 million. Table 3.3 shows a sampling of program locations for the lowest and highest annual budgets. Note that some programs, such as those housed in community mental health centers, were unable to report budget information for the crisis intervention unit separate from that for the overall agency. The great variation in budget and staff size among the respondents was not surprising given that some are part of an established community mental health center, others are suicide prevention hotlines providing telephone crisis services, and still others are small voluntary crisis support services (such as the Samaritans).

Funding sources. Table 3.4 shows the number and percentage of responses in each funding category. The two most frequently mentioned sources of funding were the United Way (47, or 46%) and county or state deficit funding (46, or 45%). Private donations reported by close to one third of the centers accounted for the third largest funding category (32, or 31.4%), followed by private foundation grants (27, or 26.5%). Direct client payments were cited by only 15 centers (14.7%).

Administrative coordinator. Of the responding programs, 98 provided information regarding the professional degree held by the administrative coordinator of their center (see Table 3.5). One program indicated that this position was shared by two staff members, resulting in a total of 99 professionals. Nearly two thirds of the crisis services (65) indicated that they were coordinated by a person holding a master's degree, with 29 (44.6%) having either an M.A. or an M.S. degree and 22 (33.8%) an M.S.W. degree. One quarter of the coordinators had a bachelor's-level degree. Of these, the vast majority (19, or 76%) had a B.A. or a B.S. degree, and 4 (16%) had a B ˆ.W. degree. Six coordinators held a Ph.D.

TABLE 3.3 Comparison of Services in High and Low Budgetary Ranges

Geographic Location	Population	Type of Client Contact	1988 Budget	Number of Paid Staffers Full-Time	Part-Time	Number of Volunteer Staffers Full-Time	Part-Time
Four services in the over $1 million range							
Minneapolis, Minn.	370,951	T, D, O	$1,000,000	13	30	0	0
Lakewood, Calif.	74,654	T, D	4,002,000	7	8	0	0
Port Huran, Mich.	33,981	*	1,200,000	26	3	3	0
Pinellas Park, Fla.	32,811	T, D, O	4,677,400	72	5	0	0
Six services in the under $50,000 range							
Milwaukee, Wis.	636,212	T, D	11,000	*	*	*	*
Colorado Springs, Colo.	215,000	T, D	43,000	1	0	0	4
San Bernardino, Calif.	118,000	T	40,600	1	0	0	40
Tuscaloosa, Ala.	73,267	T, D	16,000	*	*	*	*
Keene, N.H.	21,449	T, D	30,900	0	4	0	45
Capitola, Calif.	9,095	T	5,800	0	0	0	50

NOTE: T = telephone service; D = direct contact; O = outreach.
*Service did not provide these data.

TABLE 3.4 Funding Sources

Source	Frequency	Percentage
Title XX	9	9
Third-party payments	18	18
County or state deficit funding	46	45
Municipal court contracts	3	3
Direct client payments	15	15
Private foundation grants	27	27
Other:		
United Way	47	46
Private donations	32	31
Fund-raising	11	11
Contracts	10	10
Department of Mental Health	16	16
Grants	7	7
City	4	4
Fees for training	2	2
Title XIX	1	1
F.E.M.A.	1	1
S.O.A.	1	1
Local liquor tax	1	1
O.A.D.A.P.	1	1
Interest	1	1
Self-generated	1	1

NOTE: This is based on 257 responses from 102 respondents.

TABLE 3.5 Professional Degree of the Administrative Coordinator

Degree	Frequency	Percentage
Bachelor's level	25	25.2
B.A. or B.S. (19)		
B.S.W. (4)		
B.S.N. (2)		
Master's level	65	66.3
M.A. or M.S. (29)		
M.S.W. (22)		
M.B.A. (3)		
M.Ed. (6)		
M.Div. (4)		
M.S.N. (1)		
Ph.D. level	6	6.1
No degree	3	3.0

NOTE: This is based on 99 responses from 98 services.

Volunteer staff. Slightly over three quarters of the 99 centers that provided staffing information indicated that they rely on volunteer workers, with a total of 5,667 volunteers reported. Although volunteer staff outnumbered professional staff by more than six to one, it should be recognized that volunteers may work as little as a half day per week. Program administrators indicated that volunteer staffers are an asset to centers when the funding enables paid staff members to do careful screening and to provide adequate training and support. Because of the rapid turnover rate and attrition of volunteer staffers, however, caution should be used in relying heavily on volunteers.

Case Examples

A brief description of four crisis programs is provided here, including the sources and amounts of funding, staffing patterns, the number and types of services they provide, and areas of self-identified strengths.

Gryphon Place Crisis Intervention Center

This private, nonprofit center is located in Kalamazoo, Michigan. It has been in operation since 1970 and provides telephone and direct contact as well as professional outreach services. The program employs 11 full-time, 5 part-time, and 10 contractual staff members and has 65 part-time volunteers. During the 1987 fiscal year, this center provided services to approximately 7,000 clients. Its strongest self-reported program features are having a "strong volunteer force backed by a highly professional emergency staff" and a "strong relationship with other providers." It listed the following funding sources for the 1987 fiscal year:

Funding Source	Amount	Percentage of Budget
County and state contracts	$350,000	70
United Way	85,000	17
Private foundation grants	25,000	5
Unspecified other	20,000	4
Donations	10,000	2
Training grant	6,000	1
Title XX	6,000	1
Total	$502,000	100

The Samaritans of Keene, Inc.

Located in Keene, New Hampshire, this center has been in operation since 1981, providing a 24-hour-a-day, 7-day-a-week telephone suicide prevention service as well as limited direct contact with clients. In 1986, the staff—consisting of 3 part-time codirectors and 45 volunteers—answered approximately 11,000 calls. The program is located in a building with other social services. The Samaritans of Keene identified its major strength as "dedicated, well-trained volunteers." It listed the following funding sources for 1988:

Funding Source	Amount	Percentage of Budget
United Way	$17,598	57
Donations	12,500	40
Unspecified other	800	3
Total	$30,898	100

Emergency Service—Mental Health Center

Located in southern Wisconsin, this organization began providing emergency crisis-oriented services in 1968 and is housed at the local community mental health center. The program provides telephone, direct contact, and professional outreach services to its clients, which numbered 2,950 in 1986. The center employees 7 full-time and 17 part-time staffers and has 3 volunteers. It considers its strongest features to be the "easy availability and outpatient orientation" of the center and the fact that "clients are followed until resolution of the crisis situation." The funding sources for 1987-1988 were as follows:

Funding Source	Amount	Percentage of Budget
County and state funding	$700,000	95
Third-party payments	20,000	3
Title XX	10,000	1
Direct client payments	5,000	1
Total	$735,000	100

Crisis Intervention Unit (Triage Program)
of the Englewood Community Mental Health Center

This unit, located in the western section of Chicago, was established in 1984 and now provides 24-hour, 7-day-a-week telephone crisis intervention as well *as direct contact with clients. Most callers indicate that their primary problem is an acute psychiatric emergency, depression, or behavioral crisis. During the 1987 fiscal year, the staff of six full-time social workers, nurses, and behavioral clinicians served 1,205 clients. The director of this unit indicated that in the past they were not able to provide adequate service to victims of violent crimes, rape, child physical and sexual abuse, vehicular accidents, woman abuse, or the homeless. But in 1988, as a result of a special grant, this unit was able to expand services to rape/trauma victims and also recently initiated a case management interagency program for the homeless.*

SUMMARY

Survey results indicate that crisis centers continue to provide valuable services in their communities. All of the respondents provide telephone hotline services. Many also provide such services as face-to-face counseling and outreach. Although staffing patterns vary greatly among the programs, many use volunteers to supplement the paid professional staff. Respondents reported that volunteers are a valuable asset as long as they are carefully selected, trained, and supervised.

Although most of these critically needed crisis intervention programs seem to respond effectively to the crisis-oriented needs of depressed and suicidal callers, there are three vulnerable groups of persons in crisis that were not adequately served by crisis centers during 1986 and 1987. Of the respondents, 42 indicated that they were not able to provide crisis services to homeless persons, 18 indicated that they were not able to serve victims of violent crimes, and 15 reported that they were not able to serve vehicular accident victims. The respondents stated that they needed additional resources to meet the crisis needs of these groups.

The centers' most significant challenge is to maintain adequate service levels for increasing numbers of clients with limited full-time staff and less than adequate funds. Inadequate funding was identified as one of the top three problems by 87 respondents; 53 of them ranked funding as the number one problem.

PART II

Crisis Intervention
in Life-Threatening
and High-Risk Situations

Stalking Victims and Survivors

Identification, Legal Remedies, and Crisis Treatment

SOPHIA F. DZIEGIELEWSKI

ALBERT R. ROBERTS

The professional literature and news articles are frequently limited to reviews of celebrities being stalked, antistalking laws, pending legislation, and case studies. These articles are useful for social policy makers, social workers, psychologists, police officers, and researchers to obtain background information on the nature and extent of stalking, and the legal remedies. Unfortunately, there is a scarcity of published articles on the strengths and limitations of antistalking laws as well as methods of crisis intervention designed to aid stalking victims. Our focus in this chapter is to (a) review the recent legislation, (b) present a typology of three types of stalking victims, (c) present detailed case examples, and (d) describe the general application of cognitive time-limited crisis intervention with stalking victims.

Given that very little research has been done on the phenomenon of stalking, this chapter and our typology of stalking should be viewed as a beginning stage of analysis. Typologies can provide a tool for improving assessment of dangerous stalkers and planning treatment for victims.

The major advantage of typologies and other assessment schemata is that they provide clinicians with diagnostic indicators so that they can intervene before problem behaviors and potentially violent episodes are intensified.

RECENT LEGISLATION
AND ANTISTALKING STATUTES

The concept of "stalking" is a fairly new phenomenon in our society, and the first legislation in the United States to aid stalking victims was enacted in 1990 when California became the first state to approve a law creating the crime of "stalking" (National Institute of Justice, 1993). The California law was drafted in response to a succession of five unrelated homicides of women, all of whom had been stalked (Carmody, 1994; Sohn, 1994). Included among the victims was Rebecca Schaeffer, the young television star of the TV series *My Sister Sam.* Following California's lead, stalking laws were passed by 29 states in 1992 and 18 states in 1993. By early 1994, a total of 48 states and the District of Columbia had passed antistalking statutes.

Almost all of the antistalking laws require that the alleged stalker must have exhibited the criminal intent of inducing fear in the victim. The state stalking laws also usually require a "course of conduct," which simply stated means a series of acts directed toward a victim and taking place over a period of time. The course of conduct of the stalker must be "willful," "purposeful," "intentional," and/or "knowing." Most states require that the victims be fearful for their personal safety and/or fearful of bodily injury or death resulting from the stalker's threats and/or actions. Generally, the two primary components of most stalking laws include threatening behavior patterns and criminal intent of the perpetrator.

Prior to the passage of the aforementioned legislation, stalking victims had to wait until the stalker actually attacked, injured, or caused bodily harm to them before the police would arrest the stalker. In most of the states that have passed these laws, stalking is either a felony or a misdemeanor offense. In general, stalking is viewed as a felony either when a restraining order is violated or for a second stalking conviction; otherwise, it is considered a misdemeanor.

The following is a description of two of the toughest antistalking statutes, as enacted in Florida and New Jersey. The Florida legislature unanimously approved its antistalking law on July 1, 1992. To file a charge against an alleged stalker in Florida, the victim simply has to prove that he or she has been repeatedly followed or harassed by another person, regardless of whether the alleged perpetrator made any overt threats of killing or seriously injuring the victim (Fla. Stat. Ann. § 784.048, 1992). Simple stalking, without a credible or overt threat, is a misdemeanor of the first degree and could result in a fine of $1,000 and up to 1 year in a county jail. The Florida statute considers an act to be aggravated or felonious stalking when a person is guilty of "willfully, maliciously, and repeatedly" following or harassing another person, and making a "credible threat with the intent to place that person in reasonable fear of death or bodily injury" (Fla. Stat. Ann. § 784.048-3, 1992). The penalty for aggravated stalking, a third degree felony, is a fine of up to $5,000 and 5 years in prison. The person who commits the crime of stalking as a result of violating a protective order is also considered to be an aggravated stalker. The Florida statute may well serve as a useful tool to law enforcement officers in their efforts to protect the public, particularly because the police do not have to have a warrant to arrest an individual for stalking.

The New Jersey antistalking law, like the statute in Florida, makes it easier for police officers to arrest stalkers. The New Jersey law gives the police the authority to arrest an alleged stalker for any type of conduct that frightens the victim and serves no lawful purpose (N.J. Stat. Ann. § 2C:12-10-C, 1993). New Jersey's antistalking law is viewed as one of the toughest in the nation, primarily because it defines "credible threat" to include implicit as well as explicit or overt threats, thus making it much easier for the police to arrest the suspect.

One of the main differences between the way the New Jersey law was written and that of other states (such as California) is that, although an implicit or vague threat will result in the arrest of an alleged stalker in New Jersey, an implicit threat is not sufficient for arrest under the California statute.

In general, the most successful of the antistalking laws provide for the following: immediate and effective protection for the victim, appropriate sanctions for the convicted stalker, and appropriate clinical treatment for the stalker aimed at preventing the behavior from recurring.

In many cases, although the arrest of the stalker provides immediate relief to the victim, that relief is only temporary. Unfortunately, the accused stalker can be released prior to trial and may then present even more of a threat to the victim. States have been urged to review their pretrial release provisions and have been asked to determine whether they should be changed to provide more adequate protection for victims and their families. In response to this call, a small but growing number of states, such as California, Florida, and New Jersey, set prison sentences of 2 to 5 years for persons deemed guilty of aggravated stalking; upon arrest, there was either no bail or a very large bail amount set in an attempt to keep the perpetrator away from the victim and his or her family.

POLICE RESPONSES
TO STALKING INCIDENTS

To learn about police agencies' responses to the problem of stalking, the Police Executive Research Forum (PERF) did an international survey of 95 U.S. police agencies and 50 police agencies in Australia, Canada, Great Britain, and New Zealand. The survey found that most law enforcement agencies have charged stalking perpetrators with multiple offenses and this seems to result in an end to the stalking (National Institute of Justice, 1993, p. 38). The most common multiple charges were trespassing, simple assault, and stalking.

In regard to the incidence of stalking, the overwhelming majority of complaints are investigated by detectives, investigators, or patrol officers. After a report has been filed, 82% of police agencies in states with antistalking laws and 60% of agencies in states without such laws reported that they do a follow-up investigation (National Institute of Justice, 1993). Unfortunately, only approximately 50% of the police departments with antistalking laws provide formal training to their patrol officers. This lack of training may leave police enforcement officials feeling frustrated when confronted with the dynamics of stalking episodes.

Many police departments have been reluctant to arrest alleged stalkers for fear of arresting an innocent person and being sued for false arrest. Many of the original stalking laws required the arresting officer to obtain evidence of highly specific behavior and specific intent on the part of the stalker, that is, evidence that the victim was in fear of death or bodily injury. Therefore, the difficulty in establishing this evidence prior to the actual arrest may have complicated the ability of police officers to make constitutionally valid arrests. Another problem with the current legislation is that stalking is generally categorized as a misdemeanor—rather than a felony. This leaves stalkers with only minor sanctions for their behavior such as a paying a small fine. In some cases, the court has the option to place a convicted stalker on probation, with no jail time or fine. Unfortunately, in large cities, the probation officer typically has a caseload of 100-180 clients. As a result, the probation officer usually does not even get to see the stalking offender until the police call with information on the stalker's arrest for another offense.

Today, a few selected cities have developed model programs designed to assist and protect stalking victims. For example, as of 1990, the Los Angeles Police Department had established a four-member "Threat Management" unit (or Stalking Squad) as part of the Mental Evaluation Unit of the department's Detective Headquarters Division (Lane, 1992, p. 27). This program was developed in response to a number of stalking incidents against celebrities in the Los Angeles area, with particular attention paid to the stalking episodes that resulted in the murder of actress Rebecca Schaeffer.

Another model program developed in several areas of the United States to assist the victims of battering and/or stalking was generated by ADT Security Systems. Two of the sites that implemented this type of program were Providence House in Toms River, New Jersey, and the Spring Women's Shelter in Tampa, Florida. In such places, the victim is instructed to wear a pendant that contains a small beeper; when the victim spots the stalker, she is instructed to press the pendant. This action triggers an alarm at the local ADT monitoring station, and the monitoring station immediately informs the police. There are several drawbacks to the use of this device. The first is that no matter how quickly the police are notified, a time delay will always exist; second, if the stalker tampers with the phone lines in the victim's home, the device could be disconnected.

IDENTIFICATION AND TREATMENT

The acknowledgment of stalking is a relatively new phenomenon with few and varied legal consequences. Although stalking is not a new occurrence, it has recently received national attention. It has been particularly highlighted by the media in regard to famous individuals who have reported being stalked, as well as in movies and television shows. Movie reviews of *Fatal Attraction* with Glen Close said it echoed what was referred to as "every man's worst nightmare." In the final scene of the movie, the stalker openly confronts the wife of the victim and the victim himself with a knife. The violence that erupts is so lifelike and believable that the audience is left stunned. To support the viability of this type of scenario in real life, the friends and family members of Nicole Brown Simpson have also described a possible form of stalking. Several of them have stated that Nicole feared for her life and reportedly that her estranged husband O. J. Simpson was known to erupt in violent outrage at the presumption of her being with another. In an attempt to better understand, define, and therefore treat the victims of stalking, the following typology is proposed. Based on the literature and the legal statutes, those who participate in stalking behavior generally fall into three major areas, which include (a) the domestic violence stalker, (b) the erotomania and/or delusional stalker, and (c) the nuisance stalker.

Domestic Violence Stalker

In *domestic violence stalking*, the stalker is generally motivated by the need to continue or reestablish the domestic relationship, in which he or she can have or maintain control of the victim. Thought patterns and statements that reflect an attitude of "if I can't have him or her, no one else can either" are often noted. Many times the stalker is consumed with intense conflictual emotions of hate and love. There may also be intense feelings of anger and fear about the uncontrollable desire felt toward the victim.

Case example. When asked what brought her to the shelter for abused women, Sara, who was visibly shaken, began to cry. "I think he is going to kill me, and I know it is only a matter of time," Sara stated with tears running down her face. Sara did not understand why it had to be this way and how her 2-year marriage had turned into such a "living hell." According to Sara, the marriage was wonderful in the beginning; Donald was very loving, considerate, and attentive. After about 6 months, however, things began to change. Due to financial constraints, Sara decided to get a job. Donald really didn't want her to work but agreed that they needed the money. Sara got a job at a local convenience store as a clerk, working the day shift. To assist with transportation to her job, Sara's parents gave the couple their old family car. Sara reported that for the first week things seemed to remain quiet on the "home front," and on pay day Donald was really pleased to get the extra money.

After a while, however, Donald began to make statements that reflected that he was upset about Sara's using the car as well as about her absences from their home. Sara stated that she wasn't sure when the jealousy and suspiciousness actually began, but she could remember specific incidents. For example, one evening on her drive home, Sara got rerouted because of an accident. She ended up using a detour and taking an unfamiliar way home. She estimated that she was about 30 minutes late arriving home. When she arrived home, she found Donald standing in the driveway, furious. He immediately checked the car's odometer and demanded to know where she was and where the four extra miles had come from. Sara was very upset and she believes it was probably at that point that she realized Donald had deliberately been monitoring the mileage she used on her trips away from home.

That night, they fought continuously and Sara's eyes were swollen from crying the next morning when she went to work. At work the next day, it became very obvious to her coworker, Jane, that Sara had been crying. Jane hugged Sara and asked her what had happened. Sara was sobbing when she looked up. Much to her shock, in the shadows of the parking lot, she could swear she saw a man standing there watching. When she looked directly toward the man, he seemed to duck behind a tree. Suspecting a robbery, Sara and Jane called the police. The police found no one there. When Sara got home, Donald was very angry and questioned her about her day and wanted to know exactly what she had done. They began to fight and Sara never told him about the incident. This same incident, of a man lurking in the shadows outside her job, happened several other times, but no one was ever identified.

Over the next few weeks, Sara began to feel very restless and Donald became more insistent in his demands to know everything she had done at work. He was particularly interested in the details of whom she had talked to and what was discussed. Once while driving to the grocery store, Sara thought she saw Donald several cars behind her, but when she asked him he denied being there. Later that night, after fighting about Sara's wearing too much makeup, they went together to Donald's office holiday party. Donald was an auto mechanic who worked at a local car dealership about 5 miles from Sara's job. Sara said she became shocked at the party when she overheard a conversation between two of Donald's coworkers. They were discussing Donald's repeated short absences from work, and how he was about to lose his job over it because his boss was looking for him yesterday afternoon "and as usual he was not around."

Sara wanted to ask Donald about what she had overheard but she was afraid because she knew how their discussions always became so volatile. The last incident, which precipitated Sara's leaving, happened when Sara and Jane were standing in the parking lot near their cars. Jane was aware of Sara's problems and had agreed to help Sara leave town and stay with a friend. As they were speaking, Sara heard the sound of a car and when she looked up she saw the car speeding directly for them. Sara stated that when she saw the car coming it must have been instinct that helped her to push Jane and herself from its path. As the car screeched off, Sara was horrified to see that the car looked just like hers and, although she did not see the driver, she knew in her heart it was Donald. Sara admitted herself to the abuse shelter because she did not want to take the chance of endangering any more of her friends or family members.

Unfortunately, in domestic violence, stalking cases like this one are not unusual. Many times, the stalker is a former boyfriend or girlfriend, husband or wife, family member or household member who in desperation of maintaining or reinitiating the relationship threatens or harasses the victim. As has happened in several documented cases, stalking behavior can often end in violence or even death. This makes the crime scene one familiar to the victim, often either the victim's home or place of employment. Therefore, as in this case example, it is not uncommon for the crime scene to be in close proximity to either of these areas. Many times, the familiarity of the crime scene to the victim may leave the victim feeling safe and protected, and may leave the victim more open and vulnerable to the possible retaliation of the stalker than an unfamiliar environment.

Erotomania or Delusional Stalker

The second type of identified stalking is referred to as *erotomania* or *delusional stalking*. Here the motivation for the relationship is based on the stalker's fixation (e.g., doctor, local FBI agent, anchorman and/or anchorwoman, or simply someone who represents the unobtainable ideal). Generally, the target person is someone who is considered to be of higher status than the stalker (Anderson, 1993). It is important to note, however, that even though the victim is the center of attention, other persons close to the victim may also be in danger, particularly if the loved one is viewed by the stalker as coming between the erotomania or delusional stalker and her or his target. Potential unanticipated victims could be a husband or wife, a child, a parent, or any other person seen as receiving love, affection, and attention from the victim.

Case Example

Mr. Foster is a 40-year-old licensed clinical social worker who engages in private group practice. When he first met Mary, now his former client, he had been married for 4 years and his wife was pregnant with their first child. Professionally, Mr. Foster is fairly well renowned with over 15 years of clinical experience and a very long list of private patients. Fellow professionals describe Mr. Foster as an "impassioned" clinician who really cares about each of the clients he serves. Mary is a 32-year-old female who was referred to Mr. Foster for divorce adjustment therapy. Mary had recently been divorced from her husband after 1 year of marriage. Mary talked about the loss she felt and her anger that they did not try to have children because of her ex-husband's selfishness. After the first session, Mr. Foster noted in her chart that Mary was genuinely depressed and exhibited several dependent and possible borderline personality traits. Mary and Mr. Foster together formulated the goals to address in treatment and Mr. Foster had charted that all was progressing well.

Mary came early for the second session. It was during this session that while discussing the divorce she began to cry and reached over and squeezed Mr. Foster's hand to emphasize her frustration. Mr. Foster slowly withdrew his hand from Mary and directed her attention back to what she had been saying. No further mention of the incident was made.

On the third session, Mary came approximately 20 minutes early and upon arrival told the secretary that she really needed her session. When in the session, Mary asked Mr. Foster several questions about how he would have handled her problems. Mr. Foster continued to redirect Mary's attention back to helping her problem solve. Mary listened intently to what was said, worked hard in the session, and thanked Mr. Foster repeatedly for his help. On her way out of the session, she turned and hugged Mr. Foster briefly. Mr. Foster stated that he felt awkward and surprised and, although he did not push her away, he did not hug her back.

It was about this time that Mr. Foster's wife began complaining about receiving phone calls in which the caller would listen to her voice and then hang up. Jokingly, Mr. Foster's wife asked him if he was having an affair. Mr. Foster also started getting calls at home and at work in which the caller just listened until he or his wife hung up. The calls sometimes came at night, preventing them from sleeping. In an effort to stop this nuisance, the Fosters had their previously listed telephone number changed to an unlisted number. The new number was given only to the appropriate people—work, family, and so on. Finally, the calls stopped.

In the fourth session, Mary seemed a little upset and asked if he wanted to continue seeing her. Mr. Foster was a bit confused by this and asked if Mary was feeling rushed in the therapy sessions. Mary said she was. During the session, Mary seemed very distracted and began to ask what Mr. Foster considered to be personal questions about his wife and his relationship that had no bearing on her therapy. Mary resisted any of his attempts at redirection. At the end of the session, Mary stated that she needed more time and became angry that Mr. Foster had scheduled another client so soon after her. After the session was over, Mr. Foster talked with his supervisor, stating that he just did not feel "right" about Mary's conduct and progress in therapy. With the agreement of his supervisor, they agreed to recommend transfer of the client to another social worker in the office.

In the next session, Mr. Foster suggested to Mary that another social worker might be of more help to her at this point. Before he could finish, Mary got up and upon leaving the office screamed at him, "I let you in and you lied to me." She turned and ran from the office. Mr. Foster just stood there as his supervisor and colleagues came out of their offices to see what all the commotion was about.

Several nights later, there was a robbery in the office. It was believed that the burglars must have been interrupted because the only major thing removed was a typewriter from the secretaries' office and several other small items. Mr. Foster reported missing his microcassette tape player and a gold-plate-framed picture of his wife and him. Several days later, Mr. Foster found Mary waiting by his car. She was crying and stated that she really needed to see him again. Mr. Foster remained clear and gave her the name and number of his referral colleague and left.

When he got home that day, his wife complained about the phone calls having started again. This time, music could be heard on the other end of the phone. The words of the song that could be distinguished said something like "you cheated, you lied, you never did love me." Mr. Foster told his wife about Mary and that he suspected it might be her. His wife was very upset and asked him if he had had an affair with her. After Mr. Foster reassured her, they agreed it was time to call the phone company and see if the calls could be traced. That night, a car was heard racing up the street and a brick was thrown through Mr. Foster's car window. The police were notified but no links to Mary could be established. The harassment continued for weeks and Mr. Foster often felt that he was being followed. One time, his wife screamed into the phone for the caller to stop and the caller's response was only to make the music louder. Mr. Foster had his number changed for the second time and this time the calls ceased. Mr. Foster reported thinking that he had seen Mary several times afterward. Several months after the therapy ended, Mr. Foster received a card from Mary thanking him for his help and saying she had reunited with her husband. That was the last time Mr. Foster had heard from Mary.

In this case example, Mr. Foster was able to benefit from the client's finding another outlet for her stalking behavior. The intentions reported by Mr. Foster had the appearance of innocence, yet, as in most cases of stalking, the stalker misinterpreted them as being meaningful. From a cognitive perspective, as described in Chapter 1, the stalker may have formed a schema that resulted in a distorted cognition. A *schema* is generally referred to as the cognitive structure that organizes experience and behavior (Beck et al., 1990). Schemas involve the way individuals view certain aspects of their lives, including relationship aspects such as adequacy and the ability of others to love them. As in this case, the schema that one subscribes to can have a profound effect on the behaviors and emotions that are exhibited.

Beck et al. (1979) discussed the types of systematic errors that can lead to emotional distress. In this case, the stalker can make systematic errors such as *arbitrary inferences*. Here the erotomania stalker may reach conclusions that are not based on accurate supporting evidence. For example, in this case, the stalker may have concluded: "Mr. Foster is kind and interested in my well-being; therefore, he must love me." The second type of systematic error described by Beck et al. (1979), *selective abstraction*, could also have occurred. Here the stalker focuses on one or more details in a situation that was taken out of context while seeming to ignore the more pronounced features of the incident or situation. For example, when Mr. Foster quietly pulled his hand away from the stalker's, she may have perceived it as his inability to show her how he really feels. The stalker may have further *overgeneralized and magnified and/or minimized* the reality of the situation. The stalker may believe that Mr. Foster really cares, no matter what he says or does, and that Mr. Foster's behavior merely reflects his inability to deal with his feelings and emotions. Here the stalker distorts the reality of the situation, inappropriately representing what has actually happened.

As exemplified, comprehension of the schema the stalker subscribes to is essential in predicting future behavior. Individuals can and do distort reality based on how they perceive it, and these cognitive distortions can result in negative feelings, maladaptive behaviors, and, if carried to the extreme, psychopathology (Liese, 1994). In this case, as in others, the stalker truly believes that her interpretation of what has happened is the valid one. And many times, based on the schema subscribed to, the stalker may feel the need for revenge toward the target who is repelling the stalker's attentions.

Nuisance Stalker

The third type of stalker is the nuisance stalker. In this type of stalking, the victim is targeted and continually harassed by the stalker. Interaction attempts are often made through use of the telephone. Here the stalker might hang up, use obscene language, or simply verbally torment and harass the victim. In an attempt to be in proximity with the targeted victim, continuous physical appearance at the target's residence, place of employment, or other public places might also occur. There have also been numerous reported cases of contact through the mail with unsigned letters, cards, and so on.

Case Example

Marsha, who came for treatment based on a court order, gave her initial complaint as "feeling as though she was becoming possessed and could not control the thoughts and feelings that she was having toward her old friend Janice." Marsha believed that Janice had some kind of power over her and she was being forced to retaliate. According to Marsha, she and Janice had grown up together in the same town. Janice later married Marsha's old sweetheart. At first, Marsha didn't care because she had broken off with the man but after years of thought she had come to believe that Janice had influenced her to do so. After the death of her husband, Marsha began to become very depressed and generally stayed indoors. She had very few friends and lived meagerly off her husband's death benefits. She believes it was about this time that she started to call Janice on the phone. She stated she remembered clearly that the first time she called Janice and heard her voice she became infuriated. Janice sounded so happy. Marsha started calling her on a regular basis. At first, she would just hang up but then she started doing little things to make it exciting. One day while watching a movie, she heard a male actor curse and threaten the female actor. She recorded what was said on tape and began playing it when Janice would answer the phone. She could tell that Janice was upset and with each attempt felt some satisfaction in continuing. Marsha wrote down the words that the actor had said and mailed them to Janice in an unmarked envelope. Marsha wanted to hurt Janice as she had been hurt. Eventually, Janice was able to link the calls and letters to Marsha and filed charges against her. Marsha stated that, even though she had been forced to come in for therapy by the court, she really wanted to do something about what was happening to her.

As exhibited in this case example, the stalker may realize that what she is doing is harassment but the activity itself becomes addicting. Several stalkers have reported that the activity provided excitement and, in a bizarre sort of way, challenging entertainment.

CRISIS INTERVENTION
WITH THE STALKING VICTIM

Roberts and Roberts (1990) note that the clinician who works with the crisis victim should have an understanding of crisis theory and the methods of crisis intervention to effectively address the client's needs. Most victims of stalking have been forced to encounter sustained abuse, which may end with a serious and severe personal attack, resulting in the victim entering a crisis state. In this crisis state, the "precipitating or hazardous event" will be followed by a time of tension and distress.

The three most common precipitating events that will bring the victim of stalking in for treatment are (a) escalation in the incidence or severity of the episodes, (b) injury being inflicted whether purposeful or accidental, and (c) relationship and/or employment disturbance. Roberts and Roberts (1990) state that the precipitating event(s) is generally viewed as the *last straw*. Once the precipitating event has occurred, the client generally tries his or her usual coping methods, and when these fail, the resultant active crisis state follows (Roberts, 1990a).

In crisis theory, it is paramount that the atmosphere underlying the process of therapy be one of respect for the client. The goal of crisis work is to enable the client to regain the "capacity to deal effectively with the crisis" and "to increase his/her mastery over his/her own behavior and gain greater self awareness" (Getz, Wiesen, Sue, & Ayers, 1974, p. 43). Although interventions based on crisis theory seek to restore the client to a level of functioning that existed prior to the crisis, Roberts (1990) saw the end result for the victim as a "person returning to their pre-crisis state or growing from the crisis intervention so that she/he learns new coping skills to utilize in the future" (p. 27).

IMPLEMENTATION OF TREATMENT

As described earlier, treatment to be initiated with the victim of stalking must take into account the probable crisis state that the victim has encountered. For possible treatment of the stalking victim, a time-limited crisis intervention model is suggested. In highlighting the focus of this type of treatment, three additional topics need to be addressed.

It is crucial to note, however, that before any of these three topic areas is accomplished, the safety of the victim needs to be ensured at all times.

First, the victim of a stalker should immediately let the stalker know that a relationship is not desired. The sooner and more explicitly this point is made the better. *Second*, when confronting the stalker, the victim must be encouraged to be as direct as possible. Many times, the victim who is in a crisis state cannot think clearly and may need assistance with this. Behavioral rehearsal of what and how it will be said is an excellent starting point for the therapeutic intervention. The stalker should be told in as few words and with as little emotion as possible. This brevity and shallowness of affect allows for the least amount of misinterpretation by the stalker. It is important for the victim not to give reasons for his or her decision, because reasons can give hope and leave room for negotiation and argument. It is suggested that the therapist help victims write down exactly what they want to say and practice reading it as written on a piece of paper. This helps clients to feel reassurance and control over what will they will say at a very emotionally laden point in time.

When confronting the stalker, it is important to advise the stalking victim not to meet him or her in a private place. No matter how careful the victim is in trying to control the confrontation, she or he should always choose a safe place in case the stalker in anger decides to retaliate. This means picking a place where help (if needed) is immediately available. One suggested way to communicate this message is over the telephone, so that victims can say what they have planned and hang up. In this way, victims will not have to look at the stalker, and will only have to deal with the sound of his or her voice. It is important to remember, however, that no matter how well the situation is handled, the stalker may try to retaliate, and it remains important to plan that, once this communication is delivered, a safe place will be secured.

Even if the victim is currently in a "safe" place such as a shelter, the home of a relative, or the like, the treatment provided for the victim must carefully evaluate the risk of retaliation and involve the joint development of a safety plan. This is a crucial step to take in the first session, given the possibility that the stalker may retaliate. The clinician can evaluate risk to the victim by asking the victim whether the stalker might be suicidal or homicidal, or if the stalker has a weapon and what it is (Schecter, 1987). Questions should also focus on how obsessive the stalker is regarding the victim, her or his access to the victim, and to the best of the victim's knowledge the presence of rage, depression, or drug and alcohol dependence or abuse in the stalker.

The *third* issue that must be addressed is establishing agreement with the victim of a stalker to *cease all contact* with the stalker. The stalker may misinterpret any communication with the victim, and this communication, whether positive or negative, may be viewed as rewarding. This may mean changing the victim's usual routine (as much as possible) so that he or she will not be subject to a predictable pattern of behavior. Therefore, the stalker will also be forced to develop new patterns for reaching the victim and in doing so may reevaluate the productivity of this endeavor.

Once these three topics have been discussed and addressed, the focus of treatment must return to the mental health status of the victim. It is possible that the victim may be suffering from post-traumatic stress disorder, or, depending on the type, intensity, and frequency of the stalking, the victim may also have developed some type of dissociative reaction in response to pain (Geffner & Pagelow, 1990; Walker, 1984). Some authors have compared the behavioral and emotional reactions of these victim to those of hostages. Those exhibiting symptoms of the "Stockholm Syndrome" react with "frozen fright" and "psychological infantilism." Victims suppress their rage for survival purposes and suffer a "traumatic depression" after escape. The victim may therefore take on the perspective of the victimizer (Graham, Rawlings, & Rimini, 1988). Therefore, as with all victims of violence, the stalking victim's behavior may be influenced by low self-esteem, denial of the seriousness of the stalking behavior, and/or an inability to trust (Bolton & Bolton, 1987). There may also be an unhealthy sense of dependency on the stalker. This is particularly so if there has been any length of time during which familiar patterns of behavior between the victim and the stalker have developed.

Based on all the things that may have happened to the victim, it is always important to assess the potential for suicide. It may be unclear how much damage has been caused by the stalker to the victim's relationships, employment, and so on. Many times, the victim of a violent episode may view suicide as a permanent solution to a seemingly unsolvable problem (Dziegielewski & Resnick, in press b).

Consistent with the principles of crisis intervention, treatment for the stalking victim remains similar to working with any type of survivor and should include (a) helping the client to define and address the problem situation, (b) maintaining an action orientation, (c) setting limited goals, (d) providing support to the victim, (e) assisting with focused problem solving, (f) beginning to assess and help the victim increase self-image, and (g) working with the victim to foster as much independence and responsibility for his or her own actions as possible (Dziegielewski & Resnick, in press b).

In the *middle phase* of treatment, the social worker and client should set up goals and objectives. Goals must be stated in measurable terms, and a way to evaluate progress must be designed. Goals should include the development and enacting of an action plan for the stalking victim. It is vital that the social worker stress the danger that could develop, and continued emphasis must be placed on maintaining a safety plan. The stalking victim may need assistance in getting help from various organizations and institutions, including the legal system, with the benefits and pitfalls of going to court.

It is important, particularly in domestic violence stalking, that treatment include intervention to increase assertiveness and promote self-esteem. A focus on strengths and assets helps to offset the strong dependency and feeling of worthlessness that have been conditioned as part of this abusive cycle (Geffner & Pagelow, 1990).

In the final sessions, or the *ending phase*, of treatment, overall progress should be summarized at the conclusion of each session with an emphasis on empowerment of the stalking victim. The practical concerns of the client in terms of accessing resources are discussed while an atmosphere is maintained that engenders hope and fosters independence. In assessing the effectiveness of the treatment method, the social worker will want to consider whether the client has been returned to a precrisis level of functioning. If treatment has been effective, clients should be able to give the social worker a basic explanation of the dynamics of the stalking experience and should leave armed with information, including referrals. The victims' experience should have been validated by the social worker so they realize that what happened to them was not their fault. Treatment has also been effective if stalking victims are able to highlight their own core strengths and ways to handle this type of situation in the future.

FUTURE DIRECTIONS

The proposed typology of stalking experiences identified here is designed to provide the reader with the basic information needed to begin to understand, diagnose, and treat this type of phenomenon. It is important to remember that the identification and treatment of stalking is a relatively new phenomenon with societal identification and recognition primarily focused within the last 5 years. The victims of stalkers, similar to those of rape and domestic violence, are often traumatized and left to wonder "what could they have done differently." What they did or did not do—does not really matter. Many times, the cognitions of the stalker may be systematically distorted and simple things that the victim does may have been misrepresented or misunderstood by the stalker. By learning to understand the patterns of stalking behavior, the dysfunctional thought patterns that may surround this type of systematic thinking, and the forms of time-limited cognitive treatment available to the victim, we as professionals may be able to decrease some of the premeditated violence resulting from the stalking encounter.

5

Brief Cognitive
Therapies for Rape Victims

PATRICIA A. RESICK

MINDY B. MECHANIC

Susan was raped 4 weeks before calling for therapy. Although distressed, she expressed ambivalence about seeking treatment. Twice during her initial telephone call, she expressed this ambivalence by stating that she wasn't sure that she needed therapy, and she just wanted to put it behind her and forget that it ever happened. Susan indicated that she decided to seek help because her sister pressured her into it. The intake counselor determined that Susan was having a great deal of difficulty sleeping, had not returned to work since the assault, and had only talked to a few people about the rape. Susan was raped by a former boyfriend who unexpectedly showed up at her apartment drunk and angry. Susan tried to get him to leave but that only made him angrier, so she tried to placate him by offering him coffee. When she turned to go to the kitchen, he suddenly tackled her to the floor, dragged her down the hallway to her bedroom, and raped her vaginally. Initially, Susan tried to fight him off but then he grabbed her by the throat with one hand and hit her across the face with the other hand.

AUTHORS' NOTE: Portions of this chapter have been adapted from Resick and Schnicke (1993) and Ellis, Black, and Resick (1992).

She went limp at that point. When he finished, he suddenly started crying and asking her to forgive him. Afraid of more violence, she said she would forgive him if he would just leave her apartment. Susan locked the door upon his departure, took a shower until the water ran cold, and crawled into her bed. She told no one about the rape until her sister called her the next afternoon. When her sister urged her to call the police, Susan refused. She did not receive any medical care, but she did call her employer, who appeared to be understanding initially. At the time she called the therapist, her boss was beginning to get impatient and said that if she didn't return to work soon, he would have to replace her.

Paula was raped 7 years before seeking therapy. She was raped at age 18 after leaving a party with a young man she knew slightly. Prior to the night of the party, she had talked to him on several occasions and was attracted to him. The night of the party, Paula talked to him quite a bit and found him interesting and exciting, though he seemed somewhat arrogant. Paula was flattered that he was paying so much attention to her. When Paula's friend, with whom she came to the party, told her that she was getting back together with an old boyfriend and wanted to leave with him, the young man said that he would drive Paula home. Instead of driving her home, however, he drove out into the country and forced her to have sex. Paula was shocked by his sudden change in behavior. She was frightened because she didn't know where she was and didn't feel that she could get away, so she didn't fight him when he raped her. He drove her back to her parents' house and dropped her off saying that he would call her sometime and that maybe they could go out again. Although she initially tried to pretend that everything was all right, she was unable to keep up the pretense. The next day, Paula told her mother about the rape. Although Paula's mother was sympathetic, her advice was to forget that it ever happened and to put it out of her mind. Paula's mother also suggested that they not tell her father. Fortunately, the young man did not go to her school, so she was able to avoid seeing him again. Paula stayed home from school with the "flu" for a couple of days and then returned, although she was anxious and depressed for several months. Eventually, the nightmares stopped and she was able to resume her school activities. In fact, she became very busy with studying, clubs, and a weekend job that left her no time to date for several years. She also refused to go to parties. Just prior to seeking therapy, Paula started dating a man she had been friends with for 2 years. As the relationship developed, Paula began to worry about having sex with him. She didn't want to lose him, but she was extremely anxious about the prospect of having intercourse. Paula had not told him about the rape because she was afraid that he would reject her if he knew about it. Paula began to have nightmares and flashbacks about the rape and felt depressed.

Micki sought therapy 2 days after being raped. She called a hotline only hours after the rape because she felt suicidal. Micki had called the police and was examined at the hospital, but the police did not appear to take her case seriously because she had been drinking heavily at the time of the rape. At her first counseling session the next day, Micki had difficulty staying focused on the assault. Although greatly distressed over the rape and angry at the police, Micki expressed an equal level of distress over the fact that she had lost her job 2 weeks previously and her friend betrayed her by not returning her phone calls. When the therapist tried to find out more about the rape, Micki responded, "The rape is just one of many things that happened to me. This is the last straw. My brother used to rape me when I was little—and this is the third time I was raped. I just can't take any more." Micki said that she went to a bar because she was upset. At the bar, a man started talking to her. He seemed very nice and sympathetic, and they talked for several hours. When she decided to leave the bar, he offered to walk her to the car. As they passed an alley, he suddenly pulled her back behind a dumpster. He had a knife and threatened to kill her if she screamed. He forced her to engage in oral sex and then raped her vaginally. He left her in the alley. After she dressed, she went back into the bar and told the bartender what happened. The bartender called the police. Micki admitted to drinking heavily in the days since the rape, and the therapist noticed old scars on various places on her arms. When asked about her background, Micki said that she did not remember very much about her childhood.

The aim of this chapter is to present current theory and data on the use of time-limited cognitive-behavioral interventions for the treatment of rape-related posttraumatic stress disorder (PTSD). To date, three variants of cognitive-behavioral therapy have received empirical support: prolonged exposure (PE), stress inoculation training (SIT), and cognitive processing therapy (CPT). Before embarking on a detailed description of the use of these cognitive-behavioral frameworks for conceptualizing and treating the psychological sequelae of sexual assault, preliminary material will be presented to lay the foundation for these therapies. In the spirit of organizational clarity, this chapter is divided into three sections. The first section, "Scope of the Problem," will focus on the scope of sexual assault, with emphasis on prevalence rates and clinical symptomatology, notably PTSD and depression. The second section, "Triage," will describe initial pretreatment considerations that apply during the early phase of the initial crisis period, including evaluating the appropriateness of time-limited cognitive approaches. Assessment of client functioning for purposes of treatment planning will also be included in the second section because this is an important early step in the therapeutic process. The third section, "Information Processing Theory," will highlight information processing models of rape-related PTSD. Three cognitive-behavioral therapies with demonstrated efficacy will be detailed along with a session-by-session description of CPT. The chapter will conclude with considerations for the therapist when treating rape victims, such as issues of gender, attitudes about victims, and secondary traumatic reactions in the therapist. The reader with extensive grounding in the PTSD and rape literatures who wishes to cover just the cognitive-behavioral interventions may wish to skim sections one and two, and skip ahead to the third section.

SCOPE OF THE PROBLEM

Sexual assault is a common experience in the lives of many women. Sexual assault prevalence estimates vary from study to study depending on how it is defined, how it is measured, and who is asked about their experience. The role of these critical issues in obtaining valid estimates of the prevalence of rape and sexual assault will be considered below.

Accurate Assessment of Prevalence

Definition. As generally used, the term *sexual assault* is a broad category that includes not only completed rapes but also an array of other unwanted sexual behavior, such as fondling and attempted rape. Broad definitions of sexual assault, including attempted rape, or unwanted sexual advances, have been used in some studies, whereas restrictive definitions of rape have been used in others. Restrictive definitions of rape are generally consistent with the legal provisions of rape statutes requiring forcible penetration of the vagina, mouth, or anus. In a recent national study known as the "National Women's Study," Kilpatrick, Edmunds, and Seymour (1992) used a conservative definition of forcible rape that would meet most statutory requirements: *"an event that occurred without the woman's consent, involved the use of force or threat of force, and involved sexual penetration of the victim's vagina, mouth, or rectum."*

With this restrictive definition, Kilpatrick et al. obtained a rate of 683,000 forcible rapes per year in a large sample of adult women. This figure translates to an estimated 12.1 million women, or 13% of women, who have experienced at least one *completed forcible rape* in their lives. According to Kilpatrick and his colleagues, a little more than half (56%) of these women experienced one rape during their lives, whereas 39% reported more than one rape. When definitions of rape are not restricted to completed forcible rapes, multiple studies using different populations and methodologies reveal that 25% to 54% of women have been the victim of some form of sexual assault in their lifetimes (e.g., Kilpatrick, Saunders, Best, & Von, 1987; Koss, Gidycz, & Wisniewski, 1987; Russell, 1984). Despite the breadth of definition, these data concur that sexual assaults occur with an alarming frequency.

How questions are asked. Differences in the way questions are asked have a major impact on the rates of sexual assault reported in a given study. For example, the question, "Have you ever been raped?" yields substantially fewer endorsements than the question, "Has anyone ever used physical force or threat of force to make you have unwanted sexual contact, no matter what your relationship is to that person?" Estimates of rape obtained in the National Women's Study (NWS) were 5.3 times higher than those obtained by the National Crime Survey (NCS) and the FBI Uniform Crime Reports (UCR) for the comparable period of time, despite the fact that those data sets included attempted rape, whereas the NWS was limited to completed rapes. Because the NCS study specifically asked the victims if they were raped, whereas the NWS employed the behavioral description above, differences in phrasing most likely accounted for these discrepant rates. Faulty beliefs, myths, and stereotypes held by the public about what constitutes rape and who can be considered a rapist are among the reasons that asking about rape directly leads to gross underreporting of the crime. Some examples of these myths are that "rape is committed only by strangers" or that "someone you love and trust wouldn't rape you." Results of research by Koss (1985) found that many victims do not label their experience as rape, particularly if the rape was committed by someone the victim had an intimate relationship with, such as a boyfriend or husband. Only one in four women in the Koss et al. (1987) national survey of college women labeled their experiences of unwanted coercive sexual contact as rape. Moreover, until recently, many states did not legitimize spousal rape as a crime, so that women raped by their husbands would have been unlikely to label unwanted, forced, sexual contact as rape. If a woman fails to label the experience as rape, she undoubtebly will say no to a specific question about rape, although she might acknowledge the experience when the question is framed in terms of specific behaviors and the option is given to identify an intimate or acquaintance as the perpetrator. This issue is important not only in research on rape prevalence but also in clinical, legal, and health care settings, where it is essential to assess victimization history accurately.

Sample selection. The third important consideration for obtaining valid estimates of rape focuses on who is asked and how they are identified. The National Women's Study described above sampled only adult women; girls under age 18, boys, and men were excluded from the study. Because an estimated 60% of rapes in women's lives are believed to occur in childhood, the 683,000 annual rate of forcible rapes reflects only about half of the rapes that are estimated to occur (Kilpatrick et al., 1992). The strategies used to identify rape victims vary across studies. Sampling methods include large-scale population surveys, college campus surveys, and samples of women identified as rape victims from police departments, rape crisis centers, and hospital emergency rooms. Population surveys offer significant advantages over strategies that require rape victims to file police reports or seek medical treatment or psychological services. The percentage of rape victims who report their crimes to the police has been estimated to be as low as 5% in Koss's national study of college women (Koss et al., 1987), 7% in a representative sample of women in a small southern city (Kilpatrick, Saunders, et al., 1987), 9.5% in a representative sample of women in San Francisco (Russell, 1984), and 16% in the National Women's Study. A mere 12% of the women in the NWS sample reported the rape to the police within 24 hours of the rape. Similarly, most rape victims do not seek medical attention: 17% of the women surveyed by Kilpatrick et al. (1992) in the NWS sought a medical examination, and only slightly more than half of those who sought medical services (60%) did so within 24 hours of the assault. Alarmingly, one third of the women failed to notify the examining physician that they had been sexually assaulted.

One reason women seldom seek police and medical attention is that, contrary to stereotypes, the majority of rapes are committed not by strangers but by men who are known to their victims. Rapes committed by strangers accounted for only 17% of the rapes in Russell's (1984) study of 930 women in the San Francisco area, and 22% of the rapes in the National Women's Study.[1] The reluctance of women to report rape increases when the perpetrator is known to the victim. In the NWS, a significantly greater proportion of the women who were raped by strangers (32.4%) reported their rape to police, compared with those raped by known assailants (19%) (H. Resnick, personal communication, January 21, 1994).

Symptoms and Recovery Patterns

Sexual assault is a highly traumatic event from which many victims never completely recover. Typical post-rape reactions include depression, problems with self-esteem and interpersonal relationships, and sexual dysfunction (see Resick, 1993, for a review of psychological reactions to rape). However, the most frequently observed disorder that develops as a consequence of sexual assault is PTSD. Because of the high frequency of PTSD and depression following sexual assault and their use as target symptoms in most cognitive-behavioral interventions, we will review these reactions in the following section.

Posttraumatic stress disorder. The *DSM-IV* (American Psychiatric Association, 1994) articulates four criteria necessary for a diagnosis of PTSD. Criterion A, newly amended in the *DSM-IV*, has two component parts that must both be present: "1) the person experienced, witnessed, or was confronted with an event or events that involved actual or threatened death or serious injury, or a threat to the physical integrity of self or others" and "2) the person's response involved intense fear, helplessness, or horror" (pp. 427-428). Criterion B consists of reexperiencing phenomena, such as flashbacks, nightmares, and intrusive recollections, which may or may not be triggered by reminders of the assault. Strong physiological reactions in the presence of trauma-related cues, previously diagnosed as a Criterion D symptom, has been relocated among the Criterion B reexperiencing symptoms. Criterion C delineates a range of avoidance behaviors: avoidance of memories of the event, numbing of affect, amnesia, and diminished interest or pleasure in activities (the latter overlapping with symptoms of depression). Finally, Criterion D represents physiological overreactivity, such as problems falling or staying asleep, hypervigilance, and exaggerated startle responses. To meet criteria for PTSD, a victim must have at least one reexperiencing symptom as well as three avoidance and two arousal symptoms, and these symptoms must co-occur for at least 1 month. In addition, the individual must suffer from clinically significant distress or some form of occupational or social impairment as a result of the symptoms. The diagnosis of PTSD cannot be made until at least 1 month has elapsed following the trauma. Recent theoretical developments in the PTSD literature have posited information-processing models to account for the cardinal symptoms of PTSD. These models, which serve as the basis for cognitive-behavioral interventions, will be articulated in the third section of this chapter.

Acute stress disorder. The *DSM-IV* introduced a disorder that can be diagnosed in the *immediate aftermath* of a traumatic event: acute stress disorder (ASD) (American Psychiatric Association, 1994). In addition to requiring several of the reexperiencing, avoidance, and arousal symptoms of PTSD, to meet diagnostic criteria for ASD the individual must also experience three of five dissociative symptoms (derealization, depersonalization, dissociative amnesia, subjective sense of numbing, reduction in awareness of surroundings) during or immediately after the traumatic event. The disturbance must last for at least 2 days, but less than 1 month. ASD was proposed in response to research on victims of natural disasters, such as the firestorms in California (Koopman, Classen, & Spiegel, 1994), but has not yet been evaluated with victims of sexual assault. There are some indications that ASD may be a precursor to PTSD; for example, recent research found an association between dissociative symptoms in the early aftermath of trauma and the severity of PTSD symptoms 7 months later (Koopman et al., 1994). Future research using more sophisticated methodologies needs to docu- ment the nature of the relationship between ASD and PTSD in other trauma populations, including survivors of criminal victimization.

Course and recovery from PTSD. With regard to PTSD, within the first week of the assault, 94% of rape victims met symptom, but not duration, criteria for post-traumatic stress disorder. At 3 months postcrime, 47% of victims still met diagnostic criteria for PTSD (Rothbaum, Foa, Riggs, Murdock, & Walsh, 1992). In our own prospective study of rape victims, 84% ($N = 62$) met full (71%) or partial (13%) symptom criteria for PTSD within 2 weeks postrape (Mechanic, Resick, & Griffin, 1993). To date, 39 women were available for a 3-month follow-up evaluation: 25% were fully recovered, 35% were partially recovered, and 38% met full criteria for PTSD. Of those women with full or partial PTSD at 2 weeks ($N = 32$), 43% remained symptomatic, 46% improved, and 11% became more symptomatic. Most studies have found that recovery occurs within the first 3 months postcrime. After that, there is very little additional recovery (Atkeson, Calhoun, Resick, & Ellis, 1982; Calhoun, Atkeson, & Resick, 1982; Kilpatrick, Resick, & Veronen, 1981). In their recent study, however, Rothbaum et al. (1992), using weekly assessments, found that those women who developed PTSD showed no further recovery after 1 month postcrime while those who recovered continued to show steady improvement over the 3 months of assessment. In examining the rates of PTSD following trauma in the general female population, Resnick, Kilpatrick, and Lipovsky (1991) surveyed 4,009 adult women by telephone. They found that 35% of rape victims met criteria for PTSD at some point in time and 9.6% met criteria at the time of the interview. The likelihood of developing crime-related PTSD increases significantly when the victim is injured or her life is threatened, and is even more likely when the victim is injured *and* her life is threatened during the assault (Resnick, Kilpatrick, Dansky, Saunders, & Best, 1993).

Differences in rates of PTSD found in the Rothbaum et al. (1992) study and the Resnick et al. (1991) study are probably accounted for by differences in the methodologies of the two types of studies. Prospective studies follow individuals who have been recently victimized and assess the course of their symptoms over time. Prospective studies, therefore, measure current symptomatology more accurately without memory bias but sampling is limited to those who report the crime to some agency. Retrospective studies that ask respondents about past incidents of victimization and previous symptomatology include more representative samples but participants may not remember accurately how distressed they were or the exact symptoms they experienced with events that may have happened many years previously.

Depression. The other major disorder that frequently co-occurs with PTSD in rape victims is depression. Although depression is also very common following rape, cases of diagnosable clinical depression do not appear to be as prevalent as rape-related PTSD. Resick and Schnicke (1992) found that in treatment-seeking rape victims who came to therapy an average of almost 7 years after being raped, almost all met full criteria for posttraumatic stress disorder and 60% also met criteria for current major depressive disorder. Diagnosable cases of depression may be fewer in non-treatment-seeking samples. In a non-treatment-seeking sample of rape victims evaluated within 2 weeks of the rape, 35% met criteria for a current major depressive disorder (Mechanic et al., 1993). Moreover, all of the women with clinical depression showed symptoms of PTSD. Preliminary data indicated that, compared with nonclinically depressed women, the clinically depressed women were less likely to recover from PTSD symptoms when evaluated at a 3-month follow-up. The complicated relationship between clinical depression and PTSD needs to be evaluated further.

The extent of depression in rape victims has been evaluated in a number of studies, and a number have found that depressive reactions are fairly short-lived. In one study (Frank, Turner, & Duffy, 1979), 44% of the rape victims studied scored in the moderately or severely depressed range within the first month postrape. In a second study, Frank and Stewart (1984) found that 56% scored in the moderately or severely depressed range on the Beck Depression Inventory (BDI). With the use of a semistructured interview, 43% were diagnosed as suffering from major depressive disorder. These depressive reactions diminished by 3 months postrape. Atkeson et al. (1982) found similar results. They assessed rape victims and a matched comparison sample for 1 year and found that the two groups differed at 2 weeks, 1 month, and 2 months postcrime, but not thereafter. At 2 weeks postcrime, 75% of the victim sample was moderately to severely depressed according to the BDI.

Chronic depressive reactions following rape have been observed in other studies. Kilpatrick and Veronen (1984) found differences between rape victims and nonvictims for 1 year after the crime. Resick (1988) also found that rape victims reported significantly more depression than robbery victims for 18 months after victimization. In a clinical follow-up to a random population survey, Kilpatrick, Veronen, et al. (1987) found that rape victims were more likely to be depressed than nonvictims (mean length of time postrape was 21.9 years). They also found that 8.6% of victims of one rape and 20% of victims of two rapes met criteria for major depressive disorder at the time of the interview: 46% of single incident and 80% of multiple incident victims met criteria for a lifetime diagnosis of depression.

Suicidal ideation and behavior are serious concerns when working with rape survivors, particularly in victims who have not recovered rapidly. Frank et al. (1979) reported that 2.9% of rape victims experienced suicidal behavior within the first month of a rape. This contrasts with the 27% of rape victims who admitted to suicidal ideation or behavior in the Frank and Stewart (1984) study. Ellis, Atkeson, and Calhoun (1981), however, reported that 50% of rape victims who were assessed from 1 to 16 years postrape had considered suicide. Resick, Jordan, Girelli, Hutter, and Marhoefer-Dvorak (1988) found that 43% of treatment-seeking rape victims had considered suicide and 17% had made an attempt. Kilpatrick et al. (1985) reported very similar findings in a random population survey of 2,004 women. In their sample, 19% of those who had been raped had made a suicide attempt and 44% reported suicidal ideation.

TRIAGE

Crises experienced by sexual assault victims vary greatly and require different types of intervention. Initially, *triage* (rapid assessment and prioritizing of needs) is necessary to determine what type of intervention is appropriate and whether some approaches are contraindicated. A number of considerations about the appropriateness of brief cognitive-behavioral treatment should be evaluated. For example, the developmental and legal concerns that arise in the treatment of young girls and adolescents are important and must be taken into consideration in treatment planning. The specific developmental issues that arise in the context of treating young girls are formidable, and so they are beyond the scope of this particular chapter. Concerns about treatment with adult sexual assault victims will be described below.

Possible Contraindications for
Brief Cognitive-Behavioral Interventions

Therapeutic approaches with demonstrated effectiveness for treating rape-related PTSD are stress inoculation training (Kilpatrick, Veronen, & Resick, 1982), prolonged exposure (Foa, Rothbaum, Riggs, & Murdock, 1991), and cognitive processing therapy (Resick & Schnicke, 1992). Both of these latter two approaches include an exposure component in which the client processes her memories of the event, along with the emotions that are connected to the memories. While in crisis, however, some clients are too fragile to handle exposure and may need to be stabilized before exposure is appropriate. Some clients are at risk for decompensation, suicide, or other parasuicidal behavior if they become overwhelmed by memories and lack sufficient coping resources.

Case Examples

The three case examples cited at the beginning of this chapter are illustrative of different types of clients and presenting crises. Susan sought therapy in the initial stages of recovery from sexual assault. Intense initial crisis reactions like Susan's are normative and are to be expected by the therapist. Reactions like these are almost universal, rather than pathological. It is important for the therapist to normalize these intense reactions and describe a normal course of recovery so the client doesn't erroneously assume she is having an abnormally bad reaction.

A therapist's goal for Susan would be to facilitate recovery and help prevent a chronic pattern from developing by urging her to return to normal patterns of activity, if relatively safe, and to help her express her emotions so they can run their natural course and diminish over time. The client should be urged to refrain from developing strategies to avoid reminders or thoughts of the rape. Because rape victims think about the rape most of the time, clients in the initial stages of recovery can handle exposure techniques unless they are actively suicidal. Most rape victims are able to talk about their experience in detail and may be frustrated because their loved ones are not able to tolerate hearing about the event in detail. It is important for the therapist to be able to listen attentively to the client's description of the sexual assault. If the therapist conveys the message that he or she doesn't want to hear the gory details, the message delivered to the client is that the rape is a stigmatizing event that can't be coped with.

The second case example, Paula, portrays the client with more chronic disruption, driven by avoidance. Currently in crisis because of her conflict between trying to avoid reminders of the crime and her desire to develop an intimate relationship, the therapist will need to help Paula break up her avoidance patterns, feel her emotions about the rape, and challenge any beliefs that have become disrupted and maladaptive over time. The therapist will need to help Paula examine how her relationships have been affected by her reactions to the rape. Cognitive processing therapy or prolonged exposure are appropriate therapies for this type of victim (Foa et al., 1991; Resick & Schnicke, 1992, 1993).

Finally, Micki is representative of the fragile, repeatedly victimized client who has developed a pattern of maladaptive mechanisms to cope with her memories and emotions. Crisis intervention in this case should not include any uncovering or exposure-based techniques but should focus on helping Micki stabilize and develop adaptive coping mechanisms in preparation for longer term therapy. Coping skills training, such as stress inoculation (e.g., Foa et al., 1991; Kilpatrick et al., 1982) and stabilization techniques (e.g., having the client keep a regular schedule, meals, contracting), is most appropriate for helping this type of client through the immediate crisis and into therapy. Hospitalization may be necessary for this type of client if she is actively suicidal or addicted to alcohol or drugs.

Screening: Practical Tips

When a woman first calls seeking treatment, she may be reluctant to say on the phone what has happened to her. A straightforward, matter-of-fact approach is recommended, particularly if the woman is having difficulty stating her reasons for seeking therapy. She may need to speak to a female therapist if she is feeling uncomfortable disclosing information to a male therapist. Once she affirms that she has been victimized, the therapist can ask when it occurred. This is important because the therapist will need to respond differently depending on the recency of the crime and whether the client is an incest survivor.

Regardless of the time elapsed since the assault, the therapist should screen for suicidal ideation if the client is in crisis or sounds particularly depressed. As mentioned earlier, suicidal ideation is fairly common in rape victims. It is possible that suicidal thoughts precipitated the contact to seek treatment. If this is the case, the therapist will need to make a verbal contract with the victim until they can meet, or may need to consider hospitalization if the client cannot assure that she will be safe until the session.

If the client is an incest survivor who has subsequently been raped, short-term treatment for the rape may not be beneficial because of the greater length of time needed for trust to develop in the therapeutic relationship, and the greater likelihood of additional psychopathology (e.g., personality disorders). It may also be difficult for the client to focus only on the rape without triggering unresolved incest-related issues. The therapist will have to use her or his clinical judgment, therefore, to determine what a particular client can handle. Recently, there have been pilot studies reporting that short-term treatments for incest-related PTSD can be effective in reducing PTSD symptomatology (Dancu & Foa, 1993; Smucker & Niederee, 1993).

If there is no reported history of incest and the crime occurred some time ago, the therapist may want to ask if something particular precipitated the client's decision to seek treatment. If there is no crisis situation to deal with, a session can be scheduled with only brief telephone contact. Even without a discussion of symptoms, the therapist should inform the client that she may experience an increase in symptoms before the first session and that she may have the urge to avoid the session. It is important to tell the client to come to the session regardless of how she is feeling. The therapist should start treatment with the very first telephone contact by informing the client that her avoidance strategies will delay recovery. If the rape occurred many years ago, the therapist should gently remind the client that what she has been doing (i.e., avoiding) hasn't been working, and that even though the idea of talking and thinking about the event is frightening, it will get easier. Rape victims are less likely to show up for the session unless this is anticipated, discussed, and normalized.

When someone calls within the first week after a rape, the therapist needs to respond to the crisis situation, provide immediate information, and intervene more directly on the telephone. If the victim calls very soon after the rape, it is appropriate to ask whether she has reported the crime to the police. Although reporting the crime is each woman's decision, she should be aware that if the rape is not reported very soon after it was committed, she probably will not be able to press charges later. Also, in our state (Missouri), rape victims are eligible for victim compensation funds, which pay for therapy and medical expenses, but only if victims report the crime within 48 hours. Therapists should be aware of laws in their own state regarding victim compensation.

Finally, the woman's decision not to report the rape to the police may indicate to the therapist that the client is struggling with issues regarding self-blame, is concerned that she won't be believed, or is trying to avoid labeling the event as a rape or as a crime. This information may help the therapist to begin to formulate the client's conflicts.

Recent victims, whether they report the crime or not, should be urged to seek medical attention. Internal injuries, possible pregnancy, and venereal diseases (including AIDS) are all potential effects that need to be addressed in the aftermath of a sexual assault. Women need to be examined and treated twice: (a) immediately after the crime and (b) several weeks later. AIDS testing will need to be done 6 months after the crime and the woman will need to be instructed in safe-sex practices until she knows that she has not contracted the virus.

Therapists are also in a position to help prevent the development of PTSD in that they can provide normalizing information about symptoms and their course, can help the client activate her social support network, and can help intervene (e.g., "It wasn't your fault!"), thus preventing the formation of potentially damaging cognitions. Clients should be urged to feel their feelings and to talk about the crime and their reactions as much as possible. It will be possible for them to receive better social support immediately after the rape than months or years later when others won't understand why they are still upset.

Initial Interview

Although we have a standardized initial interview for data collection purposes, an unstructured interview is sufficient for clinical purposes. The first purpose of the initial interview is to gather information about the incident, reactions to the assault, social support, and history of other traumatic events. A second purpose is to begin normalizing reactions. Most rape victims arrive at therapy with the secret belief that they are going crazy. Asking about PTSD symptoms and labeling them accurately (flashbacks rather than hallucinations) helps to alleviate the client's concern that she is having a uniquely bad reaction.

A calm, supportive, matter-of-fact manner on the part of the therapist also leads to rapport-building and to the expectation on the part of the client that her problems are not insurmountable. This therapist reaction, the third purpose of the interview, serves as a corrective reaction to others' negative reactions. If the therapist doesn't react with shock, blame, fear, and so on, she or he is sending the message that this event is not too big to handle. Unfortunately, we have seen too many clients who have come from other therapists who have reacted in a negative and damaging fashion by either overreacting to or ignoring the clients' disclosure.

Assessment

Assessment is a very important therapeutic tool, and we conduct assessments with the clients we see in therapy who are not part of our research studies. Furthermore, we assess clients at the end of treatment, and sometimes during treatment, as well as at the beginning of therapy. At the beginning of therapy, it is important to determine the level of symptomatology and the extent of distress the client is experiencing. The presence of depression as well as PTSD may indicate more pervasive patterns of cognitive disruption, more problems with self-esteem, and greater hopelessness. Of the PTSD symptoms, we hope to see greater intrusion and relatively less avoidance. This suggests that the client is actively processing the event (even though she might be stuck or distressed) and is not avoiding her affect. If the client scores high on avoidance but low on intrusion, she may not have the event in active memory and is likely using a coping style that is more resistant to therapy. The therapist may have to work with the client more to help her overcome her long-term tendencies to avoid her affect and cognitions, not just regarding the rape but on other topics as well. The specific cognitive disruptions that have ensued as a result of the rape are not directly assessed in the preliminary assessment procedures. In cognitive processing therapy, for example, the evaluation and correction of distorted beliefs is a direct component of the therapeutic process, and the continued assessment of cognitive distortions is endemic to the therapy process. Thus, at some level, assessment is an ongoing feature in some cognitive-behavioral treatments.

We have learned through experience that it is often helpful for the client to see objectively the progress she is making in therapy. Sometimes during therapy a client will become so preoccupied with a particular conflicting belief or more general issues (e.g., esteem or intimacy) that she may not notice that she is no longer having flashbacks, intrusive recollections, or numbing of affect. By conducting a reassessment, during and at the end of therapy, the client, as well as the therapist, can see the progress she has made. On the other hand, no change in scores may indicate to the therapist that core constructs have not changed and that the therapist may have to probe behind superficial conflicting beliefs for larger maladaptive core assumptions. Pronounced avoidance may indicate a core assumption that emotions are bad and should not be experienced or that they are so overwhelming that the client cannot cope with them.

The symptom scales we are currently using in our research project are as follows:

- *Structured Initial Interview* (Resick, 1988): The structured interview we use contains the following sections: Demographics, Sexual Assault Information, Social Support, History of Victimization, Psychological History, and Problems and Treatment Since Crime. The purpose of the interview is to attempt to determine the factors that have affected the severity of the woman's reactions and those that have facilitated or hindered her recovery from the crime. For example, negative reactions from others may compound the trauma and increase trust and intimacy difficulties as well as self-blame.

- *Structured Clinical Interview for DSM-III-R—Non-Patient Version,* mood disorders modules (SCID; Spitzer, Williams, & Gibbon, 1987): The SCID was developed to assess Axis I disorders based on *DSM-III-R* criteria. The mood disorders modules are used to make formal diagnoses of current and lifetime depressive, manic, and dysthymic disorders.

- *Clinician Administered PTSD Scale* (CAPS; Blake et al., 1990): The CAPS is a 30-item structured diagnostic interview designed to assess the core features of PTSD: reexperiencing, avoidance, and arousal, as well as features hypothesized to be associated with PTSD. Ratings for each symptom are made on two independent dimensions: frequency and intensity. Scores on both dimensions contribute to rating the symptom's clinical significance. Evidence of reliability and validity for this measure is detailed in a recent report by Blake et al. (1995).

• *PTSD Symptom Scale* (PSS; Foa, Riggs, Dancu, & Rothbaum, 1993). The PSS has 17 items and comes in two versions: interview and self-report. The scale is based directly on the *DSM-III-R* criteria for PTSD and has three subscales that reflect the three major symptom criteria: intrusion, avoidance, and arousal. It is a very easy scale both to administer and to understand, has good concurrent validity with the SCID and IES, and has good test-retest reliability. We use a modification of the PSS that includes assessment of the frequency and intensity of PTSD symptoms (MPSS-SR; Falsetti, Resnick, Resick, & Kilpatrick, 1993, 1994).

• *Impact of Event Scale* (IES; Horowitz, Wilner, & Alvarez, 1979): The IES is a 15-item self-report scale consisting of two subscales measuring cognitive intrusion and avoidance. Although the IES cannot be used to diagnose PTSD because it only measures cognitive intrusion and avoidance and does not assess arousal symptoms, it is a widely used scale in the trauma literature. In addition, the subscales can give the clinician a good idea of the relative strength of intrusive versus avoidant symptoms.

• *Symptom Checklist-90-Revised* (SCL-90-R; Derogatis, 1977): The SCL-90-R is a 90-item Likert self-report scale that measures the level of overall distress and has nine subscales with the original scoring. The nine subscales assess somatization, obsessive-compulsive symptoms, interpersonal sensitivity, depression, anxiety, hostility, phobic anxiety, paranoid ideation, and psychoticism. An additional PTSD scale was developed by Saunders, Arata, and Kilpatrick (1990) from the original 90 items. The SCL-90-R has been used widely in rape research providing good norms for typical responses following rape (Kilpatrick et al., 1981; Resick et al., 1988).

Clinicians using the scale should be aware that high scores on paranoia and psychoticism subscales are quite common in rape victims with PTSD and are not indicative of severe pathology. Symptoms of PTSD are likely to elevate scores on those two subscales because rape victims are suspicious and lacking in trust (someone *was* out to get them!), and flashbacks are often perceived and labeled as hallucinations, so strange experiences are endorsed on the psychoticism scale.

• *Beck Depression Inventory* (BDI; Beck, Ward, Mendelson, Mock, & Erbaugh, 1961): The BDI is the most widely used self-report scale for measuring depressive symptoms. This 21-item scale has established cutoffs for measuring the severity of depression and norms for rape victims measured over time (Atkeson et al., 1982; Resick & Schnicke, 1993).

For clinical purposes, we recommend the following battery for diagnosis and assessment of PTSD and depression, the battery we use in our clinic with crime victims in crisis:

- Initial interview
- PTSD Symptom Scale
- Beck Depression Inventory

Both of these scales take only minutes to administer and score, and provide a good indication of the severity of PTSD and depressive symptomatology.

INFORMATION PROCESSING THEORY

The theory of PTSD that has received the greatest attention in the past few years is information processing theory (Chemtob, Roitblat, Hamada, Carlson, & Twentyman, 1988; Foa, Steketee, & Rothbaum, 1989; McCann, Sakheim, & Abrahamson, 1988; Resick & Schnicke, 1992, 1993). Information processing theory is concerned with the way in which information is organized, stored, and retrieved in memory. Recently, more attention has been given to the content of the memories and the meanings they hold for trauma victims. Drawing upon work from other cognitive theorists/therapists, Resick and Schnicke (1992, 1993) have proposed that traumatic events are schema-discrepant; that is, they conflict with preexisting beliefs and expectations about oneself and the world. Symptoms of PTSD, particularly the intrusive symptoms and subsequent arousal and avoidance to reduce this arousal, are thought to be caused by the person's inability to reconcile the traumatic event with other salient beliefs. Flashbacks, nightmares, and other intrusive recollections reflect the continued presence of the traumatic memory in active memory and the conflict that this event creates within the person. To reconcile the event and resolve the conflict, the person must either distort the event to be consistent with prior beliefs (assimilation) or change her beliefs to adjust to this new information (accommodation). Resick and Schnicke also proposed that it is possible to go overboard in accommodating to the event such that beliefs are changed too much in an attempt to feel safer ("No one can be trusted." "I am never safe."). They refer to this as overaccommodation.

An example of assimilation is illustrated by the rape victim who questions whether her experience was really rape or who blames herself for causing the assault. In the examples at the beginning of the chapter, Susan had difficulty labeling her experience as rape because the rapist was a former boyfriend whom she invited in to her apartment. Furthermore, at the time she initiated therapy, she had amnesia for the period of time from when she tried to placate him until the sexual acts occurred in the bedroom. Susan couldn't remember how they had gotten into the bedroom; she was afraid to remember because she feared that perhaps she had acquiesced. To the contrary, the amnesia covered the part of the event that defined it as a rape, the brutal assault. The amnesia is part of the assimilation process. Because of the nature of the assault, Susan was afraid to be home alone and had strong startle reactions whenever someone rang the doorbell. After the assault, she stayed with her sister as much as possible and began to believe that she was unsafe all of the time (overaccommodation).

In the example with Paula, her primary conflict, which she had difficulty admitting to the therapist, was her attraction to the young man who subsequently raped her. On one hand, she wondered if her attraction to him had been noticed by him and presumed to be consent for sex. On the other hand, she wondered what was wrong with her to have been attracted to someone who could do something like this. She vowed never to trust anyone again (overaccommodation). In addition to her own distortions, her mother discouraged Paula from speaking about the event, thereby ensuring that no one would challenge her erroneous beliefs.

Micki, because of her prior negative experiences, already believed that people were not to be trusted and would harm her if they could. Even more so, she believed that she was a trauma magnet who would always have bad things happen to her. In this case, the rape was not schema-discrepant but schema-congruent. To Micki, the rape was confirmation of her preexisting negative beliefs. Although Micki was in crisis at the time she sought therapy, she was in crisis over all of the victimizations she was subjected to, not just the most recent rape. The recent event also triggered memories and strong emotions stemming from other unresolved victimizations. In her case, distortions about the rape were concerned with the recent assault being further evidence of her worthlessness, the hopelessness of the future, and distrust for the motives of all people. Each of these distortions is an example of overaccommodation.

Given this theoretical position, the goal of either crisis intervention or delayed treatment is to assist the client to refrain from assimilating (distorting the event to fit prior beliefs), and to accommodate schemata to the new information without overaccommodating. For example, in the cases described at the beginning of the chapter, it is clear that the women are having difficulty accepting that the rape happened within the context of their lives. The therapist's goal is to have the clients remember the rape, accept that it happened, and experience their emotions about it. It is important for clients to find balance in their beliefs about themselves and the world, so that everything is not viewed through the lens of the rape.

To date, three short-term cognitive-behavioral therapies have been found to be effective in reducing the symptoms of PTSD in rape victims. Although all three therapies are compatible with an information processing model, each one approaches the therapeutic goals from a slightly different perspective.

Prolonged Exposure

Prolonged exposure (PE) allows for the reprocessing of the emotions connected to the traumatic memory. PE directly confronts the client's fears and memories through repeated, prolonged exposure to strong fear-inducing cues. The exposure to feared stimuli can be imaginal or in vivo. Repeated exposure teaches the client that the fear cues do not signal aversive consequences. Once the client learns that the fear-inducing cues do not necessarily predict negative consequences, the fear response and avoidance will diminish (Foa & Kozak, 1986).

A study by Foa et al. (1991) demonstrated the effectiveness of PE as a treatment for PTSD in sexual assault victims. Foa et al. compared the effects of PE, stress inoculation training (SIT), supportive counseling, and no counseling (waiting list control group). The supportive therapy group did not discuss the trauma and served as a control for the general effects of therapy. Clients were randomly assigned to these groups. Individuals who were raped less than 1 month before treatment were excluded from the study to control for natural recovery.

Results indicated that all groups showed some improvement, but those involved in SIT and PE showed significant improvement. Immediately following treatment, the SIT group exhibited significantly fewer PTSD symptoms than the PE group. At 3 months follow-up, however, the individuals who had undergone PE showed significantly more improvement than those in the stress inoculation group. Foa et al. (1991) explained these results using information processing theory. Stress inoculation provides immediate anxiety reduction while PE evokes anxiety in therapy. PE may provoke permanent changes in the traumatic memory, however, due to the emotional and cognitive processing occurring during exposure.

During the PE procedure, clients relive the rapes by imagining them as vividly as possible and by describing them aloud in the present tense. Clients continue to repeat their narratives of the incidents for 1 hour. Each session is taped and clients are instructed to listen to the recordings at least once a day. In addition, they are asked to engage in in vivo exposure to avoided situations that are determined not to be dangerous. Foa et al. included two sessions of treatment planning and seven PE sessions.

Stress Inoculation Training

Stress inoculation training (SIT) provides education about anxiety reactions plus skills for managing fear and breaking up learned patterns of avoidance. A cognitive component teaches clients to confront maladaptive beliefs and to develop more effective strategies for coping with stress. To learn more about stress inoculation training, readers may consult Martin (1982) and Meichenbaum and Cameron (1983). Stress inoculation training has been adapted for use in group therapy format (Resick & Jordan, 1988).

Research has documented the effectiveness of SIT for treating the symptoms experienced by rape victims. Clients who completed SIT improved on measures of anxiety, hostility, and mood (Veronen & Kilpatrick, 1983). Most of these clients identified SIT as the preferred treatment when offered SIT, peer counseling, and systematic desensitization. Another study compared SIT with assertion training, supportive psychotherapy, and a wait-list control group (Resick et al., 1988). Rape victims in each treatment group demonstrated equal degrees of symptom improvement compared with the wait-list control group, which showed no change.

Recent findings suggest that SIT is the preferred treatment for rape-related symptoms in the short term when compared with PE, supportive counseling, and a wait-list control group (Foa et al., 1991). This study, described earlier in the discussion of PE, concluded that SIT was superior to PE immediately posttreatment. PE, however, appeared more effective at a 3-month follow-up. The authors concluded that a combination of the two approaches might provide the most comprehensive treatment and are currently testing the combined procedure (Foa, 1986). Given the effectiveness of SIT and its popularity among clients, this treatment modality is an important therapeutic tool. The drawback of SIT, however, is that it does not ensure that clients reprocess their rapes. With SIT, it might be possible for clients to avoid thinking about the events or to use coping skills to facilitate avoidance rather than confront the memories. The therapist who uses SIT with rape victims needs to be cognizant of this possibility and to make sure that clients are not avoiding reminders, feelings, or thoughts about the crimes. On the other hand, SIT may be the preferred treatment for crisis intervention for those clients who are too fragile for the exposure work necessary for reprocessing. The coping skills taught through SIT may be very helpful for assisting the client to stabilize using appropriate, rather than maladaptive, strategies. Once stabilized and able to cope better with affect, the client could then move on to process the memories directly.

SIT begins with an educational phase, which describes how the fear response develops. This initial phase includes a discussion of classical conditioning, fear cues, and avoidance reactions. Clients are encouraged to identify personal cues that elicit anxiety and avoidance. The therapist explains that fear can be expressed in physical reactions, in thoughts, and in behavior. Clients learn skills that address each of those areas.

Following the educational phase, SIT concentrates on teaching the client various coping skills to manage anxiety. Clients learn various relaxation techniques, such as progressive relaxation and brief relaxation. Readers unfamiliar with these techniques might review Morris (1986) and Stroebel (1983). These skills are combined with cognitive approaches to anxiety management, such as thought-stopping and guided self-dialogue (consult Resick and Jordan, 1988, for a description of these skills). Homework assignments encourage clients to practice and apply the techniques discussed in therapy.

Following training in how to cope with physical reactions and unwanted thoughts, clients learn covert rehearsal and role-playing techniques to address behavioral avoidance. Victims of crime are likely to generalize from the trauma and view many situations as dangerous. Clients learn to use imagery and role-playing to practice coping in fear-producing situations. The therapist should discuss the difference between anxiety that is appropriate and reality based, and anxious feelings that occur in response to reminders of the crime. Victims of crime often view innocuous situations as dangerous because of their conditioned fear reactions and restrict their lifestyles to avoid such situations. To disrupt patterns of avoidance, clients should be encouraged to use their coping skills in conjunction with the stress inoculation procedure. The therapist should explain the steps in stress inoculation, which are as follows:

1. Assess the actual probability of the crime happening again.
2. Manage the overwhelming avoidance behavior.
3. Control self-criticism and self-devaluation.
4. Engage in the feared behavior.
5. Reinforce yourself for attempting the behavior and for following the protocol.

The therapist should review how each coping skill can be applied to accomplish the steps in stress inoculation (e.g., use guided self-dialogue to control self-criticism).

To further empower clients, the therapist can use creative problem-solving techniques, such as the approach described by Goldfried and Davison (1976). Victims of crime commonly feel confused, helpless, and powerless in the aftermath of trauma. This component of the treatment encourages clients to engage in decision making and to take action to master problems.

Finally, the concept of a fear hierarchy is introduced with the explanation that fearful situations can be broken down into smaller steps. The therapist helps clients to develop fear hierarchies; the method uses role-playing, covert rehearsal, and anxiety management skills to work on each step. Upon termination, the therapist reviews the client's coping skills and encourages her to practice the techniques learned to prevent avoidance patterns from becoming entrenched.

Cognitive Processing Therapy

Because of the cognitive nature of many of the symptoms of PTSD, Resick began to search for more a cognitively oriented treatment based on information processing theory. The result is a specific treatment package consisting of exposure to the traumatic memories, training in challenging cognitions, and modules on the topics that are most likely to be affected by the rape: safety, trust, power, esteem, and intimacy. This approach aims to alleviate PTSD and depression by helping clients to process the trauma fully, to accept that the traumatic event happened, and to adapt existing schemata to include new information. A major focus of the therapy is on identifying and modifying clients' "stuck points" or areas of incomplete processing. Stuck points are often expressed in terms of faulty cognitions such as denial ("It wasn't really a rape"), self-blame ("I caused the rape by drinking at the party"), and overgeneralization ("All men are dangerous"). Stuck points are assessed in an ongoing fashion throughout the therapy process, particularly in the middle sessions.

Several circumstances may give rise to stuck points. Usually, stuck points occur because the trauma conflicts with prior schemata. For example, Susan, one of the case examples at the beginning of the chapter, had stuck points regarding trust. She was stunned that someone she had cared about and thought she could trust, suddenly attacked her. She also had conflict because she always thought that she was a good judge of character, but she never suspected he could do such a thing. She had frequent flashbacks composed of images of his face, distorted with rage as he grabbed her throat and hit her. Incomplete processing also occurs when others impose conflicting information on the client (e.g., blame the victim for the trauma). Some clients may be predisposed to use avoidance as a defense, resulting in inadequate processing of the trauma. Other clients may be unable to process the event because it is so foreign and they have no meaningful schemata in which to categorize the event.

Although symptoms often occur because a trauma conflicts with prior schemata, they may also result when a trauma appears to confirm prior negative schemata. Clients whose schemata were disrupted by earlier traumas develop distorted and negative beliefs. Later traumas may serve as further evidence to support those maladaptive views (McCann et al., 1988). To facilitate processing of the trauma, CPT combines education, exposure, and cognitive restructuring components. Therapists provide education about PTSD and establish the connection between thoughts and emotions. The approach uncovers stuck points by eliciting memories of the trauma, including the accompanying affect. Then, faulty or conflicting beliefs are challenged and resolved. The therapist focuses particularly on the trauma's impact upon the five areas of functioning identified by McCann et al. (1988): safety, trust, power, esteem, and intimacy. The example of Micki at the beginning of the chapter illustrates the client with prior traumatic experience and negative beliefs and, although this has yet to be studied, it is our clinical impression that it is easier to restore disrupted positive beliefs than it is to dismantle entrenched negative beliefs.

Preliminary findings indicate that CPT is an effective treatment for rape victims (Resick & Schnicke, 1992, 1993). In Resick and Schnicke (1992), 19 sexual assault survivors were assessed for PTSD and depression pretreatment, immediately posttreatment, and 3 and 6 months posttreatment. After receiving CPT in a group format, clients showed significant improvement on posttreatment measures of both PTSD and depression. The 6-month follow-up assessment revealed that clients maintained their improvements. A waiting list control group of 20 women showed no change in symptoms across two assessment periods. Follow-up analyses presented in the treatment manual using both individual and group treatment on 45 women resulted in similar success rates. At pretreatment, 96% of the women met full symptom criteria for PTSD and 60% met criteria for major depression. At 6 months posttreatment, only 8% still met criteria for PTSD and 11% were depressed. Using the stringent criteria of therapy completion and posttreatment assessment, there was only a 12% dropout rate from therapy (Resick & Schnicke, 1993). Controlled evaluations of treatment efficacy are in progress and the long-term benefits of treatment await confirmation through empirical research.

CPT is designed to be conducted in 12 sessions. Because this approach is relatively new, a session-by-session description of CPT follows. For more detailed information about CPT, including case studies, homework handout sheets, and examples of modules for the five areas of functioning, see Resick and Schnicke (1993). For a session-by-session description of CPT as it was implemented in the context of an actual case, the reader should consult Calhoun and Resick (1993). Therapy begins after an initial interview and assessment session. Therefore, the therapist already knows whether the client has PTSD, depression, and or other disorders.

Session 1. The therapist has two tasks during the first session: to provide education about PTSD and to normalize clients' reactions. The therapist begins by summarizing the symptoms of PTSD and reviewing the types of symptoms that constitute each cluster: reexperiencing, avoidance, and hyperarousal. The therapist follows the description of each symptom cluster with questions about how those symptoms manifest themselves for the client. Results of the assessment are also shared with the client. Clients are reassured throughout the descriptions of symptoms that these symptoms are normal reactions to a traumatic event and make sense. Many clients fear that they are "going crazy" and feel quite relieved when they discover that their symptoms are common and can be treated. The therapist then gives an explanation for the development of the symptoms based on information processing theory.

After this description of information processing and symptom development, the therapist explains the goals of therapy: to help the client accept the rape without overaccommodating; to have her experience her feelings about the rape, allowing them to diminish; and to modify any distorted beliefs the client has developed about herself or the world. For homework, the therapist has the client write at least one page about what it means to her to have been raped.

Session 2. The therapist begins by having the client read her "impact statement" aloud. While discussing the impact statement, the therapist and client should begin to identify "stuck points," or places where the rape conflicts with prior beliefs. Next, the therapist makes sure the client can identify different emotions and can discriminate them from thoughts and behaviors.

For the next session, the client completes several A-B-C sheets. A-B-C sheets are handouts divided into three columns with the first column designated "A" for the activating event, the second as "B" for beliefs and self-statements, and the third "C" for consequences, including emotions and behavior. At least one sheet should be completed on her thoughts about the crime. These sheets will help the client to understand how her interpretations affect her emotions and behavior.

Session 3. The therapist and client review the client's A-B-C sheets, emphasizing the relationship but distinction between thoughts and feelings. The therapist pays attention to themes that indicate stuck points. At this point, the therapist does not forcefully challenge irrational beliefs or stuck points other than to point them out or gently question their validity.

For the next session, the client is asked to write a detailed account of the rape. She should include as many sensory details as possible as well as her thoughts and feelings during the incident. She should be encouraged to experience her feelings while writing rather than trying to avoid them. The therapist should point out that clients commonly experience intense reactions during this exercise because they have had many emotions recorded with their memories of the event that never ran their natural course (i.e., they didn't extinguish because of avoidance of them). The therapist needs to reassure the client that the intense feelings will subside with repeated exposure.

Many clients can't complete the assignment in one sitting because their emotions seem overwhelming. If clients need several writing sessions to complete the assignment, they are asked to draw a line on the page when they feel that they need to stop writing. These lines may indicate stuck points. Before the next session, the client should read the account every day and experience the feelings it elicits. She should bring the written (or taped) account to the next session.

Session 4. The therapist should have the client read her account aloud during the session. She should be encouraged to express her feelings and thoughts about the event. The following are some particularly helpful questions: "What was the most frightening part for you?" and "Is there some aspect of the incident that you shy away from recalling?" These questions aid in the processing of the trauma by eliciting the memories and accompanying affect. The therapist should inquire about points at which the client stopped writing because they may indicate stuck points. During a rape, many clients experience a particular moment when they realize that they might die or when they feel powerless and hopeless about preventing the rape. Such moments are likely to be stuck points in processing the trauma and are accompanied by intense affect.

For homework, the client writes about the entire incident at least once more and is encouraged to include more sensory details and her thoughts and feelings during the rape. Additionally, she should record her current thoughts and feelings in parentheses while writing the essay. If the client was victimized more than once, she should be encouraged to begin writing about the other incident(s).

Session 5. The client reads the new account of the rape. The therapist should help her to compare her current feelings about the rape with the emotions she experienced during the event. The therapist should also compare her reactions to writing and reading the second version with those she experienced while writing and reading the first version. Her emotions should have decreased in intensity. At this point in therapy, the emphasis shifts from memory retrieval and expression of affect to an analysis and challenging of cognitions. To help the client alter stuck points, the therapist provides her with a list of Challenging Questions that have been adapted from Beck & Emery, 1985. The questions encourage clients to challenge their ideas using cognitive therapy strategies. The therapist demonstrates the technique for the client by applying the questions to one of the stuck points that has already been identified during the therapy. For the next session, the client is asked to apply the list of questions to two stuck points and bring written answers to the Challenging Questions to the next session. She should also be encouraged to continue writing her account of the rape, if she has not yet finished that assignment.

Session 6. The client and therapist review the homework with the therapist praising effective analysis and helping the client to confront her stuck points with the Challenging Questions. The therapist should use the questions to clarify the client's underlying expectations and cognitive conflicts. This exercise often provides a deeper understanding of the sources of clients' stuck points. Next, the therapist moves from challenging one thought or belief to looking for more generalized patterns of faulty thinking patterns such as overgeneralizing and exaggerating the meaning of an event (Beck & Emery, 1985). Using a different worksheet that describes common faulty thinking patterns, the therapist gives a few examples of these patterns and has the client begin to identify her own tendencies. For the next session, the client is to note examples of each thinking pattern as she identifies them during the week.

Session 7. The seventh session begins with a review of the homework on faulty thinking patterns. The therapist and client discuss the relationship between these automatic thoughts and the client's reactions to the rape. The therapist encourages the client to identify more realistic and adaptive statements to replace the negative cognitions. Next, the therapist gives the client the Challenging Beliefs Worksheet, which is adapted from Beck & Emery. (1985). This handout expands upon the A-B-C sheet by including challenging questions and faulty thinking patterns. The client is encouraged to challenge and replace cognitive distortions. The therapist completes one sheet with the client during the session, using a stuck point as an example. For homework, the client is asked to analyze at least one stuck point each day with this worksheet.

Also during this session, the therapist should provide a brief overview of the remaining five sessions. Each session focuses on one of five themes that describe areas of functioning that may have been disrupted by the rape: safety, trust, power, esteem, and intimacy (McCann & Pearlman, 1990a). During these sessions, the client is asked to describe her beliefs concerning those areas prior to the crime, as well as how her beliefs changed after the rape. The therapist explains that each theme (safety, trust, power, esteem, and intimacy) has two components: feelings related to self and those related to others. The therapist also explains how different experiences prior to the rape will affect clients' reactions differently afterward. Next, the therapist discusses the first theme, safety, and gives the client a module to read and consider along with a number of Challenging Beliefs Worksheets. The therapist begins to explore the client's attitudes about safety before the rape and whether they were either disrupted or strengthened by the incident. For the next session, the client completes Challenging Beliefs Worksheets about safety and other stuck points.

Sessions 8-12. The format for the remaining sessions is similar. The therapist reviews the client's worksheets, identifying cognitions that she changed successfully, praising her efforts, and assisting with those in which the client has difficulty. Often, the homework reveals some beliefs that the client was unable to modify herself, frequently because the client has not recognized the faulty beliefs underlying them first. The therapist should remind the client to use the list of Challenging Questions and the faulty thinking patterns sheet to help the client alter faulty cognitions, and should provide additional information if needed. As much as possible, however, the client challenges her own beliefs. During the remaining part of the session, the next topic is introduced and discussed, and the next module and worksheets are given to the client to work with (Session 8, trust; Session 9, power; Session 10, esteem; Session 11, intimacy).

At the 11th session, the client is also given the assignment to rewrite her impact statement regarding the meaning of the rape to her. At the last session, in addition to reviewing the client's homework regarding intimacy and discussing her future goals regarding the development of friendships and intimate relationships, the client also reads and discusses her new impact statement. Finally, the therapist reviews the entire course of therapy, identifies remaining stuck points or goals the client will continue to work on, and reminds the client that she is taking over the therapy now, not quitting work on her issues.

Issues for the Therapist

Therapist gender. Therapists frequently wonder whether it is appropriate to use male therapists to conduct treatment with female victims of sexual assault. One possible benefit of using a male therapist is that a warm, empathic male therapist might help the clients to recognize distortions or overaccommodations in their beliefs about men; for example, "I was raped by a man, therefore all men are dangerous." When we used male cotherapists to provide other types of therapy in a group format, the feedback from clients was quite positive (Resick et al., 1988).

In our clinic, male therapists do provide treatment to female victims of sexual assault. It is the clients' choice as to whether they wish to have a male or female therapist. Often, male therapists provide therapy to the families, husbands, and boyfriends of sexual assault victims. Having a male therapist in the client's network may help change her overgeneralized beliefs about men, even if the male is not the primary therapist.

Therapists' attitudes and beliefs. It is essential that therapists treating sexual assault victims explore their own attitudes and beliefs about rape. Although the process is often very subtle, negative beliefs can easily be communicated to clients, especially those who feel responsible for the rape and search for cues that others also hold them responsible. Verbal and nonverbal acts that have a subtle questioning or judging quality have the power to create an atmosphere of distrust. All too often, clients come to us for treatment after having been retraumatized by well-intentioned therapists who inadvertently reinforced beliefs that (a) the client was responsible for the rape (e.g., "What were you doing out at 2 a.m. in that part of the city?" or "How intoxicated were you at the time?"); (b) somehow she could have prevented the rape from happening (e.g., "Why didn't you scream or fight him off?"); (c) it wasn't really a rape because she consented to some of the sexual acts preceding the rape (e.g., "You let him take off all your clothes, and then you told him to stop?"); or (d) she should be recovered by now (e.g., "You were raped 8 years ago and you still haven't gotten over it?"). Anytime a therapist asks "why" the client did something or did not do something, there is a subtle implication of blame or judgment.

As a way of protecting ourselves from being consciously aware of all the dangers that exist in the world, many people, including therapists, hold just-world beliefs (see Janoff-Bulman, 1992). Just-world beliefs involve the idea that good things happen to good people and bad things happen to bad people, or that we are masters of our destinies and we determine what happens to us. This sense of control is illusory. Even in the face of highly contradictory evidence, people are reluctant to surrender these beliefs. One reason people cling to these beliefs is that the beliefs foster the illusion that because we can prevent bad events from happening to us, we are indeed safe. One unfortunate by-product of this reasoning is that we also assume that other people *could have* done something to prevent the bad event from happening to them: *If only they* . . . —fought back, didn't get drunk, wore a baggier dress, weren't careless or irresponsible, didn't say yes to a sexual encounter initially, left the party alone, and so on ad infinitum. We assume that if we were in that situation (of course, we wouldn't have been in that situation), *we would have* . . . (fill in the blank for yourself). Of course, we would have emerged victorious and unvictimized.

Vicarious traumatization. This term was coined by McCann and Pearlman (1990b) to describe the cumulative effects of (indirect) exposure to the gory details of highly traumatic events (e.g., crimes, accidents, natural disasters) on therapists or other crisis responders (e.g., emergency service personnel). It is important for therapists who treat victims to consider the personal ways in which trauma exposure has affected the therapists' cognitions and feelings. Dealing with rape or other acts of violence can be very distressing, even for trained, experienced therapists. Therapists may find it necessary to expand their own schemata to account for the cruelty and violence that they have discovered humans are capable of. Vicarious trauma reactions, a parallel but less serious form of PTSD, are also possible in therapists. McCann and Pearlman (1990b) have written about vicarious traumatization and have distinguished it in significant ways from countertransference or burnout. Vicarious traumatization is a parallel form of PTSD, marked by symptoms such as intrusive recollections or nightmares that might occur after hearing graphic accounts of traumatic events during the exposure component of CPT, PE, or other therapies. This may result in anxiety and avoidance of situations perceived as potentially dangerous (being home alone, driving at night, walking through parking garages, and so on) and excessive concerns about one's safety. It might also seem that no place is safe anymore, an example of overaccommodation. Strong affect, such as sadness, anger, rage, or disgust, may also occur.

One possible consequence is that therapist reactions may be acted out in the therapeutic relationship. If the therapist has trouble listening to the details of rape, the therapist may collude with the client's avoidance, resulting in incomplete processing of the exposure component of CPT or PE. Some therapists may rationalize their avoidance of hearing about the rape by assuming that the gory details are too overwhelming for the client to handle.

These PTSD-like reactions are usually short-lived if therapists use the same therapeutic procedures with themselves that they implement with the client. We suggest that therapists working with trauma victims create mechanisms to share their reactions with supportive colleagues on a regular basis. These meetings might serve as formal or informal debriefing sessions. By building in structural opportunities for debriefing and peer support, the likelihood of developing vicarious traumatic reactions, such as PTSD, may be diminished. We also recommend reading the McCann and Pearlman (1990b) article for additional thoughts on this topic.

SUMMARY AND CONCLUSIONS

This chapter presented a cognitive-behavioral framework for the time-limited treatment of rape-related PTSD. Emphasis was placed on three therapeutic approaches with demonstrated effectiveness in treating the psychological sequelae of sexual assault, namely, cognitive processing therapy, prolonged exposure, and stress inoculation. Techniques common to these approaches include normalizing initial crisis reactions, teaching stress management skills, helping the client to fully process her memories and feelings associated with the rape, and restructuring cognitions that were distorted subsequent to the rape.

As illustrated by the case examples presented at the beginning of the chapter, sexual assault victims may present *in crisis* at any time following the assault. If repressed memories are triggered by a recent trauma or other activating stimuli in a rape victim who did not fully process a prior trauma, it may be many years after the event when treatment is sought for the first time. For example, this type of client may be extremely distraught after seeing a movie depicting a violent rape scene, yet she may not be able to acknowledge the connection between her current distress and a previous trauma in her life. Therapists must recognize that a client may be in an immediate crisis and at risk for suicidal behavior, even though the trauma occurred many years earlier. Although there are similarities in reactions to sexual assault, individual differences and personal histories affect victims' presentation, and should be considered when choosing an intervention strategy. The case examples and other material highlighted commonly observed patterns, including normal crisis reactions, delayed onset of symptoms, and chronic patterns of maladaptive behavior/cognitions stemming from unresolved trauma, personality disorder, or history of childhood incest. It is possible that these client characteristics might lead to differential response to one of the cognitive-behavior therapy variants; for example, a client with severe numbing or dissociative symptoms may fare better with prolonged exposure. To tailor therapeutic strategies to the specific pattern of client symptomatology, it is necessary to conduct controlled random-assignment treatment outcome studies assessing the impact of different therapeutic interventions in light of client characteristics. We are currently engaged in a long-term study comparing the efficacy of CPT versus PE in a large sample of rape victims. Another ofttimes illuminating, but not definitive, strategy is to study treatment failures. Evaluating interventions that fail can sometimes lead to fruitful insights about what therapy works for whom.

This chapter has largely focused on the treatment of PTSD symptoms once they have developed. As described earlier, however, close to one half of rape victims recover on their own, without therapy. Why do the other 50% develop more pathological reactions? Although research is attempting to address these vexing questions, the immediate crisis presents significant opportunities for therapists to help prevent chronic maladaptive behaviors and cognitions from developing in response to the trauma. The educational and cognitive components of CPT could easily be adapted for use with rape victims who have been victimized recently. Normalizing the experience, helping the victim to feel her feelings, and exploring the meaning of the event in the context of her schemata are all useful techniques that may prevent long-term disruption. In the immediate aftermath of the crisis when the victim is amenable to intervention, cognitive techniques, such as challenging distorted beliefs that are beginning to take hold, may help prevent a chronic pattern of maladaptive beliefs from becoming entrenched. In this way, the crisis situation might become an opportunity to facilitate recovery and perhaps to forestall the emergence of maladaptive patterns that are typical of clients who present for treatment many years after the traumatic event occurred.

NOTE

1. The following categories of perpetrators were reported in the NWS: 9% husbands or ex-husbands, 11% fathers or stepfathers, 10% boyfriends or ex-boyfriends, 16% other relatives, and 29% other nonrelatives such as friends and neighbors.

Crisis Intervention and Survival Strategies for Victims of Hostage Situations

THOMAS STRENTZ

The Federal Bureau of Investigation does not engage in the direct delivery of social work services. Yet the bureau and other law enforcement agencies around the world are directly involved in crisis intervention and thus provide some form of psychological support to people encountered at the crisis site. Most "code three," "red light," and siren responses are calls to a crisis. Personal crimes, such as rape and robbery, involve victims of a personal crisis. In addition, responses to an ongoing hostage situation also qualify as responses to personal crisis.

CASE STUDY

At 10:20 a.m. on a Friday morning in 1974, a lone gunman entered a branch of the Home Savings and Loan Association office in a western city. He approached

NOTE: Adapted from *Contemporary Perspectives in Crisis Intervention and Prevention*, edited by A. R. Roberts (Englewood Cliffs, NJ: Prentice Hall, 1991), by permission of the editor and author.

an experienced, mature, and emotionally stable teller and announced a robbery. She quickly initiated the police response by activating the silent alarm system. The police response was immediate. When two plainclothes units entered the bank, the subject placed his gun to the teller's head and ordered the police out of the building. During this initial withdrawal, the police were able to take the other employees and the customers with them. The reaction of the now trapped armed robber was typical: He added abduction charges to his offense. When negotiations were initiated, he demanded a much larger sum of money from the police than he ever expected to obtain from the robbery. He threatened to kill the teller, whom he called by name, if his demands were not met by a specified time. The negotiator gained an extension of this initial deadline and several subsequent ones. As time passed, the subject was identified as JD, and his therapist from a local psychological counseling service was located. In an attempt to gain additional time and to create a less tense atmosphere, the negotiator agreed to some of JD's demands. Money was delivered, and an opportunity to view JD and confirm his identity was created. His counselor agreed to speak with him on the telephone. When she called JD by name, he denied his identity and became more violent in his threats against his hostage. The counselor told the negotiator that JD had been diagnosed as an antisocial personality and was on parole for the second time after a series of rapes, an attempted murder, and several burglaries. As morning turned into afternoon, a subtle change was noted in the subject's threats. JD was now threatening to kill "the girl" rather than the teller he had previously called by name. He then said that if the rest of the money and the car were not delivered by 4:00, he would kill the girl. For emphasis, he added that he was looking her in the eye as he said this. JD told the negotiator that the FBI could explain to her children why Mommy would not be coming home anymore. His counselor agreed that this was a bad sign. She said that it appeared that JD was dehumanizing this victim as he had his other female victims. As late afternoon arrived and the evening rush hour approached, the subject became adamant that he be allowed to leave with his hostage. He promised to release her once he was sure that no one was following him. His counselor agreed that the life of the hostage meant nothing to JD and that allowing her to leave with him would be sentencing her to death. Shortly after 4:00, JD was shot and killed as he attempted to leave with the teller. She was not physically injured and after some counseling returned to work. She was the victim of two more armed robberies and now works in the personnel office at the same bank.

Today, a quiet surrender of the subject is a more common conclusion to such a siege. But emotional levels are high during the early hours of any such incident. It is during this traumatic period that the initial law enforcement response is achieved. Local police units are the first to arrive. During this time, the crisis is still very real. By using proper crisis intervention techniques, law enforcement can, and frequently does, begin the psychological healing process for the people involved. The first to arrive engage in ego support and family and individual counseling, encourage ventilation, clarify issues, and provide facts and a reality orientation for all of the victims. The major players are the hostages, the subject, and the responding intervenors. To some degree, all of these individuals are or can be victims in the hostage-taking crisis. Of these three primary players, the responding intervenors, the law enforcement officers, are the most prepared and certainly the best trained. Many preparation programs also exist for people who have a high potential for victimization as hostages. Generally, these private programs are attended by executives who have applied for kidnap insurance and must attend a program that focuses on prevention and survival. In the public sector, the government provides programs for airline cockpit and cabin crews, bank employees, and people assigned to our embassies (Bolz, 1987; McKinnon, 1986; Strentz, 1987; Third U.S. Army, 1985).

Many of the federal felonies investigated by the FBI are white-collar crimes. The FBI is charged with the responsibility for the enforcement of over 200 federal laws ranging from a violation of the Migratory Bird Act to violations of copyright laws and extortion of federally insured banks and savings and loan associations. Matters that may include personal crisis are also of concern to the FBI, however. Some of these more dramatic crimes are the hijacking of a commercial aircraft, robbery of a federally insured institution, and kidnapping and other forms of hostage taking. Many of these violations involve people who have been held hostage. To deal with these crises, the FBI has developed a local, regional, and national response network that includes special weapons and tactics (SWAT) teams, technical support units, and a command post to coordinate the use of these assets. This crisis response team also includes hostage negotiators, who comprise a large cadre of multilingual, carefully selected and trained male and female special agents of every race, color, and creed in 58 field offices around the country.

ORIGIN OF THE FBI'S
CRISIS MANAGEMENT PROCEDURES

Like so many other innovative law enforcement methods, hostage negotiations, SWAT, and crisis management practices are domestic forms of the so-called Pearl Harbor syndrome. Many of us tend to be more reactive than proactive. After the fire at the Coconut Grove nightclub in Boston in 1943, cities enacted ordinances covering the outward opening of doors, and mental health professionals saw the need for crisis intervention. Similarly, the FBI crisis management program grew out of a disaster. At 4:00 a.m. on October 4, 1971, special agents of the FBI responded to the hijacking of a commercial aircraft in Jacksonville, Florida. The plane had left Memphis, Tennessee, with two armed male hijackers, the hysterical estranged wife of one hostage taker, and a crew of two commercial pilots. A refueling stop in Jacksonville was scheduled. The twin-engine Aero Commander Hawk 681 landed at 5:10 a.m. at the Jacksonville International Airport, and a confrontation developed over the request for additional fuel.

The following is taken from the Federal Aviation Administration transcript of the conversation between the FBI and the tower (T) and the pilot of the hijacked airplane (P):

P: 58 November. This is the captain speaking. We're going to cut engines and we're gonna need some fuel, but I request that everyone stay away.

T: 58 November. Advise when your engines have been cut.

T: 58 November?

P: This is 58 November. Uh, this gentleman has about 12.5 pounds of plastic explosives back here, [not true] and . . . uh, I got no . . . uh, yet to join it right now so I would please expr, uh, appreciate it if you would stay away from this airplane.

T: That's a roger, 58 November. Are your engines cut?

P: Negative.

T: Stand by.

P: Where's the fuel truck?

T: 58 November?

P: 58 November. Go ahead.

T: This is the FBI. There will be no fuel. Repeat, there will be no fuel. There will be no starter. Have you cut your engines?

P: Uh, look, I don't think this fellow's kiddin' . . . I wish you'd get the fuel truck out there.

T: 58 November. There will be no fuel. I repeat. There will be no fuel.

P: This is 58 November. You're endangering lives by doing this, and, uh, we have no other choice but to go along, and, uh, uh, for the sake of some lives we request some fuel out here, please.

T: 58 November. What is the status of your passengers?

P: Ah, uh, well they're OK, if that's what you mean.

T: Are they monitoring this conversation?

P: Yes, they are.

T: Do you have two passengers aboard?

T: 58 November. What's your present fuel status on that aircraft?

P: We're down to about thirty minutes.

T: 58 November. The decision will be no fuel for that aircraft. No starter. Run it out, any way you want it. Passengers, if you are listening . . . the only alternative in this aircraft is to depart the aircraft, to depart the aircraft.

Within an hour, the discussion escalated into an argument between the hijackers and the FBI. The copilot was allowed to exit the aircraft, and he confirmed the lack of explosives as he argued for additional fuel. One hijacker also exited the aircraft to argue for additional fuel. Neither was allowed to return to the plane. Fearing that the lone hijacker was suicidal and would force the remaining pilot to crash the aircraft if it were refueled and allowed to take off, the FBI remained adamant in its refusal to provide additional fuel. The aircraft was then disabled by the FBI. Shortly thereafter, the remaining hijacker shot and killed his estranged wife and the pilot and then killed himself. Four years later, on August 8, 1975, the Sixth Circuit U.S. Court of Appeals decided that the FBI had not acted correctly, and awarded a large settlement to the widow and children of the pilot.

FBI Director Clarence Kelley, in anticipation of the court's decision and in keeping with the newest trend in law enforcement, had already ordered the FBI's Training Division to develop a program to instruct its agents in the skills and strategies of hostage negotiations. Supervisory special agents of the recently formed Behavioral Science Unit attended the New York City Police Department's (NYPD) hostage negotiation course. Other agents were developing the special weapons and tactics (SWAT) alternative, which was a modification of the Los Angeles Police Department's SWAT program. Additional crisis response resources were developed as the FBI's Training Division identified the need to deal more effectively with the developing complexities of the FBI's investigative responsibilities.

The NYPD, under the direction of Commissioner Patrick Murphy and in response to the tragedy at the Twentieth Olympiad at Munich in September 1972, had just developed a hostage negotiations program for police. The NYPD recognized that terrorist groups could strike and kill in New York with the same impunity they had demonstrated in Munich. Sergeant Frank Bolz and Officer Harvey Schlossberg (Ph.D.) had been tasked to create this first hostage negotiations program (Bolz & Hershey, 1979). They shared their expertise with the FBI and other police departments around the world. The NYPD's hostage negotiations guidelines, as they were called, were altered slightly to fit the national jurisdiction of the FBI, and training in this skill was begun at the FBI Academy. The first priority of the FBI and the NYPD was then, and is now, the preservation of human life. In other words, every decision made by the commander during a hostage siege rests on the premise that the selected course of action will do the most to preserve human life. Property damage and arrest of the hostage taker are secondary concerns. Thus, the options of negotiating, using a sniper or chemical agents, or assaulting are all considered for the goal of resolution with preservation of life as the primary concern.

TRAINING SPECIAL
AGENTS IN CRISIS INTERVENTION

As a supervisory special agent who was an instructor in the Behavioral Science Unit and later in the Special Operations and Research Unit at the FBI Academy, I was given the responsibility of creating a hostage negotiators' course. At that time, I had been a special agent in the FBI for 8 years and had a Masters of Social Work degree. The development of this course required a wide range of information, to include social work and mental health practices, philosophies, and techniques. The FBI was assisted in this developmental process by two sworn officers from New Scotland Yard who spent a month at our academy in Quantico, Virginia, and in our homes guiding us in the creation of this program.

Research into hostage situations revealed that most hostage takers in the United States were suffering from paranoid schizophrenia or extreme depression. In addition, a large number could be classified as having antisocial or inadequate personality disorders. The number of so-called political terrorists taking hostages in the United States was then, and is now, statistically insignificant (Strentz, 1984). Further, the programs developed with hostage takers who are mentally ill or monetarily motivated are easily adapted to fit the terrorist. Thus the instruction included several hours on the symptoms of the most common mental disorders of hostage takers, with law enforcement examples of these maladies. Woven into this instruction were guidelines for negotiators with ample time for closely critiqued role-playing.

GUIDELINES FOR CRISIS NEGOTIATIONS

The basis for the decision-making process for FBI executives during a hostage crisis is the preservation of human life. Preservation of property, even an expensive aircraft, is secondary. Over the years, countless lives have been saved by following several tenets that have proved their value in saving lives. Time is the most important ally of the crisis inter-venors. As time passes, the authorities gain intelligence, improve their tactical position, and incur countless other benefits from the fatigue induced in the perpetrator. His basic human needs increase and provide the crisis team with additional negotiation points.[1] As he speaks with the negotiator, his anxiety level diminishes, and he tends to become more rational. His expectations and demands tend to lower as trust and rapport develop with the negotiator. Although the passage of time can have some negative effects—for example, an unrealistic level of com-placency and boredom can develop in the command post—overall, time has a much more beneficial effect on the crisis intervenors than it has on the initiator of the crisis. Additional guidelines include the general refusal of the authorities to provide weapons or mobility to the subject as well as some reluctance to exchange hostages (Fuselier, 1981a, 1981b).

Because hostage negotiation is a skill, a widely practiced teaching technique is the use of role-playing or simulations. This application of action models is a common technique in teaching skills that cannot be learned from a lecture. One of the early leaders in the field of role-playing was J. L. Moreno (Moreno & Whitin, 1932), who is credited by many as being the founder of psychodrama. Yablonsky (1980) has discussed this technique in mental health settings. Other applications include football teams engaging in scrimmages, public speaking courses using speeches, and future negotiators practicing their skills in controlled crisis settings called field training exercises or classroom scenarios. These scenarios are simulated hostage situations based on actual incidents where role players familiar with the case play the roles of the subject, to train the new negotiators. Hostage crisis cases that are representative of typical situations are used to provide realistic training. The negotiation process is evaluated by instructors who work with the trainees during the exercise and critique them afterward. At the FBI Academy, this process is observed by the rest of the class on closed-circuit TV, which enables everyone to learn from the role-playing and to participate in the critique.

Since 1976, this type of instruction, with advanced classes for experienced negotiators, has been provided to over 1,000 domestic and foreign police officers at the FBI Academy as well as in seminars conducted at police department facilities around the world. As New Scotland Yard assisted the FBI in developing its program, the FBI assisted law enforcement agencies in Australia, Canada, Israel, New Zealand, Norway, and other democracies in Europe, Asia, and South America. Today, most nations of the free world exchange hostage negotiations staff and students regularly.

The research conducted by the FBI and other law enforcement organizations enables everyone to remain up to date on hostage-taking trends. This research indicates that over 95% of American hostage situations are successfully resolved by negotiations, usually without a shot being fired by law enforcement (Strentz, 1983b). This is accomplished through the purposeful use of crisis intervention theory and techniques by well-trained law enforcement personnel.

CRISIS COUNSELING STRATEGIES

The taking of hostages represents a crisis for the hostage taker as well as for the hostages. All of the elements of a crisis are present: an unsolved problem, disequilibrium and stress, attitudes of panic or defeat, and feelings of frustration. Efficiency is decreased, and hostage situations, like other periods of emotional crisis, are of limited duration (Puryear, 1980). Research has shown that over 92% of American hostage situations are resolved within 9 hours (Strentz, 1983b).

The procedural steps, or crisis counseling strategies, used to defuse a hostage situation are similar to those used for intervention in other crises, as discussed throughout this book. For instance, in a hostage situation, contact is made as soon as possible with the subject. This may be via a telephone call or by calling out to him if a phone is not immediately available. A telephone call is preferred to a face-to-face discussion. Very few negotiators are shot by subjects while talking to them on the telephone. The caller usually says something like, "Hello, this is John Smith of the FBI." Although it is important to identify oneself as an officer of the law, the use of rank tends to be counterproductive.

The following is an example of this initial rapport-developing process in the early discussions between an FBI negotiator, TS, and the subject, Jamie, who has taken hostages in a federal prison. Because this is a prison setting, the name of the subject is known, and quite a bit of intelligence is available on him.

TS: Hello, Jamie? This is TS of the Federal Bureau of Investigation.

Jamie: What the . . . is the FBI doing here?

TS: Well, I'll tell you Jamie. Like you, we want to see that no one gets hurt.

Jamie: Where the . . . is the warden?

TS: Beats me. Nothing but chaos out here; this place is a zoo. I think you and I are the only sane ones around.

Jamie: You have to be crazy to work here. I sure ain't here 'cause I want to be. Why are you here?

TS: They always call us in on an important case.

Jamie: Well this is an important case all right. I'm innocent and they been holding me here against my will for too long. I got my rights.

TS: Why don't you fill me in on what's been happening?

Jamie: Didn't they tell you?

TS: I want to hear it from you. . . . That way I get it straight. You know what I mean?

Jamie: Well, first off, . . .

Eventually, as rapport and trust develop, the negotiation process reaches the point where the subject begins calling the negotiator and asking for advice. The negotiation process is reflective, and the negotiator tries to keep the subject in the role of decision maker.

Ventilation is encouraged so that the negotiator can determine the subject's view of the siege. This process also allows a full exploration of the subject's emotions and some insight into his mental state by the negotiator and, in some instances, an on-scene psychological consultant. It is rare that a subject will have been involved in previous hostage situations, yet past experience in "sticky situations" is explored. Every attempt is made to discuss the various alternative courses of action in a very nondirective and nonjudgmental mode. The subject is encouraged to do most of the talking, thinking, planning, and coping with the stress of the siege. The subject is asked to provide his views on what is happening and how he would resolve the siege. The negotiator remains nonjudgmental and discusses the various options at length. Finally, he or she will say something like, "Let me run that by the boss and see what happens." This is said even if the subject wants something that the negotiator knows is unlikely to be provided, like weapons or an escape vehicle. The negotiator plays the role of arguing the case for the subject with the boss, who makes the decisions. The negotiator never says "no." The negotiator says "maybe later" or "not right now," but never "no," even if the boss has made it clear that the demands will not be met. By talking about each demand in detail, the negotiator stresses the importance of what the subject wants, and thus the importance of the subject, in this siege. In this way, the negotiator gains time and induces fatigue in the subject. Eventually, the subject is convinced of the logic of a face-saving resolution that may involve "walking out like a man." This crisis intervention process is woven into several stages of the typical siege.

FOUR STAGES OF THE CRISIS EVENT

Most authorities agree that hostage situations have stages (Derrer, 1985; Rahe & Genender, 1983; Strentz, 1984). They tend to differ on the specific number of stages, with counts ranging from three to seven. I see most hostage situations as having four steps: alarm, crisis, accommodation, and resolution. Each stage is different for each of the participants and different than each other stage, although there is some overlap. Also, it is important to realize that each hostage situation, like each crisis, is of limited duration. It has a beginning, an end, and a time in the middle when lots of things happen. It is during these middle hours that the crisis is being worked toward a successful resolution.

Alarm

The first, and probably most traumatic, period in a hostage situation is the alarm stage, and it can last for an hour or more. In many ways, particularly in the case of an armed robbery gone sour, the abductor, hostage, and police are going through similar emotional experiences. Though injury to hostages is rare, research shows that most of the hostages who are injured during the siege sustain these injuries in the opening moments when the armed robber is trying to consolidate his position or when the terrorist is intimidating his hostages to ensure control or domination of them (Jenkins, Johnson, & Ronfelt, 1977). In his desperation, the armed robber compounds his dilemma by adding kidnapping and assault charges to his list of offenses. These considerations are initially minimal to him. His emotions are running high: He wants to buy time, and in this he succeeds. A trapped armed robber usually tries to gain additional money and project the blame for the situation onto the police.

The opening moments of negotiations are usually very emotional, and generally little is achieved until the subject has settled down. It takes time for the negotiators to arrive, get the right phone number, and make the first call. Thus the initial contact may be after the alarm phase has passed. In fact, other people—the press or relatives of the hostages—may have called the subject before the negotiator arrives. In some situations, to add to the confusion, a bank of telephone lines lead into a siege site. It takes time for law enforcement to locate all the lines and obtain legal authority to cut other forms of contact. In some situations, the subject is asked to answer only one number or phone because the others are being used by people who are not authorized to call. The initial phase of negotiations may involve convincing the subject that the negotiator is the legitimate representative of law enforcement. At this point, the subject commonly vents his anger at the police, threatens to kill hostages, and demands money, transportation, and, at times, the release of friends from prison.

Contact between the negotiator and the hostage taker may be initiated by either party. Eventually, as the negotiator gains control of the crisis, the subject calls the negotiator more and more frequently. During the early contacts, the negotiator attempts to develop a relationship of trust. This trusting relationship is crucial to the successful resolution of the crisis. Although no law requires total truthfulness on the part of the negotiators, they make every attempt to be completely honest. Through discussion of the issues at hand—identity of the hostages, location, demands—the negotiator is able to engage in an initial psychological assessment of the subject.

Without taking the focus away from the subject, efforts are made to identify the hostages. In some situations, negotiations go on for hours before it is verified that there are in fact no hostages.

The subject is encouraged to tell his side of the story in as much detail as he deems necessary—in other words, to ventilate. To assist him in this process, most successful negotiators use the Carl Rogers model of active listening while negotiating. This nondirective, client-centered approach has proved most effective. Through working and carefully critiquing many foreign and domestic hostage situations, law enforcement has learned how to defuse a hostage situation. Experience has demonstrated the importance of paying close attention to the subject and his needs, desires, and dreams. It has become clear that if the negotiator does not pay close attention to the subject, the subject frequently does something to remind everyone that he thinks he is in charge of this crisis. He wants this to remain his show of force. If and when the negotiator strays from keeping him at center stage, the subject may respond by making threats against hostages, firing a shot, or injuring a hostage. Therefore, more than in most crisis experiences, the hostage taker maintains "ownership" of the siege, and negotiators endeavor to help him in this activity. He makes the decisions. The negotiator works with him in a role similar to that of a defense attorney working with a client. Because of the relationship that tends to develop between the subject and the negotiator, the negotiator is generally isolated from the command post operation. In this way, the negotiator is able to focus on the subject while working with him toward a nonviolent solution to the dilemma.

To assist the negotiator, an excellent backup system of other nego-tiators, a psychological assessment of the subject, and many other resources are made available to ensure a tranquil termination of the incident. Thus, the negotiator can concentrate on the subject and en-courage him to talk about his problems.

While talking with the subject or listening to him ventilate, the negotiator must pay close attention so as to hear not only the subject's expressed demand but also those that are instrumental. Although the subject may be talking about money and an automobile to make good his escape, one must remember that he is enjoying all the attention his demands and this crisis are garnering him. The granting of his instrumen-tal demands, allowing escape from center stage, may be the last thing he really wants. A review of hundreds of hostage situations indicates that the hostage taker really wants a quiet conclusion. If he really wanted to kill people, he probably would have already done so. Most hostage takers want an audience for their performance (Schlossberg, 1980). Like most terrorists, they want a lot of people watching, not a lot of people dead (Jenkins, 1986). Thus, simple demands should not be met quickly because the need for the audience is such that the hostage taker may then dream up new and more difficult demands to retain the undivided attention of his audience.

The subject is in a difficult situation. He wants to surrender but may not know how. To quit would cause him to lose face; he cannot admit failure. This process of hostage negotiations enables him to find an honorable solution to his dilemma. Thus, a relationship between the negotiator and the subject is slowly developed by concentrating on the subject's favorite topic, himself—what he wants, how he feels, and so on. Furthermore, the negotiator insists that the subject make the decisions on as many points of discussion as possible. Every attempt is made to keep him in a decision-making mode. This may remind some people of the practice of self-determination and the client's right to fail, but law enforcement has learned that it also provides many tactical advantages. The subject is in the center of the stage during this crisis, and every attempt is made to keep him there. Making all the decisions is a fatiguing process. His fatigue is crucial as the authorities move him toward a quiet conclusion of his crisis.

During this discussion called hostage negotiations, the negotiator helps the subject talk about his problem, how and why he came to be in this situation, and, of course, his plan for its resolution. In the process, he is encouraged to talk about whatever is on his mind. Law enforcement has all the time in the world, and the most important person in the siege is the hostage taker. Of interest, this process has also worked in those rare situations where a person trained as a negotiator has taken hostages and issued demands (Lanceley, 1988).

Hostage negotiators, because of the careful selection and training process, have a high level of confidence in their ability to resolve the crisis peacefully. This level of confidence is shared by the SWAT team. When called on to fire, they do so with the confidence that all other alternatives to end this situation in a manner designed to preserve human life have been tried and have not succeeded. This attitude is evident when the SWAT agent is debriefed in the post-traumatic incident interview and his or her psychological reactions are compared with those of others who have been involved in an equally justifiable but more spontaneous shooting. The SWAT team member has a much lower stress level. This tends to be true even when the same SWAT team member is involved in a spontaneous shooting.

Another major player in this siege is the hostage, the unsuspecting citizen who is the bargaining chip, the pawn in this dangerous dilemma. Although the basis of the hostage negotiating guidelines is the preservation of human life, and the life of the hostage is of primary importance, this value should not be communicated to the hostage taker. It is a very poor bargaining tactic to escalate the value of what you want to the person who possesses this item. The reason for the police presence is the hostage, yet the hostage taker must believe that he, not the hostage, is of primary importance to the police.

Generally, law enforcement's contact with hostages during this first phase is limited. If contact can be made, however, the negotiator tries to reassure the hostages with frequent words and expressions of concern and sympathy to help them deal with their very high level of anxiety. The alarm phase is traumatic for unprepared law-abiding citizens forced into this life-and-death situation. Suddenly their world is turned around, and they may experience near-paralyzing fear (Rahe & Genender, 1983). The police, whom one expects to help, seem to be doing nothing and could give the impression of being confused. The hostage feels let down; it all seems so unreal (Derrer, 1988). Diego Asencio, U.S. ambassador to Colombia, was taken hostage with other diplomats in the Chilean embassy. He described well the reaction to the first few minutes of a hostage situation from the victim's perspective: "The worst aspect of the ordeal was the initial trauma. In the first few minutes, all you can do to ensure survival is to lie very close to the floor." Although he was to alter his behavior later and play a more comfortable role, his most enthusiastic advice to victims of any hostage situation during the alarm stage is to disregard any notion of heroics or curiosity. "Unarmed, untrained and poorly conditioned civilians can best ensure survival by maintaining low profiles," he advised (Asencio & Asencio, 1983, p. 217).

Many hostages, while lying close to the floor in those hectic opening moments, seek immediate psychological refuge in the denial of reality. Denial is a very primitive but effective psychological defense mechanism that is put into use when the mind is overloaded with trauma it cannot handle. Each victim who copes effectively has a strong will to survive. Some may deal with the stress by believing they are dreaming and will soon wake up and it will all be over. Some deal with the stress by sleeping—somnolent withdrawal. I have interviewed hostages who have slept for over 90% of their time in captivity. Some have fainted, although this is rare. Thus, one encounters a variety of responses to the trauma of captivity. In time, some of this trauma may abate; however, some individuals, like some prisoners of war, carry the psychological scars of captivity for the rest of their lives.

Contact with family members of the hostages and the subject is common throughout the siege. From them, we obtain information about their relative to assist us in the siege and assist them in dealing with the anxiety they are feeling by providing information. We also remain available to them throughout the siege. Though the FBI does not engage in the direct delivery of social work services, an informal referral to a minister, mental health professional, or significant other is common. In some situations, like the Hanafi Muslim siege at the Washington, D.C., B'nai B'rith headquarters in 1977 and in most prison sieges, family members are provided with shelter near the site and regular briefings throughout their ordeal.

Crisis

Although this phase marks the beginning of reason for the hostage taker, many similarities to the alarm phase remain. During this phase, most subjects begin to feel a sense of growing frustration. This is particularly true if the siege is the result of a poorly planned robbery. Generally, the subject's initial demands reflect his frustration. His early dialogue may be marked by emotional outbursts and excessive demands. His level of frustration is best indicated by the amount of money demanded. A subject may have expected a few thousand dollars from his efforts at robbery. Now that the police have trapped him in the bank, he may believe that he can punish them by making them pay a large amount of money. Initial demands for hundreds of thousands of dollars are not unusual. In fact, an evaluation of the demands can provide insight into the subject's mental processes. Demands for money and other creature comforts or a car indicate a criminal orientation that generally means an antisocial or inadequate personality. Demands for impossible action, like Corey Moore's insistence in Warrensville Heights, Ohio, that all white people vacate the earth in 24 hours, suggest some mental problems. The absence of clear demands or the refusal of the subject to talk with the negotiator suggest depression and suicidal ideation.

Evidence of this pattern has emerged over the years. The subject may insist on negotiating through one of his hostages. Or he may not answer the phone or respond to other attempts at negotiation, as with the Symbionese Liberation Army in Los Angeles and many other less dramatic sieges. This lack of direct communication usually results in a violent termination of the incident. Instead of talking, he may shoot at police. Another ploy is to run from the location while threatening to shoot police. A third is suddenly to shoot a hostage and then stand by a window. One theory attempts to explain this behavior by suggesting the subject fears that he will be talked out of suicide. He uses this passive-aggressive behavior pattern to force the authorities to do to him what he cannot do to himself.

Another method of evaluating the emotional state of the subject is to identify his hostages. Because most normal people do not take their spouse or children hostage, information on the identity of his hostages may also provide psychological data.

The crisis phase is of critical importance to the survival of the hostage. The behavior pattern exhibited now creates the precedent for hostage-subject interaction that can maximize the chance of survival or ensure the demise of the victim. The stress hostages experience during this phase may be due to their personal fears of isolation, claustrophobia, the loss of a sense of time, and the clear and present danger they face. These and other hostage problems are discussed at length by several authors.[2]

Accommodation

This is the longest phase and can be the most tranquil. The personality of the hostage taker will become more evident as he talks with the negotiator. The mental stability of the hostage taker is evaluated continuously throughout the siege. Although the more normal criminal subject may bargain with authorities, the mentally ill hostage taker will engage in rambling ventilation. The depressed individual will contact the negotiator less frequently than the other types of hostage takers, and his mental state will be very clear during discussions. Some suicidal subjects insist that hostages negotiate for them.

The following is an example of an inadequate type of hostage taker. Recently, a subject took his counselor hostage in a midwestern prison. The FBI negotiator was able to delay satisfying most of the subject's wants by blaming prison bureaucracy and shift changes. During this time, the negotiator made some judgments on the personality of the subject and the likelihood of his injuring his female hostage. Part of this process involved delaying the meeting of simple demands to evaluate the subject's reaction to this type of stress. Although one may not always want to delay the gratification of a simple request, it is an excellent tactic to be prepared to negotiate the substitution of satisfying a simple demand for a difficult one when the subject seems likely to injure the hostage.

A recent example of such a transaction comes from the negotiations conducted by an FBI special agent (JD) while negotiating in Knoxville, Tennessee. The subject (Tommy) had taken his hostage at 3:00 p.m. and demanded a shotgun with a box of shells, a loaded .38-caliber revolver with extra ammunition, and an automobile. At 7:00 p.m. he also mentioned the need for coffee. The following negotiations took place at 10:45 p.m. the same day (Strentz, 1983a):

Tommy: It's been over eight hours since I requested what I requested: the car, the shotgun, and the piece.

JD: Yeah.

Tommy: The car.

JD: Just a minute, Tommy. (Talking to someone nearby yet heard by Tommy.) Did you get that coffee in to him? Dammit, you'd think you could handle something simple like that, he wants some coffee. The man needs some hot coffee.

Tommy: I want . . .

JD: A damn cup of coffee.

Tommy: Hey!

JD: Sorry, Tommy. What is it?

Tommy: We want a pot of percolating coffee. With lots of cream and sugar. Send a coffee pot down here.

JD: Coffee pot.

Tommy: We're going to need it. If you are going to keep holding out this long . . .

Eventually the subject was distracted and taken into custody while his hostage was being rescued. It is important to note that it took 8 hours to address his demands. The subject was aware of this delay and acquiesced to this tactic. This delay allowed time for the negotiator to assess the subject, induce fatigue, and enable the SWAT team to effect a rescue without injury to anyone.

This negotiating sequence, conducted by a trained negotiator, stands in contrast to those in Jacksonville a few years before.[3]

Resolution

This final phase may be one of trauma or tranquility. The mood in and outside the siege site depends on whether the siege is broken by an assault or resolved by a quiet surrender.

In the majority of situations, the subject will be fatigued by the negotiation process and will have reluctantly resigned himself to his fate, an honorable solution, not surrender.

One hostage siege in Los Angeles was resolved when the subject exited a jewelry store pushing a shopping cart he had filled with watches. It was his plan to trade these items, which he had stolen, fair and square, for a United Airlines 747 with a crew for a flight to the South Pacific, where he wanted to buy an island. He envisioned living happily ever after as he bartered with the natives for the necessities of life. His knowledge of history provided him with the Dutch precedent in Manhattan. Though he did not call himself Peter Minuit, he tried to duplicate this 1626 effort. Yet, as he exited the jewelry store with his booty, as out of touch with reality as he was, he was not ignorant of what might happen. Suddenly, on a smooth sidewalk, he accidentally tripped, and the cart of jewelry and his weapons went rolling down the sidewalk as he fell to the ground, unarmed, with his hands in full view. As the police rushed to arrest him, he remained quite still. While he was being handcuffed, he looked over at the arresting officer and said, "Hell of a way to make a living, isn't it?" This situation in May 1978 contrasted sharply with a Beverly Hills jewelry store siege a few years later during which several hostages were killed. Thus, although some generalizations can be made about typical subject and hostage behavior, each situation is a different crisis and must be treated as such to ensure a successful resolution.

It is during the process of resolution that law enforcement has the greatest and most positive psychological impact on the hostages. During the debriefing interview, law enforcement wants them to tell all they can about their experience. Most victims ventilate for some time before a sequential pattern of events can be obtained. Time is of no consequence. The postincident interview continues until all participants are satisfied that it is over, and it is usually conducted prior to hostage contact with anyone else. This is necessary to obtain their version of the incident before it is contaminated by the media and others. Rarely is a former hostage too disturbed to conduct such an interview. If some psychological or physical problems are present, the negotiator probably knew about them prior to the release, and the appropriate community resources are alerted and available at the site. Police officers and FBI agents are genuinely interested in what the released hostages have to say. One reason for this interest is the distinct possibility that the listener will have to tell a judge and a jury all about the siege. Thus, the law enforcement officer needs to know what happened.

The very positive reaction of victims to the postincident interview was especially clear when the Americans who had been hijacked on TWA 847 in June 1985 were interviewed in Germany by a number of mental health, intelligence, and law enforcement professionals. According to Dr. Robert Sokal, who was the Army psychiatrist in charge of the processing of the hostages, they said that, as victims, they felt best about their interview with the FBI agents who were so interested in their story.

Certainly one reason for their reaction was the fact that talking to the FBI gave them a chance to get even with the terrorists who had held them for so long and killed one of their fellow passengers. According to Sokal (1988, personal interview, San Francisco), the former hostages felt that by talking to the FBI, they were telling someone about their suffering who could do something to correct the wrongs they had experienced.

Although many of the hostages on TWA 847 expressed hostility toward their captors, a sympathetic reaction called the Stockholm Syndrome is also common. This is a positive reciprocal relationship that frequently develops between hostage and subject as well as between negotiator and subject. It was first identified during a bank robbery in Stockholm, Sweden, that turned into a 131-hour siege in August 1973. One definition of this reaction takes into account three phases of the experience and describes it as the positive feelings of the captives toward their captors that are accompanied by negative feelings toward the police. These feelings are frequently reciprocated by the captors (Strentz, 1979). A hostile former hostage may be the price that law enforcement must pay for a living hostage. Anti-law-enforcement feelings are not new to the police. But in a hostage situation, such feelings are encouraged to ensure the development of the Stockholm Syndrome. Hostility from people whose lives law enforcement has mustered its resources to save seems inconsistent. A human life, however, is an irreplaceable treasure and worth some hostility. A poor or hostile witness for the prosecution is a small price to pay for this human life.

CONCLUSION

The process of hostage negotiations, as engaged in by trained professionals in a variety of settings, ranging from a domestic dispute or a foiled armed robbery to a group of political terrorists who have hijacked an aircraft, is a very practical application of crisis intervention theory. Hundreds of hostage situations around the world have been successfully resolved by the application of these principles in a time-limited, traumatic event in the lives of otherwise normal human beings who just happened to be in the wrong place at the wrong time.

It is said that the Chinese character for crisis is a combination of the symbols for danger and opportunity (Puryear, 1980). In a hostage situation, the element of danger coexists with the opportunity for successful resolution and personal growth. With good mental health counseling to deal with the effects of post-traumatic stress disorders, people victimized by this trauma can grow in positive directions. They can view their captivity as a test that they passed, not a crisis in which they failed.

NOTES

1. According to the *Hostage Incident Report*, 98% of American hostage takers are male (Strentz, 1983b); males also appear to predominate as subjects overseas (Jenkins et al., 1977)—hence our assumption throughout this chapter that the hostage taker, or subject, is a male.

2. In doing this reading, one should differentiate among the reactions of prisoners of war, concentration camp inmates, and hostages (Derrer, 1988; Eitinger, 1980; Ford & Spaulding, 1973; Kentsmith, 1982; Ochberg & Soskis, 1982; Rahe & Genender, 1983; Strentz, 1979, 1983a, 1987; Symonds, 1980; Wesselius & Desarno, 1983).

3. Information on the mechanics of hostage negotiations is available in several articles on this subject written by instructors at the FBI Academy (Fuselier, 1981a, 1981b; Lanceley, 1981; Soskis & Van Zandt, 1986; Strentz, 1983a, 1986). Additional information is available in the books written by Schlossberg and Freeman (1974) and Bolz and Hershey (1979).

PART III

Crisis Intervention
With Diverse Client Groups

Crisis Response Teams in the Aftermath of Disasters

MARLENE A. YOUNG

On the morning of August 20, 1986, the National Organization for Victim Assistance (NOVA) received a telephone call from Michael C. Turpen, then attorney general of the state of Oklahoma. Earlier that day, he reported, Patrick Sherrill had entered the Edmund, Oklahoma, post office and killed 14 people before he killed himself. He left a community in chaos, and Attorney General Turpen was calling for help. Within 24 hours, NOVA had organized and dispatched its first team of seven volunteer crisis intervenors to provide assistance as needed.

Since the initial, somewhat tentative beginning, NOVA has sent numerous teams of volunteer intervenors to the sites of tragic events, including natural and technological disasters, human-caused accidents, and mass crimes.

Recently, in May 1994, NOVA was called upon to send a team to the Chicago Housing Authority as their newly established community crisis team struggled to respond to a gang-related crime spree that claimed the lives of 13 people in one weekend in the Robert Taylor Homes, the largest public housing development in the nation. In a slightly different approach, in November 1994, NOVA sent an intervenor to join a crisis team in Union County, South Carolina, whose focus was supporting law enforcement officials who had been involved in solving the case of the toddlers who had been drowned by their mother.

Different kinds of tragedies, different communities, different kinds of responses, but all illustrate the kind of work NOVA has undertaken in its National Crisis Response Team Project. It is work that is designed to address the emotional aftermath of communitywide disasters. The project is based on the premise that disasters cause individual and communitywide crisis reactions and that immediate intervention can provide communities with tools that are useful in mitigating long-term distress.

In its first 8 years of offering this service, NOVA helped 80 communities, one of them twice (see Table 7.1). Many of these disasters were precipitated by criminal events. Though there are some important differences between natural and man-made disasters and between those caused intentionally and those caused by accidents or recklessness, the commonalities of widespread emotional trauma appear to be more significant than their differences.

This chapter will review the features of crisis and stress reactions in individuals and special issues that are helpful in analyzing crisis situations, explain NOVA's guidelines in providing crisis intervention to such individuals, and describe how those guidelines are applied and adapted in a communitywide disaster.

Though readers may be familiar with the crisis reaction, a detailed understanding of its pattern is essential to NOVA's crisis intervention methodology. Teaching survivors and their caregivers elements of reaction helps them to understand the normalities of what may be experienced as abnormal.

CRISIS, STRESS, AND DISASTER SITUATIONS

Crisis Reaction

Individuals exist in a state of emotional equilibrium in their everyday lives. They establish their own boundaries for experiencing and expressing happiness, sadness, anger, excitement, and the like. Occasional

(text continued on page 161)

TABLE 7.1 NOVA National Crisis Response Project Interventions and Consultations, August 1986 to November 1994

Date	Community	Disaster
August 20, 1986	Edmond, Oklahoma	Murder of 14 people in the post office before slayer, Patrick Sherrill, committed suicide.
December 8, 1986	Mt. Pleasant, Iowa	Murder of the mayor of Mt. Pleasant and injury of two city council members by a man upset over sewer problems.
January 4, 1987	Baltimore County, Maryland	Amtrak/Conrail train crash (later found to have been caused by criminal misconduct) killed 16 people and injured hundreds.
March 26, 1987	Oxford, Mississippi	University of Mississippi "walkathon" in which a truck crashed into a car that catapulted into the walkers; five died, and several others were injured.
April 23, 1987	Palm Bay, Florida	Random murders of six individuals in a shopping mall and injuries to several others. Two police officers killed.
July 7, 1987	Inkster, Michigan	Hostage-taking and killing of three police officers.
August 10, 1987	Winter Park, Colorado	Boulder dislodged from mountainside smashed into a tour bus, killing six people and injuring 16.
August 16, 1987	Romulus, Michigan	Plane crash near Detroit airport killed 154 people; 1 survivor.
August 25, 1987	Lockport, New York	Aftermath of plane crash in Romulus. Of the 154 dead, 5 were engineers from the Harrison Radiator plant, a division of General Motors based in Lockport.
September 9, 1987	Point of Rocks, Maryland	Electrocution of a 10-year-old boy who rode his bicycle over a power line. Community members witnessed the tragedy.

(continued)

TABLE 7.1 Continued

Date	Community	Disaster
October 20, 1987	Indianapolis, Indiana	Air Force plane crash into Ramada Inn. Nine people died immediately, one later.
November 15, 1987	Denver, Colorado	Plane crash killed 26 people. NOVA's response was to Boise, Idaho, hometown of the victims.
February 25, 1988	Washington, D.C.	Sexual assault in a counseling center.
May 10, 1988	Washington, D.C.	Stabbing of a teacher in front of her students on a school playground.
May 14, 1988	Carrollton, Kentucky	Highway crash of a car into a school bus, killing 24 children and three adults. Response was to Radcliff, Kentucky, victims' hometown.
July 26, 1988	Rapid City, South Dakota	Weeklong arson-caused fire destroyed 15 homes, 42 outbuildings, and more than 40 vehicles and caused $1.3 million in damage.
January 25, 1989	Cove Neck, New York	Avianca Flight 52 crashed, killing 73 and injuring 88 passengers.
February 14, 1989	Chevy Chase, Maryland	Shooting spree in a bank. Three employees killed, one wounded. Slayer committed suicide after attack.
February 24, 1989	Honolulu, Hawaii	Door on United Flight 811 bound for New Zealand blows off at 22,000 feet as the plane climbs away from Honolulu; nine passengers killed and five others seriously injured.
March 24, 1989	Prince William Sound, Alaska	Exxon-Valdez Oil Spill; Captain Joseph Hazelwood found guilty of misdemeanor.
April 14, 1989	Sonoma County, California	Ramon Salcido killed seven people—his wife, two of his three children, his mother-in-law, two sisters-in-law,

TABLE 7.1 Continued

Date	Community	Disaster
		and a fellow worker—at Sonoma County's Grand Cru Winery.
July 19, 1989	Sioux City, Iowa	United Airlines Flight 232 crashed; 111 passengers die, 185 survive.
September 13, 1989	Kentucky	Mining explosion killed 10 miners.
September 14, 1989	Louisville, Kentucky	Joseph Westbecker shot 20 Standard Gravure Corp. workers, killing 8 before taking his own life.
September 17-18, 1989	St. Croix, Virgin Islands	Hurricane Hugo hit. Two dead and eighty hospitalized; 90% of the island's buildings were damaged. Puerto Rico hit by Hurricane as well.
September 20, 1989	New York, New York	U.S. Air Boeing 737-400 slid into the East River next to LaGuardia Airport after an aborted takeoff; 59 people survived, 2 people were killed.
September 21, 1989	Charleston, South Carolina	Hurricane Hugo hit Charleston with 135 m.p.h. winds and a 15-foot storm surge; 13 dead during the storm, 22 more die in storm-related accidents or heart attacks.
September 21, 1989	Alton, Texas	Bus crash killed 16, many children.
October 17, 1989	Bay Area, California	Loma Prieta earthquake; 55 dead in the Bay area, 6 dead in Santa Cruz, County, 37 miles from San Francisco. Three dead in aftermath.
November 16, 1989	Huntsville, Alabama	Tornado killed 22.
November 16, 1989	Newbergh, New York	Seven children killed when winds from tornado blew down a wall and glass on their lunchroom.
December 6, 1989	Montreal, Canada	Shooting in engineering building killed 14, wounded

(continued)

TABLE 7.1 Continued

Date	Community	Disaster
		13, ended in shooter's suicide.
March 25, 1990	New York, New York	Happy Land night club arson fire kills 87.
April 6, 1990	Oslo, Sweden, to Frederikshavn, Denmark	Fire (thought to be arson) broke out in a cabin of the Scandinavian Star and consumed ship. Of 385 passengers and 96 crew members, 158 died.
June 10, 1990	Birmingham, England	Wind blew out cockpit of British Airways 5390. All 82 passengers and crew survived. Captain Lancaster was sucked out of the cock-pit but passenger held on to his legs; he survived as well.
June 14, 1990	Shadyside, Ohio	Flash flood kills 26.
June 18, 1990	Jacksonville, Florida	Mass murder in General Motors Acceptance Corp. offices. James E. Plough shot 17 people, killing 10 before killing himself.
July 8, 1990	Baltimore County, Maryland	Three-year-old struck and killed by a drunk driver in the backyard of his home.
August 3 to November, 1990	Kuwait/Iraq	Hostage situation. NOVA involved in the United States with families of hostages.
August 23 to August 30, 1990	Gainesville, Florida	Four University of Florida and one Santa Fe Commun-ity College students murdered.
August 28, 1990	Joliet/Will Counties, Illinois	Tornadoes killed 28, injured 350 people. Two schools and close to 500 homes destroyed.
September 27, 1990	Berkeley, California	Mehrdad Dashti opened fire in a crowded bar near Uni-versity of California at Berkeley. One student killed, 7 wounded, and hostages taken in an all-night standoff. Dashti is killed by police.

TABLE 7.1 Continued

Date	Community	Disaster
November 13, 1990	Aramoana, New Zealand	Mass murder. David Gray killed 13 people before killing himself.
December 3, 1990	Detroit, Michigan	Plane crash between two Northwest airplanes on a runway killed eight.
December 11, 1990	Tennessee	Multicar crash killed 15 people and injured 56.
February 1, 1991	Los Angeles, California	U.S. Air plane crash with a commuter plane on the runway; 34 people dead.
March 3, 1991	Colorado Springs, Colorado	United Airlines 737 crashed and killed 20 passengers and 5 crew members. An additional body was recovered in a casket in the cargo hold.
March 4, 1991	Colorado Springs, Colorado	Crystal Spring Estates, a personal care boarding home, burned in a fire that killed nine elderly women.
March 5, 1991	Banff, Alberta, Canada	Avalanche killed 10 heliskiers.
March 22, 1991	San Diego, California	Two Navy submarine-hunting planes collided, killing 22 Navy aviators.
April 4, 1991	Stetson University, DeLand, Florida	Car crash killed three students and injured four others.
April 4, 1991	Philadelphia, Pennsylvania Suburb	Helicopter collided with a twin-engine airplane. Senator John Heinz killed along with three others in the air. The debris fell on a schoolyard and killed two children, injured nine others.
April 4-5, 1991	Sacramento, California	Florin Mall massacre. Four men take 30 hostages inside The Good Guys electronics store. After 8½ hour siege, 6 people killed (3 hostages and 3 hostage-takers) in a shootout; 13 hostages wounded.
April 5, 1991	Brunswick, Georgia	Small plane crash killed 23 people, including former Senator John Tower.

(continued)

TABLE 7.1 Continued

Date	Community	Disaster
April 26, 1991	Andover, Kansas	Tornado strike killed 19 people, destroyed 859 homes and damaged 850. Swept through Sedgwick and Butler counties.
April 28, 1991	Mt. Holly, New Jersey	Murder of assistant district attorney.
May 1, 1991	Mt. Holly, New Jersey	IMC Fertilizer Plant explosion killed eight people.
June 17, 1991	Sterlington, Louisiana	Albright and Wilson chemical company explosion; 2 dead and 33 injured, 6 critically.
July 10, 1991	Birmingham, Alabama	L'Express commuter plane crashed into the Ensley neighborhood outside the airport; 13 dead, 2 critically injured.
July 24, 1991	Milwaukee, Wisconsin	First reports of murders by Jeffrey Dahmer. Eventual discovery that he killed at least 17 young men—16 in Wisconsin and 1 in Ohio.
July 31, 1991	Camden, South Carolina	Amtrak train derailment killed seven.
August 20, 1991	Talladega, Alabama	Federal Correctional Institution. Ten-day siege by Cuban detainees. Surprise predawn raid ended it on August 30, 1991. Nine hostages held by 121 inmates.
August 27, 1991	New York, New York	Subway train wreck killed seven.
September 3, 1991	Hamlet, North Carolina	Fire in Imperial Food Products plant; 25 dead and 55 injured.
September 14, 1991	Forsyth, Missouri	Taney County Jail. Fire killed four inmates.
September 22, 1991	Montana State Prison	Inmates held five corrections officers hostage and killed five other inmates held in protective custody during a 4-hour disturbance.
October 16, 1991	Killeen, Texas	George Hennard crashed truck into Luby's cafeteria and emerged with a semi-

TABLE 7.1 Continued

Date	Community	Disaster
		automatic to kill 23 people and injure 15 more before killing himself.
October 20, 1991	Oakland, California	Brush fire killed 19; 43 people missing and 148 injured; 1,800 homes and apartments destroyed; 200 apartments damaged.
October 22, 1991	Ganeshpur, India	Earthquake killed approximately 1,000.
November 3, 1991	Iowa City, Iowa	On University of Iowa campus, a disgruntled graduate student opened fire, fatally wounding five people—four faculty and one student—before he took his own life.
February 6, 1992	Evansville, Indiana	Sixteen people killed when a C-130 military cargo plane crashed into hotel/restaurant complex; nine were guests, two were hotel employees, and five were members of the Kentucky Air National Guard. Investigation later listed pilot error as the cause of the crash.
April 10-11, 1992	East Orange, New Jersey	Discovery of four bodies over a 2-day period, possibly related to seven earlier serial killings. Task Force formed, arrest made April 12, 1992, tying the accused to five homicides and two assaults (between December 12, 1991, and April 11, 1992).
August 23-24, 1992	South Dade County, Florida	Hurricane Andrew's force covers over 165 square miles; 50-plus fatalities, 85,000 homes destroyed during the storm. Estimated damage at $30 billion.
December 15, 1992	Great Barrington, Massachusetts	Disgruntled student opened fire on campus of Simon's

(continued)

TABLE 7.1 Continued

Date	Community	Disaster
		Rock College of Bard, killing one faculty and one student, and wounding four students, before surrendering.
April 11-22, 1993	Lucasville, Ohio	Southern Ohio Correctional Facility. Fighting broke out; 13 correctional officers taken hostage. Siege brought to an end through negotiations. One correctional officer and nine inmates died. Damages estimated at over $5 million.
May 5, 1993	Passaic, New Jersey	A 7-year-old Hispanic/Latino girl kidnapped, sexually assaulted, and asphyxiated by a state parolee recently released and living in a nearby boarding house.
September 18, 1993	Arlington, Virginia	A Hispanic/Latino 19-year-old-mother shot to death by her ex-boyfriend in an apartment building laundry room in front of the victim's 16-year-old son, 4-year-old niece, and a 3-year-old boy. Assailant escaped.
December 7, 1993	Garden City, Long Island, New York	Long Island Rail Road Massacre. Five people were killed on the commuter train to Hicksville; 18 people wounded.
January 17, 1994	Los Angeles, California	Northridge earthquake killed 46 people and injured hundreds. Total property damage not yet determined.
May 9-12, 1994	Chicago, Illinois	In Robert Taylor Homes, drug-related gang war resulted in the murders of 13 people in one weekend in a single public housing development.

TABLE 7.1 Continued

Date	Community	Disaster
November 15, 1994	Union County, South Carolina	A weeklong nationwide manhunt for two young boys, Alex and Michael Smith, results in the confession by their mother that she drowned them.

stressors will stretch an individual's sense of equilibrium, but, even then, those stressors are usually predictable within the individual's frame of reference, and he or she can mobilize adequate coping mechanisms to deal with the stress.

Trauma, by contrast, throws people so far out of their range of equilibrium that it is difficult for them to restore a sense of balance in life. And when they do establish a new equilibrium, it will almost always be different than before the trauma, with new boundaries and new definitions.

Trauma may be precipitated by an "acute" stressor or a "chronic" stressor. Acute, trauma-inducing stressors are usually sudden, arbitrary, and often random events. They include many types of crime, terrorism, and man-made and natural disasters.

Among the most common trauma-inducing chronic stressors are interpersonal abuse, developmental stress caused by life transitions, long-term illness, and continuing exposure to disease, famine, or war. Chronic stressors may cause crisis reactions similar to those caused by acute stressors, with significant differences that cannot be discussed here. They should be noted, however, because they often affect the preexisting equilibrium, and individuals suffering chronic stressors are often at higher risk for emotional trauma after an acute stressor occurs.

The normal human response to trauma follows a general pattern. That pattern is characterized by both a physical response and an emotional or psychological response. The physical response is based on biological instinct and is often not within the control of an individual.

The physical reaction usually begins with a sense of shock, disorientation, and numbness. This is followed by a state of physical arousal that is triggered by a "fight-or-flight" instinct. Adrenaline begins to pump through the body. The body may relieve itself of excess materials through regurgitation, defecation, and urination. The heart rate increases. Individuals may begin to breathe rapidly and perspire. Often one sense—sight, hearing, taste, touch, or smell—becomes intense (often to the detriment of the other senses). This extraordinary sensory experience may well become an intensely vivid memory that, when rearoused, can trigger a reexperiencing of the initial crisis reaction.

Finally, the immediate physical reaction is typically ended by exhaustion. The body simply cannot sustain the state of extreme arousal for a long period of time. If individuals fail to sleep or rest, they may simply collapse with exhaustion.

The cognitive and emotional reaction to crises is very similar to the physical reaction. The first response is usually one of shock, disbelief, and denial of the trauma, with the mind trying to frame an unthreatening interpretation of the evidence it perceives. There is a sense of a suspension of reality. Not only does the mind refuse to believe what the body is experiencing, many individuals feel as though time stops or the world is in slow motion around them.

Shock may last for a few minutes or for weeks. It is usually followed by a turmoil of emotions as time goes on. The turmoil often engages emotions such as anger or rage, fear or terror, confusion and frustration, guilt and self-blame, and grief over losses suffered as a result of the crisis.

This emotional chaos often precipitates regression to a childlike state in survivors. They are, after all, in a helpless state of dependency on others or outside forces, a circumstance they may not have experienced except in childhood. This, coupled with the intensity of feelings, is overwhelming, and survivors may want a parent or parent figure to take care of things—to "kiss it and make it better."

Just as the physical reaction results in exhaustion, so does the emotional reaction. Survivors often feel as though they are on a roller coaster of extremes. At one time they are besieged with emotion and at another time they may simply feel a void or a nothingness. In defense, many constrict the range of their emotional reactions to life events, warding off pleasure and pain equally. For many, over time, they open themselves up to more emotional risks and gains, evolving from victim to survivor, establishing a new equilibrium, and constructing a new sense of self. But some face a lifetime of debilitating stress reactions as a result of the trauma.

Long-Term Stress Reactions

Long-term stress reactions tend to take one of four forms: (a) pathological, (b) character changes, (c) post-traumatic stress disorder, or (d) long-term crisis reaction. Although pathological reactions may occur in a small percentage of cases, most crises resulting from trauma-specific events do not result in pathological reactions. Such reactions may include the development of severe phobias, clinical depression, multiple personality disorder, and so forth. Psychotherapy is usually suggested in such cases.

The second type of long-term stress reaction may be the development of post-traumatic character changes. Again, these are not common reactions but they may occur, particularly in survivors of extremely shocking tragedies. Such character changes are exemplified in overcontrolling personalities, rigidity of personality, post-traumatic character decline, extreme behavior change, and the like.

The third type is post-traumatic stress disorder was described in the revised *DSM-III* (1987; see Table 7.2). The symptoms of PTSD are often seen in the loved ones of homicide victims, victims of chronic child sexual abuse, survivors of sexual assault, and survivors of catastrophic physical injury.

A final type of long-term stress reaction is one that is not often discussed by mental health practitioners but that has been most often observed in NOVA's work. Referred to as "long-term crisis reaction," it simply describes the fact that many victims do not present symptoms of PTSD or other disorders, but they are prone to reexperience feelings of the crisis reaction when trigger events recall the trauma in their lives. Trigger events may include the following situations: experiencing a physical sensation that is similar to the intense sensory perception that accompanied the initial physical reaction; anniversaries of the trauma; holidays or birthdays; developmental crises or stages of significant life events such as graduations, marriages, divorces, births, or deaths; involvement in the criminal or civil justice system as a result of the event; media events or broadcasts that are similar to the trauma; memorials of the trauma; and so on.

TABLE 7.2 Post-Traumatic Stress Disorder Definition

"A. The individual has experienced *an event* that is *outside the range of usual* human experience and that would be *markedly distressing* to almost anyone, e.g., serious threat to one's life or physical integrity; serious threat or harm to one's children, spouse, or other close relatives and friends; sudden destruction of one's home or community; or seeing another person who is being (or has recently been) seriously injured or killed as the result of an accident or physical violence.

"B. The distressing event is *persistently reexperienced* in at least *one* of the following ways:

"(1) recurrent and intrusive distressing recollections of the event (which may be associated with guilty thoughts about behavior before or during the event)

"(2) recurrent distressing dreams of the event

"(3) sudden acting or feeling as if the event were recurring (includes a sense of reliving the experience, illusions, hallucinations, and dissociative [flashback] episodes, even those that occur upon awakening or when intoxicated) (in young children, repetitive play in which themes or aspects of the distressing event are expressed)

"(4) intense psychological distress at exposure to events that symbolize or resemble an aspect of the event, including anniversaries of the event.

"C. *Persistent avoidance* of stimuli associated with the distressing event *or numbing* of general responsiveness (not present before the event), as indicated by at least *three* of the following:

"(1) deliberate efforts to avoid thoughts or feelings associated with the event

"(2) deliberate efforts to avoid activities or situations that arouse recollections of the event

"(3) inability to recall an important aspect of the event (psychogenic amnesia)

"(4) markedly diminished interest in significant activities (in young children, loss of recently acquired developmental skills such as toilet training or language skills)

"(5) feeling of detachment or estrangement from others

"(6) restricted range of affect, e.g., unable to have loving feelings

"(7) sense of a foreshortened future, e.g., child does not expect to have a career, marriage, or children, or a long life

"D. *Persistent symptoms* of *increased arousal* (not present before the event) as indicated by *at least two* of the following:

"(1) difficulty falling or staying asleep

"(2) irritability or outbursts of anger

"(3) difficulty concentrating

"(4) hypervigilance

"(5) physiologic reactivity at exposure to events that symbolize or resemble an aspect of the event (e.g., a woman who was raped in an elevator breaks out in a sweat when entering any elevator)

"E. Duration of the disturbance of at least one month.

"Specify delayed onset if the onset of symptoms was at least six months after the distressing event."

SOURCE: *DSM-III* (American Psychiatric Association, 1987).

Issues Surrounding Disasters

There are four points of analysis that are helpful in determining whether an event places an individual or a community at high risk for trauma. These points also can be useful in determining the key issues that should be addressed in strategies for intervention.

(1) The first issue is an analysis of the time dimension of the event itself. The following is a breakdown of the eight points in time that may affect the response of a survivor:

pre-event equilibrium,
threat of event,
warning of event,
event's impact,
inventory after event,
time of rescue,
time of remedial work, and
the time at which survivors can be considered to have finalized the reconstruction of their new lives.

The pre-event equilibrium is important because the more stressful that equilibrium, the greater the potential of an additional stressful event precipitating another crisis. If a trauma is preceded by a period of threat or warning to which the survivors have an opportunity to respond, there is greater possibility of guilt or self-blame if they did not respond to protect themselves or loved ones. (Conversely, if the victim can take pride in the way he or she used the warning to mitigate the harm, that can be helpful in the reconstruction process.) If there is no warning, anger may be a dominant emotion in the immediate aftermath because of the feelings of injustice and unfairness.

The time immediately following a crisis is one during which survivors will take inventory of damage and injuries suffered. There is always a stage of inventory-taking, even when rescuers appear immediately on the scene. In a medical model, that stage is called triage. If a survivor or rescuer thinks he or she has made a mistake or inappropriate assessment during the inventory stage, it may contribute to guilt or blame. And such mistakes are not uncommon; under the influence of stress hormones, humans can become oblivious to physical injuries, even life-threatening injuries.

Actions during the rescue stage or the remedy stage may also lead to guilt or anger. Rescue attempts that fail contribute to frustration and despair. The remedy stage refers to that time after the physical rescue of survivors when additional resources and services may be provided to help survivors begin to reconstruct their lives. Although it is very common for such assistance to be available in the first hours or days after a traumatic event, it is also general practice for such help to be withdrawn thereafter. This may contribute to feelings of disillusionment and outrage by survivors.

(2) The second issue for analysis is the spatial dimension of the tragedy. This is particularly critical in a communitywide trauma, for it defines and describes the community itself. One factor in the spatial dimension is the proximity of individuals or survivors to the event itself.

A tragedy may be visualized as the center of a series of concentric circles. (See Figure 7.1.) The general guideline is that the closer an individual is to the center of the tragedy, the higher the risk there is for a crisis reaction and long-term stress reactions. There is a key exception to this guideline, however. Loved ones of victims who are killed due to the disaster must be considered to be central to the tragedy even if they were not present at the time of the event. The core of their tragedy is different. It is the death notification that is the event of impact, not the actual disaster. The second spatial dimension is the phenomenon of convergence. Convergence describes the actions of individuals who come to the scene of the tragedy. When a larger number of people converge on the event, there is a greater likelihood that the event will be felt as a communitywide trauma. Conversely, when a smaller number of individuals are involved, there is more likelihood that it will be experienced as a trauma that happened to specific individuals.

In addition, it is important to examine whether the convergence was positive or negative in nature. In the most obvious terms, positive convergence occurs when those who arrive come to rescue or to help, while negative convergence occurs when voyeurs, vandals, or looters come and contribute to the chaos and damage. Negative convergence may add to feelings of anger, frustration, and loss of faith or trust in humanity. One sometimes encounters these reactions among those who came to the

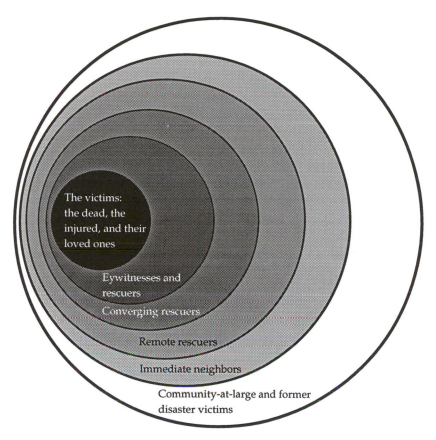

The victims:
the dead, the
injured, and their
loved ones

Eywitnesses and
rescuers

Converging rescuers

Remote rescuers

Immediate neighbors

Community-at-large and former
disaster victims

Figure 7.1. The Emotional Aftershocks of Disaster
SOURCE: © 1989 National Organization for Victim Assistance; used by permission.

scene as rescuers but rescued no one, serving only to tend to the dead and dying.

(3) A third issue to address in the aftermath of tragedy is the roles played by survivors. The more kinds of roles the survivors are forced to assume, the higher the risk of trauma.

A victim of a street mugging may have only one role in the event, that of a victim of predatory crime—and sometimes not even as an eyewitness, as is the case in many purse-snatches. In a communitywide trauma, however, it is likely that many survivors will have played multiple roles. A victim may be injured or not, an important difference in itself, but may also be a loved one of someone who was killed in the tragedy, and a witness to the event, and a rescuer who helped save others, and a resident of the neighborhood where it happened, and a caregiver who is responsible for responding to the emotional aftermath of the tragedy in the community. The roles may be further complicated by the survivor's self-perception of how well she or he performed or is performing in any of these roles; obviously, there are almost always major differences in the reactions of a rescuer who failed in the rescue attempt and a rescuer who was successful. The most dominant role from the survivor's perspective is important because it may help assess the most dominant feelings he or she has about the event.

(4) A fourth issue in the analysis of tragedy is the elements that define the uniqueness of the trauma. In examining this issue, there are several features to consider: the extent of personal impact, the type of tragedy, the duration of the trauma, the potential for occurrence or recurrence, and the ability of individuals to control the impact of the trauma in its aftermath.

The extent of personal impact can be roughly measured by answering six questions:

- How many people are dead?
- Was there a great deal of carnage or a great many people severely injured?
- What was the amount of property destruction?
- Were many people dislocated or relocated from homes, jobs, or schools?
- What was the amount of financial loss, both from the immediate disaster and due to consequent imbalance of losses and assets?
- How many people were eyewitnesses to the disaster?

The type of tragedy is defined in several ways, each of which contributes to the understanding of the impact. The cause of the tragedy is one definitive dimension. A natural disaster may cause anger at God but may also be more easily accepted because of the lack of human control over the outcome. An event seen as a man-made accident may raise concerns about human fallibility, blame, and standards for prevention or regulation. A criminal act may cause anger or outrage at human cruelty or, as with drugged or drunk driving leading to multiple deaths, at the driver's wanton, reckless disregard of human life.

The type of destruction experienced in the tragedy is another definitive dimension. Disasters accompanied by flooding or drowning raise
concerns about property destruction and bodily disfigurement of victims who have died. Fear of water and suffocation may develop in
survivors. Catastrophes that have involved fire often leave survivors
with intense memories of the smell of burning wood or flesh. Burn victims
suffer excruciating pain and, at times, awful mutilation or maiming.
Bodies of burn victims who die are disfigured and are, many times,
unrecognizable. Survivors may become preoccupied with thoughts of
hell or damnation.

A third issue is the duration of the tragedy. Duration is experienced
in three ways, each running on the "subjective time clock" of each
victim. The first kind of duration is defined by the length of time a
victim or survivor was at the point of impact of the disaster at the time
it happened. Hence, a victim who is trapped in the wreckage of a train
may be at the point of impact for hours, while a victim who was thrown
free of the train during the crash may only be at the point of impact for
a few minutes before being taken to a hospital or emergency shelter.

The second kind of duration defines how long survivors' senses are
engaged by the disaster. Survivors of arson may have been at the home
during the fire for several hours, but the smell of the burnt house may
remain with them for weeks or months after the tragedy if they continue
to occupy the home.

The third kind of duration is defined by the length of time that
survivors are involved in the aftermath of the disaster due to the response
of society. Thus, a survivor of a disaster caused by criminal attack may
be involved in the disaster for years due to participation in the criminal
justice system. *The general guideline is that the longer the survivor is engaged
in the disaster in any of these ways, the greater the likelihood for experiencing
severe crisis reaction or long-term stress reactions.*

The fourth issue of impact is the likelihood of the disaster recurring.
The greater the perceived chance of recurrence, the more likely it is that
survivors will suffer fear as a dominant emotion in the emotional turmoil.
The more impossible the event or its recurrence seems, the more likely
it is that anger will be a dominant emotion.

Finally, it is important to examine the extent to which the survivors
have control over the impact of the disaster on their own lives and futures.
Catastrophes throw the world of an individual or community out of

control. The survivors are confronted with the chaos of destruction, the chaos of the rescue response, and the chaos of lost and interrupted time. The need to reestablish a sense of control is critical to the efforts to reconstruct a new equilibrium. Although there is no control over the disaster itself, the survivors who feel they are able to control the aftermath and the events that accompany it seem better able to cope.

CRISIS INTERVENTION GUIDELINES

Crisis Intervention With Individuals

This understanding of crisis reaction, long-term stress, and special issues that help in analyzing the emotional impact of disaster helps to structure NOVA's guidelines for crisis intervention. These guidelines address the following five goals:

1. Safety and security
2. Ventilation and validation
3. Prediction and preparation
4. Rehearsal and reassurance
5. Education and expertise

The first three goals are directed at intervention in the immediate crisis reaction and the last two goals are aimed at interventions in long-term crisis reactions.

(1) Safety and security. The first goal of crisis intervention should be to help the victim reestablish a sense of safety and security. For victims who survive a disaster, there is a need to provide safety from physical harm. There is also a need to protect survivors from unwanted invasions of personal space such as their homes—to make sure, for example, that a mob of reporters and camera crews does not trespass literally or figuratively on the property of people in distress.

In addition, safety concerns include avoidance of certain sensory perceptions that might increase the severity of the crisis reaction and the provision of aid to meet basic needs for food, shelter, and clothes.

All of these safety and security activities respond to the victims' need for nurturing in their state of childlike regression.

While safety may not be an issue for survivors of loved ones who have died in a disaster, security is still a concern. Security should be provided by ensuring that there is privacy and confidentiality for survivors during death notification or while they await news of the destruction.

There are some hints for caregivers who seek to establish safety and security for victims:

- Make sure the victims/survivors feel safe or secure at the present moment of intervention.
- Do not assume that victims *feel* safe just because they are safe.
- Respond to the need for nurturing. While victims/survivors need to begin to make small decisions or take responsibility for some issues that they face to regain a sense of self-determination, they also need to be cared for.
- Just as physical rest is recommended to deal with physical injury, emotional injury calls for some emotional rest.

(2) Ventilation and validation. The second goal of crisis intervention is to give the victim an opportunity to express other feelings and reactions—to "ventilate"—and to have those reactions validated. Victims/survivors often feel as though they are going crazy when they feel the intensity of the emotional turmoil. It is important to help them identify the often-competing emotions that make up their turmoil and to give those emotions concrete names and descriptions. Diagramming the normal pattern of crisis reaction is very useful because it normalizes the feelings and lets the victims/survivors know that such reactions are legitimate. Some emotions are overwhelming, in part, because they are perceived as socially unacceptable. Examples are anger that is expressed as hatred and a desire for revenge. But those desires are common and victims/survivors should be reassured that they are normal.

To help victims ventilate and to provide validation, caregivers can employ the following tools:

- Ask the victims/survivors to describe the disaster.
- Ask them to describe where they were when it happened or when they heard about it.

- Ask them to describe their reactions and response to the tragedy.
- Avoid asking them to describe or to share their feelings. Terms such as sharing *feelings* or discussing *emotions* alienate many individuals. Most people can, however, describe *reactions* and those reactions will reveal feelings.
- List the elements of the crisis reaction (the initial response of shock, disbelief, and denial; the following emotional turmoil and its common components; the eventual reconstruction of a new equilibrium) and have individuals identify where they think they are in the crisis pattern. Draw an emotional roller coaster in which the high points are times of extreme turmoil and the low points are the times of exhaustion and feelings of numbness and depression; ask individuals to identify where they are within those ranges.
- Validate common crisis reactions and useful coping reactions.

(3) Prediction and preparation. The third goal of crisis intervention is to predict for the victims/survivors the problems, issues, and concerns they will face in the future, and to help them prepare for dealing with them. This prediction and preparation helps victims/survivors regain control over their lives and is particularly responsive to the need to restore order in the midst of chaos.

Prediction should include all practical issues that seem relevant: relocation possibilities, financial concerns, legal issues that might arise in the criminal or civil justice system, medical issues, body identification procedures, funeral concerns, media interventions, religious problems, and so forth. When the caregiver has no answers, offer to help the survivor get them.

Prediction should also include giving the survivor a road map of normal crisis and stress reactions (as have been described earlier) while emphasizing that the survivor may experience none of the symptoms described. Prediction should involve the possible reactions of significant others and casual acquaintances (including the common experience of finding warmth and sympathy initially but seeing that give way to attitudes of "you should be over that by now"). And prediction should address the problems that might be caused by normal triggering events.

Activities that help victims/survivors prepare for the practical and emotional future contribute to their sense of control.

- Encourage them to take one day at a time.
- Plan routines for dealing with each day and schedule small goals for achievement.
- A problem-solving technique helpful with victims is asking them to identify the three most critical problems facing them at the immediate time and then assisting them in thinking through what they can or cannot do to address them.
- Some intervenors develop a minicontract with victims/survivors that if they will take on one task toward the solution of one problem, the intervenor will take on a related task and together they will identify at least a temporary answer.
- Survivors/victims should be encouraged to talk and write about the disaster. Even if they cannot find someone to talk to, keeping a written or oral diary of problems, reactions, and triumphs in the aftermath can be very useful.
- Time for memories and memorials should be planned into daily or ongoing routines. Identification of a person to whom victims/survivors can turn when they face special problems is also important (sometimes the person a victim instinctively, and wisely, turns to is not a close friend or relative).
- Encourage victims/survivors to eat, sleep, and exercise regularly. Physical exhaustion precipitates emotional exhaustion and further crises.

The last two intervention goals may be used in some cases immediately after a trauma but are more useful as additional strategies in the days or weeks after a disaster.

(4) Rehearsal and reassurance. This refers to the idea of urging the victims/survivors to mentally and physically rehearse the event or expected events in the aftermath and practice reactions or behaviors that help in coping. Mental rehearsal is a matter of visualizing the event or the expected event and then visualizing reactions. Following those thoughts, individuals are asked to visualize and practice behaviors of response that are comfortable for them. At each stage of visualization, the intervenor provides comfort and reassurance for the victims/survivors.

In physical rehearsal, individuals actually role-play their reactions or planned behaviors. In some cases, they may want or need to visit the site of the disaster to role-play or to think through their responses more completely. Rehearsal and reassurance are not proposed as mental health therapy but as a practical way to plan for difficult events. It is similar to the mental and behavioral rehearsal that has been suggested for job candidates prior to an interview.

(5) Education and expertise. The final goal of crisis intervention strategies is to provide education and a sense of expertise to the victims/survivors. It has been NOVA's experience that information is a critical need in the aftermath of a disaster. Part of that information should address practical issues or strategies of response and potential involvement with institutions with which victims may become involved. In addition, ongoing education and the development of new skills may be very useful in minimizing stress and crisis over time.

One means to provide education for victims and survivors is assigning homework such as reading and writing. Articles and books on victimization, crisis, stress, and the like are often read eagerly. If victims/survivors are illiterate, an optional method is to provide them with audio- or videotapes that cover similar materials. For some victims/survivors, it is useful to encourage them to write letters to institutions that have caused them inconvenience, pain, or grief in the aftermath of the crisis.

A variety of skills can be helpful to survivors. Self-assessment skills, which may include use of stress tests, analysis of thinking patterns, aptitude tests, and the like, are often revealing and interesting exercises. Relaxation skills can aid survivors in sleeping and maintaining energy. Communication skills such as active listening, organization of thoughts, presentation of ideas, and expressing feelings usually make ongoing ventilation more productive. Problem-solving exercises are also useful. And many survivors find that the development of new physical activities such as swimming, dancing, and jogging are both physically and emotionally relieving. Not all survivors will respond to these suggestions, but they are worthwhile for caregivers to offer.

In providing crisis intervention and supportive counseling, caregivers should involve family members, friends, or neighbors when appropriate. Support networks usually provide the most effective interventions unless they are impaired by the disaster as well—and, even then, it is helpful to urge the members to be patient with one another, knowing that they may not be able to give or get the support they would normally expect of one another.

Finally, the encouragement of peer support group meetings for survivors is advised. The best source of validation of emotional reactions is the knowledge that others exposed to similar horrors reacted in similar ways.

Table 7.3 presents a sample list of phrases that should and should not be used by caregivers as they work toward the goals of crisis intervention. It is important to note that the sooner intervention is provided, the more likely that it will be effective. It is suggested that crisis intervention take place within the first 24 to 48 hours after a disaster.

Crisis Intervention Applied in Community Crises

The principles of crisis intervention can be applied in community crisis situations in a similar way as they are used with individuals. NOVA's Crisis Response Project is based on that premise.

Both the process used in sending a Crisis Response Team to a community and the procedures that the team follows are designed to address the goals of crisis intervention.

When a disaster occurs, NOVA is placed in contact with the community in one of two ways: Either the community calls NOVA, or NOVA, on hearing of the tragedy, calls the community and offers assistance.

When NOVA makes that contact, it does so through a local victim assistance program, or, if there is none, through other lead agencies (for example, police department, sheriff's office, district attorney's office, mayor's office, county commissioner's office, attorney general's office, and so forth).

No matter how the contact is made, NOVA offers three types of service: sending written materials on how to deal with the aftermath of disaster, sending the materials and providing telephone consultation to lead caregivers in the community, or sending a trained team of volunteer crisis intervenors to assist the community.

Should the community decide it wants to have a Crisis Response Team come, NOVA will only send a team if all community leaders are in agreement that the service will be useful. These initial protocols for outreach are designed to provide the community with a sense of control

TABLE 7.3 Caregivers' Speech Guidelines

DO SAY:

I am sorry this happened to you.
You're safe now (if the person is, indeed, safe).
I'm glad you're here with me now.
I'm glad you're talking to me now.
It wasn't your fault.
Your reaction is a normal response to an abnormal event.
It's understandable that you feel that way.
It must have been upsetting/distressing to see, hear, feel, smell that.
You're not going crazy.
Things may never be the same, but they will get better, and you can get better.
Your imagination can make a horrible reality worse than it is.
Its okay to cry, to want revenge, to hate . . .

DON'T SAY:

I know how you feel.
I understand.
You're lucky that . . .
    You're alive.
    You were able to save something.
    You have other children (siblings, or the like).
    You are young and can go on with your life or find someone else.
    Your loved one didn't suffer when he or she died.
    She or he led a good and full life before she or he died.
It was God's will.
He or she is better off; in a better place; happier now.
Out of tragedies, good things happen.
You'll get over it.
Everything is going to be all right.
You shouldn't feel that way.
Time heals all wounds.
You should get on with your life.

over its destiny and to affirm that whatever happens will be guided by leadership from the community, not from the outside.

The team that is sent to a community will arrive within 24 hours of the disaster, if the community so wishes. The three goals of that team are to

- help the community develop an action plan for dealing with the emotional aftermath of the disaster,

- train caregivers in crisis theory as it applies to disaster, and
- provide immediate care for populations that are at high risk for severe crisis reaction or long-term stress reactions.

The arrival of a team is usually perceived as an act of support and reassurance. The team is seen as an expression of security amidst the chaos. The team's role is to serve as advisor to the community and to teach how to conduct group interventions when necessary. The team (including the local hosts) helps mobilize the community just as an individual intervenor attempts to help an individual in crisis to regain control.

The general pattern for the team's activity is to stay in the community for no more than 48 hours after arrival. This 2-day period allows time to accomplish the team's goals but does not facilitate bonding between community members and team members. In individual crisis intervention, there is a danger that the victim may become dependent upon the intervenor unless certain boundaries are established; this danger also exists in a community crisis situation. Whether it presents a danger or a problem, 2 days together under those intense circumstances do produce bonds that last—which reaffirms the sad usefulness of the 48-hour limitation.

Within that period, ideally, the team will work to complete the following agenda in conjunction with its community hosts. First, the team will visit the site of the disaster, if possible. It has been NOVA's experience that the site visit is important to the team's understanding of the logistics involved in the disaster and also its understanding of the kind of devastation that occurred. For example, when NOVA's team went to Indianapolis in the aftermath of the air force plane crashing into the Ramada Inn, they became aware that the destruction involved not only the Ramada Inn but a bank building nearby. This meant that the bank employees were probably at risk for severe crisis reaction.

Second, at some point early on, it is recommended that the team hold a news conference. This conference serves three purposes: It lets the community at large know of the arrival of assistance; it provides an opportunity to communicate basic information about the emotional aftermath of tragedy; and it may provide an opportunity to advertise when group discussions will take place to address some of the immediate issues as well as to advertise which agencies are inviting calls for assistance. The news conference is important because many community members may not understand why they are feeling distressed if they were not at the scene of the disaster or direct victims. Information from the media can help them understand that their reactions are normal.

Third, the team will meet with community leaders and policy makers to plan the remainder of the 2 days. This planning session is critical because it symbolizes the control the community has over its immediate future. The community identifies who will be the lead and auxiliary "caregivers" to be given training by the team. It plans when and where any community debriefing sessions will take place. It identifies high-risk population groups. It designs an outreach strategy for communicating with all such groups. And it addresses any other urgent issues or concerns such as immediate memorial services or funeral services.

The only assertive role that NOVA's team takes during the planning session is to insist that there be a training session for all caregivers who will be involved with the NOVA team over the 2-day period and for any caregivers who will be involved in follow-up care after the team leaves the community. That training session is usually 3 hours in length, and it covers basic crisis and stress theory as outlined in the first section of this chapter and crisis intervention guidelines as outlined in the second section.

The training session has four purposes. First, it provides a forum for caregivers who have been exposed to the disaster to express their feelings in a safe context. Second, by reviewing crisis and stress theory, it provides validation for those feelings. Third, it usually provides validation for the services caregivers have already provided. They learn that their natural reactions have been correct. Fourth, even if the caregivers are familiar with crisis and crisis intervention, they may have forgotten their knowledge in the shock of the disaster or they may have learned such theories in a different context. It is important that all caregivers use similar words and phrases in communicating about crisis to survivors of the disaster. If they do not, they often contribute to the sense of chaos.

The planning session will generate a list of population groups that are at risk for crisis and stress. From that list, the planners will identify those with whom the team will be able to meet while they are in the community. Usually, the team tries to meet with groups such as rescuers who have been at the scene of the disaster, victims or survivors, and eyewitnesses. This may include a wide variety of groups: firefighters, law enforcement officers, Red Cross workers, paramedics, emergency medical teams, clergy, teachers, neighbors, and so forth.

Much of the remaining agenda after the training session or sessions is to conduct group debriefing sessions of those groups. In addition, the planning session usually results in at least one scheduled community-wide debriefing session. The session is a "you all come" session and is aimed at drawing individuals who self-identify their own distress and need for help.

NOVA team members generally lead the debriefing sessions, but in most cases, the local caregivers are urged to be in attendance and to serve as immediate and long-term referrals. Team members lead the sessions because, in this way, they can model the debriefing process for the caregivers.

Finally, just before the team leaves the community, NOVA recommends that there be another news conference to review what has been done in the community and to convey any lessons learned. In addition, there is usually a final session with local hosts and caregivers to help develop recommendations and strategies for the community to pursue in the weeks, months, and years to come.

The group debriefing sessions are designed to provide the participants an opportunity to express their reactions to the disaster. Group members will help to validate each other's reactions. For some, the debriefings may be sufficient to mitigate severe reactions. Others may need additional sessions or individual help as well. The local caregivers will be the source for that follow-up. The sessions are also designed to begin the process of predicting problems that may arise in the future and to help individuals begin to prepare for them.

The final planning session is devoted to predicting and preparing the community as a whole for the future. For the most part, the team's role is simply one of advisor and resource to community leaders.

Group Debriefing Process

The debriefing process in a group, again, follows the steps of individual crisis intervention with a few variations. Because it is a process of intervening in crisis, special attention needs to be paid to the logistics and the environment as well as the procedures used.

It is important to try to arrange debriefings so that they do not conflict with aftermath events such as funerals and memorials. Clearly, the goal is to encourage as many individuals to attend as possible. Night debriefings are usually better for communitywide group meetings and day debriefings are generally better for people who are employed outside of the home, homemakers, and children. It is advisable to encourage employers to give at-risk employees time off work to attend debriefing sessions. Generally, immediate postdisaster group debriefings do not take more than 2 hours each, although in some cases other debriefings may be done as a follow-up.

The location of the debriefing sessions should be assigned to promote feelings of safety and security. It is generally imprudent to use as a site for debriefing sessions one that triggers reactions to or memories of the disaster (for example, an airport conference room following a plane crash or a school gymnasium following the slaying of a student at the school).

The room for the debriefing should be accessible and comfortable for the group. Seating should be arranged in a horseshoe or circle, and local caregivers or other team members should be spread around the room. Water should be available because the intake of water can mitigate physical stress reactions. Tissue boxes should be available in case there are tears.

NOVA encourages the use of a flip-chart to record the phrases used by participants as the group interaction proceeds. These records will be given to the group at the end of the session or destroyed depending upon the group's will to preserve confidentiality. No individual's name will be attached to any reactions recorded.

Debriefing sessions should be conducted by a debriefing team of two—a leader and an assistant. The leader's role is to conduct the debriefing. The debriefing assistant's role is to provide emotional support to the debriefing leader, to record notes on the flip-charts, to take over if the debriefing leader cannot continue, and to assist individuals who may go into a crisis reaction as a result of the debriefing session itself (although it is better if local caregivers assume this role). The assistant should never be involved in conducting the debriefing unless the leader specifically requests assistance.

Once a group is assembled, the debriefing leader should begin the meeting by introducing the debriefing team and reviewing ground rules for the session. The following rules are essential for preserving the sense of safety and security:

- The group is pledged to confidentiality so that people feel they can discuss reactions freely.
- Although expressions of any feelings are legitimate, there will be no physical violence during the session. (At times, individuals may react so strongly that they may try to take out their rage and disagreement on another group member.)
- Individuals may leave the group as they need to, although they are encouraged to stay from beginning to end, and those who leave can expect someone to accompany them for support if they want it. Further, if they do leave, they are encouraged to rejoin the group when they feel they are ready.
- The group session is not a critique of how any individuals or institutions behaved during the disaster but a discussion of individual reactions.

The team's agenda is to help the group define the crisis reaction, to provide some crisis intervention, and to predict and prepare the group for possible future events. The goal is not to provide individual or group therapy, although that agenda is presented to the participants in a different form. The announced agenda is to review three things: how the participants reacted or are reacting, how their family or loved ones are reacting, and what they expect in the future.

To accomplish the aforementioned agenda, the team leader should begin the session with the following type of introduction. The introduction is accompanied by commentary to better explain the use of crisis intervention strategies:

"I am sorry that this plane crash happened here in Midville."

[This statement of sympathy is almost a mandatory introductory phrase in the NOVA protocol. It indicates to the listener that the intervenor is concerned about the listener and the tragedy. Even though it may seem trivial, many victims have said that the statement of sorrow is very important.]

"I know that if I lived here it would be terribly distressing to me. And even though I live in Center City, it is still upsetting to think that 24 people were killed."

[These introductory words are designed to validate in advance feelings
of turmoil and to acknowledge the extent of the disaster and destruction.]

"I'm John Jones, a victim advocate with the National Organization
for Victim Assistance or NOVA. With me are Susan Brown, a Crisis
Intervenor from Medford, Oregon, Larry Little, Mary Mays, and Sarah
Smith from Midville's Victim Assistance Program. Susan and I are here
as members of NOVA's Crisis Response Team Project, which sends
volunteer crisis intervenors to help communities in the aftermath of
disaster. We have assisted 18 communities since our first response in
the aftermath of the Edmund, Oklahoma post, office murders in 1986.
Larry, Mary, and Sarah are here to provide follow-up assistance if
needed in Midville."

[This part is an introduction of the individuals in the debriefing session
who will be active and the organization sponsoring them. It includes just
enough information to establish the credibility of the project and the
intervention.]

"I want to talk to you today about the impact of this plane crash on
Midville. But before we begin our discussion, it is important that
everyone here understand some basic ground rules for our talk. First, I
think it is important that everyone agrees that this discussion will be
confidential between us. That means that no one will report to others
what any named individual said about anything. You may want to tell
your spouse or a friend that certain things were discussed, or even that
someone in the group made a certain remark that you agree or disagree
with. But I'm asking you to agree that any such commentary will make
no references to names or to specific characteristics that might reveal a
person's identity. If you agree with this rule, will you please nod your
head in affirmation?"

[This rule is very important for ensuring privacy. The experience of
NOVA's team debriefing leaders is that when group members are asked
to underscore their agreement by nodding their heads, they feel more
accountable for maintaining confidentiality and others feel more trust in
their peers.]

"The second rule is that no matter what your reactions are, you
should feel free to tell us about them. But there is an exception to this

rule, and that is that you should not express your reactions through physical violence. That may sound humorous, but I have found that sometimes a tragedy like this can trigger strong anger or a desire for vengeance. Occasionally, that kind of reaction causes individuals to lash out at others without meaning to."

[This rule of nonviolence is very difficult to present. NOVA's experience has been that if the rule is presented in the positive manner as a rule of total expression with one exception, it is better received. In addition, the rule against physical violence often brings snickers or laughter because no one thinks that such a reaction would happen, but it can, so giving a caution and a reasonable explanation of the caution is a preventive strategy.]

"The third rule is that you should feel free to go and come as you please. Sometimes people need to get away from the group for a while to collect their thoughts or to think through certain things. If you want to leave for a few minutes, do so. One of our team members will follow you out just to make sure you don't need anything or that if you do, we can help you. We'd like you to return because we think your thoughts and reactions to this disaster are important, but you are not obligated to do so."

[Some people have expressed the thought that group debriefings should require that individuals who participate in them must stay for the full length of the session. It has been NOVA's experience that it is better to provide the fullest amount of freedom to participants. Any restriction takes away their sense of control. This is a time to help them reestablish their own ability to function as they see fit. At the same time, it is good practice to tell them that someone will be available to talk to them or assist them so they do not feel stranded if they leave and still need help.]

"While those are our guidelines, let me give you some more information that may be helpful. There is water, coffee, and soft drinks on the back table if you would like some refreshments during the session. The bathrooms are located down the hall and to the right. And, if you need to smoke, please feel free to do so over in that end of the room. If any of you are allergic to smoke, we suggest that you sit over at this end."

[Note that, in this section, the "rules" are referred to as guidelines. This softens the impact of the regulations. Also note that permission is given to move about the room to get refreshments, to go to the bathroom, and to smoke. Once again, this expands the sense of control the group members have over their behavior. At some training sessions, individuals have asked why NOVA allows smoking in debriefing groups. The answer is simple. Although there are good reasons to promote nonsmoking among our general population, we have observed that even reformed smokers may have a need to smoke during intense emotional sessions. We are not encouraging smoking but it is our view that the time of a disaster is not a time to curb an addiction.]

"Now, let me say once again I'm sorry that the plane crash happened in Midville. It is terrible that so many people were killed and injured. It is terrible that the destruction was so immense. But what I would like you to do at this moment is to think back over the last 48 hours and try to remember the moment—the instant—when you first saw, heard, or learned of the plane crash. I want you to try to remember where you were, who you were with, and what your reactions were. What do you remember seeing, hearing, smelling, tasting, or even touching at that time?"

[This is the critical transition to the group crisis work. There are several important factors to this transition. After the leader says that she or he wants the group to think back and remember, the leader should allow a few moments for that to happen. For some, this may be the first time they have allowed themselves to do such thinking. For others, it may be something that has been remembered over and over again. After allowing those few moments, the leader helps to structure those thoughts by stating what the group should think about. It is important to use the word *reactions* and to talk about physical reactions. These will serve as a lead to other discussions.]

"Now, I want to ask for anyone who would be willing to tell me about his or her experience. Where were you? Who were you with? And what were your reactions?"

[Repeating the questions is useful while someone in the group prepares to respond. In most cases, the leader will not have to wait for a response. In cases where no one responds immediately, however, the leader should be aware that silence is an ally, not an enemy.]

After the leader has set up the introduction, the group work begins. Usually a number of people will be ready to "tell their stories." And the normal progression of events will include a description of shock and disbelief, followed by a wide range of conflicting and congruent emotions. As a group leader, it is useful to gently interrupt individuals in their discussion of reactions after they describe the shock and disbelief stage and their physical reactions, and then proceed to the next person. This type of interruption and progression assists the validation process.

If, however, an individual seems so consumed by his or her experience that he or she must continue to describe events up to that very day, the leader should allow that. That judgment is subject to the common sense of the intervenor.

Once the discussion is under way, it is important for the leader to validate all key reactions and underscore any statements that fit within the crisis reaction framework. For example, if a person says: "I was stunned. I could not believe that it happened," a validating comment would be: "Shock is common in a disaster. How could anyone believe that such a disaster was happening to them?" It is ideal if the group itself does the validation, so that group members say, "I couldn't believe my eyes" or "I felt numb and couldn't move or think." This is the most effective validation because it comes from one peer to another; however, the leader should not be seduced into thinking that she or he should not provide validation if the group does not. Every statement that reflects normal crisis reaction should be validated.

The leader should keep an eye on the time. After about 30 minutes of introduction and descriptions of shock and disbelief, the leader should move on to reactions involving the emotional turmoil. If the discussion does not naturally flow in this direction, the leader should ask participants to describe what has happened to them in the aftermath. Again, validate anger, fear, confusion, grief, self-blame, and so forth.

The second segment of the discussion usually takes longer than the first. One reason is that there are more reactions and the emotional content of those reactions is often more intense. After about an hour, the leader should lead the discussion using questions such as the following: "What do you think will happen tomorrow or next week in your life, and how do you think you will handle it?" This last segment of the session is the predict-and-prepare segment.

In most cases, group participants will accurately predict problems and concerns on their own. In some cases, the leader may have to describe unexpected obstacles. Those obstacles may range from involvement in the criminal justice system (because the disaster involved criminal intent) to media sensationalism.

The leader should remember that an important part of the content at this stage of the discussion is to help survivors to prepare for such issues. As a result, the leader should validate good proposed coping techniques and give them a safety net for the future. In most communities, that safety net will have developed from the community's mobilization of emotional aftercare. Perhaps there will already be a plan in place for the future. No matter what the stage of preparedness is, group participants need to know there is a place to turn for help. That is the safety net for their next 24 hours and, sometimes, for the rest of their lives.

In the group debriefing process, the leader needs to be fully prepared for emotional reactions and behavioral symptoms of trauma. Participants may manifest confusion or physical and mental agitation. They may begin to cry or may become withdrawn. They may become angry and irritated. The leader needs to know that such reactions are not directed at him or her personally. The reactions are directed at the disaster. But the disaster is not controllable, and the leader is.

The leader should also be prepared for the unexplainable. In most disasters, there are stories of supernatural physical feats, messages from the dead or dying, visions of death or dying. It is not important whether such events have an explanation, it is important that the individual believes what she or he is describing.

At the conclusion of the group process, the leader should go over the agenda briefly and indicate how it was accomplished. If a flip-chart was used to record reactions, it should be used to review those reactions in the context of the normal crisis reaction. Group members will then have confirmed that their statements were reasonable. The leader should ask for any final concerns or questions from the group.

Then, the leader should distribute handouts on the crisis reaction, long-term stress reactions, and special issues.

Participants need to have something to take home with them. The group should be thanked for their participation. The confidentiality of the discussion should be repeated. And the ongoing support and interest of the host or leader's organization should be emphasized.

THE FUTURE

Understanding crisis and stress reactions, strategies for crisis intervention, and NOVA's approach to community crisis intervention should demonstrate how closely the theory of crisis and stress can translate into practice.

Disaster occurs far too often in modern life—the disaster of an individual tragedy such as a sexual assault or murder or the massive destruction of lives and property in a plane crash or multiple slayings. The impact of disasters is exponentially increased by each death, each eyewitness, each injury, each loss.

Thus, it is critical that mental health professionals, clergy, victim assistance workers, and others be prepared to respond to the emotional dimension of disaster. Without appropriate interventions, many individuals may face a lifetime of severe stress reactions. With effective help, most individuals can reconstruct a new life, one that forever carries painful memories of their losses but one into which they build new hope, pride, and gratification.

8

Repetitive Life Patterns and
Coping With the Crisis of Unemployment

ANN A. ABBOTT

This chapter examines time-limited intervention strategies for clinicians working with clients who are experiencing the impact of unemployment and downward mobility, problems that are exacerbated by the current economic climate. Two typical middle-class clients are presented for illustrative purposes together with a brief overview of current unemployment trends. Emphasis is placed on the importance of repetitive life patterns or early learned behaviors that tend to be activated as clients respond to crises or major life stressors, such as unemployment or job loss. Time-limited intervention strategies have been useful in helping clients recognize self-defeating behaviors and develop more effective coping patterns. The approach advocated here is based on a combination of problem-solving, short-term dynamic, crisis, cognitive, rational-emotive, and task-oriented modes of intervention. Special attention is given to the connection between the past (repetitive life patterns) and the present, the usefulness of cognitive restructuring and positive reframing, and the techniques for converting anxiety to action. The debilitating effects of learned helplessness and hopelessness are

recognized and confronted. Evidence is given in support of the usefulness of a time-limited approach with the unemployed middle-class client.

The Case of Ms. G.

Ms. G., a black single mother in her early thirties, had a long and successful
work history in financial planning. She had an outstanding college perfor-
mance record, excelling in a primarily white university. Her immediate family,
all college graduates, served as positive role models and strong sources of
support. Upon graduation from college, she began working in the trust depart-
ment of a major banking establishment. She was quickly promoted and, after
several years, was lured away by an outstanding offer from a competitor. After
taking this new position, Ms. G. began to feel that she had been hired on the
basis of race and gender and not on the basis of knowledge and skill. Her initial
reaction was one of withdrawal and apprehension. She became very worried
about her performance, to the point that she felt her anxiety interfered with her
ability to perform. Shortly thereafter, a major corporate merger resulted in her
being permanently laid off. Following her initial rage, she began to believe her
poor performance and race were major factors in the bank's decision to let her go.

After a job search of 6 months, she found herself in another challenging
position that again ended in corporate restructuring. She was so convinced that
she would be laid off that she resigned. Her reasons were based on race and the
possibility that her white married supervisor, who did not have children, was
biased against single black working mothers. She vowed that in the future she
would only work for an African American establishment and that, if no such
position became available, she would ride out her unemployment benefits, which
she was able to obtain in spite of the fact that she had resigned, and then resort
to welfare. Although forceful in her opinions, Ms. G. is ambivalent about her
choice of actions. She is afraid to put herself in the position of possibly suffering
another job loss; however, a major part of her identity is grounded in her role as
worker. She also wants to set the best example for her daughter, age 7. Her present
stance, which initially was fueled by anger, seems to be shifting to depression and
a fear that she will become immobilized in an all-encompassing trench.

The Case of Mr. K.

Mr. K., a senior sales representative in his late forties, was informed by his
company president that his position was being eliminated due to shifting

marketing strategies prompted by a corporate merger. Although he had always maintained an outstanding performance record, this represented the fourth time in 6 years that he was confronted with job loss. All situations directly followed leveraged buyouts and/or corporate mergers. Initially, he enthusiastically sought reemployment, finding a job almost immediately after his first and second layoffs. It took him over a year to find a position following the third layoff, and the fourth search is still in process after 11 months. Between the first and second job losses, Mr. K.'s 12-year marriage ended in divorce; between his second and third job losses, he remarried; between the third and fourth losses, it was discovered that Mr. K. had a slowly developing debilitating disease. Now, not only must he confront the challenges of the marketplace, he must do so with a somewhat noticeable handicap. His new wife, who initially served as a source of support, is now becoming disgruntled by Mr. K.'s lack of success in finding reemployment. Mr. K. is troubled by his wife's lack of understanding and support. She has threatened to leave unless he seeks help.

CURRENT WORLD OF WORK:
SHIFTING RULES AND HORIZONS

For these two workers, the traditional concept of job security no longer exists. Historically, American workers have operated under the belief that fulfilling the expectations of a job guarantees a long and fruitful life with an employer; that hard, honest work and loyalty are rewarded; and that seniority adds additional security to one's position within the workforce. These beliefs are exacerbated by the underlying ideology that success is measured in terms of economic worth, freedom is equated with the opportunity to choose one's standard of living, and justice is interpreted as everyone having an equal opportunity to obtain a satisfying job (Bellah, Madsen, Sullivan, Swidler, & Tipton, 1985, pp. 22-23). For many individuals, success in the world of work is a major component of self-esteem. At present, old adages are being challenged and new rules are being written. What was typical and predictable no longer exists; loyalty, solid performance, and longevity no longer guarantee a position within the world of work (Sherman, 1993).

Downsizing of traditional giants such as IBM, Sears, and General Motors (Mandel, Zellner, & Hof, 1993, p. 68) was totally unexpected in the eyes of loyal employees, many of whom had spent their entire working careers with one company or industry. During the 1980s, manufacturing alone lost 675,000 jobs; during the early 1990s, another 1.1 million jobs were lost. *Fortune* 500 industrial companies employed 3.7 million fewer workers in 1991 than they did a decade earlier, a loss of about one job in four (O'Reilly, 1992, pp. 63-65). Major losses occurred throughout manufacturing in textiles, fabricated metals, machinery, electrical equipment, the automotive industry, mining, and aircraft. In addition to the companies previously listed, the biggest losers were found among such former strongholds as Mobil, General Electric, USX, Union Carbide, Exxon, Ford Motor, Bethlehem Steel, Dupont, Hewlett-Packard, Rockwell International, Delta Air Lines, AT&T, General Dynamics, Walt Disney, and Aetna Life and Casualty (Brooks, 1992; O'Reilly, 1992, p. 70).

Many factors have contributed to this shift in reality: technological advances, corporate mergers, the increase in multinational firms, the dissolution of many former world trade barriers, and the current global economic recession. In the early 1980s, layoffs (which tended to be regionally based—for example, the Rustbelt industries such as the automobile and steel industries) were attributed to competitive international markets, outdated technology, high labor costs, and shortsighted government policies. In the latter 1980s and early 1990s, layoffs, which reflect comprehensive across-the-country patterns, are explained on the basis of attempts to increase profitability and to decrease expenditures following corporate mergers and acquisitions (Leana & Feldman, 1992, p. 2). The layoffs and plant closings of the early 1980s, which devastated entire communities, resulted in malaise contained within those communities; more recent layoff patterns span the country, rendering the problem a more universal one. The problem was critical locally in the 1980s; it is now more geographically pervasive.

In the 1990s, Americans not only worry about remaining employed, they also worry about staying employed in jobs that will continue to support their current standard of living (O'Reilly, 1992, p. 62). Current statistics indicate that one in five Americans of typical working age (18-65) were unemployed sometime during 1991 (Pomice et al., 1992, pp. 44-45). In addition, between 1979 and 1989, the median wage fell approximately 3% and the increase in low-wage jobs outpaced that of higher paying ones. In addition, fewer newly created jobs provide benefits such as pensions and health care. U.S. Census Bureau data indicate that in 1979 approximately one in five full-time workers held a low-wage job; currently more than one in four workers is in this category (O'Reilly, 1992).

Earlier layoffs affected primarily blue-collar workers; current patterns illustrate more numerous cuts among white-collar categories (Labich, 1993, p. 40; Leana & Feldman, 1992, p. 2).

Although middle managers represent 6% to 7% of the total workforce, they represent 16% to 17% of corporate layoffs. In the early 1980s, 90% of white-collar employees who were laid off found comparable jobs; in the late 1980s, that figure shrunk to 50%; and, currently, it is at 25% (Nussbaum, Palmer, Cuneo, & Carlson, 1992, p. 58). Similar, less severe, trends hold true for unemployed blue-collar workers, especially those who held unionized positions. The chances for finding comparable work with comparable salaries and benefits are becoming increasingly worse.

The American worker has not been prepared for the greased slide of downward mobility—destroyer of personal self-esteem and challenger of the lifelong American dream. Because of the belief that success in our society is the result of hard work, those caught in the downward slide frequently are viewed by themselves and others as being personally responsible for their predicament. Newman (1988) refers to this phenomenon of downward mobility as "falling from grace" while Ehrenreich (1989) details our "fear of falling." Both recognize the burden placed on the individual caught in the downward spiral and recognize that as an upwardly mobile society we have not provided any universal guidelines to cradle or assist the fall, other than blaming the victim.

RESPONSES OR REACTIONS
TO SHIFTING EMPLOYMENT

As clinicians, we encounter clients who are struggling in the throes of unemployment, underemployment, downward mobility, or the potential threat of such doom. These clients, who frequently are at career and employment crossroads, are forced to make decisions without the prerequisite guidance of a suitable road map. For most, the challenge is more than a personal career dilemma; it is a pervasive family problem and, in the case of massive layoffs, a community problem. Under pressure, they resort to the only road maps they know, familiar coping patterns from the past, many of which are not adequate for the task at hand.

The threat of job loss, whether real or potential, usually results in increased levels of stress. The frequently used Social Readjustment Rating Scale (SRRS) (Holmes & Rahe, 1967) gives strong support to the relationship between job change and stress. Of the 40 items making up the SRRS, almost one third are related to job loss or a change in financial status. An additional third of the SRRS items reflect changes in relationships and physical functioning that could stem from changes in employment status. Research with the SRRS has found that individuals who experience too much stress, the kind of stress related to unemployment, are at high risk for having some sort of physical or emotional problem.

The range of individual reactions to stress is infinite; however, the literature and clinical experience suggest responses or reactions that fall into three major areas: perceptual or cognitive, emotional or affective, and physiological or physical (Leana & Feldman, 1992, pp. 45-46). At the *perceptual or cognitive* level, clients attempt to explain or interpret the cause of their predicament; what it will mean for them in terms of lifestyle, position in family and society, and self-esteem; how much disruption will ensue as a result of the change; and how likely they are to recover. *Emotionally*, the unemployed worker may experience feelings of depression, anxiety, and discouragement accompanied by forms of hopelessness, helplessness, despair, and social isolation. *Physiological reactions* frequently include changes in eating patterns, sexual behavior, blood pressure, increased levels of general malaise, sleep difficulties, and increased abuse of alcohol and other substances. In addition, there may be increased incidents of social problems, such as child and/or spouse abuse and family disharmony, frequently ending in separation or divorce (Beckett, 1988; Brenner, 1973; Briar, 1976; Fleishman, 1992; Grayson, 1983, 1985; Hepworth, 1980; Justice & Duncan, 1976; Labich, 1993; Newman, 1988). How each individual responds is dependent upon existing patterns in his or her behavioral and emotional repertoire. Interpersonal problems from the past that had been difficult to handle, such as marital problems and child rearing difficulties, may now be exacerbated, and personal problems, such as overeating, drinking, or smoking, may be harder to control. In addition to reactivating preexisting conditions, the loss of a job can set in motion new stresses, problems, or challenges (Kates, 1992).

Job loss is not simply a problem for the individual worker experiencing the loss; often, it will have an impact on every member of the family. The partners and children of those who experience job loss frequently become invisible victims of loss (Berry, 1992; Fleishman, 1992; Kates, 1992; Kates, Greiff, & Hagen, 1990). Unfortunately, in many cases, insufficient attention has been paid to the impact of job loss on the worker's family system. Frequently, individual family members have been found to experience reactions to job loss similar to those of the family member who has actually lost the job (Fleishman, 1992; Kates, 1992). The spouse or children may question a worker's adequacy and may, by identification, feel that their family unit may be defective.

The literature on job loss suggests a general pattern of response to loss of employment, a stage model akin to that detailed by Kubler-Ross (1969, 1971) in explaining responses to life-threatening illness and impending death. Initially, the person experiences feelings of shock, anger, disbelief. Typically, this initial reaction is followed by a stage of optimism, accompanied by an active job search. If the job search proves fruitless, optimism and activity are followed by passivity, withdrawal, self-doubt, despondency, and depression. Ultimately, if unsuccessful in finding appropriate work, the person ends up in a state of despair with its accompanying feelings of helplessness and hopelessness and, as in the case of death and dying, being resigned that the situation is beyond one's control (Bakke, 1933, 1949; Eisenberg & Lazarsfeld, 1938; Kaufman, 1982; Leana & Feldman, 1992). Various theories suggest differing rates of progression through these stages. As clinicians, we must realize that much depends on the individual's past and present experience with loss, change, and shifting locus of control. In addition, much weight should be placed on the reaction of other family members to the job loss and the quality of support that is provided by the family and other natural support systems.

INITIAL REACTION

When confronted with loss, individuals usually try to put things into perspective. They reconstruct past events to explain their current situation. The focus that reconstruction takes typically depends on their previously developed patterns of perceiving. If people have developed the perspective from earlier life experience that they are responsible for most things that come their way, the reconstruction will contain components of heavy self-blame. If, on the other hand, people have been socialized to hold others responsible for most things, that control is out of their personal domain, the blame or responsibility for the job loss will be externally focused. To maintain the respect of those around them, there is a tendency to focus the blame on external forces even though the individuals may have strong concerns about their own personal contributions. In massive layoffs, universal early retirement packages, and plant closings, it is easier to externalize the blame (Beckett, 1988); in more individualized cuts, this proves more difficult.

Although current literature supports a changing external marketplace, which is driving current unemployment trends (Magnet, 1993), as a society we are still entrenched in a strong belief in rugged individualism, coupled with an unwillingness to challenge the status quo (Newman, 1988). In addition to thinking one is personally responsible for one's destiny, there may be additional feelings related to guilt and retribution for one's previous level of success. Views of the situation also may be influenced by the size of severance packages provided, the amount of warning time, and the emotional support of employers, family members, and friends (Mallinckrodt & Fretz, 1988). Just at a time when many unemployed workers are most in need of formal intervention and support services, they may be least able to afford them due to loss of income and accompanying benefits.

LOSS OF CONTROL AND STRESS

Jahoda (1982, p. 69), in her analysis of employment and unemployment, emphasized two basic human needs: the need to understand the world, to make sense of events, and the need for some degree of personal control over one's immediate environment. Under current marketplace conditions, both needs seem to be challenged (Labich, 1993). Lerner (1991) supports the relationship between control and manifestations of stress; the lower the control, the higher the evidence of stress. Research, such as that by Clayson and Frost (1984), illustrates that individuals experiencing these conditions—high stress and a lack of personal control—manifest lower self-concept than those with lower stress and a higher internal locus of control. In another study, stressful life events over an extended 12-month period of time resulted in impairment of both social and psychological functioning (Justice, McBee, & Allen, 1977).

CLIENT COPING PATTERNS

It is with these challenges at hand that clients typically present themselves to the clinician. Most clients present with reactive responses to stress—to loss of work, change in work status, pending change in employment status, or the threat of downward mobility. In those cases in which the client has had time to prepare for or anticipate the stressful event and possesses good problem-solving skills, responses more likely fall into the category of proactive responses (Bloom, 1984, p. 160). Reactive responses typically include use of defense mechanisms such as denial, displacement, rationalization, and turning against oneself, the outcome being withdrawal, depression, and sometimes regression, frequently accompanied by physical distress. The proactive stance involves attacking the problem directly and objectively, the result being creative successful action. It is toward this latter proactive approach, enlightened empowerment, that most intervention is directed.

Most research on job loss has been based on a "deprivation model," that is, unemployed workers are being deprived of something very important to them—work—and its accompanying accoutrements (i.e., financial security, prestige, daily structure, companionship, purpose) and workers respond specifically to this deprivation in the form of lethargy, depression, and inactivity (Jahoda, 1982; Leana & Feldman, 1992). To assume all workers respond systematically in predetermined patterns is naive. Some unemployed workers appear energized by the challenges at hand, while others become totally demoralized. The primary task for clinicians is to determine individual differences and the driving forces behind these differences. How do individuals attempt to cope and how effective are their attempts at restoring well-being, that is, reemployment, financial stability, and self-esteem?

Clients typically present a spectrum of coping behaviors ranging from problem-focused strategies, which emphasize the elimination of the stressful situation, to symptom-focused ones, which attempt to eliminate or reduce the negative consequences of a stressful situation

(Folkman & Lazarus, 1980, pp. 219-239; Leana & Feldman, 1992, p. 80). In the case of unemployment, the former includes such activities as searching for a job, retraining for another type of job, or relocating to a community with greater employment opportunities; the latter would include such activities as applying for financial assistance, seeking social support, and becoming involved in community activities to fill one's time and to soothe one's ailing self-esteem.

Typically, clients present a combination of problem-focused and symptom-focused behaviors. In many cases, any activity, whether problem focused or symptom focused, initially provides structure, reaffirms a sense of personal control and accomplishment; however, long-term relief depends on the ability of the activity to eliminate the tension-producing situation.

A question arises concerning the conditions that contribute to selected patterns of response. It is important to remember that all reactions are based on the client's perceptions of the situation; what one individual may view as a simplistic challenge, another individual may perceive as a devastating crisis. Three major factors that researchers have found to contribute to coping patterns are level of upset, locus of control, and self-esteem (Leana & Feldman, 1992, pp. 79-96). The greater the level of upset, anxiety, and negativity, the less likely one is to employ problem-focused coping and the more likely one is to rely on symptom-focused techniques. *Locus of control* refers to whether one has personal control over one's situation or whether control is in the hands of other, outside forces. The greater the sense of internal locus of control (or the belief that one has influence over life's outcomes), the greater the reliance on problem-focused strategies; the greater the sense of an external locus of control (or the belief that forces outside one's control are determining life's outcomes), the greater the use of symptom-focused coping patterns. The greater the self-esteem, the greater the likelihood of using problem-focused coping; the lower the self-esteem, the greater the likelihood of symptom-focused coping.

General reactions to job loss tend to be good predictors of the use of successful active coping techniques. For example, the greater the intensity of reaction to job loss, the less likely we are to see evidence of coping of any type (Leana & Feldman, 1992, p. 93). Workers who respond with intensity are usually too emotionally depleted to have the necessary energy required for active coping. The greater the intensity of emotional response and its accompanying immobility, the greater the likelihood of the development of a sense of learned helplessness (or the belief that one has limited, if any, control over life's events and outcomes). The longer the inactivity and the longer the period of unemployment, the greater the emotional intensity and the stronger the possibility of increased feelings of helplessness. Thus, it becomes a vicious cycle. Intensity leads to inactivity; inactivity leads to increased emotional intensity and the likelihood of increased helplessness.

Although symptom-focused strategies can provide structure and purpose, they contribute little to overall psychological well-being and satisfaction. Problem-focused interventions, more likely to result in reemployment, contribute more to psychological health and life satisfaction (Leana & Feldman, 1992, p. 9a).

We must keep in mind that active job searching, such as that facilitated by a problem-focused approach, can be very stressful. Individuals may need time to recuperate from the blow of the initial shock before identifying and activating options (Gal & Lazarus, 1975, pp. 4-20; Leana & Feldman, 1992, p. 101). Symptom-focused strategies may be helpful in this soothing process and may help ready the individual for a more problem-focused attack. The current emphasis by many companies on outplacement counseling, which stresses the importance of networking, may serve an important function in preparing the client for more problem-focused efforts.

As clinicians, we also must keep in mind the importance of additional demographic stressors confronting clients in search of reemployment: age, race, educational level, gender, sexual preference, and marital status. In addition to ageism, racism, and sexism operating in the world marketplace, there may be some pervasive differences in response patterns based on demographic factors. For example, women, because of their more nurturing interactional stance, may have a tendency to use symptom-focused coping (such as seeking social support) to a greater extent (Gilligan, 1982). Members of minority groups, who have personally felt the ravages of bias, may also exhibit a greater need for reaching out to friends and social supports coupled with decreased optimism about finding a suitable job. These various perceptions may, in and of themselves, interfere with successful reemployment.

As clinicians, we must look at individual client differences to develop a full appreciation of the challenge at hand. In addition to identifying personal data, it is important to arrive at a comprehensive view of the employment situation. For example, why was the client laid off (e.g., early retirement, plant closing, corporate merger, fired)? What are the reactions of the client's support systems and what level of support do these systems provide? What is the magnitude or pervasiveness of the problem (long term; large scale/industrywide)? What is the likelihood for reemployment in the immediate future?

REPETITIVE LIFE PATTERNS

One way of anticipating how an individual will respond to loss is to determine how he or she has responded to similar situations in the past. One's response is frequently modified by one's interpretation of reality and one's history of interacting with others. An expanded definition of the psychoanalytic concept of transference provides a useful paradigm for understanding the influential role of the past on the present.

The initial definition, or basic psychoanalytic one, for *transference* refers to the relationship between the patient and the analyst. The patient sees in the analyst an important figure from his or her childhood or early past and transfers to the analyst those feelings and reactions that applied to that earlier significant figure (Eidelberg, 1968, pp. 445-446; Freud, 1905, p. 116).

This initial psychoanalytic definition is limited and should be expanded to include a broad range of relationships, not just that of patient-analyst (client-therapist) (Brenner, 1976; Sands, 1983, pp. 26-27). People relive past emotional experiences and act as if present situations were replicas of past experiences with their accompanying complement of emotions, beliefs, and behaviors (Wolman, 1984, p. 105). A replay of early feelings and accompanying behaviors may be activated by and directed toward a range of human relationships including groups or institutions, such as professionals, hospitals, schools, and ethnic or racial groups. Transference or an activation of these earlier feelings is more likely to occur in situations of greater intimacy, such as in marriage or between siblings or with important persons in one's life such as employer or supervisor (Lane, 1986, p. 248).

This newer, more comprehensive definition should be expanded to include the concept of repetitive life patterns, which encompass a consistent replay of specific transferences (scenarios, scripts, roles), such as the passive wounded child, the exploited son, the deprived brother, the suspicious daughter, the overunderstanding sibling, and the helpful mother. As clinicians, it is our role to determine the tenor and magnitude of repetitive life patterns within clients' behavioral repertoires and the influence these repetitive life patterns have over clients' abilities to respond to loss and to arrive at successful, problem-focused responses to loss. Once these patterns are brought to the forefront, it is easier to develop an understanding of their influence on behavior and to develop appropriate intervention strategies.

RESPONSES TO CRISIS

For most workers, job loss is viewed as a crisis in need of an expedient response or resolution. Job loss, job change, or downward mobility is not a function of personality dynamics for the vast majority of unemployed workers; rather, it is directly related to the changing economic marketplace. How one responds may be a function of one's personality or entrenchment in repetitive life patterns. The intervention or goal in most instances is restoration of equilibrium or reemployment, at least at a level comparable to that which existed prior to the crisis, not a major restructuring of the personality. In some cases, an understanding of personality in the form of repetitive life patterns is useful in gauging a successful attack on the problem or understanding effective response patterns.

The nature of the problem demands intervention based on several related theories or approaches. The most important ones, considering the nature of the problem, include crisis intervention, the problem-solving approach, task-centered casework, cognitive therapy, rational-emotive therapy, and planned brief treatment or time-limited intervention.

Crisis theory is founded on the following premises: an individual is subjected to a period of increased internal/external stress that disturbs the customary state of equilibrium or balance, such as job loss, job change, or threat to financial security; this change challenges an individual's coping capacities, putting him or her in a vulnerable state; the degree of challenge or stress becomes even more challenging depending on the viability of the individual's existing repertoire of problem-solving techniques; in those instances in which an individual cannot cope, based on his or her familiar strategies and strengths, new, more adaptive options must be acquired (Golan, 1986, pp. 297-298).

Crisis intervention is designed to deal both with the problem that serves as a threat to the system and with the client's inability to cope with the accompanying increase in tension (Perlman, 1957, pp. 25-26). It is the immediacy of the need and the sudden stress that frequently render the individual more amenable to help and change. Action, which is goal oriented, focuses on the expedient resolution of the disequilibrium and emphasizes the unlearning of old, less effective patterns and the learning of new, more effective ones. The length of time between the initial shock and its resolution is short-lived, usually 4-6 weeks (Golan, 1986). With crisis intervention, the degree of stress/pain contributes to the pace of the intervention; the greater the pain, the faster the pace.

Models of crisis intervention include the seven-step model developed by Roberts (1991a) and the six-step model espoused by Gilliland (Gilliland & James, 1993, pp. 27-32). These theorists emphasize the importance of addressing client safety prior to moving toward problem or crisis resolution. The models incorporate tenets of problem solving and cognitive restructuring together with time-limited treatment. The major focus revolves around the heightened, overwhelming stress and the need for immediate action/intervention. Although both Roberts and Gilliland recognize the importance of follow-up after successful crisis resolution, Roberts emphasizes its importance by delineating it as a separate category or seventh step designed to reinforce the selected resolution.

For some individuals, being placed in the unexpected throes of unemployment constitutes a crisis. The current changing marketplace has introduced new threats for which many workers are unprepared. Even the well-adjusted individual with solid problem-solving skills can become overwhelmed or perplexed by the shift in equilibrium caused by sudden unemployment, and may need crisis intervention to help tip the scale in the direction of positive problem resolution.

The *problem-solving model*, although not geared specifically to crises, focuses on the teaching of good problem-solving techniques. It is grounded on the learning principles of John Dewey (Perlman, 1957). Similar to crisis intervention, it provides a here-and-now perspective, "beginning where the client is," focusing on the immediate problem situation as presented by the client. Problems are analyzed using a time-oriented framework that emphasizes a beginning, a middle, and an end and the importance of partializing the problem or breaking it into more manageable components (Perlman, 1986, p. 250). Like crisis intervention, the problem-solving model emphasizes and builds on an individual's strengths and the learning of more adequate, adaptive behavioral strategies. Perlman emphasizes the similarities among the problem-solving model, crisis intervention, time-limited intervention, and task-centered casework. In addition, she notes that the problem-solving model reaffirms the importance of a psychosocial perspective. In the case of unemployment or job loss, it looks at both the individual's contribution and that of the larger social environment. Individuals are taught to develop responses with both dimensions or perspectives in mind.

Task-centered social work uses a time-limited format, typically ranging from 6 to 12 sessions over a 2- to 3-month period, designed to confront a specific problem or task identified by the client (Reid, 1987). It was developed in response to research that indicated that recipients of brief time-limited treatment showed at least as much durable improvement as did recipients of long-term open-ended treatment, that most improvement associated with long-term treatment occurs soon after treatment begins, and that most voluntary treatment turns out to be short term, given the fact that clients have a tendency to drop out of treatment as soon as the crisis is reduced (Reid, 1986; Reid & Shyne, 1969). The focus of task-centered treatment entails an analysis of the client system including obstacles to problem resolution and identification of resources available to facilitate problem reduction or resolution. The prescribed format helps clients explore a problem, arrive at a goal, establish a contract, identify the tasks necessary to realize the goal of the contract, and anticipate and work through obstacles to successful resolution (Reid, 1986; Reid & Epstein, 1972; Reid & Shyne, 1969).

Variations on task-centered intervention include approaches involving entire family systems (Fortune, 1985). This approach is especially applicable to the problems confronting unemployed individuals and their families. It defines the problem as one of unemployment and the ultimate goal as reemployment. The task-centered approach provides a framework for identifying obstacles to and resources for achieving the goal and helps to delineate tasks necessary for problem resolution. The actual act of problem identification by the client serves as a source of empowerment for the client and illustrates to his or her family that the blame or cause of difficulty should not necessarily be attributed to the client but to sources outside the client. The act of involving other family members in the process also serves to empower them and to promote an organized proactive rather than a reactive stance. The fact that a time limit is placed on intervention creates a positive position implying that a solution is eminently achievable, and that the unemployed person will reenter the economic marketplace.

Cognitive therapy was initially designed to deal with the treatment of depression. Beck (1967, 1976; also see Bloom, 1992, pp. 190-203) believed that depression with its accompanying hopelessness and helplessness resulted primarily from cognitive distortions or misperceptions. These distortions provide an inaccurate basis for beliefs and accompanying behaviors. Negative distortions, based on erroneous thinking usually learned early in life, determine one's views of self, the current world, and future possibilities in life. Distortions highlighting negative self-worth, inadequacy, and doom provide powerful fodder for depression, inactivity, learned helplessness, and disempowerment. Beck and his colleagues, through cognitive restructuring therapy, provide a format for attacking erroneous negative thoughts and replacing them with positive, more accurate, empowering ones.

Loss of employment or downward mobility, resulting frequently from shifts in the economic marketplace, can easily be misconstrued as being the result of personal fault rather than changes in economic society. Many times, this self-critical view is reinforced by family and friends. If this view prevails, the outcome and ability of the unemployed to attack the underlying problem will be greatly diminished; if a more optimistic perspective emphasizing societal etiologic factors can be advanced, the chances for success are greatly enhanced. Cognitive therapy modifies existing negative or inadequate perceptions by conceptualizing a system that includes a broader range of options. An individual can only take advantage of options if they are present in his or her theoretical framework.

Rational-emotive therapy (Ellis, 1962, 1989; also see Bloom, 1992, pp. 171-179) advances a similar perspective that negative, irrational beliefs lead to self-defeating actions. The goal of treatment is to uncover these irrational beliefs, especially those leading to undesirable consequences, and to replace them with rational thoughts and accompanying positive effective behaviors and feelings that enhance success and happiness.

One's belief system is usually a long-term, firmly developed pattern of perceptions. If a person has developed a perspective based on an internal locus of control, the filter through which he or she views life's events will accentuate individual cause or responsibility and may, when not successful, contain components of heavy self-blame or inadequacy. In the case of job loss, the individual may assume individual responsibility for the loss, frequently overlooking or minimizing the role played by the shifting marketplace and the realities of downsizing, corporate mergers, or streamlining of management. Although frequently an internal locus of control can be adaptive and empowering, it also can contribute to self-blame, depression, and immobilization. The focus of treatment in rational-emotive therapy is the uncovering of such irrational thoughts or beliefs and their replacement by more accurate empowering ones, which, in turn, should lead to more successful action and problem resolution.

Both cognitive therapy and rational-emotive therapy emphasize the importance of inaccurate, ineffective beliefs as opposed to inadequate, imperfect beings. In both approaches, the worker teaches the client to recognize inaccurate, disabling perceptions and to change them to more appropriate, empowering ones.

Planned short-term treatment was designed to deal with individuals in conflict but not necessarily in crisis, although a crisis may be what prompted them to seek help in the first place (Lemon, 1983, p. 405). The identified goal of planned short-term treatment is modifying a patient's coping patterns (Bloom, 1992; Sifneos, 1972, 1992). Planned brief treatment or time-limited treatment also introduces the concept of time. An imposed limit can serve to increase optimism, which in and of itself can be empowering. In addition to setting a time limit or termination date, planned brief or time-limited treatment identifies a central issue or problem to be addressed and a plan for concrete action (Bloom, 1992, pp. 74-88; Mann, 1973; Mann & Goldman, 1982). Time-limited treatment is a combination of crisis-oriented casework, the problem-solving model, and the task-centered approach. The focus calls for partialization of the problem into clearly defined tasks, more active advice giving on the part of the human services worker, identification of repetitive life patterns, the introduction of cognitive restructuring or reframing (see Berlin, 1983; Hollon & Jacobson, 1985; Werner, 1986), greater emphasis on a product or specific action, and less emphasis on the therapeutic relationship. The worker, as in the task-centered, problem-solving, and crisis intervention models, becomes a more active educator, rather than a reflective, empathic listener.

Because of the critical, crisislike nature of job loss and the clearly defined task at hand—to achieve reemployment and financial stability as expediently as possible—a combination of crisis intervention, task-centered, problem-solving, and other time-limited strategies offers the best approach. Each individual's unique situation may prompt greater emphasis on one particular approach; however, the nature of the problem requires a combination of all.

EVIDENCE OF REPETITIVE LIFE PATTERNS

Under pressure or crisis, an individual tends to respond in a familiar, typical fashion, frequently predetermined by early childhood experiences (Mann & Goldman, 1982, pp. 21-22) and beliefs (Beck, 1967, 1976; Bloom, 1992, p. 190). Lemon (1983) noted that "former unresolved or partially resolved traumas were [are] usually activated during a state of crisis, thereby affording an opportunity for their reworking in parallel with the client's efforts to gain increased mastery of present circumstances" (p. 404). Mann (1973), reflecting a psychodynamic perspective, believes that frequently the presenting problem in time-limited treatment can be traced to difficulties originating in childhood. The fact that a time limit forces a client to think in adult time (real time) does not negate the importance of the past (child time). In fact, time-limited treatment may facilitate the unveiling or identification of repetitive life patterns. Parkinson's Law of Psychotherapy (Appelbaum, 1975, p. 427) suggests that clients stretch or shrink the amount of time required to deal with tasks depending on the amount of time available. In time-limited treatment, with its designated time limits, clients are more apt to confront obstacles to progress, such as repetitive life patterns, head-on. In long-term, open-ended treatment, it may take much longer to recognize and understand the significance of these early patterns on present behavior.

EXAMPLES OF INTERVENTION

In all cases, whether involving a short-term focus or a longer term, open-ended one, the initial task confronting the clinician involves assessment and problem identification, followed by delineation of goals and accompanying tasks and responsibilities. Identification of the client's coping patterns is included in the assessment phase, with modification of coping patterns, such as ineffective repetitive life patterns, and beliefs, being frequent targets for change.

The Case of Ms. G.

Ms. G. had presented herself for treatment with the strong fear that she was setting a course for herself that would result in permanent failure. She described her initial or primary crisis as her lack of current employment; a secondary crisis involved her fear that her current inactivity in seeking reemployment would be setting a poor example for her daughter as well as reinforcing her worst fear—that she would not reenter the world of work in a meaningful position. Although Ms. G.'s initial crisis was modified by the strong emotional and financial support she received from her family and the fact that she qualified to receive maximum unemployment benefits, the problem of reemployment still loomed into the foreground. Ms. G. tried to deny the importance of work in her life; however, it was impossible for her to put aside a lifelong perspective that what one did or achieved was an important contributor to self-esteem. Her entire family consisted of high-achieving, hardworking, successful individuals. She had tried to restore equilibrium to her life by denying her wish to return to work, stating that she was responding on a higher plane, one that was combating racism and sexism and was making the system pay for its violations. In the process, she came to feel shame for her withdrawal from action and depressed about her limited prospects for success in returning to meaningful work.

She sought help 3 weeks after her termination from employment. At the time, she complained of increased sleeplessness, increased use of alcohol, and increased irritability both with her 7-year-old daughter and with her grandparents with whom she and her daughter were currently residing.

Ms. G.'s history revealed a solid employment record, an excellent academic record, and strong personal and work references. She possessed good problem-solving skills, analytical abilities, and personal communication patterns. She presented as attractive, articulate, and well-groomed.

Initially, she stated that she just wanted to spout off about things, primarily about those "bastards" who took her job. Upon closer discussion, Ms. G. indicated that she was "sick and tired of having the rug pulled out from under her." She then changed her focus to getting even with the person(s) who drove her from her job. Her proposed way of accomplishing this was by first resigning, then winning her grievance to collect unemployment insurance, making her former employer pay her maximum unemployment benefits, and presenting the facade that the "f___ing" job meant nothing to her.

Later, Ms. G. revealed that she loved her work, was committed to it, but feared that her opportunities for fruitful employment were becoming more limited. She referred to news reports about the current job market. Having been an economics/business major in college, she astutely drew on national reports and trend lines to support her arguments. When challenged with the idea that her primary interest focused on reemployment, she initially agreed but then withdrew to the position that prevalent racism and sexism would never allow her to succeed, and, as a result, her initial goal would be to change/challenge society's biases. The clinician asked her about some of her early life experiences with racism and sexism. Although she included both in her earlier accusations, it became apparent that her primary focus was on racism.

During most of her early life, Ms. G. was in the distinct minority, being the only black child in a white school or among a handful of blacks in a primarily white university. She had no specific recollections of overt bias or discrimination in her interactions with peers or teachers, just the recollection that she had better do extremely well because the reputation of her race was resting on her performance. Her earliest recollections of bias involve strong warnings from her parents and grandparents to remember that "all eyes were on her, eager to pounce at her slightest mistake." She had not experienced the pounce, only heightened tension and the strong warning to beware, until now. She also remembered a favorite professor lecturing on the "color of poverty." Although she does not remember the instructor blaming blacks for higher reliance on welfare (in fact, she remembers the instructor stating that more whites than blacks receive public assistance), she believes that blacks are judged as being less responsible in their actions and as taking greater advantage of the system. In addition to her family responding negatively to her becoming a single parent, she was fully aware of society's negative stereotypes of black unwed mothers on welfare (or unemployment). Although a clinician cannot deny the existence of bias and discrimination, he or she can help clients restructure their own self- opinions based on reality. In this case, Ms. G., because of her own guilt at withdrawing from her typical proactive stance of tackling the task at hand, bought into the negative stereotype of black single mothers. Her family's reaction to her reinforced the appropriateness of this stereotype. When asked to expound on reality, she highlighted a solid work history, resulting in many excellent references from both black and white supervisors, a long-term relationship with her daughter's father, who consistently provided emotional and financial support for both Ms. G. and their daughter, and the reality that many workers, both white and black, were/are being laid off at both of her previous work sites.

Questions surfaced about how Ms. G. could restructure her thinking based on reality. By listing her long history of accomplishments and by recognizing her stance, poised to recognize discrimination even though personal evidence did not always verify it, she was able to capitalize on the positive and to minimize the repetitive life perspective reinforced by her family of origin. In spite of the fact that Ms. G. and the clinician both admitted that racism is rampant in our society, her reframed recognition that she had prevailed served as an empowering force. With this positive energizing reframing (or her restructuring of erroneous beliefs to more accurately reflect the positive aspects of reality) came the ability to define the problem and to outline a goal, in this case, reemployment in a suitable job.

Ms. G. could partialize the problem into reasonable tasks that she began to meet head-on. Rather than set reemployment as the only acceptable evidence of success, she reframed (or redefined) success into smaller components—initially, number of networking contacts, number of job letters sent, number of follow-up telephone calls completed. After several weeks, positive results included responses received from potential employers and interviews granted.

As Ms. G. became more involved in the job-seeking process, the activity took on a life of its own. She has not completely put aside her concern about racial bias and discrimination; rather, it has become one area in which she assesses potential employers. She has successfully reframed (or expanded) her approach to include not just the idea that employers will be interviewing her but the idea that she also will be interviewing them. Although she is still seeking employment, Ms. G. now presents as empowered, less depressed, and pleased that she is maintaining her optimistic, assertive, proactive stance.

The clinician spent considerable time with Ms. G. identifying the problem to be addressed. Had the worker not recognized the major importance of meaningful employment in determining self-esteem, it might have been easy for the clinician to be co-opted into Ms. G.'s stated fight for social justice combating racism and sexism. In the process, Ms. G. might have strayed further from a positive experience. By understanding the legitimate roots of her concerns and recognizing that not all people act in racially harmful or biased ways, Ms. G. could recognize the importance of finding reemployment, both for herself and for the larger system, including setting an example for her daughter, maintaining her self-esteem, and changing the negative forces within the workplace.

The Case of Mr. K.

Unemployment is a family problem. As in the case of Ms. G., Mr. K. did not live in isolation. The reason he came for treatment was to deal with a marital crisis prompted by the crisis of repeated job loss. Mr. K. feared his wife would desert him, unless he quickly found suitable reemployment. He initially stated the presenting crisis was his marriage; however, he added that his marital difficulties stemmed from his job losses and his medical condition. One difficulty alone was frightening, two together seemed overwhelming, and three seemed impossible.

Upon greater examination, his marriage was a strong positive source of support and satisfaction. He admired his wife and found her both sexually and intellectually stimulating. She described him in similar terms but noted that recently he became more withdrawn, greatly limiting his interaction with her. The more stressful life became, the more she wanted to talk; the more stressful life became, the less he wanted to share and interact. As stress mounted, their respective behavioral patterns became more pronounced. When asked how he typically responded to stress, Mr. K. said he would withdraw into himself.

When asked about earlier life experiences with stress, he revealed a rigid, unloving, demanding father who, by example and punishment, taught him to stand tall under pressure and fight his own battles. When he would approach his mother for support, his father would humiliate him by calling him a sissy and crybaby. His mother, who had fostered a more emotional, demonstrative approach, had died at a young age, leaving him to fight his own battles both with his father and with the rest of the world. His first wife, who reminded him of his mother in her approach to life's challenges, left him when he started to be a bit more open, stating she could not handle his burdens together with her own. As a result, Mr. K. slipped into his earlier well-established patterns of keeping a stiff upper lip and handling his own struggles independently. He has shared little with his wife about his job losses, search for reemployment, and concerns/worries about his illness. He has even found it difficult to share his concerns with his medical doctor.

His primary source of support has been a monthly meeting for men diagnosed with the same physical condition. Mr. K. worries that a prospective employer will find out about his disease or detect evidence of it, thus limiting his opportunities for reemployment. Mr. K. limited his search for reemployment for fear of rejection. When he did meet with potential employers, most of his energy was directed toward making certain his symptoms were well hidden.

Assessment revealed several problems of high priority: reemployment, resolution of marital discord, and better understanding of Mr. K.'s medical condition. To wholeheartedly seek employment, Mr. K. indicated that he needed to have his wife's support as well as an understanding of his physical limitations. In discussing his mode of interaction under stress, Mr. K. agreed that his present wife was not like his father nor was she like his first wife; however, he was treating her as if she were similar to both. He decided it would be worth the risk of trying a more open, shared stance with her. Fortunately, his openness was met by increased support on her part—the apparent beginning of a new way of relating. In addition, he risked being more open with his physician, voicing his fears and asking key questions. His physician responded positively, as did the other men in his support group. As he began to feel more secure in sharing with his doctor, he invited his wife to join them, an invitation that generated more positive support from her.

Rather than being at odds, Mr. K. and Mrs. K. are now a team actively working together on Mr. K.'s plan for seeking reemployment. She has a better understanding of his fears and hesitancies; he has a better realization of what to expect healthwise in the future. A number of men in the support group had experienced similar employment challenges. Once he shared his predicament with them, they provided knowledge that should be extremely useful to Mr. K. as he proceeds with his job search. At present, he has a plan in place for networking, a mechanism for generating job letters and resumes, and a list of potential employers, which should provide good possibilities in light of the economy and his health restrictions.

THE IMPORTANCE OF INTERVENTION

Both Ms. G. and Mr. K. were good candidates for time-limited intervention strategies (see Tables 8.1 and 8.2, case summaries). Neither client presented evidence of major psychopathology; both were articulate, motivated clients frustrated by the challenges of job loss and the search for reemployment. For both, the problem became a family problem—generating both support and criticism from their respective families. Each client responded based on his or her larger social context. For Ms. G., racism and, to a lesser extent, sexism, played major roles throughout her life. Her experience with job loss was no exception. Ms. G. recognized her initial anger—based on her programmed sensitivity to racism—and the self-defeating nature of her initial responses. Upon closer examination of her current personal reality, she was able to do some cognitive restructuring, reframing her beliefs to more accurately reflect her personal life experiences. She had been programmed throughout her life to believe that all whites were looking for blacks to make one tiny mistake, at which point the axe would fall. Throughout her life, this had been true on some occasions and not true on many others. Ms. G. also worried about being a good mother and role model for her daughter. By responding in a reactive, symptom-focused manner—directing her anger at the source of her frustration (racism in the system)—Ms. G. was missing an opportunity to serve as a problem-focused, proactive model for her daughter. Initially, Ms. G. said her anxiety and fear about additional loss contributed to her reactive stance. With brief problem-solving

TABLE 8.1 Case Summary: Ms. G.

Primary Problem: Unemployment

Overall Goal: Reemployment

Presenting problems(s) that brought client into treatment:
  a. fear of being an inadequate or negative role model for daughter
  b. depression, loss of self-esteem

Obstacles to addressing presenting problem(s):
  a. strong denial of the importance of work in her life
  b. rationalization that it is nobler to fight racism and sexism in the workplace
     by avoiding the system rather than by fighting from within the system

Resources for addressing the problem:
  a. good problem-solving skills/analytical abilities
  b. supportive family
  c. solid work history
  d. no underlying psychopathology
  e. successful past performance in a racist society

Intervention:
  a. time-limited approach (four sessions over 6-week period) focusing specifi-
     cally on obstacles to achieving her major goal of reemployment
  b. cognitive restructuring of beliefs resulting from her long history of experi-
     encing the effects of racism and, to a lesser extent, sexism
  c. reinforcing her positive repetitive life pattern of problem solving, diligence,
     and strength

---

work, she was able to shift the locus of control from one of being controlled to one of being in control, and shift her energy and talents from anxiety and fear to positive action.

Mr. K. also was strongly influenced by his early life experiences. His early training within his family of origin, to handle matters on his own without sharing feelings, proved to be self-defeating. This behavioral parameter limited important support from his wife, his doctor, and his peers. In the process, he became a prisoner of his limited knowledge about his physical condition. He was controlled by the disease to a much larger extent than was necessary. By responding to the crisis generated by his wife's threatening to leave, Mr. K. was not only able to develop better communication patterns, he also was able to get better control of two other crises—his illness and his job situation.

After a few sessions, Ms. G. and Mr. K. could recognize self-defeating behaviors, develop more effective coping patterns, restructure and/or

TABLE 8.2 Case Summary: Mr. K.

Primary Problem: Unemployment

Overall Goal: Reemployment

Presenting problem(s) that brought client into treatment:
a. fear of pending marital separation
b. fear of possible employment rejection due to visible evidence of serious illness

Obstacles to addressing presenting problem(s):
a. long-term history of behavior accentuating independence and rugged individualism (repetitive life pattern), reluctance to ask for help
b. belief that all people with whom he is close will be like his father and first wife (repetitive life pattern)

Resources for addressing the problem:
a. good problem-solving skills/analytical abilities
b. potentially supportive wife
c. membership in a supportive men's group
d. supportive, available physician
e. no underlying psychopathology

Intervention:
a. crisis intervention (eight sessions over 6-week period) focusing specifically on his relationship and communication patterns with his wife
b. cognitive restructuring concerning his beliefs about the importance of rugged individualism learned throughout his early childhood
c. rational-emotive strategies to address his assignment of inaccurate behaviors to his wife and unfounded feelings toward her that were based on his past experiences with father and first wife

---

reframe negative beliefs propelling ineffective actions, convert anxiety and fear to action, and reclaim a sense of control. For both clients, important shifts from reactive to proactive responses occurred together with shifts from symptom-focused to problem-focused patterns.

CLINICAL IMPLICATIONS

The clinician played a major role in providing a supportive problem-focused perspective. In each case, the client's strengths were emphasized together with a format for identifying important life patterns that may have been having a negative impact on solving the current crises. In addition, the clients' exposure to problem identification, partializing tasks into small manageable units, and the restructuring or reframing of inaccurate, ineffective beliefs should be transferable to new situations. Although the problem was not completely solved, in each case, time-limited intervention was instrumental in moving the situation from a level of crisis to a manageable plan of action. In a short period of time, these clients became reempowered and capable of reclaiming control. A time-limited treatment approach, based on a combination of problem-solving, short-term dynamic, crisis, cognitive, rational-emotive, and task-oriented modes of intervention, was essential in dealing with the special issues experienced by these clients in the throes of unemployment.

Clinical Issues in
Time-Limited Treatment With Women

ELAINE P. CONGRESS

Susan, a 23-year-old graduate student, was seen for an initial interview in a rape counseling center. Tearfully she reported that the previous night she had been raped by a man she had just met earlier that evening at a party given by a friend. Because she knew her friend had many bisexual friends, she was fearful she might have been exposed to AIDS. The social worker in the rape counseling center advised Susan that she could be seen for crisis intervention sessions for the next 10 weeks.

Janet McCall was employed full-time as a supervisor in the telephone company. A single mother, Janet and her 12-year-old son Brian had just been referred by the school for therapy with a clinical social worker in private practice. Ms. McCall indicated that her son's behavior at school, as well as at home, had become defiant and oppositional in the last year. The social worker and Ms. McCall agreed that they would meet for the next 8 weeks with the goal of improving Brian's behavior at home and school.

Mrs. Edwards, a 48-year-old woman employed as an administrative assistant in a nonprofit agency, presented symptoms of depression during her intake interview at the Hastings Mental Health Center. Multiple precipitating stressors were the threat of staff cutbacks in her agency, the death of her mother 6 months ago, the departure of her youngest child to a distant college, and increasing episodes of emotional and physical abuse by her spouse. The mental health team decided that she would be a candidate for short-term cognitive behavior therapy to treat her depression.

Mrs. Lyman, a 65-year-old retired department store clerk, was seen by the hospital social worker after her 70-year-old husband was hospitalized resulting from a fall in their house. Mrs. Lyman, who suffered from severe arthritis as well as diabetes, confided that it was becoming increasingly more difficult for her to give her husband, who had been diagnosed with Alzheimer's disease 2 years before, the care he needed. It was decided that Mrs. Lyman and the hospital social worker would meet for several sessions to discuss the possibility of nursing home placement for Mr. Lyman.

What all these women clients in diverse practice settings have in common is that they all were referred for time-limited treatment. Interest in and practice of time-limited treatment has mushroomed in the last decade. At least 53 models of brief treatment have been identified (Koss & Shiang, 1994).

Currently, Epstein (1992) has classified time-limited treatment into three basic types: the psychodynamic model, the problem-solving approach, and the mixed eclectic model. Psychodynamic time-limited models (Mann, 1981; Sifneos, 1987) focus on assessment, diagnosis, and treatment using ego psychology concepts. In contrast, the problem-solving method (Epstein, 1992) stresses more mutual specific problem definition and intervention using planned problem-solving strategies.

Common characteristics of time-limited treatment. In actual practice, the distinctions between models may blur and all time-limited treatment can be seen as including the following six common characteristics:

1. A positive client worker relationship is essential for ongoing treatment.
2. Problem definition and assessment occur rapidly at the beginning of treatment.
3. Intervention begins immediately and is focused and specific to the problem.
4. There are a limited number of interviews ranging from 4 sessions in some crisis-intervention and task-oriented models up to 40 sessions in time-

limited dynamic psychotherapy. Both the client and social worker know of the time limitation from the beginning of treatment.

5. Goals are specific and present oriented.
6. Interviewing style is direct and active.

APPLICABILITY OF TIME-LIMITED MODELS

Time-limited therapy models have been used for many years and originally even psychoanalysis, contrary to popular belief, was of short duration (Epstein, 1992). Earlier precursors of time-limited treatment include the functional school with its emphasis on time as an essential factor in treatment (Smalley, 1967), the problem-solving method (Perlman, 1957), crisis intervention (Parad, 1965), and the task-centered approach (Reid & Epstein, 1972).

In recent years, with the advent of managed care and service limitations in the mental health field, there has been renewed interest in time-limited treatment. The shorter number of sessions has been seen as much more cost-effective. Time-limited treatment, however, should not be considered a negative manifestation of downsizing in mental health services. Although there have been some contradictory findings and much difficulty in conducting research on brief treatment because of the diversity of models, brief treatment has been seen as quite effective with a variety of mental health symptoms (Epstein, 1992; Mancoske, Standifer, & Cauley, 1994).

For whom is time-limited treatment effective? Most proponents of time-limited treatment stress its usefulness with varied clients with problems ranging from minor adjustment problems to chronic psychiatric disorders, although some psychodynamic time-limited theorists believe that clients should have relatively intact egos (Bernstein & Lenhart, 1993). It is my belief and practice experience that time-limited treatment can be used with a variety of clients and problem situations. Even clients with severe psychiatric problems can be helped by time-limited treatment. In addition to chronic psychiatric illness, schizophrenic women often experience acute situational crisis events, as the following case example indicates.

Sally, a 22-year-old woman with a diagnosis of schizophrenia and several psychiatric hospitalizations, was seen regularly in a day program. Recently, her relationship with her parents had become more stressful and she was referred to the social worker for help in securing residential placement. The clinical social worker and Sally agreed to meet eight times during which they focused on the nature of the problem (difficult living conditions), setting a goal (securing more adequate housing), consideration of alternatives, and achievement of goal (moving into halfway house.)

WOMEN AND MENTAL HEALTH TREATMENT

Women are much more likely to be diagnosed with depression than men (Gore & Colten, 1991; Potts, Burnam, & Wells, 1991; Rothblum, Berman, Coffey, & Shantinath 1993). Furthermore, they take psychotropic medications (Aston, 1991) and are seen for outpatient mental health treatment more frequently than men (Horton, 1992).

Although there is still debate (Stoppard, 1989), time-limited treatment has been seen as an effective treatment model with women (O'Leary, Riso, & Beach, 1990). Time-limited treatment for depressed women may be either cognitive-behavioral treatment (Beck, 1991) or brief intensive psychodynamic psychotherapy (Bernstein & Lenhart, 1993).

Some clinicians have raised concerns that traditional psychoanalytic treatment is at best not helpful and at worst actually detrimental to the mental health of women clients (Ussher, 1991). Often, the psychoanalytic method fosters long-term dependency on the therapist. This dependency has been seen as nonconducive to women's mental health (Worell & Remer, 1992).

A value of time-limited treatment for women is that dependency on the therapist is minimal, because treatment is of short duration and a transference relationship is not fostered. Recent literature on women has reframed women's dependency as interrelatedness with others (Gilligan, 1993). Treatment of depressed women that focuses on balancing the need for autonomy with needs for intimacy and sharing has been effective (Carter & Kaslow, 1992). This is consistent with time-limited treatment's focus on a rapid engagement process, which is facilitated by women's ability to connect and relate to others.

Impact of Social Economic Factors on Women

Current economic and social changes contribute to the problems that women clients bring to mental health practitioners. The following changes are seen as significant:

Economic discrimination and hardships. Even though the number of women in the job force on all levels as well as the educational achievement of women have increased dramatically, women still make much less money than men (Hutton, 1994). With this discrepancy, especially during a time of economic hardship, women are much more likely to be poor (Abramowitz, 1988). Even if above the poverty level, women, especially as single-parent heads of households, are more likely to experience economic problems. Women as well as men may find themselves unemployed or forced to assume a job with less income than their education and experience might merit. Economic stress contributes to increased anxiety and depression (McCarthy, Reese, Schueneman, & Reese, 1991). The short-term nature of time-limited treatment is most appealing to women clients on a limited budget, as often in times of economic recession there are few financial resources for mental health treatment. The following women clients all had problems related to current economic stressors: a 57-year-old single woman who had been laid off from a clerical job she held for the last 20 years when the company moved out of town, a 25-year-old single mother of two young children who was having difficulty making ends meet on a minimal wage factory job, a 39-year-old married woman complaining of anxiety because of her husband's limited income and increased household expenses. All of these clients received time-limited treatment. A more detailed description of using time-limited treatment with unemployed women can be found in Chapter 8.

Changes in family structure. Traditional nuclear families (*working* fathers, housewife mothers, and children) now make up fewer than 15% of American households (Family Service Association, 1987). The number of single-parent households has doubled within the last 20 years (U.S. Bureau of the Census, 1991). Women now assume multiple roles, both within the household as single parents or within the workforce as paid employees. Often, role overload contributes to stress for women clients.

Time-limited treatment can be very helpful to the overburdened woman in helping her learn problem-solving skills and develop priorities for the many demands on her time and resources.

Increase in crisis situations. Life-cycle transitions such as pregnancy, childbirth, and parenting as well as infertility and menopause can be stressful for women (Brashear, 1990; Frank, Kupfer, Jacob, & Blumenthal, 1987; Millis & Kornblith, 1992; O'Connor & Wolfe, 1991). Women with problems of this type can often benefit from time-limited treatment to help them in coping with changed roles and responsibilities. With one out of two marriages ending in divorce, more women are continually experiencing stress related to the transition from married to single life (Brewer & Rawlings, 1993). Domestic violence often leads women to seek crisis intervention, a specific form of time-limited treatment (Roberts & Roberts, 1990). Also, as the life expectancy of women increases, there are more older women who are newly widowed and/or with chronic health problems who could benefit from time-limited treatment.

For women, rape is a major crisis event and recent positive changes in legislation related to marital and date rape have increased the number of reported rapes (Congress, 1992). Crisis intervention is often the treatment of choice for rape victims (Ben-Zvi & Horsfall, 1985; Brown & Ziefert, 1988; Koss, 1993; Lee & Rosenthal, 1983).

SOCIAL WORK VALUES, WOMEN, AND TIME-LIMITED TREATMENT

It is crucial that professional social work practice be consistent with our value base (Congress & Lynn, 1994), and respect for the individual client is a basic principle of ethical social work practice (National Association of Social Workers, 1993). For all types of time-limited treatment, developing a positive therapeutic relationship is a consistent objective. Positive regard may be especially important in work with women who may not have previously received much acceptance from significant others. Often, women have received approval conditional upon their conformity to certain standards or performance of assigned tasks.

Promoting autonomy is considered a basic, although possibly unattainable, principle of social work practice (Freedburg, 1989). Time-limited treatment tends to minimize dependency on the worker and maximize the client's participation in the definition of problem and planning for solution. This is most appropriate for women who may not always have had the opportunity to participate in planning their treatment. Despite changes in women's lives in recent years, women may still have difficulties with self-determination (Cook, 1993).

STAGES OF TIME-LIMITED TREATMENT

Time-limited treatment can be divided into three main stages:

(1) Problem definition and assessment. Although this stage occurs in all treatment models, problem definition and assessment are of special importance in time-limited treatment, as they must be accomplished quickly and accurately (Epstein, 1992). At times, time-limited treatment focuses only on a client's simple statement of perceived need, as, for example, a client's request for help with securing day care services, and at other times, time-limited models of treatment include a more thorough assessment of individual person, problem, and psychosocial situation. Furthermore, psychodynamic time-limited models in contrast to problem-solving approaches often contain a diagnosis (Epstein, 1992). In all time-limited treatment, however, assessment usually takes place in the first interview and occurs concurrently with the beginning of treatment interventions.

(2) Contracting and treatment planning. This stage occurs very early in time-limited treatment. Goals are often very specific and clients are encouraged to participate in this process. The client is very aware from the very beginning about the length of treatment and what expectations for change are possible. The focus is on the present and change is usually defined in specific, concrete terms. While encouraging the client to participate maximally, the social worker often assume a very active, direct role.

(3) Psychodynamic, cognitive-behavioral, and problem-solving time-limited treatment may vary in terms of the treatment process. The psychodynamic approaches focus on intrapsychic issues and use ego psychology

techniques including working with defenses, uncovering, exploring, and analyzing; cognitive-behavioral time-limited treatment helps clients explore irrational beliefs that lead to certain behaviors and possible alternative behaviors. Problem-solving time-limited treatment often includes a discussion of problem-solving strategies, consideration of alternatives, and removing obstacles to problem solving.

Assessment

One value of the assessment process in time-limited treatment for women is its focus on specificity of problem definition. This often helps to clarify the problem quickly and the client begins to note improvement almost immediately, as the following example indicates.

A 35-year-old woman was referred for time-limited treatment because of continued conflict with her 15-year-old daughter. In the first session, she reported that she had been in long-term therapy last year but had dropped out after 6 months because "nothing was happening." By the end of the first time-limited treatment session, the client indicated that she had greater insight into her family conflict than after her previous 6 months of treatment. In the process of more clearly defining and specifying her problem, she had learned that most of the fights with her daughter occurred when they both had to leave the house at the same time. By better clarification of the problem, she was able to begin to plan for possible solutions, such as scheduling different times for using the bathroom.

Psychodynamic approaches to brief treatment often use a *DSM-IV* diagnosis (American Psychiatric Association, 1994). The use of the *DSM* has been criticized as inaccurate, stigmatizing, and focusing only on psychopathology (Kirk & Kutchins, 1992). Despite the use of a multiaxial formulation including a statement of social and environmental problems (Axis IV) and global assessment of functioning (Axis V), the main focus of *DSM-IV* is on Axis I in which the clinical disorder is listed. Thus, the psychosocial stressors that often lead to psychological stress and bring women into treatment are often minimized. Also, *DSM-IV* focuses more on weakness, when a strength perspective is often useful in working with clients (Saleeby, 1992), as the following example illustrates.

A 28-year-old woman began time-limited psychotherapy when she was first seen at a mental health clinic with symptoms of depression, which had occurred over the last 2 months since she moved into the city. She was diagnosed as having an adjustment disorder with depressed features (DSM-IV 308.24), which was seen as caused by her psychological difficulties in adjusting to this move. Fortunately, her social worker was able to explore other factors related to her depression, which included that she had given up a good job in a distant city to relocate with her transferred husband, who had begun to drink excessively, and her 10-year-old son, who had begun to present behavioral problems in his new school. The social worker learned how this client was able to successfully relocate and resettle her family across country with limited help from her husband or other family supports and was able to use this information to encourage and increase the self-esteem of this depressed client.

An alternative classification system, PIE, has been developed to focus more on clients' problems with social role functioning rather than pathology (Karls & Wandrei, 1992). By applying this assessment system to the previous example, the social worker was able to see that much of this client's depression was related to disturbances in role functioning. The client's role as worker had been terminated. Her accustomed role of wife was threatened by her husband's increased alcohol abuse. Because of her son's school behavior, the client felt inadequate in her parental role. The use of PIE assessment is often less stigmatizing, which is a significant issue in work with women clients. A PIE assessment also is quite conducive to a time-limited approach in which the social worker needs to move quickly from an assessment of client functioning and problem areas to treatment interventions.

Contracting and Planning

An essential phase of time-limited treatment involves contracting and planning. This step usually includes

1. generating alternative goals or various solutions,
2. deciding on preferable or alternate solutions, and
3. scheduling tasks and setting priorities (Epstein, 1992).

Although important in all treatment, this phase is especially significant in time-limited work because of the fewer scheduled sessions for therapeutic work. Moreover, this stage is especially crucial for women who may previously have had limited opportunities to participate in considering alternatives, as the following case example illustrates.

> *Mrs. Dean had been abused by her alcoholic husband for many years. Until she was referred for brief treatment by the hospital emergency room and began to discuss alternatives, she had never considered the option that she could insist that her husband receive treatment or that she could move into a battered women's shelter.*

Establishing priorities is an especially important aspect of time-limited treatment. Given the impact of ongoing economic and social stress during the current recession and consequent multiple problem areas, many clients experience endemic stress, which leads to feelings of helplessness and hopelessness (Fried, 1982). Organizing problem areas and developing priorities help to empower clients in working toward solutions to their problems. This is often not an easy task, especially when clients come to social agencies with multiple, very challenging problems.

> *Mrs. Brown was referred to the brief treatment unit of a mental health center. A 35-year-old single mother of three children, Tom, 16, Susan, 12, and Daryl, 9, she recently learned that she would be laid off from her clerical job, her landlord was threatening eviction, (he wanted her apartment for his relatives), Tom was increasingly truant from school, Sue had been left back in school this year, and Daryl had been suspended 2 days for fighting in the classroom. Because of the number of severe problems, Mrs. Brown reported feeling so helpless and depressed that she could barely get out of bed in the morning. In the first session of time-limited treatment, with the help of the social worker, Mrs. Brown was able to prioritize what problems she felt needed immediate attention. She was also able to develop strategies for dealing specifically with different problem areas.*

An essential element of all contracting is that it should involve a mutual process (Hepworth & Larsen, 1993). This may be difficult to achieve, especially if time-limited treatment is with mandated clients.

At times, the goals of clients may differ from that of the social worker, as in the following example.

Mrs. Sanchez's 8-year-old son was placed in a foster home after she severely beat him when he did not come home promptly from school. She indicated that she had not wanted him to be hurt in the dangerous community in which they lived, to discipline children in this way was appropriate in the country where she was raised, and she wanted her son returned home as soon as possible. The social worker to whom she was referred for time-limited treatment articulated a goal of improving Mrs. Sanchez's parenting skills by having her attend special classes and learn alternative ways of disciplining her son. Mrs. Sanchez, on the other hand, had a very different short-term goal, that is, that her son would be returned to her care immediately.

Problem-Solving Method

The intervention phase of time-limited treatment relies primarily on problem-solving techniques or cognitive-behavioral methods (Epstein, 1992). Both methods have proven to work quite well with women clients who come to treatment with a variety of problems.

Problem-solving techniques include the use of problem-solving strategies, discussing alternatives and obstacles, evaluating progress and problems, advising and revising, and providing environmental resources. Ms. McCall, the client presented in the beginning of this chapter, was helped by problem-solving interventions.

The main problem was viewed as her 12-year-old son's acting-out behavior at home and at school. In the first session, Ms. McCall and the clinical social worker made the following decisions:

1. Greater clarification of this problem was needed. Ms. McCall discussed in detail exactly how and when Brian did not behave at home. Also, it was planned that Ms. McCall would try to learn from Brian's teacher more about his problematic behavior at school.
2. Brian would learn more about how he saw this problem and his involvement would be elicited in working on the problem.
3. Ms. McCall would delineate a specific list of behavior problems that she found unacceptable.

4. Homework assignments would be given. When Brian did not misbehave, Ms. McCall was instructed to reward Brian by, for example, taking him to a special video store he liked.

These specific strategies were all delineated during the first session. In the next session, Ms. McCall reported that she had seen his teacher, who reported that Brian often began to act out when he finished his assignment early, which happened frequently. At home, Ms. McCall observed that Brian was often argumentative on Saturdays. In the past, he had frequently gone out with his father on weekends, but recently his father, who had been separated from his mother for 2 years, had moved to a distant city and no longer took Tom out on weekends.

As planned in the initial session, Brian was seen by the social worker. He appeared very quiet and withdrawn. Although he shared little information, he did verbalize that he enjoyed weekend trips with his father.

In accordance with the initial plan, Ms. McCall began to make a list of Brian's behaviors that she found most problematic. She reported in the second session that as his behavior had been particularly disturbing the preceding week, she did not reward him at all.

As a result of this second contact with the client, the social worker decided to use alternative interventions, that is, to elicit the school's help in providing more challenging assignments and to involve Brian in joint sessions. In a subsequent session, it became evident that Brian was very resentful that his mother, who was feeling quite burdened with increased responsibilities as a single mother, did not have time to take him out on Saturdays as his father had in the past. Ms. McCall reported that she did not realize how Brian felt and that she felt guilty that she had not been more available to him. She was able to ventilate feelings of depression, anxiety, and loss related to her change in role from married to divorced woman. Through her knowledge of community resources, the social worker was able to recommend that Ms. McCall enroll Brian in a Saturday activity program for preteens. The social worker also began to work with Ms. McCall around time management so that she was able to complete household chores during the week so as to have more time on weekends to spend with Brian.

With the problem-solving method, alternatives are continually discussed and revised. In addition, the social worker takes a very active role in directing and advising the client. Input from the client is encouraged in each session, however, to maximize client's participation and commitment to change.

Cognitive-Behavioral Intervention

Cognitive-behavioral therapy has frequently been used as time-limited treatment for depressed women (Beck, 1991; Beck et al., 1979). Therapy of this type includes cognitive techniques such as eliciting maladaptive assumptions, analyzing maladaptive assumptions, and cognitive reframing, as well as behavioral techniques including scheduling activities, graded task assignments, rehearsals, role-playing, and homework assignments involving diversion activities.

The social worker assigned to Mrs. Edwards, who was presented in the beginning of this chapter, used a variety of techniques in time-limited treatment with this client. First, a number of faulty maladaptive assumptions were elicited. Mrs. Edwards became aware that she had always felt her major roles were those of daughter, mother, and wife. She felt that her role as daughter was now gone as her mother had died. Her role as mother was diminished now that her youngest child had gone to college, and her role as wife was threatened by physical and emotional abuse. While analyzing these roles, Mrs. Edwards became aware that roles could change over time and that there might be different facets of these roles for her to assume. Instead of defining herself as a failure for not succeeding or continuing in these roles, Mrs. Edwards was able to more positively reframe her roles. She now began to see herself as a loving, caring daughter who had been so supportive to her mother during her final illness. She became more aware of how her positive parenting for many years had helped launch her youngest child as a successful college student. In terms of her marriage, she became more aware that she had alternative ways of dealing with spouse abuse, that marital therapy might be an option. If her husband would not consent, she began to consider the alternative of separating from her spouse.

In working with Mrs. Edwards, the social worker also used behavioral techniques involving scheduling activities and assigning tasks. Instead of spending the day crying and blaming herself as a failure, Mrs. Edwards was helped to plan and develop a daily schedule of activities. Included in this schedule was also time for nightly discussion with her husband, which had not occurred previously. The social worker also rehearsed with Mrs. Edward ways in which she could initiate discussion with her husband about beginning marital therapy. Also, the social worker engaged in role-playing to give Mrs. Edwards more confidence and practice in assuming a more assertive role with her spouse. Finally, the social worker gave Mrs. Edwards very specific assignments for pleasurable activities. One week, Mrs. Edwards was instructed to go shopping and buy herself a new dress; during another session, Mrs. Edwards was encouraged to plan a luncheon date with an old friend.

Similar to problem-solving methods, cognitive-behavioral therapy presupposes that the therapist assumes an active, directive role in working with clients. Often, the therapist makes decisions as to what are irrational and maladaptive assumptions of the client. To avoid increasing a woman's dependence, it is essential that the client have as much input as possible into the analysis of irrational thoughts and behavior, as well as homework assignments. This is particularly important in working with women clients who may have had problems with overdependence on others. With Mrs. Edwards, for example, it certainly would have been counterproductive to exchange Mrs. Edwards's dependence on her mother, children, and spouse for dependence on a therapist.

TERMINATION ISSUES

One factor that mitigates excessive dependence on the therapist in time-limited treatment is the time factor itself. From the very beginning of treatment, the time that treatment will end is discussed. Both the woman client and her therapist enter into a therapeutic relationship with the knowledge that it will end at a certain designated time. Even though the relationship has been short term and the point of termination delineated from the very beginning, the client, nevertheless, may have intense reactions to termination (Woods & Hollis, 1990). As a result, it is crucial for the social worker using time-limited treatment to plan carefully for terminating with clients.

How should the social worker handle doorknob communication, which occurs when a client at the end of a session or nearing the end of treatment communicates information that is of crucial importance? In traditional therapy, often doorknob communication is considered a sign of resistance, because as this type of client's behavior is viewed as a pathological manifestation of the patient's desire to extend contact with the therapist at a time when treatment is scheduled to end (Shulman, 1992). Yet, in time-limited treatment, the social worker must recognize that often doorknob communication may be an important cry for additional help. Although initial treatment goals may have been met in time-limited work, the social worker must be willing to renegotiate the contract and provide an extension of time-limited treatment if indicated.

The option for additional treatment is especially relevant in work with women clients. Because women often are more focused on relationships (Gilligan, 1993), they may experience intense feelings of rejection in terminating from the therapist. The therapist who uses the time-limited model in treating women must be continually cognizant that doorknob communication is not always a negative resistance to termination but may be a positive reaffirmation of need to continue time-limited treatment.

SUMMARY AND CONCLUSIONS

Time-limited treatment has proven to be valuable in working with women clients for the following reasons:

1. Time-limited treatment is effective with a variety of problems including environmental, interpersonal, and intrapsychic problems. Women clients with minor adjustment problems as well as serious psychiatric disorders including major depression and schizophrenia can be helped with time-limited treatment. Varied settings such as mental health clinics, schools, hospitals, family service agencies, and child welfare programs have found time-limited treatment an important option in work with women clients.

2. The time-limited, focused quality of brief treatment is particularly advantageous in working with women clients, who often have very limited financial and time resources to expend in therapy.

3. Time-limited treatment does not foster overdependency on the therapist, which has been seen as problematic in long-term traditional therapy for women.

4. The direct, active role of the therapist in time-limited treatment models for women models more active, assertive behavior, which has previously been viewed as a problematic area for women clients.

5. Time-limited treatment promotes the self-determination of the client in setting appropriate, accomplishable goals. As well as being consistent with the professional social work code of ethics, this focus on self-determination is positive in working with clients who may previously have had limited ability to self-determine on their own behalf.

6. Time-limited treatment uses a strength perspective, which includes discovering and mobilizing what capabilities a woman client has to resolve a specific problem. This technique can be very helpful in empowering a woman client who is feeling helpless and hopeless about her life situation.

Because of the versatility and economy of time-limited treatment in an era of managed care, it can be predicted that more and more social agencies will provide time-limited treatment to their women clients. Consequently, professional schools of social work and psychology must remain cognizant of the importance of teaching students about using this model with women clients.

Although practice experience has demonstrated the value of time-limited treatment in clinical work with women, there is continued need for research in this area. Comparative studies of long-term treatment versus time-limited treatment should be undertaken to study the effectiveness of time-limited treatment in helping women address specific problems areas as well as more general women's issues of dependency, low self-esteem, and depression.

Crisis Intervention With
AIDS Patients and Their Families

GRACE H. CHRIST
ROSEMARY T. MOYNIHAN
LES GALLO-SILVER

Acquired immunodeficiency syndrome (AIDS) generates a spectrum of events marked by five major crises: (a) perception of personal risk, (b) confirmation of human immunodeficiency virus (HIV)-positive status, (c) onset of HIV-related symptoms, (d) diagnosis of AIDS, and (e) terminal illness. With each new crisis, people must confront and master predictable psychosocial tasks to maintain their psychological and even physical equilibrium. Effective crisis intervention—helping people to develop the cognitive and emotional strategies needed to master the crisis—requires an understanding of the psychosocial tasks that must be completed at each stage of disease (Christ, Siegel, & Moynihan, 1988). This chapter highlights the social conditions related to transmission of HIV and describes the reactions, psychosocial tasks, and interventions associated with the five major crises in the progression of AIDS.

NOTE: Adapted from *Contemporary Perspectives in Crisis Intervention and Prevention*, edited by A. R. Roberts (Englewood Cliffs, NJ: Prentice Hall, 1991), by permission of the editor and author.

SOCIAL CONDITIONS
RELATED TO HIV TRANSMISSION

Effective crisis intervention requires familiarity with the complex social conditions affecting the groups most frequently diagnosed with AIDS. Many of the stresses experienced by people in each major group relate to how HIV is transmitted.

Homosexual and Bisexual Men

The largest group of patients with AIDS, accounting for 66% of those diagnosed, consists of homosexual and bisexual men (Goedert & Blattner, 1988). Although the gay community has developed a culture, network, and language to protect its members from general public hostility, gay patients lose this protection when asked to share intimate personal information with clinicians, who are usually heterosexuals influenced by dominant cultural values. The often unconscious prejudices of clinicians may make them emotionally distant at a time when gay patients are struggling with guilt, shame, and fear. Bisexual men may experience even greater stress because they tend to be secretive about their homosexual behavior and may feel tremendous conflict about revealing it to their partner or spouse.

Because AIDS has become epidemic, most gay men know many people with the disease. The cumulative effects of watching friends and acquaintances deteriorate and die can be as great as the effects of the death of a family member. As a result, the anxiety many newly diagnosed patients feel is often increased by fears that their disease will progress in the same way. Therefore, patients should be encouraged to focus on how their disease differs from that of others and how new treatments may postpone progression of the disease.

Intravenous Drug Users

The second largest group of AIDS patients, intravenous (IV) drug users, make up 24% of all AIDS patients (Goedert & Blattner, 1988). Unlike gay men, IV drug users have no organized community to rally to their support. Many are only marginally functional and have limited support and a minimal ability to cope with the stresses of AIDS and its treatment (Christ et al., 1988). Clinicians must avoid acting on stereotypical views, and work with IV drug users as people whose different backgrounds, vocations, and life situations have led them to choose drugs as a means of solving life's problems. Despite the stereotypical belief that drug users are personally and socially irresponsible, we find that many express deep concern about sexual relations and about endangering future children.

Addictive illegal drugs can affect the efficacy of drugs prescribed for the pain, depression, anxiety, and nausea associated with AIDS. Methadone maintenance is also difficult during drug therapy for AIDS or the pain associated with the disease. Because effective AIDS treatment requires strict compliance in return for only limited benefits, patients with a limited ability to cope with emotional and physical frustration have difficulty complying with treatment. Moreover, recovering addicts may have difficulty staying off drugs while coping with physical deterioration, energy loss, neurologic impairment, ambiguity, rigorous treatment, and inactivity.

A long, debilitating illness often depletes a patient's personal financial resources, and IV drug use magnifies this problem. Therefore, health care providers must maintain liaisons with drug rehabilitation programs and self-help groups composed of former addicts. These resources are essential for ongoing consultation about drug-related difficulties and referrals for further counseling or specialized intervention.

Heterosexual Women Who Do Not Use Drugs

The incidence of AIDS among heterosexual women has increased with the increasing prevalence of AIDS among IV drug users (Goedert & Blattner, 1988). Some women are unaware of the risk of sexual intercourse with IV drug users. Many others are aware but unable to protect themselves, however, because of their own or their partner's unwillingness to practice safer sex, economic dependence on their sexual partner, or a limited ability to change their current relationship or behavior (Siegel & Gibson, 1988).

Patients Infected by Blood Transfusions

Patients with hemophilia and others exposed to HIV in blood transfusions are likely to exhibit seemingly unjustified anger and mistrust toward physicians and other health care professionals. Clinicians need to help these patients and their families deal openly with these feelings, which are often related to their intense struggle with an already debilitating disease that evokes subtle but real social prejudice.

CRISES EXPERIENCED BY AIDS PATIENTS

Perception of Personal Risk

The first crisis in the spectrum of AIDS occurs when people perceive themselves as being at risk. Risky behaviors or situations include unprotected homosexual or bisexual contacts, anonymous sexual contacts, sexual contacts with current or former IV drug users, IV drug use with needle sharing, blood transfusions, or exposure to body fluids of people infected with HIV.

Most adults in the United States are aware of how AIDS is transmitted and are eager to minimize their own risk. Those who have been involved in high-risk behaviors or situations may, however, become so immobilized by anxiety or so preoccupied with their bodies that they require intervention. For example, a midwestern salesman went to his physician's office frantically seeking treatment for AIDS. While traveling, he had sexual relations with women he did not know, and he felt guilty and frightened after hearing repeated media warnings. When he developed a cold, he became convinced he had AIDS.

Clinicians helping clients with other problems may need to educate them about their risky behavior. For example, a social worker in an urban mental health clinic became deeply concerned about a young client being counseled for depression. The client expressed growing anger that a sexual partner had engaged in prostitution to obtain money for drugs. This statement made the social worker aware that the client was unaware of his own risk of exposure to HIV.

Reactions to Concerns About HIV Infection

Psychosocial symptoms. People who have engaged in actual or perceived high-risk behavior may present with high anxiety about their wellbeing or health status and be preoccupied with bodily changes. Others present with concerns about the well-being of their needle-sharing partners, sexual partners, or unborn children.

Those who are actively involved in high-risk behavior may exhibit various levels of denial about the riskiness of their acts. Denial is most often seen among IV drug users engaged in compulsive or addictive behavior and among female partners of current or former IV drug users who believe that they cannot obtain emotional, financial, or practical support outside these relationships (Siegel & Gibson, 1988). Some gay men rationalize their risky behavior by relying on their own perceptions of what constitutes risk (Siegel, Mesagno, Chen, & Christ, 1989). If a client appears to be placing self or others at risk, the clinician may need to increase the client's level of anxiety by challenging the denial.

Cognitive reactions. New scientific information constantly alters facts about HIV infection and perceptions of personal risk. Several barriers to understanding or changing risky sexual behavior have been identified (Siegel & Gibson, 1988). These barriers include misperceptions about the risk of infection or the magnitude of that risk, cultural or personal antipathy toward condoms, the stigma associated with AIDS, confusion about the value of modifying one's sexual behavior, conflicting values, and idiosyncratic health beliefs.

Emotional reactions. Recognition of personal risk of HIV infection produces a broad range of emotional reactions. These include immobilizing anxiety, fear, and guilt; anger and suspicion; and denial of personal risk or responsibility. For example, a young pregnant woman who transferred from Chicago to Ireland with her husband received transfusions during delivery of her first child. She was extremely anxious about the safety of the blood supply in Ireland and about being far away from home and family during this medical crisis. No amount of reassurance helped; she became so preoccupied about the risk of HIV infection to herself, her husband, and her baby that she finally returned to the United States for HIV testing.

The fear of inflicting harm on others may cause people who believe they are at risk to retreat from all sexual contact or all physical contact of any kind. People with a history of IV drug use may return to using drugs to manage their anxiety, fear, or hopelessness about treatment.

Assessment

The initial assessment of a person at risk for HIV infection should be both expeditious and comprehensive. Counseling may need to be directed toward increasing a client's anxiety rather than toward the usual mental health goal of reducing it. Two goals must be balanced: maintaining a sufficient degree of anxiety in clients to force them into assessing their risky behavior and its possible danger to others, and preventing them from becoming overwhelmed and immobilized. Thus, the initial assessment should include all of the following:

- A history of the client's sexual identity and activity
- A description of the client's current sexual activities and relationships
- A history of any blood transfusions the client has received and any other situations that involve the exchange of blood or body fluids
- The client's history of drug use
- An evaluation of the personal, familial, cultural, and religious contexts of the client's high-risk sexual and drug-taking behavior
- A history of the client's crisis management skills and ego strengths
- A history of any previous psychiatric problems
- A description of the client's social, practical, and financial resources

An effective assessment depends on the attitudes of the clinician who seeks to obtain this personal, highly sensitive information. The potential for countertransference reactions to material that a client reveals is enormous. To be effective, the clinician's approach must reflect non-judgmental acceptance, empathy for the client's emotional distress, reassuring interest and concern, and support for the client's positive efforts to cope with the crisis.

Because primary prevention of a life-threatening illness requires extensive assessment and planning, at least two follow-up sessions should be scheduled with clients in crisis about their risk of HIV infection. Their sexual behavior and chemical dependency should be discussed in depth, a plan should be developed for maintaining their health and for receiving regular health monitoring, and they should be helped to decide whether to be tested for HIV infection.

Crisis Intervention Model

People who are at obvious or perceived risk for AIDS usually need help in confronting multiple psychosocial tasks. Therefore, crisis intervention will not be effective unless all these criteria are met:

- Their sexual behavior and sexual dependency must be discussed with them in detail.
- Their actual and perceived risk must be assessed.
- They must receive assurance of professional support and help.
- They must receive help in maintaining—but not eliminating—their anxiety, stress, and guilt through individual or group treatment, self-help referrals, and accurate information.
- Their myths and misconceptions about risk must be eradicated.
- They must understand how HIV is transmitted.
- They must develop plans for altering their risky behaviors and for managing changes in their relationships resulting from these alterations.
- They must formulate plans for appropriate medical care.
- They must direct their energies toward such positive goals as health maintenance and self-care.
- They must receive information about HIV testing and help in making a decision about testing.

HIV Testing

The recent development of medical treatments that may postpone the onset of symptoms in people who test HIV-positive has significantly changed attitudes toward HIV testing (Lambert, 1989). In the past, many people who engaged in risky behavior refused testing to avoid confronting a definite diagnosis of a life-threatening illness with no known treatment. Even then, however, some people chose to be tested to eliminate ambiguity, although no medical treatments were available. HIV testing, with counseling both before and after, is now recommended as a first step toward the treatment of people at risk.

Counseling before testing. The decision to undergo HIV testing may lead to intense anxiety and depression, and so represents a critical time for professional support and education. The purpose of pretest counseling is to help clients (a) realistically assess their risk, (b) make informed decisions, (c) anticipate their own negative psychological reactions and those of others if the test results are positive, and (d) develop plans to maximize the benefits of testing while minimizing its psychological and social costs. The clinician must inform clients about the significance of both negative and positive results and the problems of confidentiality and consequent vulnerability to discrimination. In addition, the clinician should emphasize that counseling is available while clients are awaiting the test results.

The following questions may be useful in guiding a client's thinking before testing:

- How would you feel if you learned that you were infected?
- How would you have to change the way you have sex?
- How would you tell your sex partner or partners?
- How would you feel if you learned that you may have transmitted the virus to someone?
- How would you deal with discrimination in seeking or maintaining employment or insurance?
- Would you have to change your pattern of IV drug use?
- Would an HIV-positive result change your feelings about having children?
- Whom could you talk with about the results of the test?

Counseling after testing. Clients also need counseling after HIV testing, regardless of whether the results are negative or positive. For those with negative tests, counseling can prevent false perceptions of immunity to the infection and emphasize the likelihood of infection if their high-risk behavior continues. For those with positive tests, yet another crisis obviously looms.

Confirmation of HIV-Positive Status

Reactions to the Crisis

Psychosocial symptoms. Even people who strongly suspected that they were HIV-positive tend to experience tremendous anxiety and depression when the test results confirm their suspicions. Because extreme reactions such as suicidal or homicidal ideation and behaviors are not uncommon, immediate reassurance of professional support and concern is essential. People who test positive must be aware from the beginning that they must control the disclosure of information about their condition to avoid discrimination and social rejection, yet be able to share their concerns. Some people feel pressured to relieve their anxiety by telling everyone they know, thus exposing themselves to social rejection and other destructive losses. At the other extreme, some people have difficulty telling anyone about their condition, even those who need to know because they shared in the risky behavior that led to the disease.

In addition, people who test positive must change their sexual and drug-using behaviors to avoid infecting others and becoming more infected themselves. Some withdraw from all physical intimacy, even hugging and kissing, to avoid transmitting the virus. Others have difficulty changing even their risky behaviors for various reasons (Siegel, Bauman, Christ, & Krown, 1988). Thus, HIV-positive status becomes a major barrier to continuing or developing the intimate relationships that are so vital to people under stress.

Cognitive reactions. Many people who test positive find the ambiguity of their medical condition—of not knowing whether or when they will develop AIDS—difficult to tolerate. Because they initially fear that any physical symptom is related to AIDS, they need to be taught how to distinguish the symptoms of AIDS from the symptoms of other, less threatening illnesses. They also need continuous access to health care, not only to receive optimal treatment but also to maintain an optimal degree of concern about their condition and to receive support for efforts to change their risky behavior without experiencing excessive, immobilizing anxiety.

Emotional reactions. When people learn that they are HIV-positive, they are often overcome with a sense of helplessness and hopelessness even if they had strongly suspected their condition. Helping such people find a way of managing their overwhelming emotions must be a major focus of crisis intervention.

Assessment

A psychosocial assessment of a person who is HIV-positive can provide a baseline description of functioning that may help the clinician identify later symptoms of AIDS such as dementia. This assessment should determine the person's (a) knowledge of the difference between being HIV-positive and having AIDS, (b) awareness of how to avoid transmitting the infection, (c) history of emotional problems or psychiatric illness, (d) ability to cope with stress, (e) access to social networks for emotional and practical support, and (f) plans for medical evaluation and ongoing monitoring.

Because people who are HIV-positive are stressed by the ambiguous diagnosis, the chronic nature of the condition, and their potential to infect others, they require one to three extended sessions—or even more—so that the clinician can develop a support network for them or engage them in a formal, ongoing support program. The primary goals are to preserve their functioning, contain their anxiety, and encourage them to change their behavior and refocus their lives.

Crisis Intervention Model

Crisis intervention after a person tests positive for HIV should include the following components: (a) a psychosocial assessment, (b) advice about how and with whom to share information, (c) suggestions about how to maintain confidentiality and manage legal, employment, and insurance problems, (d) development of plans for medical care, (e) engagement of at least one person in the social network to provide support, and (f) initiation of the process of thinking through decisions about drug use, childbearing, and communicating with sexual partners. The clinician can often assist these people by helping them establish priorities on the basis that they may have a limited life span.

Onset of HIV-Related Symptoms

Because people who are HIV-positive often develop an acute sensitivity to their bodies, become hypervigilant about any potential AIDS symptom, and do not know when a medical crisis will develop, they often say they feel like they are in state of constant alarm—that they feel like a time bomb. This chronic stress may diminish their capacity to cope with the onset of HIV-related symptoms. For example, a young lawyer wept as he rocked gently back and forth in his chair trying to control and comfort himself. His physician had just told him that although he could not yet be diagnosed as having AIDS, his recent fatigue and weight loss were caused by progression of the HIV infection.

Reactions to the Crisis

Psychosocial symptoms. Many patients experience the onset of AIDS-related symptoms as the onset of the "sick role" associated with a life-threatening disease. That is, they begin to deal with some of the realities of their situation while clinging to the hope that their current condition will not progress to a full diagnosis of AIDS. Their need to cope with aggressive medical management of symptoms often leads to a preoccupation with health and treatment problems. If they are experiencing overwhelming anxiety, they may withdraw from work, child rearing activities, and important supportive relationships. Thus the progression of the illness introduces the risk that they will lose existing sources of support.

Cognitive reactions. As patients with HIV-related symptoms struggle with emotional reactions to their changed medical status, they must also integrate complex information about the potential effects of this change on their life span and their quality of life. Patients with AIDS-related complex (ARC) often become seriously ill. For example, IV drug users frequently die of ARC without ever having been diagnosed with AIDS. Therefore, patients often need to have their medical status clarified. Have they been diagnosed as having ARC? How long will this stage of the disease continue before they are diagnosed as having AIDS? What specific changes constitute an AIDS diagnosis?

Patients may cope with their fears of progressive disease by engaging in ritualized or even obsessive behavior, such as insisting on a specific amount of sleep each night, taking large doses of vitamins and minerals, or rigidly curtailing their daily activities and relationships. Many attempt to avoid stress and "negative" emotions.

Maladaptive or obsessive efforts to take control of preserving health are illustrated by two examples. An advertising executive who complained of insomnia revealed that he believed he could prevent becoming run down and developing AIDS by sleeping for 10 hours each night. He became so anxious about his need to sleep 10 hours that he had difficulty falling asleep. A computer operator was chronically late for work in the morning because he had to count the exact number of vitamin C, zinc, and garlic pills he thought he needed to take during the day.

Emotional reactions. When confused with the symptoms of progressive disease, patients often experience a resurgence of the immobilizing anxiety, guilt, and fear they felt when they first learned they were HIV-positive. Some patients express these feelings in sudden emotional outbursts that are often directed toward coworkers, neighbors, salespeople, or others with whom they do not have a close relationship. These outbursts often represent efforts to ventilate their fear and anger about death and dying. Their families of origin, children, and others they are close to may be unable to provide comfort because the patient has not told them about their HIV status or high-risk behavior. As a 22-year-old college student asked, "How can I tell my parents I'm gay and I'm sick at the same time?"

With the onset of symptoms, patients must reevaluate decisions about who should know about their medical status. They often worry about how to tell their employer about their need to take time off for medical appointments or about disabilities caused by new symptoms. A textile worker said, "I'm always tired. Every morning I'm late for work, and my boss yells at me. But how can I tell him what's happening to me?"

To prevent their employers from learning they have AIDS, many patients choose not to use their medical insurance. Symptoms that require more intensive medical treatment, however, may force them to reverse this decision. By disclosing serious health problems to their employer, patients often confront the loss of their career momentum because of an inability to compete, to be involved in special projects, or to be promoted. These losses cause many young adults to lose their sense of purpose, which heightens their fears of being unable to function independently and of death. As a cosmetics salesman said, "After I told my boss why I needed time off, I knew I'd lost the promotion I'd been striving for years to get. When someone else got it, I felt like I died a little." At such times, former IV drug users may return to drugs to cope with powerful feelings of sadness and anger.

Assessment

Assessment after the onset of HIV-related symptoms should include (a) clarification of the patient's responses to the previous crises of HIV testing and HIV-positive status, (b) an evaluation of the patient's support network, including identification of people who have already helped and those who may help as the disease progresses, (c) possible abuse of alcohol or illegal or prescription drugs in response to emotional stress, and (d) an appraisal of the patient's ability to maintain health. Patients may neglect their medical care or avoid follow-up care. For example, a patient with hemophilia said, "For five days, I've known I had an infection in my mouth, but I was so upset I forgot to call my doctor for an appointment to get medicine for it."

Two or three sessions may be needed to develop strategies that will enable a patient to stay employed, engage in creative endeavors and child rearing activities, and increase sources of social support by disclosing the diagnosis. Joint counseling of the patient and the person identified as the key source of emotional support may help to strengthen and clarify that relationship. The clinician may need to maintain daily telephone contact with the patient if counseling sessions are scheduled several days apart.

Crisis Intervention Model

Several important steps make up the crisis intervention model for patients who develop the symptoms of progressive illness. First, the clinician should help patients disclose their condition. Selective disclosure allows them to negotiate the changes necessary in their functional responsibilities and to increase their sources of social support. Role-playing and other specialized techniques can help them search for the "right words" to use when approaching others for support and comfort. Because patients are appropriately concerned about the potential for rejection and abandonment, the clinician plays a key role in helping them identify the most likely sources of support.

Second, the clinician should help patients reinvest their energy in the tasks of daily living and in setting priorities. A task-focused approach can help them feel more normal and in control of their lives. Patients need to determine which activities need to be changed or curtailed in response to such symptoms as fatigue. Some patients, however, may not have the flexibility to alter their work schedules to accommodate reduced stamina. For example, a plastic surgeon with HIV-related symptoms said, "I can't practice anymore. Some days are good, but some are bad. That's just not acceptable to me or fair to my patients."

Third, the clinician should evaluate patients' needs for more intense specialized services. Patients often benefit from referrals for practical, financial, and psychological services from clinicians who are knowledgeable about AIDS and its progression.

Diagnosis of AIDS

AIDS is a syndrome comprising two categories of illnesses: *opportunistic infections,* which usually affect the lungs, brain, genitourinary tract, eyes, colon, or central nervous system, and *cancers,* most commonly Kaposi's sarcoma and certain lymphomas. The diagnosis of AIDS is made when the patient presents with one of these opportunistic infections or cancers.

Treatment of most opportunistic infections requires an acute hospital admission. For instance, a waiter who had been HIV-positive for several years came to the emergency room because he was short of breath. After having a chest X ray, he was told he probably had pneumocystis carinii pneumonia, an indication that his condition had progressed to AIDS. (Further tests were required to confirm the diagnosis.) His fear and sadness made him cry, which in turn made it even harder for him to breathe.

Unlike most opportunistic infections, some cancers can initially be treated on an outpatient basis. Kaposi's sarcoma, for example, proceeds slowly, and its first symptoms are often superficial.

Reactions to the Crisis

Psychosocial symptoms. Patients diagnosed with AIDS may not experience the emotional impact of the diagnosis immediately because of their need to focus on the immediate medical crisis. Only when their acute symptoms subside do they confront the reality of their diagnosis and their mortality, a reality that becomes more apparent with each successive hospital admission. As a postal clerk said, "This is my fourth bout of pneumonia. Each time I have to be admitted to the hospital, I think, 'This is it—I'm not getting out alive.' "

Although patients with Kaposi's sarcoma already know they have AIDS, they may not actually confront the diagnosis until they are hospitalized for the first time with an opportunistic infection. When a bookkeeper who had had Kaposi's sarcoma lesions on his face and arms for several years was admitted to the hospital with pneumonia, he said, "I've had AIDS for years, but it's only now that I'm in the hospital that I think it's going to kill me."

Cognitive reactions. Because patients recently diagnosed with AIDS are plagued by fears of imminent death, even though many people live several years after the diagnosis, they often focus on mortality statistics and media coverage emphasizing that AIDS is a terminal illness. The fear of imminent death may induce anger and emotional withdrawal from others. For example, a young female patient, the wife of a man with hemophilia, said, "I don't talk to anyone. No one can help me."

Even when patients are doing well (e.g., after recovering from an opportunistic infection), they may prematurely contemplate resigning from their job and making funeral arrangements. The lover of a man hospitalized for AIDS-defining meningitis said to the nurses, "He seems to get better each day, but he keeps telling me to donate all of his clothes to the church."

Emotional reactions. AIDS patients, who are usually young, fear becoming debilitated, neurologically impaired, and unable to function independently almost more than they fear death. These fears become intense when they are hospitalized for treatment of advancing disease. Some react with feelings of helplessness, hopelessness, and even suicidal ideation.

The diagnosis of AIDS increases the pressure on patients who have not yet disclosed their situation to families of origin, spouses, children, and friends. Overwhelming panic, sadness, and fear of rejection may make it difficult for them to communicate with people close to them. As a middle-aged businessman said, "After all these years, how can I tell my children that their mother and I divorced because I'm bisexual? But how can I avoid telling them now that I'm sick?" Repressed fears of having transmitted the disease to sexual partners may resurface when the disease is diagnosed.

Assessment

When AIDS is formally diagnosed, the assessment focuses on (a) clarifying distortions or misunderstandings of medical information by determining how the patient views the illness and the prognosis, (b) evaluating the patient's physical frailty, possible dementia, and environmental instability, including unresolved financial, housing, or insurance problems, and (c) appraising the patient's ability to cope with future stresses as the illness progresses, which includes identification of the patient's sources of social support and previous coping abilities.

Two or three sessions are usually required to help patients cope with the crisis of the formal diagnosis. Patients must be helped to move from denial and panic to constructive processing of medical information and planning for self-care. The goal is to continue to reduce their social isolation by helping them disclose information to appropriate individuals and agencies to maintain ongoing support. Clinicians must ensure that patients' formal and informal supports are adequate to sustain them through acute medical episodes over what may be a period of years.

Crisis Intervention Model

Interventions with newly diagnosed patients should be directed toward reducing their negative identification with other AIDS patients, containing their anxiety, and increasing their realistic feelings of hope and sense of control. The clinician can assist them in achieving these goals in the following ways.

Help them to understand the medical information they are given and to organize their lives around their new status. Asking them to write down questions and concerns may help to identify misunderstandings and gaps in information about prognosis and treatment that are caused by confusing reports in the media. The clinician also can help them formulate additional questions and learn to anticipate their reactions to new information.

Help them develop and maintain as normal a daily schedule as possible. Mastery of life-focused tasks promotes a sense of control and normalcy and helps prevent an immobilizing preoccupation with the threat of death.

Ensure that they have adequate home care, financial assistance, and other support services. Patients often experience a loss of self-esteem when they recognize that they need support services. Therefore, the clinician should offer them the opportunity to grieve over their losses of work, income, and independence and encourage them to view support services as resources for promoting an optimal degree of personal control and quality of life rather than as reasons for feeling helpless and dependent. This approach helps prepare them to accept home care and nursing if these services are needed.

Terminal Illness

Patients diagnosed with AIDS can live many years with the disease under control. When treatment fails, however, they enter the final stage of the disease, terminal illness, which presents another series of tasks. At this stage, they are faced with maintaining a meaningful quality of life despite the disease and the threat of death, coping with disfigurement and loss of function, and attempting to answer complicated existential and spiritual questions related to lifestyle, unmet responsibilities, and potential separation and loss (Moynihan, Christ, & Gallo-Silver, 1988).

CONCLUSION

The psychosocial tasks confronting people who are affected by AIDS will continue to evolve as more effective treatments are developed. In addition, changes in the social context of the disease will have powerful effects on these patients. Thus, clinicians involved in interventions at each stage of the crisis must be aware of these changes and integrate that knowledge into their interactions with patients.

PART IV

Intervention by Telephone

Handling Client Crises
Effectively on the Telephone

JUDITH WATERS

ERIC FINN

CASE STUDY

2:00 a.m., Sunday morning: The setting is a suicide prevention hotline in a suburban community mental health center. The phone has rung several times since midnight. Each time the counselor has answered, the caller has hung up immediately. Finally, the counselor can hear a sobbing voice speak so low that the words are almost unintelligible. The counselor, a clinical psychology graduate student in his early thirties, begins to speak calmly and slowly, encouraging the caller to talk to him and tell him what the problem is. Eventually, after about 4 or 5 minutes, the caller, who sounds like a young woman, gives him her first name and says that she has just learned that she is pregnant and thinks she is HIV positive. She says she wants to kill herself and her baby that night. The counselor continues to engage her in talking about herself and the people in her life. Because she sounds as if she might hang up again if pressured, he is careful in his attempts to find out where she is.

3:00 a.m.: The caller is still on the phone. By this time, her voice is stronger. Since she and the counselor have established a trusting relationship, she has told him where she lives and that she will wait for the police to come and take her to the suicide prevention unit of the local hospital. The counselor tries to keep her on the phone while another counselor contacts the police. The caller, however, says she's tired of talking and hangs up.

3:15 a.m.: The police call. The address was an empty warehouse.

CASE STUDY

This is the third time that Howard has called the hotline on this day. He has been calling the crisis intervention hotline for 30 years. He is a paraplegic who suffered a stroke when he was in his early twenties. He worked as an aerospace engineer and was an avid skier. When he calls, he talks about his operation, and the doctors' prognoses when he first had the stroke. Although he also talks about his family, the theme of his life is his disability. If he goes out at all, he must be transported in his wheelchair in a special van. Most of the time, he is home in bed listening to the radio.

All the counselors know Howard very well. If there are no other calls, a counselor can listen to Howard's stories, but must cut him off or put him on hold to take another call. Sometimes, they even ask him to call later. For Howard, the hotline counselors are his personal support group, his only reliable and concerned contact with the outside world. If he were prevented from calling, it is probable that his quality of life would decline and his morale would deteriorate rapidly.

DIARY OF A HOTLINE COUNSELOR

There is nothing to compare with answering hotline calls on the graveyard shift on a Saturday night. I mean, you get all kinds of calls. Sometimes, a group of drunk teenagers will see the television ads and call the line as a joke, making up an outrageous story, and asking for someone to please, please help! These calls get easier to spot with experience. There is usually rowdy noise in the background, the caller may give vague answers to simple questions, or contradictions may appear in the caller's narrative. Many times, when I first started working on the hotline, my earnest attempts to be of assistance would be cut off by loud bursts of laughter from the other end of the line, and I knew the joke was on me.

The hotline I work for is primarily an information and referral service run in conjunction with a psychiatric hospital. When a call comes in, I try to get an idea of what the caller wants. If the caller needs help in dealing with a specific problem, I'll give him or her the number of a hotline that has people trained in handling that problem. If the caller is seeking treatment for a psychiatric illness, either I'll get some information from the person for our admissions department, or I'll refer the caller to an appropriate facility. Most of the calls I get, however, are from people who are confused and don't know where to turn for help or who just need to talk to someone. I think that it's reassuring for a person who's awake at four in the morning wrestling with a problem to know that someone else is there.

Sometimes the calls can just break your heart, like the one I received this past Christmas. Christmas fell on a Saturday, so I was working the phones that night. A 12-year-old girl called at two in the morning, crying and nearly hysterical, saying that her mother was drunk again, and was throwing things around the house. The police had already been to the house twice that night, having been called by the neighbors due to the noise. Because the police had judged that the mother was not dangerous to her self or the child, however, they were reluctant to take any action against her. Consequently, my options in handling the call were severely limited. Usually, if I have reason to fear for the caller's safety (i.e., if the person appears suicidal or is being threatened by someone's actions), my first course of action is to find out where the caller is and then call in some sort of emergency personnel. In this case, however, the police had already been involved, and as they saw no reason to take action against the mother, I knew that they would not go out again. The child told me that when the police came, her mother had put on an "act" designed to fool them into thinking everything was all right. Also, she stated that, although her mother had never hit her, she had locked herself in her room before calling the hotline.

It is at times like these that the limitations of hotline intervention become painfully obvious. I mean, there is only so much you can do. Despite the fact that she had locked her door to make the call to the hotline, I was reasonably reassured that the child was in no immediate danger, so I tried to gauge the strength of her support system. It turned out that her father was home, but he was also drunk and passed out in his bedroom. I mean, Merry Christmas kid. We ended up talking for the better part of an hour, and I think that the presence of a sane, rational adult on the other end of the phone did help, and she calmed down considerably. Still, there was not much I could do to affect her immediate situation. I gave her a couple of phone numbers for agencies that deal with adolescents in crisis, and the names and numbers of treatment programs she could give to her parents in the morning. I also told her that if things got any worse that night, she should not hesitate to call 911 or the police, and she assured me that she would. Then she thanked me for listening, and that was that. She struck me as a very resourceful young person. Growing up in an environment like that, I guess you have to be. I hope things turn out all right for her.

Working on the phones can be frustrating and stressful at times, but it can also be very rewarding. This point becomes obvious when I think about a woman I know who had a career in business when she became a volunteer on a suicide hotline. That experience of helping people in crisis so affected her that she made a career change, went back to school, and is now working on her doctorate in clinical psychology. I know the feeling, because there is nowhere else on earth where you can develop a better sense of the scope of human suffering than at a hotline.

HANDLING CLIENT CRISES
THROUGH TELEPHONE CONTACT

The 24-hour suicide prevention hotline is only one way that the telephone is used to meet the needs of clients in crisis. The earliest of the hotlines, most of which were established in the 1960s, are associated with suicide prevention (Rosenbaum & Calhoun, 1977). In the last 30 years, the use of telecommunication as a tool has been extended to hotlines with a broader set of goals than suicide prevention. These services include outreach programs to check on the status of the elderly and people with disabilities, radio and television call-in lines, information lines with recorded messages on mental health issues, coverage for vacationing therapists, "warm lines" for latchkey (self-care) children, confidential lines for runaways, contact between recovering substance abusers and their sponsors, the police emergency or 911 line, and even psychotherapy that is billed to the caller's telephone or credit card number. Telephone networks frequently reach groups who do not always use more traditional services (e.g., homebound agoraphobics) (Stein & Lambert, 1984). The proliferation of crisis lines has raised a number of serious questions that must be addressed by professionals in the field. Issues such as the use of volunteers versus professional staff, the adequacy of selection and training procedures, counselor "burnout," the need for rigorous program evaluation, and privacy and other ethical questions that have arisen with the advent of new technologies (e.g., instant caller identification) have led to honest conflict among responsible practitioners and researchers.

THE SCOPE OF THE PROBLEM

Brennan (cited in Rosenbaum & Calhoun, 1977) suggests three basic reasons for the growth of hotlines: (a) They are generally less expensive in terms of both initial establishment and ongoing operating costs than a center because they don't require a large physical facility and are generally staffed by volunteers (this latter pattern may change); (b) Their treatment goals are more general, thus lessening the need for highly trained staff; and (c) Hotlines serve a broader spectrum of problems than many centers, which makes them valuable in a great many cases (e.g., AIDS lines).

Given the most widely accepted description of a *crisis*, a state of disequilibrium in which the individual's normal coping strategies have failed, leaving him or her susceptible to the influence of others, the provision of a therapeutic intervention at the most vulnerable time has the potential to contribute to a successful resolution of the crisis, and to subsequent well-being (Bloom, 1963; Caplan, 1961). The goal of telephone services—the amelioration or resolution of crisis situations—fits the overall goal of crisis intervention, which is to focus primarily on the situation, not on the personality of the individual, although individual resources and traits cannot be completely ignored.

Although there are no accurate counts of the total number of services using both professional and volunteer workers in the United States and Canada , an estimated 5 million phone calls are made to various hotlines in the United States every year (Roberts & Comasso, 1994). Some of them deal with problems such as cocaine addiction (Cocores & Gold, 1990), and others reflect the loneliness and need for human contact that almost everyone experiences at one time or another. Many crisis calls are made during the middle of the night when most walk-in services are unavailable. For a significant number of callers, traveling to a center is either impossible (e.g., latchkey children and the disabled) or difficult due to the time of the contact or transportation problems. Given that the primary goal of crisis intervention is to intercede at the earliest possible stage for the most effective client outcomes, the immediacy of telephone counseling and referral, especially for the homebound, clearly meets that objective. What is equally important is that the hotline provides an opportunity for anonymity, which may be critical to clients who are too embarrassed to work with a counselor in person. The anonymity of the telephone service has its disadvantages, however, with respect to locating suicidal clients and deterring chronic, obscene, and prank callers.

In a study of over 6,000 contacts that occurred between 1970 and 1977, in-person contacts were compared with telephone contacts (Hinrichsen & Zwibelman, 1981). It was established that the telephone was clearly the most frequently used avenue of access to services for problems. Hinrichsen and Zwibelman (1981) reported that "walk-ins require, on the average, over twice as much time to process as do phone calls" (p. 318).

Williams and Douds (1973) have summarized the four basic ways that telephone therapy differs from traditional face-to-face psychotherapy. First, the client, in most cases, has more control over the situation because he or she can terminate contact at will. Second, as previously noted, the client can remain anonymous should he or she so wish. Third, geographic barriers, either real or psychological, can easily be overcome, and, finally, therapists can also remain anonymous, giving them added protection against hostile clients.

With respect to client issues, a person in distress may not have the energy, capability, or inclination to visit a helping agency. Moreover, because a telephone relationship is tantamount to a therapeutic encounter without commitments, it is possible that the client will be more honest than he or she would be when in close physical proximity to the counselor. Anonymity also reduces the fear of being "ridiculed or abused" (Rosenbaum & Calhoun, 1977) or being prosecuted for substance abuse, sexual problems, or other legal complications.

Therapist anonymity also has advantages because it protects the counselor from potentially dangerous clients, crank callers, obscene messages, or the masturbating caller. On the other hand, telephone counseling robs both the caller and the counselor of the information that can be derived from nonverbal behavior.

Clients may view the counselors, both volunteers and professionals, in one of two general ways: as authoritative sources of information (Center for Public Safety Studies, Inc., 1991) or as sympathetic peers who do not exhibit "the barrier of professional armor" (Caplan, 1961). If the counselor is effective in terms of displaying concern for the welfare of the client and dispensing knowledge about the situation as well as credible referrals, both roles may be successfully fulfilled.

CLIENT VARIABLES

The probability of a crisis response, and the severity of that response, is related to the individual's background, history of previous coping experiences, psychosocial resources, and cognitive appraisal of the circumstances as potentially (Dohrenwend & Dohrenwend, 1974). His or her adaptive capacity to address the situation (i.e., hardiness factor) also influences the response. It is clear that certain conditions (e.g., war, natural and manmade disasters, and the death of someone close) will induce enough anxiety in most people to interfere with their ability to function, at least temporarily. The purpose of crisis intervention is to reduce the costs of these events by early treatment before the initial maladaptive responses descend into long-term psychopathology. What could be more effective than speedy intervention by phone?

> The clear implication of most models is that crisis intervention emphasizes dealing with ordinarily adequately functioning individuals who are responding with disabling levels of anxiety to discrete environmental stressors, as opposed to chronically maladjusted individuals whose behavior seems to stem from a continuing psychiatric disorder. (Auerbach & Kilman, 1977, p. 1190)

Although it is possible to screen clients in a mental health center, diverting those in need of long-term therapy to the appropriate professionals and those in need of crisis intervention to counselors trained in those skills, telephone hotlines are generally not structured for triage decisions. The operators must deal with the crisis at hand, only later attempting to refer clients for continuing care.

CHARACTERISTICS OF HOTLINES

Hotlines are operated by a broad spectrum of facilities including hospitals, colleges and universities, religious organizations, volunteer and self-help groups, community groups, and law enforcement agencies (e.g., 911). Although many hotlines function 24 hours a day, others are available only during normal working hours or at specific and limited times (e.g., radio call-in programs). When a counselor is not available, telephone answering machines may be provided. A counselor will return the call during regular hours. If one thinks how frustrating it can be to reach the answering machine of a friend, just think how the crisis caller feels when a machine answers. Hotlines offer information, advice, and referral services according to their rules of operation. For example, hotlines based in Catholic hospitals will not dispense abortion information or referrals.

In recent years, a number of information lines have been established that employ taped messages on various physical and mental health issues (e.g., Almay's 800 Healthline). The topics covered by these information services include stress management, vocational questions, AIDS and other sexually transmitted diseases, and community problems such as housing emergencies or garbage removal.

Hotlines can be categorized in a number of ways, from their goals to their target populations. The following is a rough typology of their goals:

Hotlines dedicated to specific needs. The earliest hotlines responded to suicidal clients. It quickly became apparent that the focus could be expanded to address the problems of a broader spectrum of callers. There are still many lines dedicated to specific groups, however (e.g., runaways, suicides at high-risk sites such as bridges, the caregivers of dementia patients, and people concerned about AIDS).

Hotlines geared to dispensing information and referrals. Some of these services target the general population in a particular catchment area.

They frequently have the computer-based capability to provide appropriate referrals on a large number of problems. This type of network is usually housed in hospitals and universities or colleges. There are also lines that use taped messages.

Emergency response systems. Although the 911 line is the best known of the emergency services, there are other lines that respond to the physical and psychological emergencies of specific groups, such as patients recently released from hospitals. One of the primary goals of this type of crisis line is to give support and reduce the anxieties of people who may have been sent home too soon. Patients reporting serious symptoms will be taken by ambulance to the appropriate facility. Clearly, anonymity is not an issue.

"Warm lines." With the increasing number of self-care ("latchkey") children, the necessity to provide direct services for these children has been recognized. Calls include questions about homework, the need to talk to someone, and reports of sexual and physical abuse. Runaway crisis lines are also directed to children and youth, but can scarcely be classified as "warm lines."

Radio and television call-ins. The goal of these programs is ostensibly to provide information and referrals with the emphasis on information. Diagnosis and psychotherapy are strictly prohibited (see the section on call-in issues, below).

Outreach phone services. Most outreach networks check on the health status and needs of elderly and disabled clients. In addition, the service provides psychological support on a daily basis.

Psychotherapy. A new service has recently been developed that delivers actual psychotherapy to clients who are billed by the minute. The line is staffed by experienced and licensed professionals. Clients may recontact individual therapists by using a code.

Another way to conceptualize the various telephone services is by comparing the risk level of the clients and the nature of the situations. In many cases (e.g., most calls to traditional information and referral lines), delays are not critical to the safety of the clients and referrals for future appointments are easily made. In other cases, however, the situations (e.g., potential suicides, and children or even adults in hostile or abusive environments) require immediate action by caregivers on site. Runaways, for example, can fall into either category depending on the counselor's assessment. The operator must be able to evaluate the psychological status of the caller, and the risk components in the environment, to convince the caller of the appropriate action to take (e.g., go to a shelter or wait to be assisted). Because runaway hotlines invariably guarantee confidentiality, the persuasive skills of the counselor are very important.

Experts estimate that, depending on the size of the organization, its focus, and the length of each shift, it can take between 10 and 90 persons per week to staff a hotline. In these times of financial exigencies when people need jobs, it is increasingly difficult to recruit and maintain volunteer counselors, as emergency squads and volunteer fire departments discovered some time ago.

Organizers of hotlines do not suggest that crisis lines be substituted for more conventional psychotherapies. Most administrators would rather have their services perceived as either filling a need for clients who would not ordinarily be covered by traditional mental health agencies or as the first step in a sequence of stages in dealing with crises. For many clients, calling the hotline may be a critical phase in the move from contemplation of action or preparation for action to actually taking action in a model of behavioral change (Prochaska, DiClemente, & Norcross, 1992).

COUNSELOR GUIDELINES

According to Roberts (1990a), "The telephone crisis intervenor is trained to establish rapport with the caller, conduct a brief assessment, provide a sympathetic ear, help develop a crisis management plan, and/or refer the caller to an appropriate treatment program or service" (p. 5). All of these tasks must be accomplished with people who are so distressed that they probably should not consider driving to a center, even if it were not the middle of the night. Roberts has delineated a series of steps in a general model of crisis intervention that is applicable to hotline counseling:

1. Make psychological contact and rapidly establish the relationship.
2. Examine the dimensions of the problem so as to define it.
3. Encourage an exploration of feelings and emotions.
4. Explore and assess past coping attempts.
5. Generate and explore alternatives and specific solutions.
6. Restore cognitive functioning through implementation of the action plan.
7. Follow up.

The establishment of rapport, the assessment of the situation, the exploration of past coping strategies, and the development of a viable action plan are integral components of the crisis intervention process that must all take place within the limitations of the telephone contact. Unfortunately, in terms of follow-up, most counselors will never know whether their skills influenced positive resolutions of the clients' crises. Occasionally, counselors may be informed if a caller has made an appointment at a referral agency. "No-shows," however, do not necessarily indicate a failed intervention. Relatively stable clients may not have felt the need for further consultation. In an early study, Slaikeu used three levels of outcome (showing, not showing, or canceling subsequent appointments for face-to-face counseling) and found that callers who were relatively silent during the time period preceding the actual discussion of the referral were least likely to appear for their appointments. Thus, it is clear that one of the major tasks for the hotline counselor is to engage the client in productive communication. Slaikeu (1979) suggests that "many no-show referrals are a result of volunteers being 'blocked,' not knowing what to say or do with a caller, with referral chosen as a way out of the dilemma" (p. 194). Better counselor training that focuses on dealing with callers who have difficulty in communicating their problems is definitely in order.

The following list, adapted from Echterling and Hartsough (1989, p. 249), also delineates the phases in responding to a crisis call:

1. *Creation and maintenance of the climate necessary for the intervention* (e.g., sustaining telephone contact, the development of a helpful relationship, and the establishment of helper and caller roles)

2. *Assessment of the crisis* (i.e., identification of the actual problem and determination of the personal and environmental conditions affecting the problem)
3. *Establishment of affect integration* during which the helper assists the caller in recognizing, understanding, and expressing feelings about the crisis
4. *The problem-solving stage,* in which the helper and the caller identify goals, explore and evaluate alternatives, and make decisions regarding the appropriate next step

In exploring the dimensions of the counseling role, Roberts (1990a) suggests that training should focus on the "now and how" rather than on the "then and why." Counselors should also try to identify the precipitating event, even if the client seems reluctant to share that information. Assessing the lethality of the situation is also an important step. The overall goals of the intervention are to assist the client in resolving the current crisis and in acquiring the problem-solving skills needed to deal with future crises in an effective manner. Despite the brevity of the interaction, the counselor should attempt to improve the client's level of cognitive functioning. Good critical thinking skills involve the ability to develop a realistic perspective of the events that led to the crisis, and the personal meaning the crisis has for the caller, including irrational beliefs and distortions. Restructuring cognitions and replacing false perceptions with realistic thinking must be done with care so as to avoid alienating the caller and destroying rapport. Counselors must be careful not to be confrontational. Throughout the intervention, the counselor must remain aware that callers are frequently under the influence of drugs and/or alcohol, which interferes with the ability to engage in problem solving.

Although volunteers may range in age from adolescents to the elderly and come from all walks of life, they frequently show common characteristics such as warmth, empathy, dedication, caring, responsibility, and a commitment to help. Despite the best of motivations, extensive training is still required for effective performance. Good training programs range from 40 to 55 hours and involve both didactic and experiential material. Depending on the goals of the organization, the focus will be on listening skills and the ability to give correct information and appropriate referrals. Many training programs are based on the tenets of cognitive therapy and Rogerian client-centered therapy. The characteristics of nonjudgmental feedback are emphasized:

1. Focus on the behavior, not the person.
2. Use observations, not inferences.
3. Be situation specific when making comments.
4. Share information and ideas rather than giving advice. Giving advice frequently elicits resistance.
5. Explore alternatives rather than searching for a correct solution.
6. Alternatives should relate to the life circumstances of the caller.
7. Be careful not to overload the caller with more information and options than he or she can reasonably handle.
8. Conduct periodic checks to make sure that you have understood what the caller has actually said and meant.
9. Work toward closure. Ascertain whether or not the client has an action plan or the needed information, and that he or she is satisfied with the intervention.
10. Welcome a callback if the problem is not resolved.

Ending the Call

Most novice counselors are worried about establishing initial rapport. Given the circumstances of many hotline calls, building a working relationship is less difficult than ending the call gracefully. Some clients, for example, are not only experiencing a crisis, but are also very lonely. Therefore, they are unwilling to break the connection with a warm and caring counselor. In fact, many clinicians have the same problem with face-to-face therapy sessions. Clients often drop little "bombshells" on the way out the door in an effort to prolong the contact. When the crisis line counselor feels the time is appropriate, he or she should review the situation and the action plan (including the referral) and ask if the client is satisfied with the intervention. The counselor should give the client clues to end the call in a way that enables the client to feel in control of the situation. With chronic calls, cues are usually ignored (see the discussion of chronic callers, below).

Suicidal Clients

Although the National Institute of Mental Health has recommended that telephone services be staffed by personnel trained in crisis intervention techniques, nonprofessionals (e.g., hospital switchboard operators) must sometimes deal with phone calls from suicidal clients (Green

& Wilson, 1988). Green and Wilson remind us that the context of these calls is "highly emotional and create[s] a sense of urgency and need for action. The callers may be uncooperative and manipulative or, worse yet, abusive and threatening" (p. 310). To assist operators in dealing with suicidal calls, a set of guidelines have been developed. The overriding purpose of these guidelines is to keep the client alive and to put him or her in contact with appropriate professional help.

There are two basic rules that must be considered when dealing with potential suicides: (a) All suicidal threats must be taken seriously despite denials by the caller to the contrary, and (b) it is essential that the operator remain calm and listen carefully. Callers must be encouraged to talk regardless of their manners of speech (e.g., rambling, incoherent, or abusive). Given that alcohol and/or drugs are frequently involved in suicide attempts, the caller may be very difficult to understand. The guidelines focus on a general approach and philosophy of response, response strategies, and rallying support for the individual. According to Green and Wilson (1988), the general approach is one of caring, empathy, and genuine concern, which they feel is the best approach for developing a sense of trust and obtaining the cooperation of the caller. Because suicidal people are frequently out of control and seeking someone to help, the counselor should emphasize his or her desire to work with the caller. The worker should suggest that the caller come in to a crisis center. If the client refuses or becomes anxious or hostile, the counselor should revert to listening and attempting to help the client focus on the healthy component of his or her personality, the part that led him or her to seek assistance.

If a second operator is available, that person should contact the police or an appropriate outside party. For this to be done, the caller must be convinced to give his or her name, present location, and phone number. Local telephone caller identification systems can help the operator locate the caller (the issue of confidentiality will be discussed later). Although persons using drugs and/or living alone are at even greater risk than other callers, it is not the job of the counselor to make that type of judgment. *All calls*, as previously noted, *are serious*. The more information about the client the operator can obtain, the easier it will be to contact significant others.

In evaluating the crisis, counselors may want to ask callers if they are contemplating doing harm to themselves. It is also important to determine whether or not the individual has a plan and a weapon. This type of information is not only critical to assessing lethality but also to warning the police what to expect. There are several other questions that the operator may ask, such as whether or not the caller has recently been released from an inpatient facility (another risk indicator), whether or not he or she has ever attempted suicide before, and whether or not he or she is feeling depressed, apathetic, helpless, disorganized, confused, guilty, ashamed, angry, or hostile. The caller should be given the number of a nearby suicide prevention center for future use. Finally, all information should be recorded.

COUNSELOR ROLES

Having reviewed over 100 articles on the topic of crisis telephone services and having served both as a volunteer and a trainer for two years, France (1975) postulated three roles for lay volunteers as "referral sources, helpers, and technique-equipped behavior changers" (p. 198). To function successfully as a referral source, the individual must have a thorough knowledge of community resources. The efficiency of novices as referral sources is easily facilitated by computerizing the information so that it can be accessed as needed. The role of helper is further described by France as requiring "a caring individual whose goal is to express genuine, warm, empathic concern to the caller" while a technique-equipped behavior changer must be trained in some type of change strategy. Many theorists cited in France (1975) consider referral to be the primary goal of suicide prevention and/or crisis services. Although many clients do not use the referrals that they receive, it may be sufficient that they know help is available.

The helping role is also called "Clinical Effectiveness" (CE) and has been defined as "the creation of a positive relationship with the caller" (McGee et al., 1972, p. 171, cited in France, 1975, p. 201). France reviewed Tanley's study of the telephone counseling relationship based on training that emphasized Rogerian theory during lectures and role-plays. Composure, competency, and comfortableness were among the factors rated. In evaluating the counselor's performance, judges listened to the entire taped phone call. It may be that the caller's responses influenced the assessment of the counselor's competence. There are clearly times when the caller seems to have his or her own agenda regardless of what the counselor says or how he or she says it.

The Fowler Technical Effectiveness Scale (Fowler & McGee, 1973) was designed to assess the major functions of the counselor from establishing communication to evaluating the caller's condition (especially with respect to potential suicide) and developing a plan of action. The performance score is based on answering "yes" or "no" to a list of questions (e.g., "Did the volunteer communicate that he is willing to help?"). There is considerable variability in how counselors are rated using this scale.

TRAINING ISSUES

There are several issues relating to the training of telephone counselors. France (1975) has listed three important questions with respect to the education of lay volunteers. The first concerns whether or not counselors are actually doing what their trainers and administrators expect them to do. For example, are they providing appropriate referrals or assisting the caller in making realistic plans? The second question concerns how effective the counselors are in what they do accomplish. After gaining experience, counselors may develop techniques that they find useful regardless of training. And finally, we must ask, especially if the counselors are not using the techniques they have been taught, what types of training would produce the desired performance? Consequently, to borrow a term popular in management journals, *management by objectives* must be instituted. First, the objectives need to be clearly defined. Trainers and program planners need to listen to experienced counselors before designing new guidelines.

REQUIREMENTS FOR REFERRALS

According to France (1975), the minimum standards for referrals should be to give accurate information that is appropriate to the problem and to the caller's needs. Complete information needed to contact an organization includes not only the name, address, and phone number of the agency but also any restrictions on the services such as fee structure or location.

The evaluation apprehension or performance anxiety of counselors must be overcome before the efficiency of telephone services can be improved. Volunteers may be unrealistically anxious about being evaluated. Therefore, it is important that trainers and administrators explain the need for evaluation and training to improve performance.

THE ROLE OF GENDER

The question of gender with respect to both clients and counselors has been investigated with mixed results. The specific issues range from which gender is more likely to ask for help and under what conditions (e.g., the gender of the helper). In a study of a crisis center telephone line, Salminen and Glad (1992) found that calls received by female counselors lasted longer than those received by males. The interaction between caller and counselor gender was, however, not statistically significant. The authors found that the most important gender differences were related to the caller. For example, both male and female counselors were able to help male callers by simply listening to their problems, but female callers were helped more with empathic understanding. Women callers were usually troubled by family, alcohol, or sexual issues. The men frequently called to "renew a contact or just to disturb" (Salminen & Glad, 1992, p. 132).

COUNSELOR CHARACTERISTICS

Butcher and Maudal (1976) described the effective crisis worker as a directive helper who is able to assess the situation quickly, intervene decisively, and generally assume a problem-solving or task-oriented approach to the situation. In 1989, Young published a study of callers' perceptions of the counselor behaviors that they considered helpful. The subjects were 80 callers who gave their permission to be interviewed immediately following their own calls to the hotline. The results indicated that clients rated listening and feedback, understanding and caring, appropriate climate, nonjudgmental support, and directiveness as the most helpful behaviors. Directiveness was, however, more closely related to positive change than nonjudgmental support (Young, 1989).

Crisis worker performance is frequently measured for Technical Effectiveness (TE), Clinical Effectiveness (CE), and Situational Effectiveness (SE). The Fowler Technical Effectiveness Scale (Fowler & McGee, 1973) was developed to rate workers on the degree to which they engage in a set of functions while answering a call. These tasks include establishment of communication, specification of the problem area, assessment of the lethality of the situation, evaluation of resources available to the client, and formation of an action plan.

Clinical Effectiveness involves assessment of the qualities of empathy, warmth, and genuineness. These qualities are typically more difficult to evaluate than those of Technical Effectiveness, which deals with the quality of the referral. Evaluations of counselor effectiveness depend on the behavior of the client. Observers look for an immediate reduction in the emotional dysfunction of the client, improvement in his or her coping skills, some evidence indicating that long-term improvement or adjustment is possible, and self-reports of satisfaction with the intervention and referral.

It may be that the personal attributes of the crisis worker, most of whom are nonprofessional volunteers with some training, are the salient characteristics with respect to generating successful outcomes. Because such traits as empathy and warmth are the very factors that motivated the individual to volunteer to serve on a hotline, almost instant rapport can be established. Consequently, once trained novices gain experience, they learn to move quickly to problem solving and other tasks such as referral. Several researchers cited in Stein and Lambert (1984) noted that, without training and guidelines, experience with hotlines does not facilitate empathy, genuineness, or warmth. The authors point out, however, that phone workers are usually evaluated as helpful by clients sometimes despite lack of training, inexperience, and even when being rated as low on empathy, warmth, and genuineness by researchers. The possibility exists that external observers may be too critical and expect spontaneity in the counselor and a fresh approach to each call when the client has no such criteria.

Although some authors have postulated that the most effective approach to the training of nonprofessionals is to engage in a "minimal degree of didactic training followed by a rapid introduction into the work situation" (Elkins & Cohen, 1982, p. 84), the most extensively used model combines a strong educational component, albeit one that varies in length of time, with supervised experience. Elkins and Cohen (1982) demonstrated that both counselor skills and counselor knowledge increased significantly immediately following training but did not improve further after 5 months of experience. They also found that some variables such as the acceptance of others and dogmatism (negatively related to both counselor skill and counselor knowledge) did not change as a function of either training or experience. One may thus draw the implication that, despite the pressing need for volunteers, procedures that identify dogmatism as a trait should be used in a selection process.

HANDLING ESPECIALLY DIFFICULT CALLS

Sometimes clients have motives other than getting help for a crisis when they call a hotline, or they may have a personality style that makes the job of the counselor particularly difficult. The *Morris County Hotline Training Manual* (n.d.) deals with a number of "games that callers play" based on Berne's (1964) list of games that people play.

The first of these troublesome situations involves so-called manipulation games. During these calls, the client challenges the counselor to prove that he or she is capable of handling the client's problem. The client may also try to make the counselor explain how it is possible for someone who does not know the caller to be genuinely concerned with his or her problems. One way to diffuse the caller's insecurities (real or imagined) on the latter issue is to work the issue into the intervention. Try saying, "It sounds as if you are worried that I won't be able to relate to you. Let's talk about that for a while" (p. 80). Thus, what is a potential source of conflict becomes a component of the intervention process.

The second problem concerns attempted role reversal. The client may ask the counselor about his or her own life history and emotional reactions. If the counselor is not wary, he or she can end up disclosing personal problems.

Another game is titled "Yes, but . . .". The "yes, but" response can frustrate even the most experienced counselor. Although the client seems to accept the alternatives, information, and/or referrals provided by the counselor, the acceptance is immediately followed by a list of excuses and explanations, frequently plausible, about why the suggestions won't work. The best strategy is to reflect back to the client the negativism being expressed and assist the caller in doing an effective job of developing viable alternatives that will overcome the barriers that he or she has presented.

Every hotline has to deal with repeat callers. There are two general approaches to working with chronic callers. One position is that they are to be discouraged at all costs because they drain the resources of the service. At the other end of the continuum are those who strongly believe that a crisis line is designed to respond to whomever calls. There are a few strategies that may help counselors. For example, clients can be reminded of the urgency of other people's calls; they may be restricted to a specified time limit; or they may be required to focus only on the presenting problem. It is also possible to transfer the call to another counselor. Because chronic callers frequently ask for a specific counselor, they may be encouraged to speak to any available volunteer, assuming there is more than one counselor.

Counselors may also respond to prank and obscene calls. According to the *Morris County Hotline Training Manual* (n.d.), counselors are to "treat all calls as if they were serious concerns to the person, regardless of how ludicrous they may appear" (p. 85). The authors of the manual suggest that if prank calls are treated seriously, the caller will probably hang up. If the hotline counselor were to terminate the call, the prankster or the chronic caller would continue to call back. When an obscene call comes in, however, the counselor must be free to hang up. Another strategy would be to use Rogerian techniques and reflect caller's feelings. One might say, "You sound very angry. Would you like to talk about what is bothering you?" Not every counselor can handle every call. After a real attempt has been made to address the caller's issues, it may be necessary to terminate the call, especially if the caller is obviously masturbating during the call. Putting the phone down and switching to another line is also possible.

The silent caller or caller who hangs up before speaking to a counselor is probably not a prankster. Frequently, very distressed clients will ring the hotline several times before working up the courage to speak to a counselor. If it is clear that someone is on the line, the counselor might say, "We are here to help you. Won't you tell me what's the matter?"

Counselors are not expected to memorize scripts and therefore must be prepared to use language with which they are comfortable. Nor are they expected to be spontaneous and original with each client. Training

and experience will help each individual develop his or her own repertoire of skills.

COUNSELOR BURNOUT

Given the nature of crisis phone calls (e.g., suicide attempts and
spouse abuse), it is to be expected that volunteers, however motivated
and well trained, may suffer from stress and, eventually, from burnout.
Crisis calls are frequently single events with no opportunity for the
counselor to ascertain the outcome of the intervention. Thus, there is
little opportunity for positive feedback and the personal gratification
that traditional psychotherapists and counselors experience. For volunteers, the frustrations and disconfirmed expectations associated with
treating high-risk clients can quickly lead to absenteeism and the desire
to stop working altogether. Cyr and Dowrick (1991) used a survey of
volunteers to identify the factors that may reduce or modify burnout
and those that increase overall satisfaction with hotline interventions.
Their results indicate that high initial expectations and subsequent
stagnation and frustration in attempting "to help people when they
don't seem to get any better" (p. 347) as well as "negative emotional
and physical reactions to the volunteer work" (p. 347) were mentioned
most frequently. Apathy, which includes a "lost feeling of caring/con-
cern for clients" (p. 347), was noted by 28% of the sample of crisis hotline
volunteers. The turnover rate in volunteers was one of the highest rated
sources of stress (44% of the respondents). Seeing other volunteers quit
and terminating peer relationships can be very distressing. Lack of
confidence in one's own skills was another negative factor.

On the positive side, the subjects discussed emotional growth,
human contact, and the ability to use helping skills as factors that
contribute to satisfaction. Both supervisory support and a sense of being
appreciated by one's supervisors were considered important variables
by two thirds of the respondents. Having the demands of the job clearly
delineated, being sufficiently well trained, realizing that it is not possible to "produce miraculous changes in the client's life" (p. 348), and
recognizing that clients cannot always benefit from the help available
were also listed as factors contributing to satisfaction. In sum, being
properly trained and supervised, and having realistic expectations about

the demands of the job and the nature of clients, prevented burnout or contributed to the management of stress. One of the most useful sections of the article reviewed the respondents' own strategies for dealing with burnout. Among the techniques listed were

1. setting limits on involvement;
2. avoiding high expectations, and "venting" with peer volunteers and staff;
3. requesting performance evaluations;
4. taking time off;
6. altering volunteer responsibilities;
7. attending to health; and
8. engaging in relaxing activities (adapted from Cyr & Dowrick, 1991, p. 347).

Holding more volunteer staff meetings, improving supervisory skills, delivering more realistic and effective training, and encouraging volunteers to take better care of themselves are all approaches that hotline administrators can employ to improve satisfaction, decrease stress and burnout, and reduce volunteer turnover.

ROLE OF ADMINISTRATORS

Although the role of counselors is to be focused on the needs of the caller, many of the administrative and managerial goals must, of necessity, relate to the viability of the organization. Auerbach and Kilman (1977) delineated the concerns of senior-level program staff. For example, administrators must simultaneously be aware of the level of satisfaction of personnel in other associated community agencies, the degree to which the program meets the needs of the community, the visibility of the service, and the degree to which the target population is even aware that the service exists. Sometimes the general population in the area does know about the program, but the group the program is designed to serve (e.g., elementary and/or high school students) is not familiar with the fact that the crisis line even exists. Especially with "hard-to-reach" groups, maintaining high hotline use rates often depends on the efficacy of an intensive media approach (Ossip-Klein, Shapiro, & Stiggins, 1984).

Some researchers are justifiably concerned about administrative or structural issues with respect to the management of the service. More than 20 years ago, McGee (1972) suggested that such considerations as record keeping systems, provisions for confidentiality, and training (presence or absence) were reflections of the efficacy and planning of a program and should be taken into consideration. Computer-facilitated record keeping procedures in human services organizations have become much simpler in recent years, thus allowing for accurate process and outcome evaluation (Waters, Robertson, & Kerr, 1993).

ISSUE-DIRECTIVE VERSUS NONDIRECTIVE COUNSELING STYLES

What is considered effective by professionals in any field, especially counseling and psychotherapy, depends very much on one's theoretical orientation. Stein and Lambert (1984) point out that the issue of directive versus nondirective counseling style is a perfect example of the problem. Those advocates of a directive, task-oriented, problem-solving style would find the strategies used by Rogerian therapists to be very unproductive. On the other hand, being too directive and potentially authoritarian can lead to the development of resistance and self-defeating behaviors on the part of the client. The most potentially facilitative approach may be to exhibit humanistic traits during the initial stages of the interaction and shift carefully into a directive role as the intervention progresses. The demographic characteristics of the client (e.g., age and sex) must also be taken into consideration, as well as the magnitude of the crisis and the client's perception of threat or challenge. Some people may only need some advice or information, but others who may expect miracles over the phone will need to be referred for possible inpatient treatment. Client evaluations of the skill of the counselor clearly reflect the reality of the situation.

SPECIAL POPULATIONS AND SERVICES

An increasing number of hotlines are designed to address the problems of specific groups. The following sample of programs is representative of the types of hotlines being implemented at the present time.

Substance Abuse

Cocores and Gold (1990) describe the 800-COCAINE hotline as a national drug abuse treatment referral and information service that receives calls from almost every region in the United States. Established in 1983, this 24-hour-a-day operation deals with almost half a million calls a year. In addition to providing information, crisis intervention, assessment, and assistance in obtaining treatment, the existence of the service has helped to increase public awareness concerning cocaine use. The line has also been used to collect important data with respect to the incidence of physical and psychological symptoms, dysfunctional behavior, marital and relationship problems, involvement with the criminal justice system, and, for adolescents, school-related difficulties and suicide attempts (Washton, Gold, Pottash, & Semlitz, 1984).

Media Call-Ins

The Child Care Switchboard (Ball, 1984) was designed to bring clients into instant contact with experts in issues related to child development. It began with phone-in radio programs in six areas in England (Bristol, Nottingham, Leeds, London, Derby, and Manchester). The idea behind the phone service was that if children or parents were in difficulty and did not know whom to contact, they could call the local radio station. People could call during one of the programs or could call a private hotline at the station. Calls were answered by a variety of experts including teachers, social workers, community police officers, and physicians, and originated from a number of different sites (public and residential phones, gas stations, offices, and factories). The average length of time for the calls to the private hotline was 20 minutes. Subsequent to the experiment with the Child Care Switchboard, other similar hotlines were established, sometimes on a temporary basis and sometimes as a permanent service.

Henricks and Stiles (1989) describe the verbal interaction between program hosts and callers during call-in radio programs. Call-in radio or television programs differ from hotlines in that they are designed as entertainment as well as the sources of personal advice and information on psychological issues. In this article, the authors are concerned with violations of the ethical guidelines established by the American Psychological Association in 1981, which permit educational content and "prohibit conducting mass media psychotherapy with callers" (p. 315). In 1986, interviews with 30 callers to six radio programs were audio-taped and analyzed according to eight categories: disclosure, edification, advisement, conformation, question, acknowledgment, interpretation, and reflection. The authors' major finding was that "edification" was the most common verbal response mode. It was used to present information, research findings, and theories of psychopathology. "Advisement" was also a major category, which may demonstrate the need to be directive in short term contact (10 minutes or less). One of the problems with analyzing these data is that the talk show host, even when a credible psychologist, is the "star" of the show and is not only expected to be entertaining but also to dominate the interaction. After all, the host's popularity is what generates ratings and determines the longevity of the program.

With respect to observance of the ethical guidelines, the authors find that it is difficult to distinguish between giving "personal advice" and "individual diagnostic and therapeutic services" because providing advice involves the diagnostic process to make recommendations.

Police Emergency Calls

A training program for 911 operators (Center for Public Safety Studies, Inc., 1991) deals with effective telephone techniques and the basics of radio broadcasting skills for police officers. The issues covered include proper tone of voice, rate of speech, and even potential sources of liability. The 911 operator is under considerable pressure to determine whether or not the statements made by the caller are actually true because dispatching the scarce resources of a police department for a false report is a serious problem. One of the difficulties with 911 is that the more experienced the operator, the more likely he or she is to draw inferences based on assumptions derived from previous patterns of calls. The operator must be careful not to make false assumptions, for example, when the caller sounds like a teenager. On the other hand, questioning all of one's assumptions can prove to be dysfunctional. The primary pressure felt by all 911 operators is to be able to process the pertinent information, classify the nature of the complaint, and follow through on the data obtained. Operators also have an advantage in that the public generally assumes that they constitute the voice of authority, and will attach a great deal of importance to what the operator says and how it is said (Nasser, 1991, p. 5).

Police emergency operators must learn to use techniques that enable them to "take charge of the conversation, sense the need of the caller, cut off superfluous wordage, ask pertinent questions of the caller, and [deal] with hysterical (emotional) callers" (p. 5). A measure of success for a 911 operator is to gather the most accurate information in the shortest amount of time. By comparison, the goal of the crisis line counselor is to keep the caller talking as long as possible, because the length of contact is usually related to positive outcomes.

Despite the fact that there are clear guidelines for addressing emergencies, newspapers are all too frequently filled with accounts of mistakes made by poorly trained and/or inexperienced 911 operators. Some of the cases appear to be a function of individuals who did not follow their "ministerial duties" (i.e., situations in which nothing is left to the discretion of the operator; "simple and definite duty, imposed by law, and arising under conditions admitted or proved to exist," p. 8), and some of the cases arise from failure to use good judgment in a "discretionary act" (i.e., "those acts wherein there is no hard and fast rule as to course of conduct that one must or must not take" p. 8). Only training and experience can reduce errors in discretionary acts.

Suicide Prevention at a High-Risk Site

Glatt (1987) describes some of the prevention methods that have been used to reach suicidal individuals prior to the actual attempt. With respect to the various sites that appear to be so "enticing" that they almost have "demand characteristics" (e.g., bridges or the observation decks of high buildings), easy access can be somewhat limited through the installation of barriers. The Mid-Hudson Bridge in Duchess County, New York, has become one of the sites chosen by potential suicides. To reduce the incidence of suicide, the Duchess County Department of Mental Hygiene and the New York State Bridge Authority installed a "dedicated line" call box that would connect the caller with the Psychiatric Emergency Service. No dialing, coins, or operator assistance were involved.

Dramatic signs ("DESPERATE? LIFE IS WORTH LIVING. PICK UP HELPLINE. 24 HOURS A DAY. Duchess County Mental Health Center") were placed near to and directly above the phone. The area around the phone was painted bright orange to increase visibility. The radio-phone system itself is designed for maximum operating reliability, to be vandal- and tamper-proof, for easy operation and maintenance, and with the ability to identify the phone location. When the caller is evaluated to be potentially suicidal, police are sent to the bridge while the counselor continues to maintain contact with the caller. Most of the people who used the phone were considered to need some form of treatment. In one case, a fire was reported, and in another, the driver of a disabled vehicle was helped. The author concludes that the system is effective and a "legitimate means for a potential suicide to make a non-destructive cry for help" (Glatt, 1987, p. 308). He recommends that the program be considered for other high-risk suicide sites.

Career Hotline for Rural Residents

The economic crises being faced by large segments of our population have led to the establishment of several career-oriented hotlines, most notably for groups such as aerospace industry workers and farmworkers (Heppner, Johnston, & Brinkhoff, 1988). Data analysis of the telephone services provided for farmers in Missouri yielded a number of themes that are also typical of others in crisis. Many callers, for example, exhibited "a wishing and hoping syndrome in which the person wishes he or she could go back to more simple times or ahead to a brighter future rather than deal with the present" (p. 341). Clients also frequently expressed the belief that someone or something would appear to save the person from the crisis (the sort of "deus ex machina" so popular in Greek drama). Many callers were cynical, resigned, and passive about the possibility of change. A number of them lacked previous experience with "life transitions," which is particularly threatening for a population that is usually stable. They were frustrated by the career change process and wanted direct solutions and single "right" answers. Finally, it was clear that they were going through a grief process similar to that associated with other types of personal loss.

Hotlines for the Elderly

As Wolf-Klein and Silverstone (1987) note, the implementation of strategies (e.g., Diagnostic Related Groups) designed to reduce hospital costs in the American health care system has promoted ambulatory care as an alternative to hospitalization for many elderly patients. These strategies are not without serious problems, especially when the frail are discharged into the community too early in the recovery process. To address the emergency needs of geriatric patients in a suburb of New York City, a 24-hour-a-day hotline was established. The service is used to request medical interventions including hospitalization, and is considered cost-effective.

The psychological value is in the security that the emergency hotline provides. Losee, Auerbach, and Parham (1988) discuss the effectiveness of a peer counselor hotline for the elderly. In evaluating callers' perceptions of the counselors' skills, the authors found that volunteers who were rated high on Technical Effectiveness (TE) after training were better at helping clients resolve their problems and in giving appropriate referrals, "but did not produce greater subjective feelings of satisfaction in callers. The reverse finding was obtained for volunteers who attained high levels of Clinical Effectiveness (CE) after training" (p. 428).

The process of aging is not only associated with many myths and stereotypes that need to be addressed, but also with some very serious life events that inevitably lead to stress responses that only serve to exacerbate the situation. The reality faced by many of even the healthiest of today's elderly population is loss of work identity and the income and social status that are an integral component of one's job role, illness, bereavement, substance abuse, and disrespect from society (Drew & Waters, 1987). It has been estimated that almost a third of the elderly are in need of mental health services. The elderly, as well as adolescents, are at risk for suicide. Moreover, although a growing number of professionals have dedicated their careers to gerontology, there are not enough to deal with the special needs of this group. In addition, many elderly people do not feel comfortable talking to younger counselors who may not have experienced some of the events that the client has faced. Trained peer counselors would seem to be the obvious solution to the staffing problem. Losee et al. (1988) report that although "telephone reassurance programs for the elderly have become increasingly common, caller-initiated hotlines directed at this population are still un-usual" (p. 29).

The HIV and AIDS Hotline

The National AIDS Hotline (NAH), a toll-free information service of the Centers for Disease Control (CDC), has received more than 1.4 million calls per year since it was established in October 1987. The NAH employees are called "information specialists" and are supported by the CDC's National AIDS Clearinghouse databases, both for referrals and for ordering publications. Not only does the service play an important role in AIDS prevention by providing information on how the virus is transmitted and how transmission can be prevented, but it also "reduces callers' fears by giving information on how HIV is *not* trans-mitted" (Waller & Lisella, 1991). The overall advantages of hotlines are relevant to the use of the AIDS service in that the caller has control over the situation, anonymity is assured, geographic barriers are not a problem, and the operator can also remain anonymous. Wark (cited in Waller & Lisella, 1991) states that "anonymity seems to enable the caller to take larger risks in the expression of painful feelings more quickly than in the face to face setting" (p. 629).

Although the NAH was initially run by volunteers, it is currently staffed by paid employees. Performance evaluations are conducted by using monitoring equipment that allows supervisors to listen to the complete interaction. Although the information specialists focus on the facts, the nature of the calls requires that "those facts be delivered in a context of concern, sensitivity, confidentiality, and trust" (Walker & Lisella, 1991, p. 633).

Services for Children and Adolescents

Nichols and Schilit (1988) describe a telephone service for a segment of the estimated 6 to 10 million self-care children in the United States. Self-care or, as they are more popularly known, "latchkey" children, spend several hours every day at home without any adult supervision. This population is expected to increase given the number of single parents in the workforce as well as the number of households where both parents are employed. In many of our embattled urban centers, there are "vagabond" children who have lost both parents to AIDS, substance abuse, crime victimization, and criminal penalties (e.g., jail and/or prison). They live in "crack houses" earning money as runners, or with neighbors, sometimes at a different address each night. In homes where parental authority is acknowledged, severe rules and restrictions may be established for the safety of latchkey children. Because these limitations reduce opportunities for social contact, latchkey children frequently report feelings ranging from boredom to loneliness to fear. In the best of all possible worlds, there would be child care alternatives such as extended schooldays. Although as a society we have not developed low- or no-cost child care options, however, some communities have instituted what they call "warm lines." Nichols and Schilit (1988) describe KIDLINE, a telephone program that supplies information, support, or assistance especially for self-care children. According to the authors, the program objectives are to

1. enable actually or potentially abused, dependent, or delinquent children to mature in as healthy and normal a manner as possible;
2. provide telephone help line services to children, ages 6 to 17, especially (but not limited to) those whose parents are out of the home, either on an emergency or an ongoing basis;
3. at all times, provide an interested, intelligent, listening ear and, when appropriate,
    a. teach children home safety and instruct in 911 usage;
    b. use supportive listening skills;
    c. provide guidance for homework, problems, accidents, illness, and so on; and
    d. make referrals to other community resources;
4. gather data for analysis that may lead to further community action (Nichols & Schilit, 1988, p. 50).

School officials and police personnel try to make sure that children are aware of the service, which is also advertised on television and promoted by celebrities such as the late Michael Landon. KIDLINE, which is based in Tucson, receives an average of 1,500 calls per month. The type of call ranges from serious safety issues to children who need to share the news of a good report card. Some children require adult guidance in how to handle a conflict, while others are worried about strange noises or parents who are late getting home. In a few cases, the police or another child protective service must be contacted; in others, the counselor can provide the service.

Kliewen, Lepore, Broquet, and Zuba (1990) analyzed the calls to a community help line for children in terms of developmental and gender trends in support-seeking behaviors during middle childhood. The growing numbers of children without responsible adult supervision have led to the development of a number of community support services, including crisis lines (Williams & Fosarelli, 1987). There has also been a concomitant increase in research concerning the effects of social support on the physical and mental health of children. The crisis lines provide informational services, referrals for emergency situations, a concerned listener for emotional problems, or distractions for lonely and bored youth. In fact, 61% of the calls in the study by Kliewen et al. (1990) were classified in the "nonproblem" category. Some children seemed to be bored or "just wanted to talk" (not very different than many adolescent and adult hotlines), or "called to hear a joke or story." The younger children (6- to 8-year-olds) were more likely to call out of boredom than the older children (11- to 12-year-olds). There were, unexpectedly, no significant gender differences. It is, of course, possible that the younger children were less capable of expressing their true needs, which may have sounded like boredom but were actually more serious. There were also fewer calls by younger children (6- to 8-year-olds) than the other age groups for a variety of reasons. Explanations range from an inability to use the phone, to the probability that fewer of the younger children are left in their own care than those in the 8- to 12-year-old category.

Teenline is a peer response telephone information service. Boehm, Chessare, Valko, and Sager (1991) report that in its first year of operation, 2,270 phone calls were recorded. Two thirds of the callers were young women; 96% of the calls were concerned with such typical adolescent issues as peer relationships and family dynamics; and some of the callers just wanted someone "to talk to." Only 4% of the calls actually dealt with crisis situations such as potential suicide and physical abuse. Although not designed as a source of therapy, *Teenline* does provide a distressed adolescent with a peer who is trained to listen to problems and help the caller use problem-solving techniques that put the situation into perspective, which serves as a model process for the resolution of future problems. The hotline also maintains an updated referral file of needed community services. The volunteers are trained to address typical issues (peer relationships and family dynamics) as well as drug and alcohol abuse, sexuality, mental illness, death and suicide, and, as the sponsoring group is a local church youth group in the Midwest, questions of spirituality.

University-Based Hotlines

Stewart and Glenwick (1992) report on a university-based peer-operated hotline. Most of the calls involved hetero- and homosexual personal relationships (22.5%), miscellaneous and school-related issues (15.2%), academic performance (11.9%), sexual performance (10.6%), and potential suicide (8.5%). Suicidal thoughts were more frequently reported by upperclassmen (juniors and seniors) than by freshmen and sophomores. Seniors in general, however, called the hotline less than the other groups.

The University of Texas at Austin Counseling and Referral Service uses self-help tapes as a component of their telephone counseling service (Chiauzzi & Carroll, 1982). The program provides a series of prerecorded tapes on a variety of physical and mental health issues. The tapes, which range from 5 to 10 minutes in length, are divided into five categories: sexuality, self-help for depression and anxiety, interpersonal skills, crises such as suicide and rape, and substance abuse. Each tape defines or describes the problem and delineates potential strategies for handling the issues and available resources. After the phone counselor has either played the requested tape or read a transcript of the material, he or she will ask if the caller desires further assistance. If the caller responds in the affirmative, the rest of the session is treated as a typical hotline call. The authors report that students have responded favorably to the service, and that the most frequently requested tapes address sexuality, self-help needs, and interpersonal skills.

Telephone Treatment for Agoraphobics

McNamee, O'Sullivan, Lelliott, and Marko (1989) report on a telephone treatment program for housebound agoraphobics. The study involved a random assignment investigation of two treatment strategies: self-exposure and telephone guided self-relaxation. The subjects, agoraphobics who stated that they were unable to attend a clinic, constituted a set of "unusually severe and unmotivated cases" (p. 491). Despite that fact, the authors hypothesized that the telephone was a potentially useful medium for supplying treatment. The results, although not as strong as in some face-to-face strategies, did demonstrate that with the use of an exposure manual, telephone treatment is an effective way to help agoraphobics with panic disorder who are unable to attend a clinic.

Information and Referral for Dementia Caregivers

Not all of the people calling hotlines are the actual patients or clients. Family members, significant others, and friends frequently call 1-800-COCAINE. The hotline for dementia patients (Alzheimer's and other related illnesses) is called by caregivers (44% of calls), family members of caregivers (31.2%), professionals who deal with dementia patients (10.4%), and individuals interested in dementia (4.8%) (Coyne, 1991). Not only are the callers interested in information and referrals, but they are also concerned about the pressures on caregivers. The predominant number of callers are middle-aged daughters and daughters-in-law who are responsible for the day-to-day supervision and direct care of the patients. The author expresses the hope that the knowledge acquired "contributes both to the well-being of both caregivers and care recipients" (Coyne, 1991, p. 388).

An Employee Assistance Hotline

In these times of organizational change, employees working for Bellcore in New Jersey can call the Employee Assistance Program (Reid, 1994). Needless to say, all employee assistance sessions are kept strictly confidential. The director of Bellcore's Employee Assistance Program, Dr. Robert I. Lynn, emphasizes the importance of open communication and supervisor sensitivity to human resource issues. The hotline is one way of ensuring that these goals can be met.

Telephone Therapy

What is reported to be the first national 24-hour professional counseling service using the telephone was established at the end of 1993 (Dr. Robert Maronne of the Summit Services Network Solutions Line, personal communication). Maronne describes the Summit Solutions Line as being directed toward clients who are not in desperate need of treatment but who could benefit from a brief counseling session every once in a while. He anticipates that the anonymity will appeal to men, in particular. The controversial service presently costs $3.99 per minute or $240 per hour.

The Summit Solutions Line is staffed by 300 licensed psychologists, social workers, and marriage and family therapists with an average of 17 years of professional experience. It is anticipated that calls will average about 15 minutes each (approximately $60). To alert the client, who might lose track of time, a tone will sound every quarter hour. Should the client wish to talk to the same therapist on a future occasion, a code number is provided. Given the nature of the brief interaction, the focus is on problem solving, not on uncovering underlying dynamics. Telephone therapy is not a new concept. Whenever therapists go on vacation or are unavailable, someone answers their crisis calls. Therapists themselves may have to deal with a crisis situation by phone (e.g., when a patient or client threatens suicide). In the case of a professional who is covering for a colleague, he or she must be responsive to the needs of the client. Unless the situation is a clear emergency, however, it would be unwise to interfere with the primary therapist's program of treatment. In many cases, the substitute therapist is engaging in a "holding action" until the therapist who is more familiar with the client's case can be reached. Now, with beepers and such technologies as "call waiting," therapists can be contacted almost anywhere almost anytime.

Tel-Med is a telephone "encyclopedia of health advice" (Clines, 1994). The caller can choose from a variety of topics including "Fears of the After-40 Man," "How to Fall Asleep," and "How to Prevent Mugging."

THE IMPORTANCE OF
GOOD PROGRAM EVALUATION

Evaluation research assesses whether or not a specific program is meeting its own goals, delivering promised services, and achieving aims that are consistent with the aims of the field. Process and outcome evaluation are used to justify continued financial support for the organization's functions. Formative evaluation, which should be conducted early in the development of the program, is used to make changes to improve the process. The competition for scarce mental health funding resources, and the pressure for accountability, have made accurate evaluation even more important in recent years than it was when these programs were first founded.

The use of telephone hotlines is most frequently justified on theoretical and pragmatic bases rather than on the results of empirical research. Many of the existing studies suffer from some serious methodological flaws. More important, follow-up research would compromise one of the main advantages of crisis lines—the anonymity of the caller. Although the concept of telephone hotlines and other related services may be justifiable, the issue of the effectiveness of such programs and the quality of counselor skills is still open to question. The basic question about the techniques used by counselors is whether or not these strategies actually reduce psychological stress and enhance coping behavior (Auerbach & Kilman, 1977). It is extraordinarily difficult to evaluate the effectiveness of hotline operations without compromising the anonymity of the callers. The problem is due to the nature of the callers, who may be rape victims, parents who have abused their children, children who have been abused themselves, runaways, drug and alcohol users, friends and family of drug and alcohol users, suicidal individuals, and others who are experiencing serious sexual, social, and even economic problems.

The dependant variables in most outcome evaluations include client self-reports of satisfaction with the intervention or perceptions of counselor effectiveness, "shows" versus "no-shows" following referrals, suicide rates, counselors' ratings of their own effectiveness, and the ratings of independent judges of simulated or real interventions.

Although most telephone services have developed specific goals, many of them also serve tangential functions that are not always evaluated. For example, although the stated objectives of one agency may be to provide information and referrals to its clients, the counselors may also generate a warm, empathic, therapeutic environment that contributes to the successful outcome of the contact and motivates the client to take further action.

The literature suggests that crisis line counselors perceive themselves to be from moderately to extremely helpful (Stein & Lambert, 1984). Counselors may, in fact, be quite accurate in their self-assessments. Self-reported distress ratings correlate well with perceptions of distress by observers. When counselors evaluate their own interventions, they frequently rely upon their perceptions of client's spontaneous outcomes rather than on formal questions concerning the caller's satisfaction with the interaction in general or the referral specifically. The client might have expressed gratitude, reported feeling relieved or more self-confident, reported thinking more clearly, or reported having gained emotional awareness, ventilated feelings, and developed a plan of action. He or she might also have accepted the helper's referral and/or received needed information rather than terminating the call at an earlier stage in the intervention. Thus, the length of the intervention is, in most cases (but not 911 calls), related to the outcome.

One of the major questions about the efficacy of hotlines relates to the differences between professional and volunteer staff. Echterling and Hartsough (1989) found that counselors with some professional training did not differ significantly from nonprofessionals in either behavior or efficacy. With repeat calls, however, the professionals who focused on problem-solving strategies were generally more successful than the nonprofessionals. The critical issue is that repeat callers frequently have chronic problems that need the attention of a professional. The conclusions are that volunteers need more training both initially and on a regular basis, and that, if possible, chronic callers should be routed to the most experienced counselors or referred to a more appropriate mental health service. The author unexpectedly found that there appears to be little need to spend excessive time on establishing rapport because, in most cases, verbal contact is easily developed.

The Crisis Call Outcome Rating Scale (CCORS) was developed by Bonneson and Hartsough (1987) to measure the outcomes of a hotline intervention. It was designed from critical incidents supplied by an initial pool of volunteers. The Crisis Call Outcome Form (CCOF) is used to measure objective statements such as "the caller said he or she felt better" and "the caller stated a specific plan of action." It also uses subjective assessments such as "the caller sighed in relief when he/she realized what to do" and "the caller's frustrated (or tense, or strident) sounding voice was constant throughout the call."

Record Keeping

Another difficulty in conducting credible evaluations concerns poor record keeping in many human services agencies. Sometimes, there are no immediate outcome data, much less long-term follow-up information. Hotlines, as well as many other mental health facilities, are loath to dedicate treatment dollars to evaluation (Waters et al., 1993). They must also be convinced that external evaluators will not destroy programs with criticism because they don't understand how difficult it is to maintain a hotline.

TELEPHONE TECHNOLOGIES

Berman (1991) discusses relatively new telephone technologies that can affect the philosophy and operation of hotline services. These technologies include Caller Identification (Caller ID), which displays the number of each incoming phone call and is usually limited to in-state or local calls; Call Block, which can prevent the connection of calls from specified numbers; and Call Trace, which can trace the "current or most recent in-coming call" (p. 407). Each one of these technologies raises philosophical issues that must be considered, especially with respect to anonymity. Among the obvious questions is the right of the hotline to use phone numbers for further interventions (however well intentioned) or the right of the hotline to prevent incoming calls from certain people who may be abusing the service. Caller ID can alert counselors to the fact that an incoming call is from a particularly difficult repeat caller, thus allowing them a few extra seconds to prepare themselves. Call Block enables the service to avoid a difficult call rather than deal with it. In other words, the technologies allow the counselors to protect themselves from harassment and avoid calls they don't want to take. If a hotline defines its role as a "rescue mission," it could use Caller ID to locate abused children. In most cases, when a life is not at stake, both the callers and the counselors may value confidentiality more than the advantages to be gained from using telephone technologies to extend the intervention. "Even in times of crisis, individuals can, and need to be, empowered rather than coerced or compelled" (p. 411).

In the concluding commentaries in Berman's article, G. Lee Judy, executive director of Life Crisis Services in St. Louis, Missouri, writes that "the paramount factor in successfully handling hotline calls is not technological capacity but the listening skills of the volunteers. By listening and clarifying, listeners can achieve the delicate work of a hotline, including preserving life" (p. 412).

Berman feels, however, that hotlines are negligent when they do not use every available strategy to save the caller's life. He writes that "there isn't a hotline worker that wouldn't rather have used Caller ID to save a life than read in the paper that the caller had killed herself or himself. That's what is at stake" (p. 413). It is clear that responsible professionals have vastly disparate views on the incorporation of new technologies into the hotline programs.

In the search for quality control, uniformity in the delivery of services, and the ability to conduct credible research, we may lose the capability to address the individual needs of some clients and to match clients to appropriate services.

In all probability, crisis hotlines and other telephone services will remain an important component in the mental health treatment process. We still need credible evaluations of counselor performance, however, as well as improved selection and training procedures.

CONCLUSIONS

There is clearly sufficient empirical evidence to attest to the utility of hotlines and other telephone responses (e.g., therapy lines). Telephone contact has several distinct advantages, a primary one being the immediacy of response. Another asset for many clients is the anonymity of the relationship. Although anonymity and lack of visual contact allow some clients increased freedom of expression, they can be a disadvantage in at least three ways. First, counselors lose important information based on nonverbal communication and the physical appearance of the caller. The client also loses the benefits of face-to-face interactions. Another disadvantage of anonymity is that there is an opportunity for prank phone calls or for chronic clients to tie up the counselors unfairly. Finally, on the asset side of the scale are two or more factors. First, the cost of the hotline is borne by the organization, not the caller, and, second, there is accessibility for people who cannot travel, especially at night. There are many individuals who are homebound and who would otherwise have no contact with a counselor. *For them, the hotline is literally a lifeline.*

In addition to the telephone hotline, modern science is also, for example, involved in the prevention of and intervention in crises. Members of Alcoholics Anonymous have used such systems as "Compuserve" for the establishment of self-help groups. The major difficulty encountered is the need for fairly sophisticated keyboard skills. Future developments (e.g., the widespread use of "phonevision") may overcome some of the disadvantages of telephone and computer-based programs and make these cost-effective systems even more useful than they are today.

Sex-Related Hotline Calls

Types, Interventions, and Guidelines

ANNE L. HORTON

CASE EXAMPLES

"I've never hurt anyone, but I find myself attracted to young boys and pornography. When I pass an adult book store I am almost sucked inside and feel I have no control. I have been thinking about approaching my next door neighbor—a kid about 10 years old who really seems to like my company. What kind of legal trouble could I get into for this?"

"My boyfriend and I have been going together for over a year and I am trying to remain a virgin. He says that oral sex isn't the same as intercourse and that he is really having some nervous problems as a result of our situation. Is he right? I'm not sleeping well anymore and cry a lot but I don't want him to leave me, but should I give in? And what about AIDS?"

"I am really unhappy and suicidal because of some sexual addiction problems I have that will eventually destroy my family and I'm in all kinds of legal hassles. I'm so confused about who I am and what I want. . . . I can't go on like this any longer . . ."

"I have been involved sexually with my 10-year-old granddaughter and I am afraid she may tell someone. If I go to get counseling I understand the counselor will have to report me and I'll be sent to prison. What can I do?"

"I found my 11-year-old son trying on his sister's bra. I am really embarrassed, but I have to know. Does this mean he is homosexual? Should I get him counseling?"

"I believe my wife is sexually involved with our 16-year-old foster son. He is very street-wise and she spends so much time alone with him in his room. . . . I accused her of being too affectionate but she says I'm perverted. Who has the problem—her or me?"

"A houseguest of mine over Christmas called me yesterday and told me he had AIDS. Is there any danger to me and my family? Can I get the disease from french-kissing or if I ate a bean dip he made for the party?"

"My wife just had a hysterectomy six weeks ago. She doesn't want to talk about it and won't let me near her. Will sex ever be normal again? Just what should I do for her now? She cries all the time."

Sexuality is a lifelong, ongoing part of one's existence, yet each individual has a completely unique and private sexual development. Thus, this important aspect of life is often misunderstood and abused. Unlike other critical areas of learned behaviors, parents do not—nor can they—directly model normal sexual interactions nor do they encourage their children to rehearse these activities as they do other important life tasks. As a result, children often receive inaccurate, inappropriate, exploitative, or limited information, and develop behaviors and desires that can result in sex-related crises that have severe, long-term effects and even present later life-threatening situations and decisions. Appropriate channels for correct information gathering and proper, responsible investigation are usually unknown, embarrassing, or forbidden. As a result, both children and adults often struggle to identify proper coping skills and stress management for their sexual behaviors throughout life. Because many people are often driven by passion and confusion rather than reason and knowledge, all manner of sexually related crisis scenarios emerge.

Today, the availability and anonymity of crisis intervention and hotline services offer those suffering from personal concerns and traumas related to sexual behaviors new, more confidential access and hope for help and relief. The many forms of sexual exploitation, sexual confusion and identity issues, sexually related diseases, and sexual crimes make serious demands for sufficient triage skills to meet the needs of these individuals. Unlike many callers whose crises are private and focused on their intrapsychic needs, crisis workers often have a twofold responsibility in respect to sexually related hotline inquiries: a responsibility to the crisis of the caller, and a responsibility for the potential crisis to other potentially endangered parties.

Regrettably, many professionals generally, and hotline workers specifically, lack the knowledge, skills, training, and willingness to meet these challenging calls appropriately. Often, as a result of ignorance, embarrassment, or unresolved transference/countertransference issues, the untrained crisis worker will blame the caller for being inappropriate in approaching a sexual issue rather than accepting the considerable challenge of helping someone in a sensitive, private, and critical area of life. Such rejection may damage these callers irreparably in the future by shaming them, discouraging them from seeking further help, and causing more harm than has been previously acknowledged.

Sex therapists currently report that the majority of the fears and concerns individuals experience and bring to their attention often require education and information, not drawn-out treatment for sexual dysfunction. Thus, an informed crisis worker can prove an invaluable, reassuring partner in distress, who reduces a potential serious sexual impairment to a mere inconvenience, rather than causing years of miscommunication and poor sexual resolution. With proper instruction and reassurance, the worker may reduce a fearful, precrisis concern for the caller to a normal, common question or misunderstanding, kindly reassuring him or her that many people have the same concern. A worker's ignorance or embarrassment must not cause more harm than good. Just as the one type of caller may be identified as innocent and normal, however, dangerous callers must be identified also. Careful training is critical because insensitive, untrained listeners may also leave others unnecessarily at risk. The informed line worker can learn how to differentiate the specific types of sexual callers and provide appropriate hotline services and referrals.

This chapter consists of the following sections:

1. First, the scope of the problem is presented, that is, an introductory, broad overview of the spectrum of sexually related calls that deserve crisis assistance and appropriate treatment and referral.

2. Second is the crisis model and its theoretical importance, that is, applying Roberts's model and related principles to these specific callers. Following the recent decades of sexual experimentation, diseases, alternative lifestyles, and deviant sexual practices, new skills in crisis application are required of crisis workers. An understanding of theory prepares good listeners to be more expert partners in these crises.

3. The general procedures section offers guidelines for the direct, specific application of Roberts's seven-step model for responsible hotline workers in working with a sex-related call.

4. Desirable qualities and skills of well-trained line workers in approaching sex-related callers are explored.

5. The final section discusses treating 10 specific types of sex-related calls and appropriate guidelines. This section also discusses what services should be offered by responsible crisis workers.

SCOPE OF THE PROBLEM

Today, sexual behaviors are involved in many crisis situations and often lead to severe personal and criminal consequences that must be responsibly addressed in crisis training. Yet, most trained counselors are unprepared to identify and treat them. Therefore, new line workers in particular should be reassured that the breadth of information they possess will no doubt initially be lacking in many areas. Nevertheless, opportunities for prevention and precrisis intervention in serious sex-related situations, even crimes, offer compelling incentive for providing and developing a sufficient and constantly growing knowledge base.

Because sexuality is generally regarded as a taboo topic, many line workers themselves state that they have little experience discussing these topics. This gap in line worker comfort must be addressed as a major training concern. Many graduate students and casework training classes will laugh and minimize the importance of role-playing sex-related callers, of discussing routine sexual behaviors in practice sessions, and of learning the basics of human sexuality. Although humor and minimization are common defenses most people use when they are uncomfortable discussing topics, trainers must be particularly sensitive to these obvious attempts at avoidance. Thus, this portion of the training is essential and must not be downplayed. It is better to openly confront someone's discomfort in training than to risk poor crisis management later. Therefore, it is critical to stress that listeners who have their own sexual issues and questions poorly resolved are inappropriate crisis workers and need to be identified as quickly as possible. Even child protective service workers who work exclusively with sexual abuse indicate they have problems discussing these aspects of sexuality and this is the thrust of their training (Lynn, Jacob, & Pierce, 1988). Yet, adequate education and understanding in these sensitive areas will greatly enhance prevention, intervention, and empowerment.

Currently, many callers reach out to crisis lines as their only confidential hope of information services and change when traditional services appear inaccessible or problematic. Because sex-related crises are so varied in their nature, no one specific group can be targeted, but a brief overview of sex-related statistics may jolt the reader's awareness. A few initial in-depth examples are described below, followed by a broader overview of the general nature of sex-related calls.

> The Gays Counselling Service (GCS) of New South Wales is a grassroots, homosexual, self-help, community organization that is committed to serving the needs of Australia's gay and lesbian populations. Staffed entirely by volunteers, who range from adolescents to middle-aged adults, GCS provides a number of programs. The Gayline, GCS's basic service, is a telephone hotline that operates daily between 4 p.m. and midnight. The Gay Crisis Network offers support and care to victims of legal harassment, violence, and rape. The AIDS Counselling Service is made up of five components. Among these are: 1) peer-counseling support for patients with Acquired Immune Deficiency Syndrome (AIDS); 2) the Community Support Network which coordinates home-help services for AIDS patients; 3) the Bobby Goldsmith Foundation which raises money to be used to assist AIDS patients directly; 4) Gay Counselling Workshops acquaint helping professionals with specific aspects of counseling gays and lesbians; and 5) Information Services which produce the annual "Sydney Gay Guide," a resource manual. (Goulden, 1985)

The AIDS epidemic alone has provided ample need for crisis and precrisis information that is incalculable in its scope. Because death is the inevitable outcome for this disease, no lives will be untouched by this tragic problem. The resulting pain, suicides, shame, loneliness, and traumas that are AIDS related demand ongoing crisis training and compassion on the part of all crisis workers. Information gathering and the ability to apply crisis skills to this specific disease should be part of a responsible crisis workers' continual effort to improve their skills, knowledge, and expertise. Most larger communities have various services available and many offer an AIDS "101" information class that should be part of all current in-service training for crisis workers.

In a national study of services to incest perpetrators, hotlines were considered to be among the "least helpful" resources by the offenders reaching out for help. According to perpetrators, hotlines were widely criticized primarily because of their inability to advise and their overall insensitivity to offenders' needs. While clearly not all agencies can meet the needs of all perpetrators, most offenders' complaints about current crisis lines involved the listener's lack of understanding, lack of empathy and lack of knowledge about incest.

Major complaints regarding clinical services were: 1) counseling professionals did not know enough about incest; 2) they were untrained about its dynamics and causation; 3) they did not understand the problem or the perpetrator; 4) they held many myths about incest; 5) some expressed open hostility toward the perpetrator; and last, but most distressing, 6) the counselors did not know what to suggest, many denied or minimized the problem, assuming that recognition or expressed remorse constituted a cure. Perpetrators themselves suggested and responsible crisis line trainers felt it would certainly seem advantageous today, with the large number of child sexual abuse reports, for the treatment community to combat this problem by creating a "hotline" or emergency service for perpetrators or incestuous families on a 24-hour-a-day basis, have crisis workers who are specifically knowledgeable about incest, and offer all new workers appropriate training.

Perpetrators, like all clients, want trained professionals who understand the problem and are in touch with appropriate referrals and interventions. Statements such as "you should be locked up," "leave your family," "many men have feelings like those you've expressed—it's normal," or "it sounds like you've learned your lesson" were defined as unsatisfactory. Offenders preferred to get a true evaluation of their offense and to deal with hard realities, rather than have it either lightly dismissed or overexaggerated. (Horton, Johnson, Roundy, & Williams, 1990, p. 161)

Today, sex-related mental health crises also often involve lesbian and gay clients, and line workers may have important and sometimes lifesaving roles to play in the psychological well-being and empowerment of gay people. Studies suggest that up to 30% of adolescents who kill themselves are gay; this is three times the national average rate. Because gay teenagers are usually shamed by friends, peers, and family, quite often these teenagers suffer alone and hesitate to seek help. Often, crisis workers too do not approach the issue of sexual orientation; instead, they inquire about other associated problems such as school failure, depression, social isolation, and substance abuse, rather than the primary concern.

Other sex-related calls address issues ranging from intimacy and relationship concerns to self-esteem, pornography, and the media. Crisis workers must be ever watchful of the growing breadth of knowledge concerning sexuality and never dismiss a client's call, fear, or threat as inappropriate or unimportant. Today, the number of therapists who do clinical work as exclusively qualified specialists in the area of human sexuality has expanded incredibly. The well-trained, sensitive clinician must quickly recognize that the complexity of sex-related problems demands continual study of a wide range of areas and an openness to explore specific journals as well as appropriate popular media. Each of the many specific sex-related concerns may demand unique research on the line worker's part to assist with these special needs.

The potential scope of the problem is incredibly challenging. Although no line worker can be expected to be an all-knowing expert, he or she can be vigilant, clinically astute, and take these concerns seriously. The following are only a few of the sex-related issues a crisis worker may encounter:

Abortion and teenage pregnancy. Statistics for these problems are higher than at any other period in history. This severe method of birth control and the fear of pregnancy, however, may be devastating not only to the pregnant or formerly pregnant female but also to the male involved as well.

Child sexual abuse. Assistance for victims and abusers always represents a crisis and the growing amount of information in this area demands constant awareness and study.

Rape/sodomy/date rape/marital rape. New laws, the rising number of reports, special dynamics, and the criminal aspects of this crisis area demand trained specialists to guide line workers and explain agency protocol.

Special in-service training should focus on the critical areas of immediate medical and legal concern as well as the emotional and physical trauma.

The rise in sex-related crimes and behaviors. In the past 10 years, the prison population for sex-related crimes has more than tripled.

Additional potential areas.

- Homosexuality, cross-dressing, gender confusion
- Prostitution
- Treatment in ERs for sex perversion
- Sexual identity issues/physiology concerns
- Sexual practices/education/expectations
- Sex-related dysfunctions/pathological sexual practices/crimes
- Diseases/addictions
- Harassment/sexual exploitation
- Pornography

THE CRISIS MODEL FOR
SEX-RELATED CALLERS: ROBERTS

Like other forms of crisis, those related to sexual distress take many forms but certainly fit the overall crisis (theory) model promoting an initial careful, holistic assessment of the individual and his or her problem (Roberts & Roberts, 1990, 1991). Because Roberts's "seven-stage model" (Roberts & Roberts, 1991) offers responsible treatment steps for crisis intervention workers generally and is explained at other points in this text (i.e., see Chapter 1, which offers a review of this step-by-step approach), this chapter focuses solely on sex-related issues, stressing information, education, and empowerment as well as other prompt (24-hour), action-oriented interventions.

In addition, as sexual behavior is so closely linked with morality, legality, and values, and because it involves such a complex emotional range of responses, levels of dangerousness, and room for individual differences, the appropriate modification steps in the seven-stage model as well as specific theoretical considerations will be offered on a case-by-case, level-by-level approach for better reader understanding and application. These aspects will be discussed specifically and coupled with each intervention under consideration. Proper emphasis will be stressed to protect the caller, hotline volunteer, and community.

Unlike other forms of crisis, from a theoretical standpoint, it is critical to remind personnel that these sex-related calls represent an extremely challenging responsibility. Although, by definition, most crises are "time limited" and not lifetime problems, and the line worker is not expected to provide or "be" a specific form of therapy, these clients still represent appropriate hotline inquiries, albeit somewhat nontraditional and atypical. In addition, unfortunately, the period of imbalance, the accompanying symbolic meaningfulness of the event, and the threatening quality of these experiences to these callers may extend into dysfunctional repeated life beliefs or behaviors. These may create unnecessary pain for a victim with sex-related concerns for a lifetime and recur periodically. Finally, a specific, identifiable event that triggers most crisis inquiries often is not simply extracted, immediately diagnosed, or easily understood. Sexual difficulties or crises may happen years after the crisis event. Victims of post-traumatic stress disorder are good examples of this phenomenon. A line worker's respect for privacy and sensitivity to the caller's discomfort must be uppermost in the worker's mind and remain present as an important ongoing factor. Callers often "lose their nerve" partway through an intervention. Practice will help listeners learn how to collect necessary, specific, and direct information without offense but it is always a primary line worker consideration.

GENERAL PROCEDURES
AND GUIDELINES FOR HOTLINE LISTENERS

Starting Where the Counselor Is

A number of years ago, Carl Rogers advised that therapy begin "where the client is." Treating sexual issues in crisis-related situations, however, requires solid crisis intervention skills and healthy sexual attitudes that emphasize self-awareness—a willingness to examine personal stereotyping biases and sensitivities.

Therefore, in addressing sexually related calls, healthy crisis workers must be certain how comfortable they are with (a) their own sexuality,

(b) any unresolved sex-related issues of their own, and (c) any overall sexually related topics, and they must possess (d) an ability to discuss sexual issues dispassionately and in keeping with an overall responsible treatment plan. All line workers should begin evaluating their effectiveness in this area by taking a personal inventory as their first step. Some suitable opening questions would include the following:

1. Ask yourself: *Is this call appropriate? Do I feel comfortable with it?*
2. Ask yourself: *How much do I know about the caller's concern?*
Note: Often we feel uncomfortable because
   a. we lack knowledge;
   b. we lack experience (ideally, all line workers would have a basic course in sexuality training);
   c. we lack credibility (i.e., being unmarried or sexually inactive, young, or the like);
   d. we lack proper emotional distance;
   e. we've been taught not to discuss these things; or
   f. transference and countertransference.
Therefore, if we lack knowledge, experience, or information, we must learn to seek it diligently—to do our homework.

3. *Do I have good resources available by the phone? And am I constantly working to increase my knowledge?* To do so, you should establish a responsible reference file:
   a. There should be at least three recent, reputable books on human sexuality (i.e., *Human Sexuality* by Masters & Johnson, 1988; "Sexual Trauma and Psychopathology" by Shapiro & Domeniak, 1992; *Our Sexuality* by Crooks & Baur, 1990, as well as many others).
   b. There should be an organized and continually updated, alphabetically arranged topic file addressing just sexuality issues, that is, AIDS, bestiality, bisexuality, contraception, and so on with easily identified, more focused subtopics (e.g., "lesbians in abusive relationships," "genital herpes"). These should be categorized by specific reference for easy and speedy retrieval.

4. *Does my agency offer an entire training session with specific role-plays and exercises emphasizing sexual awareness and sexuality attitudes?* This is strongly recommended at the outset of line worker training. Certainly it should be emphasized that we do not have equal comfort levels with each delicate or sensitive area. Nonetheless, each worker should identify his or her own weaknesses, biases, stereotypes, myths, and value judgments early on before imposing them on callers.

5. *Do I* trust *my client? Do I* trust myself? Although clients will usually focus on revealing information to you that presents them in the best light, careful listening and genuine respect and interest must be extended to every caller. Kindness and reassurance concerning their own abilities—based primarily on your initial "gut"-level feeling about their situation—should always encourage you to give the clients' and your assessment skills adequate faith in that you and the clients have usually given this concern more thought than anyone else. Remember, you are a fellow traveler to help guide their journey, not a tour director expected to run it.

6. *Do I* validate *each caller and the purpose of the call? dispel embarrassment or anxiety about seeking help?* The following are examples of comments that are reassuring: "Your concern is certainly an important one but I can hear in your voice that it is hard for you to talk about it. . . ." or "Isn't it interesting how important sex is in our lives and how hard it is to talk about at first?" or "I think if you can just consider it an information call . . . and we get lots of them . . . it might be easier." In the course of all crisis workers' careers, they will find their "caring" and willingness to be involved often offers more—far more—meaningful long-term solutions than a straightforward answer. Ideally, you can accomplish both.

7. Don't be afraid to say you don't know, but don't let it go at that. Seek more answers as a partner with the callers, not an expert. Let them know you truly care about their challenge and arrange to get the information for them or refer them appropriately.

8. Also, because clients are generally so motivated toward change during crises, it is an excellent time to learn the information together. It will soon be obvious that your information may be limited or even incorrect. Nonetheless, when callers can *trust* you to be honest with them, they are generally quite accommodating about waiting a few hours and will call you back while you consolidate your resources.

9. Own your own discomfort—don't ever make a caller feel guilty for asking a question. Admit that you have never discussed a particular area and don't feel as knowledgeable as you would like but that you want to help and if the caller can help explain a bit more thoroughly, you will work with him or her to find the solution. Reassure callers that no problem is insurmountable and you will search for the answer with them.

10. Talk to others who have had similar specific problems if firsthand knowledge is not available to you. Then encourage your caller to check back with you or put the caller in touch with these more knowledgeable resources.

11. Don't discuss a topic when you cannot overcome the loathing or distaste you initially feel. Make an immediate, appropriate referral when you feel squeamish, disgusted, or downright embarrassed or call in a colleague. I hope this warning will encourage you to get some more information or know yourself better in a specific area but meanwhile it must not be done at the caller's expense.

12. Don't give double messages: "This decision is yours but because you asked what I would do . . ." or "Of course, I can't advise you to leave your husband."

13. Always refer to good resources—check them out beforehand. A well-researched resource file following careful personal investigation and a personal interview is essential. It is most helpful to have a personal working relationship with a few professionals who are readily available to you as consultants.

14. Talk to a friend to desensitize yourself about discussing topics that you know you are sensitive about yourself (divorce, hemorrhoids, and so on).

15. Do not be self-righteous, judgmental, condescending, or *presumptuous*. Ask questions. Be clear, not vague. Remember, however, that you are discussing a sensitive issue so move considerately. Make certain all your questions are specifically related to the crisis situation and are in no way voyeuristic or improper. Ask questions without embarrassment and be direct. Many sexually related problems are ignored because the callers and/or the worker were too uncomfortable to mention the problem.

16. Do not state you know how someone else feels or relate your own personal experiences. Intimate topics require candid advice and open communication but must not involve intimate revelations. Appropriate boundaries are very important and the crisis listener must set them. Relationships with certain intimate components often lead vulnerable clients to further victimization. Tragically, today, even the clergy and therapists themselves are sexually exploiting many victims.

17. Listen to the caller very carefully. Get to know his or her concerns, background, and perspective. Cultural differences have a great impact

on this communication and also influence sexual expectations, feelings of entitlement, and additional exploitation.

18. Select your choice of words carefully. Our nonverbal cues are the most powerful and our level of familiarity establishes a role pattern. At what level do you speak concerning sexual acts and behaviors—street? common? technical? Be careful of innuendoes and nonverbal cues. Be approachable but professional.

19. Be aware of implications—intentional or unintentional. Be tolerant and flexible.

20. Some topics are emotional no matter how carefully approached. For instance, how do you tell a 16-year-old to wear deodorant without offending? Or encourage less provocative clothing styles? Yet, these delicate, important concerns need sensitive consideration at the same time that you provide direct, accurate information.

DESIRABLE QUALITIES FOR CRISIS WORKERS IN ADDRESSING SEX-RELATED TOPICS

Crisis workers in many respects have the most demanding mental health positions in working with crises in family life and they are on duty 24 hours a day. They often must make crucial clinical assessments and decisions instantly and then have full accountability for the outcome. Hotlines are always understaffed and depend on all other community services to support and help them with their various client problems. Whether a young woman has been brutally sexually assaulted or a wiener was forced into a young bride's vagina or if a young man is suicidal because his lover is HIV-positive; crisis, pain, and problem solving must be promptly provided.

Therefore, ideally, the crisis worker, who no doubt will face repeated sexual behavior and crisis-related calls that sound improbable, will soon gather a potpourri of skills, talents, and compassion that will be necessary to good crisis response in these areas. Ideally, this line worker will focus on the following:

1. Create a comfortable, open, and trusting relationship—offer warm and friendly help, yet always be honest and speak directly about unpleasant consequences when appropriate. Always discuss serious problems directly; avoid evasion.

2. Be comfortable in discussing any sexual topic. More training time needs to be focused on the "basics" and good referrals in each of the areas you address as a line worker. Study your own body language when you discuss touchy topics. Your actions, tone of voice, and expressions must be congruent with what you are saying.

3. Positive attitudes, respect, and personal regard for any sexually perceived groups or belief systems must allow clients to still possess a genuine, intrinsic worth while discouraging the undesired behaviors.

4. Know your referral services and stay close to them. Make complete referrals so that the client is not left hanging or is unable to negotiate the system adequately. Always follow up.

5. Be prepared for the wide range of sexual practices, preferences, and logical sexual tie-ins to other more commonly expressed forms of sex-related crises. Be open to other positions and perspectives.

6. Be able to ask about specific direct sexual concerns and their obvious implications. Also be willing to explore the distasteful. Identify atypical behavior quickly.

7. Develop the ability to place emphasis on how well certain behaviors work for people and what effects these behaviors have. Being nonjudgmental does not mean having no judgment at all.

8. All workers are as unique as their clients when it comes to their personal sexualization. More emphasis needs to be placed on conflict or crisis resolution rather than what is "normal" versus what is pathological.

9. Experience, comfort, and skill in processing sexual problems and problem solving allow clients to speak freely. Listen closely to them and hear their specific "unstated" concerns as well as the more obvious ones. Focus on the issues, not on moralizing, minimizing, or degrading the caller.

10. Be flexible, creative, and accepting. Tolerance and support, if presented properly, are not the same as condoning another's inappropriate behavior.

Crisis line workers who are carefully and specifically trained can then easily follow Roberts's seven-stage model. All his suggestions should be sensitively and professionally considered and appropriately applied. Because sex-related issues are so sensitive, trained line workers should avoid

a. preaching or lecturing/judging;
b. stating that they know exactly how the caller feels or that it is *wrong* for the caller to feel specific feelings;
c. rushing clients or hurrying them to reveal painful, intimate concerns;
d. minimizing or dismissing a problem or telling the client that it should be resolved by now;
e. blaming, threatening, or disturbing the caller; and
f. advising clients toward simplistic conclusions or that they should not be concerned.

TREATING TEN SPECIFIC TYPES OF SEX-RELATED CALLS: PROCEDURES AND GUIDELINES

Sex-Related Callers: Who Are They?

Hotline callers who introduce sex-related issues represent an important cross section of users because many of them are potentially "at risk," vulnerable, or dangerous clients. Because sexual behaviors are so private and hidden, sexual exploitation, highly destructive practices, and criminal sexual behaviors often go undetected and unreported. Certainly most are not announced in advance. Some painful situations are never exposed because the public and even others in one's own closest social circles cannot be trusted to understand the behaviors. Also, sexual problems can create such despair and embarrassment to victims and offenders that they may result in other life-threatening crises. Daily, however, more people are coming forward to share experiences concerning sexual behavior that are unacceptable or undesired or that created long-term disturbances that were previously never brought up. Specific types of callers are as follows:

- The healthy, but uninformed—"all you wanted to know about sex but were afraid to ask" (with the crisis line becoming the information connection)
- Victims—those being sexually exploited or abused
- Abusers—those abusing others in some sexual manner or who are considering such behavior
- Family/friends—intimates who have fear about the sexual behaviors or attitudes of others but who are not directly involved
- Law enforcement, religious leaders, treatment providers—all secondarily involved in unusual sexual activities

Ten Specific Types of Sex-Related Callers: What Do They Want? What Will Help?

(1) Information callers are the most common sex-related crisis line users. Because many callers have no other known resources, they call out of desperation, confusion, or lack of adequate knowledge and skills. Their questions are appropriate ones that need to be treated with respect, appropriate warmth, and professionalism.

Examples:

Can I get pregnant if I'm still nursing my baby?

Can I get AIDS from french-kissing or a bean dip made by someone who has it?

Can I have sex if I get a hysterectomy?

Specific interventions and suggestions. Often, extensively trained clinicians may know the appropriate answer. Others may need to refer the caller to the reference sources they have prepared for themselves. Seldom are referrals to sex therapists or gynecologists necessary for information calls. If your knowledge is incomplete, however, it is always appropriate to make good referrals and risk giving callers too much information as opposed to too little.

(2) A strong need to talk. Many callers lack trusted listeners and need to discuss sensitive topics that are very much on their minds. They may wish to get something off their chests but not wish to have the information generally known or risk a lifetime of questions and reminders about some sexual concern that has long since past. Often, these callers do not want advice but affirmation and validation of their concerns.

Examples:

My husband told me he's having an affair . . .

In a letter my daughter wrote her girlfriend she admits to being intimate with her boyfriend. I am beside myself . . .

I just found some pornographic magazines in my son's drawer.

Specific interventions and suggestions. Patience and good listening skills are usually all that is required under these circumstances. Clinicians must always attend the caller closely, however, as there may be some underlying concerns that won't be readily volunteered. Clients are also very sensitive about discussing these problems, so paying close, informed attention is critical.

(3) Fear. Young people as well as elderly people and often others who live alone are particularly vulnerable to sexual fears and the unknown. Many callers are afraid of their own feelings or desires. Certainly the media set up a lot of opportunity for late-night insecurities. These sexual fears need to be addressed but often involve a lot of feelings.
    Examples:
        What if I'm pregnant . . .
        I am afraid someone may break in and rape me.
        I am attracted to another girl and don't know how to change. It will kill my parents but I am so lonely when she is gone.

Specific interventions and suggestions. In addition to good listening skills and diagnostic practices, sexual fears, which are often triggered by recent experiences, need sensitive exploration and more in-depth discussion. Careful history taking and a discussion of recent sexual practices may help dispel these sexual fears. Further referrals may be required if medical, psychiatric, or legal advice is needed but often it is possible to reassure the caller if he or she is confused, lonely, or misinformed. Listen closely for the "unstated" content in callers' fears. Also remember that when people are afraid, even diagnosed as paranoid, there is usually a grain of truth to their concerns so do not dismiss sexual fears and inquiries too lightly.

(4) Decision making. Although moral questions are often very subjective and value-laden, a good crisis line listener can help a caller with problem-solving skills and support for the difficulty of deciding.
    Examples:
        Should I have sex with my boyfriend?
        Should I tell my daughter she was born out of wedlock?
        Is masturbation really wrong?

Specific interventions and suggestions. Most therapists and line workers consider providing information and discussing alternatives as the major focus of their services and most advisable where decision making is involved. Value judgments, religion, and morality are usually not considered appropriate areas to influence or discuss with callers. Nonetheless, with callers who are concerned with these subjects, avoiding or refusing to talk about them may also mean denying a caller much needed services. Of interest, beyond listening carefully and discussing options with a client, many therapists feel that hotline listeners have an obligation to the caller and the community to provide advice about the "responsible" use of sexuality and carefully detail the severe consequences of sexual exploitation. Beyond weighing the factors involved in making the decisions, the following is the surprising response by youth worker specialists to the question:

> "Should professionals—therapists/educators/ministers/researchers, etc. —take a position against young teenagers, 12 to 17, engaging in sexual intercourse?" was asked of subscribers to *Children and Teens Today* (in May 1986). Of the first 258 responses, an overwhelming majority—73 percent—said, "yes," they supported that position. Twenty-five percent said, "no"; an additional two percent did not answer the question.
>
> Those who took a yes-position in support of telling teens not to engage in sexual intercourse, explained their reasons for doing so as follows:
>
> "I see alcoholism and sexuality struggles most often in my work with teens. I would love to get more support in the fight against teenage sexual activity." Topeka, Kansas.
>
> "I am not a moralist, but I think there are strong physical, emotional and spiritual reasons why teen sexual intercourse can be very damaging." North Suburban, Illinois.
>
> "Sex between teenagers always leads to many problems. Of course, professionals should try to help by sharing with them the intended purpose for sex and the consequences of participating in it outside of marriage. The home is where our youth should learn about sex. I've yet to see any sure evidence that sex education in the schools has helped at all." Wabash, Indiana.
>
> "Not an extreme position—but advise against it—help kids to see disadvantages, make own decisions." North Bay, California.
>
> "I'm very conflicted about my answer to #1. I believe contraceptives and abortion should be available, but the best solution is to delay intercourse." North Jersey, New Jersey. . ." ("Youth Workers," 1986)

Clearly, line workers have quite a bit of room for discretionary behavior in these instances, according to this study. Those listeners who clearly are unwilling to allow an open discussion of alternatives or refuse to consider various moral alternatives (i.e., abortion, homosexuality, and so on), however, are obviously limited by their own belief systems and may need to refer those callers to other line workers.

Certainly it is critical for well-trained workers to avoid

a. regarding their own opinion as being "common sense" and the only rational alternative,
b. approaching the listener or inquiry with a closed mind,
c. confusing opinions with facts, and
d. stereotyping and judging.

It is helpful for the well-trained line worker to recall the following:

The only way in which a human being can make some approach to knowing the whole of a subject, is by hearing what can be said about it by persons of every variety of opinion, and studying all modes in which it can be looked at by every character of mind. No wise man ever acquired his wisdom in any mode but this. (John Stuart Mill)

(5) To get attention or testing. Adolescents, borderlines, and more dramatic callers are well aware that sex catches interest. Often, if they feel their problems lack interest to the hotline worker, they will inappropriately add spice to their calls. At other times, they are afraid of rejection and poorly approach a subject of real importance to them.

Examples:

I don't suppose you'd want to talk to me if you knew I'd had an abortion.

My husband wants to have sex at least three times a day.

No one is as promiscuous as I am!

Special interventions and suggestions. Attention-getting and testing behaviors in the area of sexuality can really challenge the boundaries of good, concerned line listeners and line workers who are naive, too invested, or who have their own sexual problems to address. As soon as the crisis worker detects any sexual innuendoes and sexual drama, it must be confronted and clearly defined as inappropriate. Sometimes these callers are tricky and may be genuinely worried about a sexual matter. If the caller is genuinely fearful of being judged or disliked because of previous sexual practices, a reasonable measure of reassurance is appropriate.

When callers dwell on and emphasize sexual issues to hold a line worker's attention, however, their comments and concerns need to be immediately addressed and identified as inappropriate. Then statements like the following ones can be used to follow up:

"We have been discussing your financial and child rearing problems. Why are you now bringing up your husband's sex preferences? Is this a primary concern? If so, I need to refer you to an expert because that isn't relevant to what you originally stated was your problem."

"I am not concerned about your past sexual behavior unless it is relevant to our current topic. Is your promiscuity really important or do you wonder if I might think less of you because of your past? To help you, we must define the problem, not worry about judging you. I always admire someone who tries to improve her situation. Let's get back to discussing your major concern."

Sometimes the line worker may be confused on the proper responses to these types of callers, but experience and awareness will be very helpful. Review the overview of guidelines as well and trust your "gut response" on these matters. You will intuitively learn to sense inappropriate calls and danger, and to confront them as quickly as you are aware of them.

The final types of calls are more serious in their nature and need careful monitoring, sufficient training, and special precautions:

(6) Seduction or intimacy: Confusing the role of the worker, and masturbation. Often callers may be repeaters and are known to the agency or to specific listeners. Occasionally, the caller may attribute more to the intimate nature of the relationship than is appropriate. Such situations need monitoring. Unfortunately, this occasionally results in worker-client double messages and inappropriate meeting:

Examples:

We get along so well. I feel you really understand me. Could we meet somewhere and discuss this further?

You really sound pretty to me. Why don't you describe what you are wearing for me?

Do you know how exciting it would be to be on a bear rug in front of a roaring fire with me?

Special interventions and suggestions. See situation type 5.

(7) Shock or upset worker. These calls occur in all agencies on occasion, and a direct, aggressive protocol should be in place for the following:
  Obscene suggestions
  Vulgar language
  Heavy breathing

Special interventions and suggestions. See situation type 5.

(8) Call for help when callers are calling with fear of no self-control or as a potential victim. Some abusers or potential abusers may call for assistance in alleviating their dangerousness to self or others. It is particularly important to work with those seeking early interventions.
  Examples:
      I was an incest victim and I'm afraid of what I might do to my own daughter . . .
      I feel like exposing myself to someone again.
      I've thought of raping someone and I'm afraid I might do it.

Special interventions and suggestions. When perpetrators or callers contemplating any extreme, dangerous behavior toward another are calling for assistance, immediate support should be offered for their wisdom in calling and an available trained professional must be involved. When dangerousness to oneself or others is contemplated, needs for help should be addressed in the following order:
  a. Help must be provided for the victim.
  b. Support and treatment must be offered to the caller.
  c. Others affected by the sexual experience may receive assistance.

Trained professionals and agency protocol should be in place to protect all concerned in this situation. Backup degreed personnel must make these more complex diagnostic and referral decisions. (Do *not* overstep your expertise.)

(9) When reporting is mandatory. Because the crisis worker does not have complete information on clients, the worker's responsibility to report is limited. Nonetheless, workers must know the laws and advise the client accordingly:

Examples:

> I have been involved with a 10-year-old neighbor girl and I'm afraid someone might catch me.
>
> When my wife and her boyfriend walk out of this motel I'm going to blast him with a shotgun.

Special interventions and suggestions. Mandatory reporting today consists of several legal dictates that line workers must be advised of and trained about thoroughly. The major areas that need specific sessions explaining current agency and community practices are

a. duty to warn and protect, and privileged information

b. child abuse and neglect

c. confidentiality

d. dual relationships

Because line workers usually do not know their client's identity, the rules and ethical standards will vary from state to state and in keeping with their situational limitations. Nonetheless, agencies and line workers are obliged to offer the best possible and most responsible services to these clients and to the community. Specific training and protocols are a must for line workers. *Never* deviate from prescribed policy.

(10) Dangerous and pathological calls. These callers, like all dangerous individuals, are unpredictable and unstable. There must be no delay in reporting practices and pursuing appropriate actions:

Example:

> Threats—to you or others

Special interventions and suggestions. See situation type 9.

CONCLUSION

Sexuality patterns and practices continue to change but responsible crisis line workers manage to uphold consistent patterns that attempt to assist callers and empower them to resolve pressing challenges in these specific areas of their lives. Because there is no such thing as "normal" or "correct" in regard to most sexual behaviors except in certain legal instances, the line worker must constantly meet the challenge of learning what we do know, not bemoaning the areas we still do not understand. Following the preceding correct principles is a positive and important step in that direction.

References

Abramowitz, M. (1988). *Regulating the lives of women*. Boston: Southland.

Aguilera, D. C., & Messick, J. M. (1982). *Crisis intervention: Theory and methodology* (4th ed.). St. Louis, MO: C. V. Mosby.

American Psychiatric Association. (1987). *Diagnostic and statistical manual of mental disorders* (3rd ed., rev.). Washington, DC: Author.

American Psychiatric Association. (1994, March). *Diagnostic and statistical manual of mental disorders* (4th ed.). Washington, DC: Author.

American Psychological Association. (1981) Ethical standards of psychologists. *American Psychologist, 36*, 633-638.

Anderson, S. C. (1993). Anti-stalking laws: Will they curb the erotomaniac's obsessive pursuit? *Law and Psychology Review, 17*, 156-185.

Appelbaum, S. A. (1975). Parkinson's law of psychotherapy. *International Journal of Psychoanalytic Psychotherapy, 4*, 426-436.

Asencio, D., & Asencio, N. (1983). *Our man is inside*. Boston: Little, Brown.

Association for Media Psychology. (1982). *Guidelines*. Santa Monica, CA: Author.

Aston, H. (1991). Psychotropic drug prescribing for women. *British Journal of Psychiatry, 158*(Suppl. 10), 30-35.

Atkeson, B., Calhoun, K. S., Resick, P. A., & Ellis, E. (1982). Victims of rape: Repeated assessment of depressive symptoms. *Journal of Consulting and Clinical Psychology, 50*, 96-102.

Auerbach, S. M., & Kilman, P. R. (1977). Crisis intervention: A review of outcome research. *Psychological Bulletin, 84*(6), 1189-1217.

Bakke, E. W. (1933). *The unemployed man*. London: Nisbet.

Bakke, E. W. (1949). *Citizens without work*. New Haven, CT: Yale University Press.

Ball, R. (1984). The child care switchboard experiment. *Early Child Development and Care, 13*, 185-191.

Beck, A. T. (1967). *Depression: Clinical, experimental, and theoretical aspects.* New York: Hoeber.

Beck, A. T. (1976). *Cognitive therapy and the emotional disorders.* New York: International Universities Press.

Beck, A. (1991). Cognitive therapy: A 30 year retrospective. *American Psychologist, 46*(4), 368-375.

Beck, A. T., & Emery, G., with Greenberg, R. (1985). *Anxiety disorders and phobias: A cognitive perspective.* New York: Basic Books.

Beck, A. T., Freeman, A., & Associates. (1990). *Cognitive therapy of personality disorders.* New York: Guilford.

Beck, A. T., Rush, A. J., Shaw, B. F., & Emery, G. (1979). *Cognitive therapy of depression.* New York: Guilford.

Beck, A. T., Ward, C. H., Mendelson, M., Mock, J., & Erbaugh, J. (1961). An inventory for measuring depression. *Archives of General Psychiatry, 4,* 561-571.

Beck, A. T., Wright, F. D., Newman, C. F., & Liese, B. S. (1993). *Cognitive therapy of substance abuse.* New York: Guilford.

Beckett, J. O. (1988). Plant closings: How older workers are affected. *Social Work, 33*(1), 29-33.

Bellah, R., Madsen, R., Sullivan, W. M., Swidler, A., & Tipton, S. M. (1985). *Habits of the heart: Individualism and commitment in American life.* New York: Harper & Row.

Bengelsdorf, H., Levy, L. E., Emerson, R. L., & Barile, F. A. (1984). A crisis triage rating scale: Brief dispositional assessment of patients at risk for hospitalization. *Journal of Nervous and Mental Disease, 172*(7), 424-430.

Ben-Zvi, R., & Horsfall, E. (1985). Adolescent rape: The role of rape crisis counseling. *International Journal of Adolescent Medicine and Health, 1*(3-4), 343-356.

Berlin, S. (1983). Cognitive-behavioral approaches. In A. Rosenblatt & D. Waldfogel (Eds.), *Handbook of clinical social work* (pp. 1095-1119). San Francisco: Jossey-Bass.

Berman, A. L. (1991). New technologies and telephone hotlines. *Suicide and Life-Threatening Behavior, 21*(4), 407-413.

Berne, E. (1964). *Games people play: The psychology of human relationships.* New York: Grove.

Bernstein, A., & Lenhart, S. (1993). *The psychodynamic treatment of women.* Washington, DC: American Psychiatric Press.

Berry, S. (1992, October 14). Firing just one worker can mean upending a whole family. *Philadelphia Inquirer,* sec. D, p. 1.

Blake, D. D., Weathers, F. W., Nagy, L. M., Kaloupek, D. G., Gusman, F. D., Charney, D. S., & Keane, T. M. (1995). The development of a clinician-administered PTSD scale. *Journal of Traumatic Stress, 8,* 75-90.

Blake, D. D., Weathers, F. W., Nagy, L. M., Kaloupek, D. G., Klauminzer, G., Charney, D. S., & Keane, T. M. (1990). A clinician rating scale for assessing current and lifetime PTSD: The CAPS-1. *Behavior Therapist, 13,* 187-188.

Bloom, B. L. (1963). Definitional aspects of the crisis concept. *Journal of Consulting Psychology, 27*, 498-502.

Bloom, B. L. (1992). *Planned short-term psychotherapy: A clinical handbook.* Boston: Allyn & Bacon.

Bloom, M. (1984). *Configurations of human behavior: Life span development in social environments.* New York: Macmillan.

Boehm, R., Chessare, J. B., Valko, T. R., & Sager, M. S. (1991). Teenline: A descriptive analysis of a peer telephone listening service. *Adolescence, 26*(103), 643-648.

Bolton, F., & Bolton, S. (1987). *Working with violent families: A guide for clinical and legal practitioners.* Newbury Park, CA: Sage.

Bolz, F. (1987). *How to be a hostage and live.* Secaucus, NJ: Lyle Stuart.

Bolz, F., & Hershey, E. (1979). *Hostage cop.* New York: Rawson Wade.

Bonneson, M. E., & Hartsough, D. M. (1987). Development of the Crisis Call Outcome Rating Scale. *Journal of Consulting and Clinical Psychology, 55*(4), 612-614.

Boren, C., & Zeman, P. (1985). Psychiatric triage. *Connecticut Medicine, 49*(9), 570-573.

Brashear, D. (1990). Time-limited cognitive therapy with women in crisis of reproductive failure. In A. Roberts (Ed.), *Crisis intervention handbook: Assessment, treatment, and research* (pp. 236-254). Belmont, CA: Wadsworth.

Brenner, C. (1976). *Psychoanalytic technique and psychic conflict.* New York: International Universities Press.

Brenner, H. (1973). *Mental illness and the economy.* Boston: Harvard University Press.

Brewer, B., & Rawlings, E. (1993). Feminist therapy with single again mothers: A case analysis. *Journal of Training and Practice in Professional Psychology, 7*(1), 26-34.

Briar, K. H. (1976). *The effect of long-term unemployment of workers and their families.* Unpublished doctoral dissertation, University of California, Berkeley.

Briere, J. N. (1992). *Child abuse trauma: Theory and treatment of the lasting effects.* Newbury Park, CA: Sage.

Brooks, N. J. (1992, October 14). The class of "92" is still looking for that 1st job. *Philadelphia Inquirer,* sec. D, p. 1.

Brower, A. M., & Nurius, P. S. (1993). *Social cognitions and individual change: Current theory and counseling guidelines.* Newbury Park, CA: Sage.

Brown, K., & Ziefert, M. (1988). Crisis resolution, competence and empowerment: A service model of women. *Journal of Primary Prevention, 9*(1-2), 92-103.

Bureau of Justice Statistics. (1987). *Lifetime likelihood of victimization* (Technical Report No. NCJ 104274). Washington, DC: Government Printing Office.

Bureau of Justice Statistics. (1992). *B.J.S. national update.* Washington, DC: U.S. Department of Justice.

Burgess, A. W., & Baldwin, B. A. (1981). *Crisis intervention theory and practice.* Englewood Cliffs, NJ: Prentice Hall.

Burgess, A., & Holstrom, L. (1979). Adaptive strategies and recovery from rape. *American Journal of Psychiatry, 136,* 1278-1282.

Burns, D. D. (1980). *Feeling good.* New York: William Morrow.

Butcher, J. N., & Maudal, G. R. (1976). Crisis intervention. In I. B. Weiner (Ed.), *Clinical methods in psychology* (pp. 591-648). New York: John Wiley.

Calhoun, K. S., Atkeson, B. N., & Resick, P. A. (1982). A longitudinal examination of fear reactions in victims of rape. *Journal of Counseling Psychology, 29,* 655-661.

Calhoun, K. S., & Resick, P. A. (1993). Post-traumatic stress disorder. In D. H. Barlow (Ed.), *Clinical handbook of psychological disorders* (pp. 48-98). New York: Guilford.

Caplan, G. (1961). *An approach to community mental health.* New York: Grune & Stratton.

Carkhuff, R. R. (1969). *Helping and human relations: A primer for lay and professional helpers* (Vol. 2). New York: Holt, Rinehart & Winston.

Carmody, C. (1994, September). Deadly mistakes. *ABA Journal,* pp. 68-71.

Carter, A., & Kaslow, N. (1992). Phenomenology and treatment of depressed women. *Psychotherapy, 29*(4), 603-609.

Center for Public Safety Studies, Inc., in conjunction with the Apco Institute, Inc. (1991). *Student manual: Apco Institute, Inc./New Jersey edition, 24 hour telecommunicator training course.* South Daytona, FL: Apco Institute, Inc.

Centers for Disease Control. (1993). *AIDS information: Statistical projections/ trends.* Atlanta, GA: Author.

Chemtob, C., Roitblat, H. L., Hamada, R. S., Carlson, J. G., & Twentyman, C. T. (1988). A cognitive action theory of post-traumatic stress disorder. *Journal of Anxiety Disorders, 2,* 253-275.

Chiauzzi, E., & Carroll, B. P. (1982). Self-help tapes as an adjunct to hotline counseling services: A preliminary analysis. *Journal of College Student Personnel, 23*(1), 25-28.

Christ, G. H., Siegel, K., & Moynihan, R. T. (1988). Psychosocial issues: Prevention and treatment. In V. T. De Vita, Jr., S. Hellman, & S. A. Rosenberg (Eds.), *AIDS: Etiology, diagnosis, treatment, and prevention* (2d ed.). Philadelphia: Lippincott.

Clark, D. C., & Fawcett, J. (1992). Review of empirical risk factors for evaluation of the suicidal patient. In B. Bongar (Ed.), *Suicide: Guidelines for assessment, management & treatment* (pp. 16-48). New York: Oxford University Press.

Clayson, D. E., & Frost, T. F. (1984). Impact of stress and locus of control on the concept of self. *Psychological Reports, 55*(3), 919-926.

Clines, F. X. (1994, February 6). Dr. Telephone explains it all for you. *New York Times,* sec. 1, p. 39.

Cocores, J. A., & Gold, M. S. (1990). Recognition and crisis intervention treatment with cocaine abusers: The Fair Oaks Hospital model. In A. R. Roberts (Ed.), *Crisis intervention handbook* (pp. 177-195). Belmont, CA: Wadsworth.

Congress, E. (1992). Unmet needs, service delivery, and practice issues with rape victims. *Justice Professional, 7*(1), 1-15.

Congress, E., & Lynn, M. (1994). Group work programs in public schools: Ethical dilemmas and cultural diversity. *Social Work in Education, 16*(2), 107-114.

Cook, E. (1993). *Women, relationships, and power: Implications for counseling.* Alexandria, VA: American Counseling Association.

Corcoran, K., & Fischer, J. (1994). *Measures for clinical practice: A source book* (2nd ed.). New York: Free Press.

Cormier, W. H., & Cormier, L. S. (1991). *Interviewing strategies for helpers* (3rd ed.). Pacific Grove, CA: Brooks/Cole.

Coyne, A. C. (1991). Information and referral service usage among caregivers for dementia patients. *The Gerontologist, 31*(31), 384-388.

Crooks, R., & Baur, K. (1990). *Our sexuality.* Menlo Park, CA: Benjamin Cummings.

Cyr, C., & Dowrick, P. W. (1991). Burnout in crisisline volunteers. *Administration and Policy in Mental Health, 18*(5), 343-354.

Dancu, C., & Foa, E. (1993, October). Cognitive behavioral treatment of survivors of childhood sexual abuse with PTSD. In J. Niederee (Chair), *Innovative approaches in the treatment of adult survivors of childhood sexual abuse experiencing PTSD.* Symposium presented at the 9th Annual Meeting of the International Society for Traumatic Stress Studies, San Antonio, TX.

Dattilio, F. M., & Freeman, A. (Eds.). (1994). *Cognitive-behavioral strategies in crisis intervention* (pp. 1-22). New York: Guilford.

Derogatis, L. R. (1977). *SCL-90: Administration, scoring and procedure manual-1 for the R (revised) version.* Baltimore: Johns Hopkins University, School of Medicine.

Derrer, D. (1985, May). Terrorism. *Proceedings/Naval Review,* p. 198.

Derrer, D. (1988, May). [Victim training session, Camp Pendleton, CA].

Dixon, S. (1979). *Working with people in crisis.* St. Louis, MO: C. V. Mosby.

Dohrenwend, B. S., Dohrenwend, B. P. (Eds.). (1974). *Stressful life events.* New York: John Wiley.

Drew, B., & Waters, J. (1987). Aging and work: Perceptions of low income Puerto Rican adults and high school seniors. In H. Strange & M. Teitelbaum (Eds.), *Aging and ethnic diversity* (pp. 131-152). New York: Bergin and Garvey.

Dublin, L. I. (1933). *To be or not to be: A study of suicide.* New York: Random House.

Dublin, L. I. (1963). *Suicide: A sociological and statistical study.* New York: Ronald.

Dziegielewski, S., & Resnick, C. (in press a). Crisis assessment and intervention with adult survivors of incest. In A. R. Roberts (Ed.), *Crisis management and brief treatment.* Chicago: Nelson-Hall.

Dziegielewski, S. F., & Resnick, C. (in press b). Crisis assessment and intervention: Abused women in the shelter setting. In A. R. Roberts (Ed.), *Helping battered women.* New York: Oxford University Press.

Echterling, L. G., & Hartsough, D. M. (1989). Phases of helping in successful crisis telephone calls. *Journal of Community Psychology, 17,* 249-257.

Ehrenreich, B. (1989). *Fear of falling.* New York: Pantheon.

Eidelberg, L. (1968). *Encyclopedia of psychoanalysis.* New York: Free Press.

Eisenberg, P., & Lazarsfeld, P. E. (1938). The psychological effects of unemployment. *Psychological Bulletin, 39,* 358-390.

Eitinger, L. (1980). The concentration camp syndrome and its late sequelae. In J. E. Dimsdale (Ed.), *Survivors, victims and perpetrators* (pp. 127-161). Washington, DC: Hemisphere.

Elkins, R. L., & Cohen, C. R. (1982). A comparison of the effects of prejob training and job experience on nonprofessional telephone crisis counselors. *Suicide and Life-Threatening Behavior, 12*(2), 84-89.

Ellis, A. (1962). *Reason and emotion in psychotherapy.* New York: Stuart.

Ellis, A. (1989). Using rational-emotive therapy (RET) as crisis intervention: A single session with a suicidal client. *Individual Psychology, 45,* 75-81.

Ellis, E. M., Atkeson, B. M., & Calhoun, K. S. (1981). An assessment of long-term reaction to rape. *Journal of Abnormal Psychology, 90,* 263-266.

Ellis, L. F., Black, L. D., & Resick, P. A. (1992). Cognitive-behavioral treatment approaches for victims of crime. In P. A. Keller & S. R. Heyman (Eds.), *Innovations in clinical practice: A sourcebook* (pp. 23-38). Sarasota, FL: Professional Resource Exchange.

Epstein, L. (1992). *Brief treatment and a new look at the task-centered approach.* New York: Macmillan.

Erikson, E. (1950). *Childhood and society.* New York: W. W. Norton

Estrada, E. G. (1981). Triage systems. *Nursing Clinics of North America, 16*(1), 13-24.

Ewing, C. P. (1978). *Crisis intervention as psychotherapy.* New York: Oxford University Press.

Falsetti, S. A., Resnick, H. S., Resick, P. A., & Kilpatrick, D. G. (1993). The modified PTSD symptom scale: A brief self-report measure of posttraumatic stress disorder. *Behavior Therapist, 16*(6), 161-162.

Falsetti, S. A., Resnick, H. S., Resick, P. A., & Kilpatrick, D. G. (1994). *The modified posttraumatic stress disorder symptom scale: A study of validity and reliability for use with clinical and community samples.* Manuscript submitted for publication.

Family Service Association. (1987). *The state of families II: Work and family.* Milwaukee, WI: Family Service America.

Farberow, N. L., & Shneidman, E. S. (Eds.). (1965). *The cry for help.* New York: McGraw-Hill.

Fischer, J. (1978). *Effective casework practice: An eclectic approach.* New York: McGraw-Hill.

Fleishman, J. (1992, April 13). Laid off, some take it out on families. *Philadelphia Inquirer,* sec. A, p. 1.

Florida Statutes Annotated, § 784.048 (West, 1992).

Foa, E. B. (1986). *Rape victims: Persistent reactions and their treatment* (Grant No. MH42178). Bethesda, MD: National Institute of Mental Health.

Foa, E. B., & Kozak, M. J. (1986). Emotional processing of fear: Exposure to corrective information. *Psychological Bulletin, 99,* 20-35.

Foa, E. B., Riggs, D. S., Dancu, C. V., & Rothbaum, B. O. (1993). Reliability and validity of a brief instrument for assessing post-traumatic stress disorder. *Journal of Traumatic Stress, 6*, 459-473.

Foa, E. B., Rothbaum, B. O., Riggs, D. S., & Murdock, T. B. (1991). Treatment of post-traumatic stress disorder in rape victims: A comparison between cognitive-behavioral procedures and counseling. *Journal of Consulting and Clinical Psychology, 59*(5), 715-723.

Foa, E. B., Steketee, G., & Rothbaum, B. O. (1989). Behavioral/cognitive conceptualizations of post-traumatic stress disorder. *Behavior Therapy, 20*, 155-176.

Folkman, S., & Lazarus, R. S. (1980). An analysis of coping in a middle-aged community sample. *Journal of Health and Social Behavior, 21*, 219-239.

Ford, C. V., & Spaulding, R. C. (1973). The Pueblo Incident. *Archives of General Psychiatry, 29*, 340-343.

Fortune, A. E. (Ed.). (1985). *Task-centered practice with families and groups.* New York: Springer.

Fowler, D. E., & McGee, R. K. (1973). Assessing the performance of telephone crisis workers: The development of a technical effectiveness scale. In D. Lester & G. W. Brockopp (Eds.), *Crisis intervention and counseling by telephone* (pp. 287-299). Springfield, IL: Charles C Thomas.

France, K. (1975). Evaluation of lay volunteer crisis telephone workers. *American Journal of Community Psychology, 3*(3), 197-220.

Frank, E., Kupfer, D., Jacob, M., & Blumenthal, S. (1987). Pregnancy-related affective episodes among women with recurrent depression. *American Journal of Psychiatry, 144*(3), 288-293.

Frank, E., & Stewart, B. D. (1984). Depressive symptoms in rape victims: A revisit. *Journal of Affective Disorders, 7*, 77-85.

Frank, E., Turner, S. M., & Duffy, B. (1979). Depressive symptoms in rape victims. *Journal of Affective Disorders, 1*, 269-277.

Freedburg, S. (1989). Self determination: Historical perspectives and effects on current practice. *Social Work, 34*, 33-38.

Freeman, A., & Dattilio, F. M. (1994). Introduction. In F. M. Dattilio & A. Freeman (Eds.), *Cognitive-behavioral strategies in crisis intervention* (pp. 1-22). New York: Guilford.

Freud, S. (1905). A case of hysteria: IV. Postscript. In *The complete psychological works of Sigmund Freud* (Vol. 7, pp. 112-122). London: Hogarth.

Fried, M. (1982). Endemic stress: The psychology of resignation and the politics of scarcity. *American Journal of Orthopsychiatry, 52*(1), 4-19.

Fuselier, G. D. (1981a). A practical overview of hostage negotiations. *Law Enforcement Bulletin, 50*(6), 2-6.

Fuselier, G. D. (1981b). A practical overview of hostage negotiations: Conclusion. *Law Enforcement Bulletin, 50*(7), 10-15.

Gal, R., & Lazarus, R. S. (1975). The role of activity in anticipating and confronting stressful situations. *Journal of Human Stress, 1*, 4-20.

Geffner, R., & Pagelow, M. (1990). Victims of spouse abuse. In R. Ammerman & M. Hersen (Eds.), *Treatment of family violence: A source book* (pp. 113-135). New York: John Wiley.

Getz, W., Wiesen, A., Sue, S., & Ayers, A. (1974). *Fundamentals of crisis counseling*. Lexington, MA: D. C. Heath.

Gilligan, C. (1982). *In a different voice.* Cambridge, MA: Harvard University Press.

Gilligan, C. (1993). *In a different voice* (2nd. ed.). Cambridge, MA: Harvard University Press.

Gilliland, B. E., & James, R. F. (1993). *Crisis intervention strategies* (2nd ed.). Pacific Grove, CA: Brooks/Cole.

Glatt, K. M. (1987). Helpline: Suicide prevention at a suicide site. *Suicide and Life-Threatening Behavior, 17*(4), 299-309.

Goedert, J. J., & Blattner, W. A. (1988). The epidemiology and natural history of human immunodeficiency virus. In V. T. De Vita, Jr., S. Hellman, & S. A. Rosenberg (Eds.), *AIDS: Etiology, diagnosis, treatment, and prevention* (2nd ed.). Philadelphia: Lippincott.

Golan, N. (1972). Social work intervention in medical crisis. *Hospital and Community Psychiatry, 2*, 25-29.

Golan, N. (1986). Crisis theory. In F. J. Turner (Ed.), *Social work treatment: Interlocking theoretical approaches* (3rd ed.). New York: Free Press.

Goldfried, M. R., & Davison, G. C. (1976). *Clinical behavior therapy.* New York: Holt, Rinehart & Winston.

Gore, S., & Colten, M. (1991). Gender, stress, and distress: Social relational influences. In J. Eckenwode (Ed.), *The social context of coping* (pp. 139-163). New York: Plenum.

Gorin, S., & Moniz, C. (1992). The national health care crisis: An analysis of proposed solutions. *Health and Social Work, 17*(1), 37-43.

Goulden, T. (1985). The gays counselling service of N.S.W. *Australian Social Work, 38*(2), 38-41.

Graham, D., Rawlings, E., & Rimini, N. (1988). Survivors of terror-battered women, hostages and the Stockholm Syndrome. In K. Yllo & M. Bograd (Eds.), *Feminist perspectives on wife abuse* (pp. 217-233). Newbury Park, CA: Sage.

Grayson, J. P. (1983). The effects of plant closure on the stress levels and health of workers' wives: A preliminary analysis. *Journal of Business Ethics, 2*(3), 221-225.

Grayson, J. P. (1985). The closure of a factory and its impact on health. *International Journal of Health Services, 15*, 69-93.

Green, L. W., & Wilson, C. R. (1988). Guidelines for nonprofessionals who receive suicidal phone calls. *Hospital and Community Psychiatry, 39*(3), 310-311.

Greenstone, J. L., & Leviton, S. C. (1993). *Elements of crisis intervention: Crises and how to respond to them.* Pacific Grove, CA: Brooks/Cole.

Haughton, A. (1968, July). Suicide prevention programs in the United States: An overview. *Bulletin of Suicidology*, pp. 25-29.

Henricks, W. H., & Stiles, W. B. (1989). Verbal processes on psychological radio call-in programs: Comparisons with other help-intended interactions. *Professional Psychology: Research and Practice, 20*(5), 315-321.

Heppner, M. J., Johnston, J. A., & Brinkhoff, J. (1988). Creating a career hotline for rural residents. *Journal of Counseling and Development, 66*, 340-341.

Hepworth, D., & Larsen, J. (1993). *Direct social work practice: Theory and skills* (3rd ed.). Chicago: Dorsey.

Hepworth, S. (1980). Moderating factors of the psychological impact of unemployment. *Journal of Occupational Psychology, 53*(2), 139-145.

Herman, J. L. (1992). *Trauma and recovery.* New York: Basic Books.

Hinrichsen, J. S., & Zwibelman, B. B. (1981, July). Differences between telephone and in-person peer counseling. *Journal of College Student Personnel*, pp. 315-319.

Hoff, L. A. (1989). *People in crisis: Understanding and helping* (3rd ed.). Redwood City, CA: Addison-Wesley.

Hollon, S. D., & Jacobson, V. (1985). Cognitive approaches. In M. Hersen & A. S. Bellack (Eds.), *Handbook of clinical behavioral therapy with adults* (pp. 169-199). New York: Plenum.

Holmes, T. H., & Rahe, R. H. (1967). The Social Readjustment Rating Scale. *Journal of Psychometric Research, 11*, 213-218.

Horowitz, L. M. (1994). Schemas, psychopathology, and psychotherapy research. *Psychotherapy Research, 4*(1), 1-19.

Horowitz, M., Wilner, N., & Alvarez, W. (1979). Impact of event scale: A measure of subjective stress. *Psychosomatic Medicine, 41*, 209-218.

Horton, A. L., Johnson, B. L., Roundy, L. M., & Williams, D. (Eds.). (1990). *The incest perpetrator: A family member no one wants to treat.* Newbury Park, CA: Sage.

Horton, J. (Ed.). (1992). *The women's health data book: A profile of women's health in the United States.* Washington, DC: Jacobs Institute of Women's Health.

Hutton, S. (1994). Men's and women's incomes: Evidence from survey data. *Journal of Social Policy, 23*(1), 21-40.

Jahoda, M. (1982). *Employment and unemployment: A social-psychological analysis.* Cambridge, UK: Cambridge University Press.

Janoff-Bulman, R. (1992). *Shattered assumptions: Towards a new psychology of trauma.* New York: Free Press.

Janosik, E. H. (1984). *Crisis counseling: A contemporary approach.* Monterey, CA: Wadsworth.

Jenkins, B. M. (1986). [Lecture to *Fortune* 500 vice-presidents, Los Angeles].

Jenkins, B. M., Johnson, J., & Ronfelt, D. (1977). *Numbered lives: Some statistical observations from seventy-seven international hostage episodes.* Santa Monica, CA: RAND.

Justice, B., & Duncan, D. F. (1976). Life crisis as a precursor to child abuse. *Public Health Reports, 91*(2), 110-115.

Justice, B., McBee, G. W., & Allen, R. H. (1977). Life events, psychological distress and social functioning. *Psychological Reports, 40*(2), 467-473.

Karls, J., & Wandrei, K. (1992). PIE: A new language for social workers. *Social Work, 37*(1), 80-85.

Kates, N. (1992, May). *Unemployment and families: The forgotten victims.* Paper presented at the meeting of the American Orthopsychiatric Association, New York.

Kates, N., Greiff, B. S., & Hagen, D. Q. (1990). *The psychosocial impact of job loss.* Washington, DC: American Psychiatric Press.

Kaufman, H. G. (1982). *Professionals in search of work.* New York: John Wiley.

Kentsmith, D. K. (1982). Hostages and other prisoners of war. *Military Medicine, 147,* 969-971.

Kilpatrick, D. G., Best, C. L., Veronen, J. L., Amick, A. E., Villeponteaux, L. A., & Ruff, G. A. (1985). Mental health correlates of criminal victimization: A random community survey. *Journal of Consulting and Clinical Psychology, 53,* 866-873.

Kilpatrick, D. G., Edmunds, C. N., & Seymour, A. K. (1992). *Rape in America: A report to the nation.* Arlington, VA: National Victim Center.

Kilpatrick, D. G., Resick, P. A., & Veronen, L. J. (1981). Effects of a rape experience: A longitudinal study. *Journal of Social Issues, 37,* 105-121.

Kilpatrick, D. G., Saunders, B. E., Best, C. L., & Von, J. M. (1987). Criminal victimization: Lifetime prevalence reporting to police, and psychological impact. *Crime and Delinquency, 33,* 479-489.

Kilpatrick, D. G., & Veronen, L. J. (1984, February). *Treatment of fear and anxiety in victims of rape* (Final report of NIMH, Grant No. MH29602). Bethesda, MD: National Institute of Mental Health.

Kilpatrick, D. G., Veronen, L. J., & Resick, P. A. (1982). Psychological sequelae of rape. In D. M. Doleys, R. L. Meredith, & A. R. Ciminero (Eds.), *Behavioral medicine: Assessment and treatment strategies* (pp. 473-498). New York: Plenum.

Kilpatrick, D. G., Veronen, L. J., Saunders, B. E., Best, C. L., Amick-McMullan, A. E., & Paduhovich, J. L. (1987). *The psychological impact of crime: A study of randomly studied crime victims* (Final report, NIJ Grant No. 84-IJ-CX-0039). Washington, DC: National Institute of Justice.

Kirk, S., & Kutchins, H. (1992). *The selling of DSM: The rhetoric of science in psychiatry.* New York: Aldine de Gruyter.

Kliewer, W., Lepore, S. J., Broquet, A., & Zuba, L. (1990). Developmental and gender differences in anonymous support-seeking: Analysis of data from a community helpline for children. *American Journal of Community Psychology, 18*(2), 333-339.

Kliman, A. S. (1978). *Crisis: Psychological first aid for recovery and growth.* New York: Holt, Rinehart & Winston.

Koopman, C., Classen, C., & Spiegel, D. (1994). Predictors of posttraumatic stress symptoms among survivors of the Oakland/Berkeley Calif. firestorm. *American Journal of Psychiatry, 151*(6), 889-894.

Koss, M. P. (1985). The hidden rape victim: Personality, attitudinal, and situational characteristics. *Psychology of Women Quarterly, 9,* 193-212.

Koss, M. (1993). Rape: Scope, impact, interventions, and public policy responses. *American Psychologist, 48*(10), 1062-1069.

Koss, M. P., Gidycz, C. A., & Wisniewski, N. (1987). The scope of rape: Incidence and prevalence of sexual aggression and victimization in a national sample of higher education students. *Journal of Consulting and Clinical Psychology, 55,* 162-170.

Koss, M., & Shiang, J. (1994). Research on brief psychotherapy. In S. Garfield & A. Bergin (Eds.), *Handbook of psychotherapy and behavior change* (pp. 664-700). New York: John Wiley.

Kubler-Ross, E. (1969). *On death and dying.* New York: Macmillan.

Kubler-Ross, E. (1971). What is it like to be dying? *American Journal of Nursing, 71*(1), 54-61.

Labich, K. (1993, March 8). The new unemployed. *Fortune, 127*(5), 40-49.

Lambert, B. (1989, August 16). In shift, gay men's health group endorses testing for the AIDS virus. *New York Times,* p. 32.

Lanceley, F. (1981). The antisocial personality as a hostage taker. *Journal of Police Science and Administration, 9,* 28-34.

Lanceley, F. (1988). [Lecture to FBI hostage negotiators course, FBI Academy, Quantico, VA].

Lane, F. M. (1986). Transference and countertransference: Definitions of terms. In H. C. Meyers (Ed.), *Between analyst and patient* (pp. 237-255). Hillsdale, NJ: Analytic Press.

Lane, J. C. (1992, August). Threat management fills void in police services. *Police Chief,* pp. 27-31.

Leana, C. R., & Feldman, D. C. (1992). *Coping with job loss: How individuals, organizations, and communities respond to layoffs.* New York: Lexington.

Lee, J., & Rosenthal, S. (1983). Working with victims of violent assault. *Social Casework, 64,* 593-601.

Lemon, E. C. (1983). Planned brief treatment. In A. Rosenblatt & D. Waldfogel (Eds.), *Handbook of clinical social work* (pp. 401-419). San Francisco: Jossey-Bass.

Lerner, M. (1991). *Surplus powerlessness: The psychodynamics of everyday life . . . and the psychology of individual and social transformation.* Atlantic Highlands, NJ: Humanities Press.

Liese, B. S. (1993). Coping with AIDS: A cognitive therapy perspective. *Kansas Medicine, 94*(3), 80-84.

Liese, B. S. (1994). Brief therapy, crisis intervention and the cognitive therapy of substance abuse. *Crisis Intervention and Time Limited Treatment, 1*(1), 11-29.

Liese, B. S., & Larson, M. W. (1995). Coping with life-threatening illness: A cognitive therapy perspective. *Journal of Cognitive Psychotherapy: An International Quarterly, 9,* 19-34.

Lindemann, E. (1944). Symptomatology and management of acute grief. *American Journal of Psychiatry, 101,* 141-148.

Losee, N., Auerbach, S. M., & Parham, I. (1988). Effectiveness of a peer counselor hotline for the elderly. *Journal of Community Psychology, 16,* 428-436.

Lynn, M., Jacob, N., & Pierce, L. (1988). Child sexual abuse: A follow-up study of reports to a protective service hotline. *Children and Youth Services Review, 10,* 151-165.

Magnet, M. (1993, March 8). Why job growth is stalled. *Fortune, 127*(5), 51-57.

Mahoney, M. J. (1991). *Human change processes: The scientific foundations of psychotherapy.* New York: Basic Books.

Mallinckrodt, B., & Fretz, B. R. (1988). Social support and the impact of job loss on older professionals. *Journal of Counseling Psychology, 35*(3), 281-286.

Mancoske, R., Standifer, D., & Cauley, C. (1994). The effectiveness of brief counseling services for battered women. *Research on Social Work Practice, 4*(1), 53-63.

Mandel, M. J., Zellner, W., & Hof, R. (1993, February 22). Jobs, jobs, jobs. *Business Week,* pp. 68-74.

Manderscheid, R. W., Rae, D. S., Narrow, W., Locke, B. Z., & Reiger, D. (1993). Congruence of service utilization estimates from the epidemiologic catchment area project and other sources. *Archives of General Psychiatry, 50,* 108-114.

Mann, J. (1973). *Time-limited psychotherapy.* Cambridge, MA: Harvard University Press.

Mann, J. (1981). *A casebook of time-limited psychotherapy.* New York: McGraw-Hill.

Mann, J., & Goldman, R. (1982). *A casebook in time-limited psychotherapy.* Washington, DC: American Psychiatric Association.

Martin, R. A. (1982). A primer on stress inoculation. In P. A. Keller & L. G. Ritt (Eds.), *Innovations in clinical practice: A sourcebook* (Vol. 1, pp. 112-125). Sarasota, FL: Professional Resource Exchange.

Masters, W. H., & Johnson, V. (1988). *Human sexuality.* Glenview, IL: Scott, Foresman.

McCann, L. I., & Pearlman, L. A. (1990a). *Psychological trauma and the adult survivor: Theory, therapy and transformation.* New York: Brunner/Mazel.

McCann, I. L., & Pearlman, L. A. (1990b). Vicarious traumatization: A framework for understanding the psychological effects of working with victims. *Journal of Traumatic Stress, 3,* 131-149.

McCann, I. L., Sakheim, D. K., & Abrahamson, D. J. (1988). Trauma and victimization: A model of psychological adaptation. *Counseling Psychologist, 16,* 531-594.

McCarthy, P., Reese, R., Schueneman, J., & Reese, J. (1991). Counselling working class women. *Canadian Journal of Counselling, 25*(4), 581-593.

McGee, R. K. (1974). *Crisis intervention in the community.* Baltimore: University Park Press.

McKinnon, D. (1986). *Everything you need to know before you're hijacked.* San Diego, CA: House of Hints.

McMullin, R. E. (1986). *Handbook of cognitive therapy techniques.* New York: Norton.

McNamee, G., O'Sullivan, G., Lelliott, P., & Marks, I. (1989). Telephone-guided treatment for housebound agroaphobics with panic disorder: Exposure vs. relaxation. *Behavior Therapy, 20,* 491-497.

Mechanic, M. B., Resick, P. A., & Griffin, M. G. (1993, October). Rape-related PTSD: Comorbidity of DSM-III-R Axis I disorders and associated symptoms. In D. E. Hearst (Chair), *Collateral symptoms in women with PTSD: Depression, physical health, sexual and interpersonal adjustment.* Symposium presented at the 27th Annual Association for the Advancement of Behavior Therapy Convention, Atlanta, GA.

Meichenbaum, D., & Cameron, R. (1983). Stress inoculation training: Toward a general paradigm for training coping skills. In D. Meichenbaum & M. E. Jaremko (Eds.), *Stress reduction and prevention* (pp. 115-154). New York: Plenum.

Mezza, I. (1992). Triage: Setting priorities for health care. *Nursing Forum, 27*(2), 15-19.

Millis, J., & Kornblith, P. (1992). Fragile beginnings: Identification and treatment of postpartum disorders. *Health and Social Work, 17*(3), 192-199.

Moreno, J. L., & Whitin, E. S. (1932). *Plan and technique of developing a person into a socialized community.* New York: National Committee on Prisons and Prison Labor.

Morris County Hotline Training Manual (n.d.). (Available from St. Clare's Hospital, Denville, NJ)

Morris, R. J. (1986). Fear reduction methods. In F. H. Kanfer & A. P. Goldstein (Eds.), *Helping people change: A textbook of methods* (pp. 145-190). New York: Pergamon.

Moynihan, R. T., Christ, G. H., & Gallo-Silver, L. (1988). AIDS and terminal illness. *Social Casework, 68,* 380-387.

Narrow, W. E., Reiger, D. A., Rae, D. S., Mandersheid, R. W., & Locke, B. Z. (1993). Use of services with mental and addictive disorders. *Archives of General Psychiatry, 50,* 95-107.

National Association of Social Workers. (1993). *Code of ethics.* Washington, DC: Author.

National Institute of Justice. (1993). *Project to develop a model anti-stalking code for states.* Washington, DC: Author.

New Jersey Statutes Annotated, § 2C:12-10-C. (West Supp., 1993).

Newman, K. S. (1988). *Falling from grace: The experience of downward mobility in the American middle class.* New York: Free Press.

Nichols, A. W., & Schilit, R. (1988). Telephone support for latchkey children. *Child Welfare, 67*(1), 49-59.

Nussbaum, B., Palmer, A. T., Cuneo, A. Z., & Carlson, B. (1992, March 23). Downward mobility: Corporate castoffs are struggling just to stay in the middle class. *Businessweek*, pp. 56-63.

Ochberg, F. M., & Soskis, D. A. (Eds.). (1982). *Victims of terrorism*. Boulder, CO: Westview.

O'Connor, D., & Wolfe, D. (1991). From crisis to growth at midlife: Changes in personal paradigm. *Journal of Organizational Behavior, 12*(4), 323-340.

O'Leary, K., Riso, L., & Beach, S. (1990). Attributions about the marital discord/ depression link and therapy outcome. *Behavior Therapy, 21*(4), 413-422.

O'Reilly, B. (1992, August 24). The job drought. *Fortune, 126*(4), 62-74.

Ossip-Klein, D. J., Shapiro, R. M., & Stiggins, J. (1984). Freedom line: Increasing utilization of a telephone support service for ex-smokers. *Addictive Behaviors, 9*, 227-230.

Parad, H., et al. (1990). *Crisis intervention: The practitioner's sourcebook for brief therapy*. Milwaukee, WI: Family Service Association of America.

Perlman, H. (1957). *Social casework: A problem-solving process*. Chicago: University of Chicago Press.

Perlman, H. H. (1986). The problem-solving model. In F. J. Turner (Ed.), *Social work treatment: Interlocking theoretical approaches* (3rd ed., pp. 245-266). New York: Free Press.

Persons, J. B. (1989). *Cognitive therapy in practice: A case formulation approach*. New York: Norton.

Pollun, R. L., & Labbage, L. A. (1992). Psychiatric hospitalization: Treatment or triage? *Military Medicine, 157*(12), 634-636.

Pomice, E., Black, R. F., Collins, S., & Newman, R. J. (1992, January 13). Is your job safe? *U.S. News and World Report*, pp. 42-48.

Potts, M., Burnam, M., & Wells, K. (1991). Gender differences in depression detection: A comparison of clinician diagnosis and standardized assessment. *Psychological Assessment, 3*(4), 609-615.

Prochaska, J. O., DiClemente, C. C., & Norcross, J. C. (1992). In search of how people change: Applications to addictive behaviors. *American Psychologist, 47*(9), 1102-1114.

Puryear, D. A. (1980). *Helping people in crisis*. San Francisco: Jossey-Bass.

Rahe, R. H., & Genender, E. (1983). Adaptation to and recovery from captivity stress. *Military Medicine, 148*, 577-585.

Reid, K. (1994). How to make sense out of change. *NEWS* (Bell Communications Research), *11*(8), 3.

Reid, W. J. (1986). Task-centered social work. In F. J. Turner (Ed.), *Social work treatment: Interlocking theoretical approaches* (3rd ed., pp. 267-295). New York: Free Press.

Reid, W. J. (1987). Task-centered approach. In A. Minahan et al. (Eds.), *Encyclopedia of social work* (pp. 757-763). Silver Spring, MD: National Association of Social Workers.

Reid, W., & Epstein, L. (1972). *Task-centered practice.* New York: Columbia University Press.

Reid, W. J., & Shyne, A. W. (1969). *Brief and extended casework.* New York: Columbia University Press.

Reiger, D. A., Narrow, W. E., Rae, D. S., Manderscheid, R., Locke, B. Z., & Goodwin, F. K. (1993). The defacto US mental and addictive disorders treatment system. *Archives of General Psychiatry, 50,* 85-94.

Resick, P. A. (1988). *Reactions of female and male victims of rape or robbery* (Final report, Grant No. 85-IJ-CX-0042). Washington, DC: National Institute of Justice.

Resick, P. A. (1993). The psychological impact of rape. *Journal of Interpersonal Violence, 8*(2), 223-255.

Resick, P. A., & Jordan, C. G. (1988). Group stress inoculation training for victims of sexual assault: A therapist manual. In P. A. Keller & S. R. Heyman (Eds.), *Innovations in clinical practice: A sourcebook* (Vol. 7, pp. 99-111). Sarasota, FL: Professional Resource Exchange.

Resick, P. A., Jordan, C. G., Girelli, S. A., Hutter, C. H., & Marhoefer-Dvorak, S. (1988). A comparative outcome study of behavioral group therapy for sexual assault victims. *Behavior Therapy, 19,* 385-401.

Resick, P. A., & Schnicke, M. K. (1992). Cognitive processing therapy for sexual assault victims. *Journal of Consulting and Clinical Psychology, 60,* 748-756.

Resick, P. A., & Schnicke, M. K. (1993). *Cognitive processing therapy for rape victims: A treatment manual.* Newbury Park, CA: Sage.

Resnick, H. S., Kilpatrick, D. G., Dansky, B. S., Saunders, B. E., & Best, C. L. (1993). Prevalence of civilian trauma and posttraumatic stress disorder in a representative national sample of women. *Journal of Consulting and Clinical Psychology, 61,* 984-991.

Resnick, H. S., Kilpatrick, D. G., & Lipovsky, J. A. (1991). Assessment of rape-related posttraumatic stress disorder: Stressor and symptom dimensions. *Psychological Assessment: A Journal of Consulting and Clinical Psychology, 3,* 561-572.

Roberts, A. R. (1970). An organizational study of suicide prevention agencies in the U.S. *Police, 14,* 64-72.

Roberts, A. R. (Ed.). (1975). *Self-destructive behavior.* Springfield, IL: Charles C Thomas.

Roberts, A. R. (1990a). *Crisis intervention handbook: Assessment, treatment and research.* Belmont, CA: Wadsworth.

Roberts, A. R. (1990b). An overview of crisis theory and crisis intervention. In A. R. Roberts (Ed.), *Crisis intervention handbook: Assessment, treatment and research* (pp. 3-16). Belmont, CA: Wadsworth.

Roberts, A. R. (1990c). *Helping crime victims: Research, policy and practice.* Newbury Park, CA: Sage.

Roberts, A. R. (1991a). Conceptualizing crisis theory and the crisis intervention model. In A. R. Roberts (Ed.), *Contemporary perspectives on crisis intervention and prevention* (pp. 3-17). Englewood Cliffs, NJ: Prentice Hall.

Roberts, A. R. (1991b). *Contemporary perspectives on crisis intervention and prevention*. Englewood Cliffs, NJ: Prentice Hall.

Roberts, A. R., & Comasso, M. J. (1994). Staff turnover at crisis intervention units and centers: A national survey. *Crisis Intervention and Time Limited Treatment, 1*(1), 1-9.

Roberts, A. R., & Roberts, B. (1990). A comprehensive model for crisis intervention with battered women and their children. In A. R. Roberts (Ed.), *Crisis intervention handbook: Assessment, treatment and research* (pp. 106-123). Belmont, CA: Wadsworth.

Roberts, A. R., & Roberts, B. (1991). A comprehensive model for crisis intervention with battered women and their children. In S. M. Stith, M. Williams, & K. H. Rosen (Eds.), *Violence hits home: Comprehensive treatment approaches to domestic violence* (pp. 25-46). New York: Springer.

Rosenbaum, A., & Calhoun, J. F. (1977). The use of the telephone hotline in crisis intervention: A review. *Journal of Community Psychology, 5*, 325-339.

Rosenbluh, E. S. (1986). *Crisis counseling: A handbook for practice and research.* Dubuque, IA: Kendall/Hunt.

Ross, J. (1992). Health: Who is in control? *Health and Social Work, 17*(1), 3-6.

Rothbaum, B. O., Foa, E. B., Riggs, D. S., Murdock, T., & Walsh, W. (1992). A prospective examination of post-traumatic stress disorder in rape victims. *Journal of Traumatic Stress, 5*, 455-475.

Rothblum, E., Berman, J., Coffey, P., & Shantinath, S. (1993). Feminist approaches to therapy with depressed women: A discussion. *Journal of Training and Practice in Professional Psychology: A Discussion, 7*(1), 100-112.

Rotheram-Borus, M. J., & Bradley, J. (1991). Triage model for suicidal runaways. *American Journal of Orthopsychiatry, 61*(1), 122-127.

Rowe, J. A. (1992). Triage assessment tool. *Journal of Emergency Nursing, 18*(6), 540-544.

Rund, D. A., & Rausch, T. S. (1981). *Triage.* St. Louis, MO: C. V. Mosby.

Russell, D. E. H. (1984). *Sexual exploitation: Rape, child sexual abuse, and workplace harassment.* Beverly Hills, CA: Sage.

Safran, J. D., Crocker, P., McMain, S., & Murray, P. (1990). Therapeutic alliance rupture as a therapy event for empirical validation. *Psychotherapy, 27*, 154-165.

Safran, J. D., & Segal, Z. V. (1990). *Interpersonal process in cognitive therapy.* New York: Basic Books.

Saleeby, D. (1992). *The strength perspective in social work practice.* New York: Longman.

Salminen, S., & Glad, T. (1992). The role of gender in helping behavior. *The Journal of Social Psychology, 132*(1), 131-133.

Sands, R. G. (1983). Transference reconsidered. *Arete, 8*(2), 18-29.

Saunders, B. E., Arata, C. M., & Kilpatrick, D. G. (1990). Development of a crime-related post-traumatic stress disorder scale for women within the symptom checklist-90-revised. *Journal of Traumatic Stress, 3*, 439-448.

Schecter, S. (1987). *Guidelines for mental health practitioners in domestic violence cases.* Washington, DC: National Coalition Against Domestic Violence.

Schlossberg, H. (1980). Values and organization in hostage crisis negotiation teams. *Annals of the New York Academy of Sciences, 347*, 113-116.

Schlossberg, H., & Freeman, L. (1974). *Psychologist with a gun.* New York: Coward, McCann & Geoghegan.

Schmitt, B. (1995, January 22). Man talks woman into sex: Or is it rape. *Tennessean, 91*, 1A and 10A.

Schneider-Braus, K. (1987). A practical guide to HMO psychiatry. *Hospital and Community Psychiatry, 38*(8), 876-879.

Shapiro, S., & Domeniak, G. M. (1992). Sexual trauma and psychopathology. In *Private practice, psychiatric social worker.* Springfield, MA: Lexington.

Sherman, S. (1993, January 25). A brave new Darwinian workplace. *Fortune, 127*(2), 50-56.

Shulman, L. (1992). *The skills of helping individuals and groups* (3rd ed.). Itasca, IL: F. E. Peacock.

Siegel, K., Bauman, L., Christ, G. H., & Krown, S. (1988). Patterns of change in sexual behavior among men in New York City. *Archives of Sexual Behavior, 17*, 481-497.

Siegel, K., & Gibson, W. (1988). Barriers to the adoption of modifications in sexual behavior among heterosexuals at risk for AIDS. *New York State Journal of Medicine, 88*(2), 66-70.

Siegel, K., Mesagno, F. P., Chen, J. Y., & Christ, G. H. (1989). Factors distinguishing homosexual males practicing risky and safe sex. *Social Science and Medicine, 28*, 561-569.

Sifneos, P. E. (1972). *Short-term psychotherapy and emotional crisis.* Cambridge, MA: Harvard University Press.

Sifneos, P. (1987). *Short term dynamic psychotherapy: Evaluation and technique.* New York: Plenum.

Sifneos, P. E. (1992). *Short-term anxiety-provoking psychotherapy: A treatment manual.* New York: Basic Books.

Simpson, O. J., & Schiller, L. (1995). *I want to tell you.* Boston: Little, Brown.

Skinner, B. F. (1953). *Science and human behavior.* New York: Macmillan.

Slaikeu, K. A. (1979). Temporal variables in telephone crisis intervention: Their relationship to selected process and outcome variables. *Journal of Consulting and Clinical Psychology, 47*(1), 193-195.

Smalley, R. (1967). *Theory for social work practice.* New York: Columbia University Press.

Smucker, M., & Niederee, J. (1993, October). Imagery rescripting: Modifying traumatic memories of childhood sexual abuse. In J. Niederee (Chair), *Innovative approaches in the treatment of adult survivors of childhood sexual abuse experiencing PTSD*. Symposium presented at the 9th Annual Meeting of the International Society for Traumatic Stress Studies, San Antonio, TX.

Sohn, E. F. (1994, May-June). Anti-stalking statutes: Do they actually protect victims? *Criminal Law Bulletin*, pp. 203-241.

Soskis, D. A., & Van Zandt, C. R. (1986). Hostage negotiation: Law enforcement's most effective nonlethal weapon. *Behavioral Science and the Law, 4*, 423-435.

Spitzer, R. L., Williams, J. B. W., & Gibbon, M. (1987). *Structured clinical interview for DSM-III: Non-patient Version (SCID-NP-V)*. New York: New York State Psychiatric Institute, Biometrics Research Department.

Stein, D. M., & Lambert, M. J. (1984). Telephone counseling and crisis intervention: A review. *American Journal of Community Psychology, 12*(1), 101-125.

Stewart, A. M., & Glenwick, D. S. (1992). Patterns of usage of a university-based, peer-operated hotline. *Journal of College Student Development, 33*, 547-553.

Stoppard, J. (1989). An evaluation of the adequacy of cognitive-behavioral theories for understanding depression in women. *Canadian Psychology, 30*(1), 67-76.

Strentz, T. (1979). The Stockholm Syndrome: Law enforcement policy and the ego defenses of the hostage. *Law Enforcement Bulletin, 48*, 2-12.

Strentz, T. (1983a). The inadequate personality as a hostage talker. *Journal of Police Science and Administration, 11*, 363-368.

Strentz, T. (1983b). *A statistical analysis of American hostage situations*. Unpublished handout, FBI Academy, Quantico, VA.

Strentz, T. (1984). Preparing the person with high potential for victimization as a hostage. In J. T. Turner (Ed.), *Violence in the medical care setting* (pp. 183-208). Rockville, MD: Aspen.

Strentz, T. (1986). Negotiating with the hostage taker exhibiting paranoid schizophrenic symptoms. *Journal of Police Science and Administration, 14*, 12-16.

Strentz, T. (1987). A hostage psychological survival guide. *Law Enforcement Bulletin, 58*, 2-10.

Stroebel, C. F. (1983). *Quieting reflex training for adults: Personal workbook*. New York: DMA Audio Cassette Publications.

Symonds, M. (1980). The second injury to victims. *Evaluation and Change* (Special issue), pp. 36-38.

Third U.S. Army. (1985). *Terrorism, security, survival handbook*. Washington, DC: Government Printing Office.

Treatment Team. (1991). *Management of HIV infection handbook* (Update). New York: World Health Communications.

Turner, P. M., & Turner, T. J. (1991). Validation of the Crisis Triage Rating Scale for psychiatric emergencies. *Canadian Journal of Psychiatry, 36*(9), 651-654.

U.S. Bureau of the Census. (1991). *Household and family characteristics*. Washington, DC: Author.

Ussher, J. (1991). *Women's madness: Misogyny or mental illness?* Amherst: University of Massachusetts Press.

Veronen, L., & Kilpatrick, D. (1983). Stress management for rape victims. In D. Meichenbaum & M. E. Jaremko (Eds.), *Stress reduction and prevention* (pp. 341-374). New York: Plenum.

Walker, L. (1984). *The battered woman syndrome*. New York: Springer.

Waller, R. R., & Lisella, L. W. (1991). National AIDS hotline: HIV and AIDS information service through a toll-free telephone system. *Public Health Reports, 106*(6), 628-634.

Washton, A. M., & Gold, M. S. (1986). Recent trends in cocaine abuse: A view from the national hotline, 800-COCAINE. *Advances in Alcohol and Substance Abuse, 6*(2), 31-47.

Washton, A. M., Gold, M. S., Pottash, A. C., & Semlitz, L. (1984). Adolescent cocaine abusers. *Lancet*, 746.

Waters, J., Robertson, J. G., & Kerr, D. (1993). Computer-assisted drug prevention and treatment program evaluation. *Computers in Human Services, 9*(1-2), 155-162

Wells, R. A. (1994). *Planned short-term treatment* (2nd ed.). New York: Free Press.

Werner, H. D. (1986). Cognitive theory. In F. J. Turner (Ed.), *Social work treatment: Interlocking theoretical approaches* (3rd. ed., pp. 91-130). New York: Free Press.

Wesselius, C. L., & Desarno, J. V. (1983). The anatomy of a hostage situation. *Behavioral Science and the Law, 1*, 33-45.

Whitlock, G. E. (1978). *Understanding and coping with real-life crisis*. Monterey, CA: Brooks/Cole.

Williams, T., & Douds, J. (1973). The unique contribution of telephone therapy. In D. Lester & G. W. Brockopp (Eds.). Crisis intervention and counseling by telephone. Springfield, IL: Charles C Thomas.

Wolf-Klein, G. P., & Sliverstone, F. A. (1987). A hotline emergency for the ambulatory frail elderly. *The Gerontologist, 27*(4), 437-439.

Wolman, B. B. (1984). *Interactional psychotherapy*. New York: Van Nostrand Reinhold.

Woods, M., & Hollis, F. (1990). *Casework: A psychosocial study*. New York: McGraw-Hill.

Worell, J., & Remer, P. (1992). *Feminist perspectives in therapy: An empowerment model for women*. Chichester, UK: John Wiley.

Yablonsky, L. (1980). *Psychodrama: Resolving emotional problems through role playing*. New York: Basic Books.

Young, J. E. (1994). *Cognitive therapy for personality disorders: A schema-focused approach* (2nd ed.). Sarasota, FL: Professional Resource Exchange, Inc.

Young, J. E., & Lindemann, M. D. (1992). An integrative schema-focused model for personality disorders. *Journal of Cognitive Psychotherapy: An International Quarterly, 6*(1), 11-23.

Young, R. (1989). Helpful behaviors in the crisis center call. *Journal of Community Psychology, 17*, 70-77.

Youth workers: 73% say professionals should take a position against teens engaging in intercourse. (1986, June). *Children and Teens Today*, pp. 1-2.

National Directory of Crisis Hotlines

Toll-Free Crisis Hotlines

Children and Adolescents

Adolescent Runaways, Crisis Victims, & Battered Women
Victims Service Agency
2 Lafayette St.
New York, NY
1-800-999-9999

Child Find
New York State hotline: 1-800-426-5678
1-800-292-9688

Childhelp / Forrester National Child Abuse Hotline
1-800-4-A-CHILD

I Search of Illinois (missing children)
Illinois Dept. of Law Enforcement
200 Armory Building
Springfield, Illinois 62706
(214) 782-6429
Hotline for sightings: 1-800-843-5763

Metro Help Agency
(information on runaways)
Chicago, IL
U.S. except Illinois: 1-800-621-3860

Missing Children Help Center of Florida
410 Ware Boulevard, Suite 303
Tampa, Florida 33619
In Florida: (813) 623-KIDS
Outside Florida: 1-800-USA-KIDS

National Center for Missing and Exploited Children
2101 Wilson Blvd., Suite 550
Arlington, VA 22201
1-800-THE-LOST
1-800-843-5678

National Child Safety Council
Missing Children International
Jackson, MI
MI, 313, 517, 616, UT: 1-800-872-7875

National Child Safety Council
Jackson, MI
U.S.: 1-800-327-5107

National Clearing House and Information Center on Missing and Murdered Children and Sexual Exploitation of Children Including Pornography and Teenage Prostitution
Hotline number: 1-800-843-5678
TDD hotline (for deaf persons): 1-800-826-7653

National Resource Center on Child Abuse and Neglect
U.S. except Colorado: 1-800-227-5242

National Runaway Switchboard
Chicago, IL
Nationwide call: 1-800-621-4000

National Resource Center on Child Sexual Assault
1-800-542-7006

Parents Anonymous (self-help groups for parents who are, or fear that they may become, out-of-control in disciplining

their children and abusive)
1-800-421-0353

Health and Mental Health Including Addictions

AIDS All Prevention Center
(also see National AIDS Hotline)
Palm Beach, FL
U.S.: 1-800-322-8911

Crisis Hotline
Biddleford, ME
Maine: 1-800-345-3498

Crisis Line HSA Hartford Hospital
Nevada, MO (eating disorders / food addiction information
treatment centers, ABTEC Services, Inc., St. Louis, MO)
U.S. except MO: 1-800-222-2832
AR, IA, IL KS, KY, MO, NE, OK, TN: 1-800-492-2139

National AIDS Hotline
Durham, NC
U.S.: 1-800-342-AIDS
or 1-800-342-2437
Spanish Speaking AIDS Hotline: 1-800-344-SIDA
For Hearing Impaired: 1-800-AIDS-TTY

National Clearinghouse for Alcohol and Drug Information
1-800-729-6686

National Hotline for Cocaine and Crack Users
Fair Oaks Hospital
Summit, NJ
1-800-COCAINE

National Information System for Health Related Services
Columbia, SC
U.S. except SC: 1-800-922-9239
SC: 1-800-922-1107

New Jersey Council on Compulsive Gambling
1-800-GAMBLER

Occupational Health Services
New York, NY
U.S. except NY: 1-800-445-6737
Oakland, CA; U.S.: 1-800-327-7526

Rare Disorders
National Organization for Rare Disorders
1-800-447-6673

St. Claire's Hospital and Health Center Aids Hotline
New York, NY
U.S.: 1-800-433-2437

Spokane Poison Center
Spokane, WA
CA, 309, 408, 415, 707, 916, ID, MT, NV, OR: 1-800-424-8802

Victims and Violence

MADD (Mothers Against Drunk Driving)
1-800-438-MADD

National Domestic Violence Hotline
Washington, DC 20037
1-800-333-SAFE

National Resource Center on Child Sexual Assault
1-800-542-7006

National Resource Center on Child Abuse and Neglect
U.S. except Colorado: 1-800-227-5242

National Resource Center on Domestic Violence
2401 Virginia Avenue, N.W. Suite 305
Washington, DC 20037

1-800-537-2238
(202) 293-8860

National Sheriff's Association Victim / Witness Program
Alexandria, VA
U.S.: 1-800-424-STAR

National Victims Center
(technical assistance and legislative database related to
victimization and criminal justice)
1-800-FYI-CALL

New Jersey Hotline for Battered Women
Trenton, NJ
1-800-572-SAFE

Parents Anonymous (self-help groups for parents who are, or
fear that they may become out-of-control in disciplining
their children and abusive)
1-800-421-0353

Rape Abuse and Incest National Network
1-800-656-4673

Women's Center
Warren, PA
U.S.: 1-800-338-3460

Hotlines for Addiction and Treatment Centers

Al-Anon Family Groups
Headquarters, Inc.
New York, NY
U.S.: (212) 302-7240

Alcohol and Drug Treatment Prevention
College Park, MD
U.S., Monday-Friday, 9 a.m. to 4 p.m. EST: 1-800-635-7619

American Council on Alcoholism
5024 Campbell Blvd, Suite H
Baltimore, MD 21236
U.S., 24 hrs., 7 days a week: 1-800-527-5344

Bethany Center (addictions treatment)
Bethany, PA
U.S.: 1-800-345-5550
or (717) 253-9600

Brattleboro Retreat—Addiction Treatment Center and Psychiatric Hospital (adolescent alcohol and drug abuse treatment program)
P.O. Box 803 75 Linden Street
Brattleboro, VT
U.S., 24 hrs.: 1-800-345-5550

Care Unit Hospital Program
Adult & Adolescent Treatment Programs Available Nationwide
U.S. except CA: 1-800-854-0318
Northern CA: 1-800-422-4427
Southern CA: 1-800-422-4143

Charter Medical EAP Services
Corona, CA
U.S.: 1-800-622-9299

Hazelden Foundation
Center City, MN
General Info.: Minneapolis, MN
U.S. except MN: 1-800-257-7800
Admissions (U.S. except MN)—24 hr.: 1-800-262-5010
—Jane Fedderly, Supervisor

Koala Center
Nashville, TN, & Indianapolis, IN
U.S. except TN: 1-800-423-9499

Life Center of Galax (addictions treatment)
Galax, VA
U.S. except VA: 1-800-345-6998
VA: 1-800-542-8708
—Chester Gross, Marketing Director

National Council on Alcoholism
New York, NY
U.S.: 1-800-622-2255

NCA & Other Dependencies
Southfield, MI
U.S.: 1-800-542-2237

Schick Shadel Hospital (addictions treatment)
Santa Barbara, CA (U.S.): 1-800-322-5796
Fort Worth, TX (U.S.): 1-800-772-7516
Seattle, WA (U.S.): 1-800-426-7516
or 1-800-542-4202
800 CHANING (U.S.): 1-800-272-8464

Seabrook House
Seabrook, NJ
NJ: 1-800-582-5968
—Matt Wolf, Director of Admissions
1-609-455-7575

Sierra Tuscon
Tuscon, AZ
U.S. except AZ: 1-800-624-9001
U.S.: 1-800-624-4624

Spofford Hall Rehabilitation
Center Spofford, NH
CT, MA, ME, NJ, NY, 212, 315, 516, 518, 607, 718, 914, RI, VT:
1-800-451-1716
New Hampshire: 1-800-451-1717

Stonington Institute
N. Stonington, CT
DC, DE, MA, MD, ME, NH, NJ, NY, OH, PA, RI, VA, VT,
WV—Admissions Only: 1-800-832-1022

Talbot Place
Hammelstown, PA
CT, DC, DE, MA, MD, NC, NH, NY, OH, RI, VA, VT, WV:
1-800-441-5458

Turning Point Care Center
Moaltrie, GA
AL, FL, KY, MS, NC, SC, TN: 1-800-847-5822
GA: 1-800-342-1075
or (918) 985-4815

Crisis Centers and Suicide Prevention Hotlines

Alabama

Contact Mobile
P.O. Box 66608
Mobile, AL 36660-1608
—Executive Director: Donna Bennett
Monday-Friday, 8:30 a.m. to 4:30 p.m.: (205) 431-4189

Crisis Center, Inc.
(Jefferson Co.)
3600 8th Avenue, S. Suite 501
Birmingham, AL 35222
—Acting Director: Michael Falligante
24 hrs.: (205) 323-7782

Crisis Line / Tuscaloosa
P.O. Box 2190
Tuscaloosa, AL 35401

—Director: Jean Cobb
5:00 p.m. to 8:00 a.m.: (205) 345-1600

Alaska

First Call for Help
341 W. Tudor, Suite 106
Anchorage, Alaska 99503
—Executive Director: Lynn Fairy-Caswell
(907) 562-4048

Arizona

Interfaith Counseling Service
Suicide Prevention Center
1232 E. Broadway
Tempe, AZ 85282
—Director: Ilene L. Dode, Ph.D.
24 hrs.: (602) 784-1500

Casa De Yuma
Suicide Prevention Hotline
Center Against Sexual Assault
P.O. Box 4201
Yuma, AZ 85366
—Program Coordinator, Kathy Bierl
—Director: Sandy Conrad
(602) 783-1860
24 hr. hotline: (602) 782-7273

Arkansas

Life Preservers, Inc.
825 W. 3rd Street
Little Rock, AR 72201
—President, Kathy Churchill
(501) 374-5134

Northwest Arkansas Crisis Intervention Center
P.O. Box 1618
Springdale, AR 72765
—Executive Director: Bergean Burlington
(501) 756-1995
Hotlines: 1-800-640-2680
or 1-800-756-2337

California

Contra Costa Crisis / Suicide Intervention
P.O. Box 4852
Walnut Creek, CA 94596
—Executive Director: Dennis Lepak
(415) 939-1916
Hotline, 24 hrs.: (415) 939-3232

The Crisis Team
P.O. Box 85524
San Diego, CA 92138-5524
—Coordinator: Pamela Blackwell, M.A.
(619) 236-4576
Hotline, 24 hrs.: (619) 236-3339
San Diego area only: 1-800-479-3339

Help in Emotional Trouble
P.O. Box 4282
Fresno, CA 93744
—Executive Director: Renee Clift
9 a.m. to 5 p.m.: (209) 486-4703
24 hr. hotline: (209) 485-1432

Hotline Help Center
P.O. Box 999
Anaheim, CA 92805
—Executive Director: Rev. Rick Gastil
10 a.m. to 10 p.m.: (714) 778-1000

San Francisco Suicide Prevention
3940 Geary Blvd.
San Francisco, CA 94118
—Executive Director: Eve Meyer
(415) 752-4866
Hotline, 24 hrs.: (415) 221-1423

Santa Clara Suicide & Crisis Service
2220 Moorpark Avenue
San Jose, CA 95128
—Director: Meg Paris
(408) 299-6250
Hotline, 24 hrs.: (408) 279-3312

SPC of Family Service of Los Angeles
626 S. Kingsley Drive
Los Angeles, CA 90005
—President: Tony Lufrano
Crisis line, 24 hrs.: (213) 381-5111

Suicide & Crisis Intervention Service
1669 N. "E" Street
San Bernardino, CA 92405
—Program Coordinator: Barbara J. Cameron
Hotline, 24 hrs.: (714) 886-4889

Suicide Prevention & Crisis Center
Serving Monterey & San Benito Counties
P.O. Box 52078
Pacific Grove, CA 93950-7078
—Executive Director: Pat Garrigues
(408) 375-6966
Hotline, 24 hrs.: (408) 649-8008

Suicide Prevention / Crisis Intervention of Alameda County
P.O. Box 9102
Berkeley, CA 94709
—Director: Dr. Ronald Tauber

(415) 848-1515
Hotline: (415) 849-2212

Suicide Prevention Services of Sacramento
P.O. Box 277815
Sacramento, CA 95812-0448
—Executive Director: Lou Ziskind
Hotline, 24 hrs.: (916) 368-3111

Teen Line
Thalians Mental Health Center
8730 Alden Drive, C301
Los Angeles, CA 90048
—Director: Elaine Leader, Ph.D.
(213) 855-3401
6 p.m. to 10 p.m.: (213) 855-4673
Hotline: 1-800-852-8336

Colorado

Pueblo Suicide Prevention Center, Inc.
801 N. Sante Fe Avenue
Pueblo, CO 81003
—Director: Eleanor Hamm
(719) 545-2477
Hotline, 24 hrs.: (719) 544-1133

Suicide & Crisis Control
2549 South Ash
Denver, CO 80222
—Executive Director: Bill Anderson
Hotline, 24 hrs.: (303) 756-8485

Connecticut

Hotline, Inc.
120 E. Putnam Avenue
Cos Cob, CT 06807

—Executive Director: Gilda Press
(203) 661-4378
Hotline, 24 hrs.: (203) 661-HELP

Info Line of Southwestern Connecticut
83 East Avenue Suite 107
Norwalk, CT 06851
—Director: Sherrie Winkworth
(203) 853-9109
Hotline, 24 hrs.: (203) 853-2525

The Wheeler Clinic, Inc.
Emergency Services
91 Northwest Drive
Plainville, CT 06062
—Unit Coordinator: Alan Kennedy
(203) 747-6801
Hotline, 24 hrs.: (203) 747-3434

Delaware

Contact-Delaware, Inc.
P.O. Box 2939
Wilmington, DE 19805
—Executive Director: Patricia P. Tedford
(302) 656-6222
Hotline, 24 hrs.: (302) 575-1112

Kent / Sussex Mobile Crisis Unit
P.O. Box 912
Milford, DE 19963
(302) 422-1133
Hotline—Delaware only: 1-800-345-6785

Mental Health Assoc. in Delaware
1813 N. Franklin Street
Wilmington, DE 19802

—Executive Director: Marjorie Medrick
Monday-Friday, 8:30 a.m. to 4:30 p.m.: (302) 656-8308

New Castle Community Mental Health
801 West Street
Wilmington, DE 19801
—CMHC Reg. Director: Neil McLaughlin
(302) 577-6490

District of Columbia

The Samaritans of Washington, Inc.
P.O. Box 9814
Washington, DC 20016
—Executive Director: Ellen Weinberg
(202) 362-8858
Hotline, 24 hrs.: (202) 362-8100

Florida

Alchua County Crisis Center
730 N. Waldo Road Suite 100
Gainesville, FL 32601
—Director: Marshall Knudson
(904) 372-3659
Hotline, 24 hrs.: (904) 376-4444

Children / Adolescents Crisis Service
1660 NW 7th Ct.
Miami, FL 33136
—Director: Dr. Anna Rivas-Vasquez
Hotlines, 24 hrs.: (305) 545-2305
or (305) 324-1900

Crisis Line Information and Referral Services, Inc.
P.O. Box 3588
Lamtanta, FL 33465
—Director: Sheryl Lenz

Hotline, 24 hrs. (North): (407) 547-1000
Hotline, 24 hrs. (South): (407) 245-1000

Family Resources Helpline
P.O. Box 13087
St. Petersburg, FL 33733
—Program Manager: Jennifer Sewell
Hotline, 24 hrs.: (813) 531-4664

First Call for Help / Broward County
1300 So. Andrews Avenue
P.O. Box 22877
Fort Lauderdale, FL 33335
—Executive Director: Arthur J. Ellick
Hotline, 24 hrs.: (305) 467-6333

HelpLine, Inc.
P.O. Box 2186
Key West, FL 33045-2186
—Executive Director: Jo Pine, M.A.
Hotline, 24 hrs.: (305) 296-HELP

Hillsborough County Crisis Center, Inc.
2214 E. Henry Avenue
Tampa, FL 33610-4497
—Executive Director: Jerry J. Vasquez
(813) 238-8411
Hotline, 24 hrs.: (813) 238-8821
Rape hotline: (813) 238-RAPE

Lakeside Alternatives
434 W. Kennedy Blvd.
Orlando, FL 32810
—Director: Duane Zimmerman
Hotline, 24 hrs.: (407) 875-3700

Pinellas Emergency MHS, Inc.
11254 58th Street North

Pinellas Park, FL 34666-2606
—Executive Director: Thomas C. Wedekind, M.S.W.
(813) 545-5636,7
Suicide prevention hotline, 24 hrs.: (813) 791-3131

Suicide / Crisis Hotline
Crisis Services of Brevard, Inc.
P.O. Box 1108
Rockledge, FL 32955
—Executive Director: Elizabeth Donoghue
(407) 631-9290
Hotline, 24 hrs.: (407) 631-8944

Suicide Prevention Center / Jacksonville
2218 Park Street
Jacksonville, FL 32204
—Director: Jim Fortenberry
(904) 353-2012

Telephone Counsel and Referral Service
P.O. Box 20169
Tallahassee, FL 32316
—Executive Director: Randall S. Nicklaus
(904) 681-9131
Hotline, 24 hrs.: (904) 222-NEED

Georgia

Emergency Mental Health Services
Fulton County Health Department
99 Butler Street, S.E.
Atlanta, GA 30303
—Director: Alan T. Burrell, Ph.D.
Hotline, 24 hrs.: (404) 730-1600
Hotline, 24 hrs. (TTY): (404) 730-1611

Hawaii

Suicide and Crisis Center
680 Iwilea Road, Suite 430
Honolulu, HI 96817
—Center Director: Sue Atta, M.A.
(808) 536-7234
Hotline, 24 hrs.: (808) 521-4555

Idaho

Canyon Suicide Prevention Hotline, Inc.
1512 12th Avenue Road
Nampa, ID 83686
—Director: Myron McDaniel
2 p.m. to 2 a.m.: (208) 465-2121

Illinois

Call for Help
Suicide and Crisis Intervention
9400 Lebanon Road
Edgemont, IL 62203
—Executive Director: Joann Pisel
Hotline, 24 hrs.: (618) 397-0963

Champaign County Mental Health Center Crisis Line
P.O. Box 429
Champaign, IL 61820
—Coordinator: Wilma Bryant
Hotline, 24 hrs.: (217) 359-4141

Contact of Rockford
P.O. Box 1976
Rockford, IL 61110
—Director: Earl Hollander
(815) 964-0400
Hotline, 24 hrs.: (815) 964-4044

Crisis of Will County
P.O. Box 2354
Joliet, IL 60434
—Executive Director: Charlene Lockowitz
Hotline, 24 hrs.: (815) 744-5280

Emergency Crisis Intervention Team
McLean Co. Center for Human Services
108 W. Market Street
Bloomington, IL 61701
—Program Director: Cheryl Gaines
Hotline, 24 hrs.: (309) 827-5351

In-Touch Hotline
Counseling Center
University of Illinois at Chicago Circle
P.O. Box 4348
Chicago, IL 60680
—Director: Dr. Barry Greenwald
(312) 996-3490
Hotline, 6 p.m. to 3 a.m.: (312) 996-5535

Indiana

Mental Health Associates
2506 Willowbrook Parkway Suite 100
Indianapolis, IN 46205
—Coordinator: Mary Hoffman
(317) 251-0005
Hotline, 24 hrs.: (317) 251-7575

Southwestern Indiana Mental Health Center, Inc.
415 Mulberry Street
Evansville, IN 47713-1298
—Clinical Director: Richard Paul, A.S.C.W.
Hotline, 24 hrs.: (812) 423-7791

Iowa

Community Telephone Services
Crisis Line Service of the American Red Cross
2116 Grand Avenue
Des Moines, IA 50312
—Program Director: Margie Dunlap
Hotline, 24 hrs.: (515) 244-6700

Crisis Services / Waterloo
2530 University Avenue
Waterloo, IA 50701
—Coordinators: Angi Stuckenberg and Renee Else
Hotline, 24 hrs.: (319) 233-8484

Kansas

Headquarters, Inc.
1419 Massachusetts Street
P.O. Box 999
Lawrence, KS 66044
—Director: Marcia Epstein
Hotline, 24 hrs.: (913) 841-2345

Sedgwick County Department of Mental Health
1801 E. Tenth Street
Wichita, KS 67214-3197
—Director: Herman Bruce
(316) 383-8251
Hotline, 24 hrs.: (316) 686-7465

Kentucky

Crisis and Information Center
Seven Counties Services, Inc.
101 W. Muhammad Ali Blvd.
Louisville, KY 40202
—Coordinator: Linda Hazelap

(502) 589-9630
Hotline, 24 hrs.: (505) 589-4313

Louisiana

Baton Rouge Crisis Intervention Center
4837 Rever Avenue
Baton Rouge, LA 70808
—Executive Director: Frank Campbell
(504) 924-1431
Hotline, 24 hrs.: (504) 924-3900

River Oaks Admission and Referral Center
1525 River Oaks Road W.
New Orleans, LA 70123-2199
—Director: Lois Laughlin, R.N.
Hotline, 24 hrs.: (504) 734-1740 ext. 357

Maine

Crisis Stabilization Unit
38 North Avenue
Skowhegan, ME 04976
—Director: Bette Parsons
Hotline, 24 hrs.: (207) 474-2506

Tri-County Mental Health Services Crisis Intervention Unit
106 Campus Avenue
Lewistown, ME 04240
—Director, Crisis Intervention: John Coffin
Hotline, 24 hrs.: (207) 783-9141

Maryland

First Step Youth Services Center
8303 Liberty Road
Baltimore, MD 21207
—Executive Director: David Goldman

(301) 521-4141
Hotline, 24 hrs.: (301) 521-3800

Grass Roots
6700 Freetown Road
Columbia, MD 21044-4014
—Director: Andrea Ingram
(301) 531-6006
Hotline, 24 hrs.: (301) 531-6677

Montgomery County Hotline
c/o Mental Health Association
1000 Twinbrook Parkway
Rockville, MD 20851
—Director: Ann Reiss
Hotline, 24 hrs.: (301) 738-2255

Massachusetts

Crisis Center, Inc.
P.O. Box 652
Worchester, MA 01602
—Acting Executive Director: Timothy J. Kelley
(508) 791-7205
Hotline, 24 hrs.: (508) 791-6562

The Samaritans
500 Commonwealth Avenue
Boston, MA 02215
—Director: Peggy O'Neill
(617) 536-2460
Hotline, 24 hrs.: (617) 247-0220

Samaritans of Fall River-New Bedford
386 Stanley Street
Fall River, MA 02720
—Director: Ellie Leite
Hotline, 24 hrs.: (508) 673-3777

Samaritans of Merrimack Valley
169 East Street
Metluan, MA 01844
—Director: Margaret F. Serley
Hotline, 24 hrs.: (508) 688-0030

Samaritans of South Middlesex, Inc.
73 Union Avenue
Framingham, MA 01701
—Executive Director: Tim Hunt
Hotline, 24 hrs.: (508) 875-4500

Samaritans on Cape Cod
P.O. Box 65
Falmouth, MA 02541
—Director: Mary Clenindon
Hotline, 24 hrs.: (508) 548-8900

Tri-Link, Inc.
51 Everett Street
Southridge, MA 01550
—Executive Director: Karl Gustafson
Hotline, 24 hrs.: (508) 765-9101

Michigan

Gryphon Place
1104 S. Westnedge
Kalamazoo, MI 49008
—Director: William Pell
(616) 381-1510
Hotline, 24 hrs.: (616) 381-4357

Macomb County Crisis Center
5th Floor, County Building
Mt. Clemens, MI 48043
—Director: Gary Burnett
Hotline, 24 hrs.: (313) 573-2200

NSO Emergency Telephone Service
Suicide Prevention Center
220 Bagley, Suite 626
Detroit, MI 48226
—Director: Sharon Jamal
(313) 963-7890
Hotline, 24 hrs.: (313) 224-7000

Operation L.I.F.E. Foundation
2012 Glendale Avenue
Flint, MI 48503
—President: Rose Ann MacDonald
Referral service: (313) 767-9418

Psychologists Helping Psychologists
Networking Education Research and Referrals for Doctoral
Level Psychologists and Graduate Students with a Substance
Abuse Problem
23439 Michigan Avenue
Dearborn, MI 48124
(313) 278-1314

Minnesota

Crisis Intervention Center
Hennepin County Medical Center
701 Park Avenue South
Minneapolis, MN 55415
—Psychologist: Zigfrids T. Sielmachers
(612) 347-3164
Hotline, 24 hrs. (crisis): (612) 347-3161
Hotline, 24 hrs. (suicide): (612) 347-2222

Missouri

Community Counseling Center
402 S. Silversprings Road
Cape Girardeau, MO 63701

—Director: Roger Henry
8:00 a.m. to 4:30 p.m.: (314) 334-1100

Life Crisis Services, Inc.
1423 S. Big Bend Blvd.
St. Louis, MO 63117
—Executive Director: Mr. Lee Judy
(314) 647-3100
Hotline, 24 hrs.: (314) 647-4357

Nevada

Clark City School District Crisis Intervention Center
2625 E. St. Louis Avenue
Las Vegas, NV 89104
—Coordinator: William Miller
7:00 a.m. to 5:00 p.m.: (702) 799-7449

Suicide Prevention & Crisis Call Center
P.O. Box 8016
Reno, NV 89507
—Executive Director: Roger Simon
(702) 323-4533
Hotline, 24 hrs. (Nevada only): 1-800-992-5757
Hotline, 24 hrs.: (702) 323-6111

New Hampshire

Emergency Services / Concord CNHCMS, Inc.
P.O. Box 2032
Concord, NH 03302-2032
—Director: Mark J. Ciocca, Ph.D.
Hotline, 24 hrs.: (603) 228-1551

Help Line / Merrimack County
Community Service Council of Merrimack County
2 Industrial Park Drive
Concord, NH 03301

—Director, Community Program: Arlene Pinkos
Hotline, 24 hrs.: (603) 225-9000

The Samaritans of Keene
25 Lamson Street
Keene, NH 03431
Hotline, 24 hrs.: (603) 357-5505

New Jersey

Contact-a-Friend-Line (for children)
(609) 261-2220
Information and referral line
9 a.m. to 5 p.m.: (609) 234-2223

Contact Burlington County
P.O. Box 333
Moorestown, NJ 08057
—Executive Director: Gail Breshohan
(609) 234-5484
Hotlines, 24 hrs.: (609) 234-8888
(609) 871-4700
(609) 267-8500
(609) 261-2220

Contact-We Care, Inc.
P.O. Box 37
Westfield, NJ 07091
—Executive Director: Candy Santo
(908) 232-2936
Hotline, 24 hrs.: (908) 232-2880

Gambler's Anonymous
P.O. Box 283
Kearny, NJ 07031
Hotlines, 24 hrs.: (908) 756-1171
(609) 429-6516

N.J. Self-Help Clearing House
St. Clare's Riverside Medical Center
Denville, NJ 07834
(201) 625-9564 *or* 1-800-FOR-MASH
(mutual aid self-help)
TDD, for the hearing impaired: (201) 625-9053

St. Mary's Community Mental Health Center
St. Mary's Hospital Community Mental Health Center
314 Clinton Street
Hoboken, NJ 07030
—Director: Michael Swerdlow
—Assistant Director: Sally Davis, R.N., M.S.
(201) 792-8200
Crisis hotline, 24 hrs.: (201) 795-0800

Steininger Center
Kennedy and Lords
19 E. Orchard Avenue
Cherry Hill, NJ 08021
—Director, Crisis Program: Charles Graham
(609) 428-1300
Lords crisis hotline, 24 hrs.: (609) 541-2222
Kennedy crisis hotline, 24 hrs.: (609) 428-4357

New York

Child and Adolescent Psychiatric Center
350 Main Street
Buffalo, NY 14214
—Director: Shepard Goldberg, Ph.D.
Monday-Thursday (9 a.m. to 9 p.m.), Friday (9 a.m. to 1 p.m.): (718) 835-4011

Child Sexual Abuse Treatment Clinic
Westchester Jewish Community Services
20 South Broadway
Yonkers, NY 10701

—Executive Director: Oscar Rabinowitz
(914) 949-6761

CMHC Mental Health Services—Mercy Hospital
1000 North Village
Rockville Center, NY 11570
—Director: Dr. Brian Fitzsimmons
(516) 255-2331
Hotline, 24 hrs.: (516) 536-4335

Contact—Syracuse
P.O. Box 6149
Syracuse, NY 13217
—Executive Director: Janice K. Liddell
(315) 425-5138
Hotline, 24 hrs.: (315) 425-1500

Covenant House / New York
440 Ninth Avenue
New York, NY 1001-1607
—Executive Director: Bruce Henry
Hotline, 24 hrs.: (212) 727-4000

Drug Abuse Hotline
Buffalo Psychiatric Center
775 Third Avenue
Niagara Falls, NY 14302
—Director: Daniel E. Clark
Hotlines, 24 hrs.: (716) 285-3515
or (716) 285-9936

Drugs Anonymous
(formerly Pills Anonymous)
National Self-Help Group
P.O. Box 473
Ansonia Station, NY 10023
Hotline, 24 hrs.: (212) 874-0700

Dutchess County Department of Mental Health
Psychiatric Emergency Service
730 North Road
Poughkeepsie, NY 12601
—Clinical Administrator: Brian Ward
Hotline, 24 hrs.: (914) 485-9700, ext. 456

Fordham-Tremont Community Mental Health Center
2021 Grand Concourse
Bronx, NY 10453
—Executive Director: Mildred M. Allen, Ph.D.
9 a.m. to 5 p.m.: (212) 960-0300
—Clinical Director: Dr. Maura Grossman
(212) 960-0348

Lifeline Service Day Treatment for Children and Adolescents
(ages 3-13)
80-09 Winchester Blvd.
Queens Village, NY 11427
8 a.m. to 4 p.m.: (718) 740-4300

Maimonides Community Mental Health Center
Maimonides Medical Center of Brooklyn
Brooklyn, NY 11219
—Director: Marcel Biberfield, D.S.W.
(718) 283-6000

Middle Earth Crisis Counseling and Referral Center (teen crisis)
2740 Martin Avenue
Bellmore, NY 11710
—Coordinator: Diane Gorenstein, C.S.W.
Hotline, 24 hrs.: (516) 826-0244

Mobile Crisis Unit
Psychiatric Institute
Westchester County Medical Center
Valhalla, NY 10595

—Director: Dianne Alden
Hotline, 24 hrs.: (914) 285-7075

Mobile Crisis Unit
Rockland Psychiatric Center
Orangeburge, NY 10962
—Executive Director: Charlotte Oliver
(914) 359-1000

Rape Hotline
1 Police Plaza
New York, NY 10038
Hotline, 24 hrs.: (212) 267-7273

Response of Suffolk County, Inc.
P.O. Box 300
Stony Brook, NY 11790
—Executive Director: Arlene Stevens
Hotline, 24 hrs.: (516) 751-7500

The Samaritans of New York City
Madison Square Station
P.O. Box 1259
New York, NY 10159
—Executive Director: Alan Ross
(212) 673-8180
Hotline, 24 hrs.: (212) 677-3000

Suicide Prevention and Crisis Service of Tompkins County
P.O. Box 312
Ithaca, NY 14851
—Executive Director: Margaret Dyer
(607) 272-1616
Hotline, 24 hrs.: 1-800-333-4444

Suicide Prevention / Crisis Counseling Center
St. Francis Hall 33 Inpatient Unit
301 Prospect Avenue

Syracuse, NY 13203
—Coordinator: Teresa B. Domanic
Hotline, 24 hrs.: (315) 474-1333

Suicide Prevention Hotline
Mental Health Association
29 Sterling Avenue
White Plains, NY 10606
—Clinical Director: Arlene R. Stana, C.S.W.
(914) 949-6741
Hotline, 24 hrs.: (914) 946-0121

North Carolina

To Life
P.O. Box 9354
Charlotte, NC 28299
—Chief Executive Officers: Alexis Stein &
Howard R. Winokeur
9 a.m. to 5 p.m.: (704) 322-LIFE

North Dakota

Mental Health Association of North Dakota
P.O. Box 160
Bismarck, ND 58502
—Director: Myrt Armstrong
(701) 255-3692
Hotline, 24 hrs. (ND only): 1-800-472-2911

United Way's Hotline
United Way of Cass Clay, Inc.
P.O. Box 447
Fargo, ND 58107-1609
—Director: Mark Dourdon
Hotline, 24 hrs.: (701) 235-7335

Ohio

The Link Crisis Center
315 Thurston Street
Bowling Green, OH 43402
—Director: Linda Meyerholtz
Hotlines, 24 hrs.: (419) 352-1545
or (Ohio only) 1-800-472-9411

St. Vincent Charity Hospital
Psychiatric Emergency Service
2351 East 22nd Street
Cleveland, OH 44115
—Director, Psychiatric Emergency: Bahkman Sharif, M.D.
(216) 861-6200, ext. 2000
Suicide Hotline, 24 hrs.: (216) 229-2211

Suicide Prevention Services
1301 N. High Street
Columbus, OH 43201
—Director: Jack Schuster
(614) 299-6600
Hotline, 24 hrs.: (614) 221-5445

281-CARE—Crisis Care Center
Talbert House
Cincinnati, Ohio
—Program Director: Nelly Rimini
(513) 281-2866
Hotline, 24 hrs.: (513) 281-2293

Oklahoma

Teenline (Oklahoma City)
Department of Mental Health
Capital Station
P.O. Box 53277
Oklahoma City, OK 73152

—Supervisor: Viola Wells
(405) 271-7474
Hotline, 24 hrs. (Oklahoma only): 1-800-522-9054

The University of Oklahoma National Resource Center for Youth Services
202 W. 8th Street
Tulsa, OK 74119-1419
—Director: James M. Walker
Monday-Friday, 8 a.m. to 5 p.m.: (918) 585-2986

Oregon

Metro Crisis Intervention Service
P.O. Box 637
Portland, OR 97207
—Executive Director: Laura Scolar
(503) 226-3099

Pennsylvania

Agoraphobia and Anxiety Center of Temple University
112 Bala Avenue
Bala Cynwyd, PA
9 a.m. to 5 p.m.: (215) 667-6490

Albert Einstein Medical Center—N. Div.
Department of Psychiatry
York and Tabor Roads
Philadelphia, PA 19141
—Director of Research: Bonnie Frank Carter, Ph.D.
(215) 456-7312

Chester County Mental Health Crisis Intervention Service
520 E. Lancaster Avenue
Downingtown, PA 19335
—Director: Aylin Aybar
Hotline, 24 hrs.: (215) 873-1000

Childline
PA only: 1-800-932-0313

Contact Teleministries
Harrisburg, PA
(717) 232-3501

Contact York
104 Lafayette Street
York, PA 17403
(717) 845-9123
Hotline, 24 hrs.: (717) 845-3656
Hotline, 24 hrs. (PA only): 1-800-826-EARS
Teenline: (717) 845-1886

Dauphin County Crisis Intervention
25 S. Front Street
Harrisburg, PA 17101
—Director: Martin Yespy
(717) 255-2705
Hotline, 24 hrs.: (717) 232-7511

Lancaster Guidance Center
630 Janet Avenue
Lancaster, PA 17601
—Deputy Director: Joanne W. Good, A.C.S.W.
(717) 394-2631

Pennsylvania Teen Suicide Project
Div. Assist. Program / Allegheny Intake Unit
200 Commerce Court Building
Pittsburgh, PA 15219
—Program Director: Sandra Morgan
(412) 394-5837

Survivors of Suicide, Inc.
1724 Rodman Street
Philadelphia, PA 19146

—President: Sunnie Baron Freeman
Hotline, 24 hrs.: (215) 545-2242

Teen Suicide Treatment and Prevention Program
Hahnemann University Hospital, Child and Adolescent
Inpatient Unit, Mail Stop
403 Broad and Vine, 16 South Tower
Philadelphia, PA 19102
—Staff Psychiatrist: Hedy K. Singer, Ph.D.
(215) 448-7206

Women Organized Against Rape
Philadelphia, PA
(215) 922-3434

Rhode Island

The Samaritans of Providence
2 Megee Street
Providence, RI 02906
—Director: Anthony Majone
(401) 272-4044

South Carolina

Charleston Hotline
P.O. Box 71583
Charleston Hts., SC 94115-1583
—Executive Director: Charlotte Anderson
(803) 747-3007

Helpline of the Midlands, Inc.
P.O. Box 6336
Columbia, SC 29260
—Executive Director: Jane W. Key
Hotline, 24 hrs.: (803) 790-4357

Tennessee

Crisis Intervention Center, Inc.
P.O. Box 40752
Nashville, TN 37204-0752
—Director: Patricia Couto
(615) 298-3359

Suicide / Crisis Intervention Services—Memphis
P.O. Box 40068
Memphis, TN 38174
—Executive Director: Ann Knight
(901) 276-1111
Hotline, 24 hrs.: (901) 274-7477

Texas

Austin-Travis Mental Health MR Center
Crisis Hotline
2006 Gaston Place
Austin, TX 78723
—Program Coordinator: Chris Allman
(512) 926-7080

Crisis Intervention
c/o Family Service, Inc.
1424 Hemphill
Ft. Worth, TX 76104
—Director: Carol West
Monday-Thursday, 8:30 a.m. to 8:30 p.m.; Friday, 8:30 a.m.
to 5 p.m.; Saturday, 9 a.m. to 5 p.m.: (817) 927-8884

Crisis Intervention of Houston, Inc.
P.O. Box 130866
Houston, TX 77219
—Director: Pat Whitten-Lege
(713) 527-9864

Crisis Services / Corpus Christi
4906-B Everhart
Corpus Christi, TX 78411
—Acting Director: Dot Barnette
(512) 993-7416

Harris County Psychiatric Intervention
Department of Mental Health / Mental Retardation
2800 South MacGregor
Houston, TX 77021
—Social Services Administrator: Mary Etta Clark
(713) 741-6000

Rape and Suicide Crisis of Southeast Texas
P.O. Box 5011
Beaumont, TX 77706
—Executive Director: Diane Collinge
(408) 832-6530
Hotline, 24 hrs.: (409) 835-3355

Rx for Crisis
P.O. Box 272651
Houston, TX 77277-2651
—Director: Penny Crist
(713) 795-4529

Suicide and Crisis Center
2808 Swiss Avenue
Dallas, TX 75204
—Executive Director: Sheryl Pender
(214) 824-7020

Utah

Salt Lake Valley Mental Health
1228 S. 900 E
Salt Lake City, UT 84105

—Unit Manager: Lynn Whittaker
Suicide prevention line, 24 hrs.: (801) 483-5444

Virginia

Community Mental Health, Mental Retardation, and Substance
Abuse Services Board—Prevention Division
8033 Ashton Avenue
Manassas, VA 22110
—Youth Specialist: Martha Joseph
(703) 355-7730

Northern Virginia Hotline
P.O. Box 187
Arlington, VA 22210
—Executive Director: May Pearl
(703) 522-4460

Suicide Crisis Center, Inc.
P.O. Box 1493
Portsmouth, VA 23705
—Executive Director: Bonnie L. Durham
(804) 393-0502
Hotline, 24 hrs.: (804) 399-6393

TRUST—Roanoke Valley
360 Washington Avenue, SW
Roanoke, VA 24106
—Executive Director: Stuart Israel
(703) 345-8859

Washington

Crisis Clinic
1515 Dexter Avenue North, #300
Seattle, WA 98109
—Executive Director: Roy Sargeant

(206) 461-3210
Hotline, 24 hrs.: (206) 461-3222

Lifeline Institute for Suicide Prevention
910A Lakewood Drive, SW
Tacoma, WA 98499
—Director: Dolores Bialarz, MA
Emergency line, 24 hrs.: (206) 584-3733

Seattle Counseling Service for Sexual Minorities
1505 Broadway
Seattle, WA 98122
—Program Manager: Christina Coiro, M.A.
(206) 329-8737

Youth Service Prevention Center
18312 101 Street, NE
Bothell, WA 98011
—Program Director: Vicki Jung
(206) 481-0560

Wisconsin

Crisis Intervention Center / Green Bay
131 Madison Street
Green Bay, WI 54301
—Program Director: Sue Cohen
(414) 437-7071
Hotline, 24 hrs.: (414) 436-8008

Emergency Services
Mental Health Center of Dane County
625 West Washington Avenue
Madison, WI 53703
—Manager, Emergency Services: Karen H. Stevenson
(608) 251-7933

Suicide Prevention Center
1221 Whipple Street
Eau Claire, WI 54701
—Director: Susan Barnard
(715) 839-3274
Hotline, 24 hrs.: (715) 834-6040

Survivors Helping Survivors (SEWAS)
St. Luke's Medical Center
2900 Oklahoma Avenue
Milwaukee, WI 53215
—Nursing Specialist: Marcia Williams, R.N.
(414) 649-6333

Victim Service and Witness Assistance Programs

Alabama

Victim / Witness Program
Tuscaloosa Country District Attorney
410 County Courthouse
Tuscaloosa, AL 35401-1894
—Coordinator: Vicki Clawson
Monday-Friday, 8:30 a.m. to 5:00 p.m.: (205) 349-1252

Alaska

Advocates for Victims of Violence
P.O. Box 132
Valdez, AK 99686
—Director: Carolyn Dallinger
Monday-Friday, 8:30 a.m. to 5:00 p.m.: (907) 835-2980

Arizona

Maricopa County Attorney's Office
Victim / Witness Program

301 Jefferson, 5th Floor
Phoenix, AZ 85003
—Director: Carol McFaddon
(602) 506-8522

Pima County Victim / Witness Program
110 W. Congress
Tuscon, AZ 85701
—Coordinator: Viki Sharp
(602) 792-8749

Victim Assistance Services
5850 W. Glendale Avenue
Glendale, AZ 85301
—Assistant Director: T. J. Titcomb
(602) 435-4063

California

*Amador / Alpine / Calveras County Victim / Witness Assistance
Program*
108 Court Street
Jackson, CA 95642
—Coordinators: Mark McCaffrey & Barbara Elben
Monday-Friday 8:30 a.m. to 5:00 p.m.: (209) 223-6474

Butte County Victim / Witness Assistance Program
170 E. 2nd Avenue, Suite 1
Chico, CA 95926
—Director: Janet Taylor
(916) 891-2812

Contra Costa District Attorney Victim / Witness Assistance Program
725 Court Street, Room 402
P.O. Box 670
Martinez, CA 94553-0150
—Program Coordinator: Stephanie Pete
(415) 372-4521

CSP Inc. Victim / Witness Assistance Program
County of Orange
700 Civic Center Drive West
Superior Court, P.O. Box 1994
Santa Ana, CA 92702
—Director: Kathryn A. Yarnall
(718) 834-7103

Del Norte Victim / Witness Assistance Center
Rural Human Services, Inc.
811 G Street
Crescent City, CA 95531
—Program Manager: Dennis Conger
(707) 464-7441

District Attorney's Victim / Witness Assistance Center
2 South Green Street
Sonora, CA 95370
—Coordinator: Deborah Cooper
(209) 533-5642

District Attorney's Victim / Witness Assistance Program
of Santa Barbara County
118 E. Figueroa
Santa Barbara, CA 93101
—Coordinator: Joan M. Selman
(805) 963-6155

Fresno County Victim / Witness Service Center
P.O. Box 453
8th Floor Courthouse
1100 Van Ness
Fresno, CA 93709
—Program Director: Rose Marie Gibbs
(209) 488-3425

Lake County Victim / Witness Assistance Division
c/o Lake County District Attorney

755 N. Forges Street
Lakeport, CA 95453
—Coordinator: Michael R. Blakey
(707) 263-2251

L.A. City Attorney Victims of Crime Program
808 North Spring Street, 4th Floor
Los Angeles, CA 90012
—Director: Alex Vargas
Monday-Friday, 8 a.m. to 5 p.m.: (213) 485-6976

Marin County Victim / Witness Assistance Program
Room 181, Hall of Justice
San Rafael, CA 94983
—Coordinator: Dyanne Bohner
Monday-Friday, 8:00 a.m. to 4:30 p.m.: (415) 499-6482

Mendocino County Victim / Witness Assistance
Mendocino County Courthouse, Room 10
Ukiah, CA 95482
—Coordinator: Elizabeth Anderson
(707) 463-4218

Napa Victim / Witness Services
1700 Second Street, Suite 308
Napa, CA 94558
—Coordinator: Gayle O'Kelley
(707) 252-6222

NCCJ Santa Clara County Victim / Witness Assistance Center
777 N. First Street, Mezzanine
San Jose, CA 95112
—Director: Joe Yomtov
(408) 295-2656

Placer County Victim / Witness
11563 B. Avenue
Dewitt Center

Auburn, CA 95603
—Coordinator: Linda Mitcham
8 a.m. to 5 p.m.: (916) 889-7020
Hotline, 24 hrs.: (916) 889-7800

Rape Crisis Center of West Contra Costa
2023 Vale Road, Suite 2
San Pablo, CA 94806
—Director: Gloria Sandoval
9 a.m. to 5 p.m.: (510) 237-0113

Rape Treatment Center—Santa Monica Hospital
1250 16th Street
Santa Monica, CA 90404
—Director: Gail Abarbanel
8 a.m. to 5 p.m.: (310) 319-4503

Sacramento County District Attorney's Victim / Witness Assistance Program
901 G Street
Sacramento, CA 95814
—Coordinator: Veronica G. Zecchini
(916) 440-5701

San Benito Victim / Witness Program
483 Fifth Street
Hollister, CA 95023
—Director: Cynthia Fahy
(408) 637-8244

San Luis Obispo County Victim / Witness Program
County Government Center
Room 121
San Luis Obispo, CA 93408
—Victim / Witness Supervisor: Gerald O. Young
(805) 549-5822

Solano County Victim / Witness Service Center
600 Union Avenue
Fairfield, CA 94533
—Program Administrator: Suzanne Perthes
Monday-Friday, 8 a.m. to 5 p.m.: (707) 421-6844

Sonoma County Victim / Witness Assistance Program
Probation Department
P.O. Box 11719
Santa Rosa, CA 95406
—Coordinator: Linda Poggi-Lestrange
(707) 527-2002

Sutter County Victim / Witness Assistance Program
Sutter County Probation Department
446 Second Street
Yuba City, CA 95991
—Probation Officer: Edward F. Eden
Monday-Friday, 8 a.m. to 5 p.m.: (916) 741-7345

Ventura County District Attorney's Victim / Witness Assistance Program
800 South Victoria Avenue
Ventura, CA 93009
—Program Manager: Richard Harris
(805) 654-3919

Victim Center of San Mateo County
2317 Broadway
Redwood City, Ca 94063
—Program Manager: Robert E. Mantynen
8 a.m. to 5 p.m.: (415) 363-4010

Victim / Witness Assistance Center
701 Ocean, Room 250
Santa Cruz, CA 95060
—Coordinator: Judith A. Osborn
(408) 425-2610

Victim / Witness Assistance Program
316 N. Mountain View
San Bernardino, CA 92415
—Coordinator: Joann Nunez
(714) 383-2942

Victim / Witness Assistance Program
850 Bryant Street, Room 322
San Francisco, CA 94103
—Director: Donna Medley
8 a.m. to 5 p.m.: (415) 553-9044

Victim / Witness Center
South Lake Tahoe Branch
Box 14506
South Lake Tahoe, CA 95702
—Coordinator: Ivone Basus
8 a.m. to 5 p.m.: (916) 573-3083

Yolo County Victim / Witness Assistance Center
P.O. Box 1247
Woodland, CA 95695
—Program Coordinator: Karen Sufrentes
Monday-Friday, 8 a.m. to 5 p.m.: (916) 666-8187

Yuba County Victim / Witness Assistance Program
938 14th Street
Marysville, CA 95901
—Coordinator: Sandy Fonley
8 a.m. to 5 p.m.: (916) 741-6725

Colorado

Boulder District Attorney's Victim / Witness Assistance Program
P.O. Box 471
Boulder, CO 80306
—Coordinator: Marti Kovenor
(303) 441-3730

1st Judicial District Attorney's Victim / Witness Assistance Unit
1620 Jackson Street
Golden, CO 80401
—Director: Ralynee Gattmann
(303) 277-8946

Victim Assistance Program
Arapohoe County Sheriff's Department
5686 S. Court Place
Littleton, CO 80120
—Coordinator: Barbara Alexander
(303) 795-4747
Hotline, 24 hrs.: (303) 795-4711

Victim / Witness Assistance Division
District Attorney's Office
P.O. Box 1489
Fort Collins, CO 80522
—Coordinator: Pamela Garman
(303) 221-7200

Victim / Witness Program
Office of the District Attorney
326 South Tejon
Colorado Springs, CO 80903
—Coordinator: Irene Kornelly
(303) 520-6049

Connecticut

Victim / Witness Program
Office of the State's Attorney
101 Lafayette Street
Hartford, CT 06106
—Victim Advocate: Charles Lexius
(203) 566-3190
or (203) 566-4787

Delaware

Victim / Witness Assistance Program
Department of Justice
820 N. French Street
Wilmington, DE 19801
—Director: Susan Baldwin
(302) 577-2599

District of Columbia

U.S. Attorney's Office
Victim / Witness Assistance Unit
District of Columbia Courthouse
500 Indiana Avenue, NW, Room 5201
Washington, DC 20001
—Chief: Anita B. Boles
(202) 727-0497

Florida

Alachua County Rape / Crime Victim Advocate Program
730 N. Waldo Road, Suite 100
Gainesville, FL 32606
—Director: Elizabeth Jones
(904) 375-2068

Dade County Advocates for Victims
1515 N.W. 7th Street, #213
Miami, FL 33125
—Director: Catherine G. Lynch
(305) 758-2546

Palm Beach County Victim / Witness Services
307 N. Dixie Highway, Suite 500
West Palm Beach, FL 33401
—Director: Robert C. Wells
(407) 837-2418

Seminole County Sheriff's Department Victim Services
1345 28th Street
Sanford, FL 32771
—Victim Services Coordinator: Deputy F. Pisano
(407) 322-5115

Sexual Assault Assistance Program
Office of the State Attorney
Post Office Drawer 4401
Ft. Pierce, FL 33450
—Director: Harriette Rowe
Hotline, 24 hrs.: (407) 465-1814

Victim Advocacy Program
Pinellas County Sheriff's Department
P.O. Box 2500
Largo, FL 34649
—Victim Advocate Coordinator: Laura Scott
(813) 587-6279

Victim Advocate Program
Orange County Sheriff's Office
3205-B W. Colonial Drive
Orlando, FL 32808
—Advocate: Denise Hassee
(407) 836-4020

Victim / Witness Assistance Program
P.O. Box 1068
Key West, FL 33040
—Director: Meg Bates
(305) 296-2027

Victim / Witness Assistance Program
S.A.O. 1351 NW 12th Street, 6th Floor
Miami, FL 33125
—Director: Denise M. Moon
(303) 547-7230

Victim / Witness Management Program
5100 144th Avenue
P.O. Box 5028
Clearwater, FL 33520
—Contact Person: Connie Mederos-Jacobs
(813) 530-6221

Georgia

Rape Crisis Network
1609 Newcastele Street
Brunswick, CA
—Coordinator: Constance Smith
(912) 267-0760, ext. 3109

Victim / Witness Assistance Program
133 Montgomery Street
Savannah, GA 31401
—Director: Helen Pitts
(912) 652-7329

Victim / Witness Assistance Unit
District Attorney's Office
Cubb Judicial Circuit
30 Waddell Street
Marietta, GA 30090-9646
—Director: Pamela Edds-West
(404) 528-3041

Hawaii

Kauai Victim / Witness Program
Office of the Prosecuting Attorney
4193 Hardy Street
Unit 4
Lihue, HI 96766
—Counselor: Jennifer Arashiro
(808) 245-5388

Victim / Witness Assistance Program Department
Office of the Prosecuting Attorney
200 S. High Street, Wailuku
Maui, HI 96793
—Coordinator: Dr. Brian K. Owaga
(808) 244-7799

Illinois

DuPage County State's Attorney's Center
for Victim / Witness Assistance
205 Reber Street
Wheaton, IL 60187
—Coordinator: Jean A. Tuzik
(708) 682-7759

Jackson County Victim / Witness Assistance
c/o State Attorney's Office
Murphysboro, IL 62966
—Victim / Witness Advocate: Mary Hughes
(618) 684-2155

Lake County State's Attorney's Office
Victim / Witness Assistance
18 N. County
Waukegan, IL 60085
—Contact Person: Ruth Rosengarden
(708) 360-6644

Indiana

Indianapolis Police Department Victim Assistance
50 North Alabama, E142
Indianapolis, IN 46204
—Supervisor: Judy Moore
(317) 236-3331

Marion County Prosecutor's Victim Assistance Program
560 City-County Building
Indianapolis, IN 46204
—Co-coordinators: Sallie Wills & Ruth Percell
(317) 684-6300

Victim Assistance
City-County Building
Ft. Wayne, IN 46802
—Director: Patricia Smallwood
(219) 427-1205

Iowa

Polk County Victim Services
Polk County Department of Social Services
1915 Hickman
Des Moines, Iowa 50312
—Manager: Sharon Thomas
(515) 288-1050
Hotline, 24 hrs.: (515) 288-1750

Kansas

Johnson County Victim / Witness Assistance
P.O. Box 728, 6th Floor Tower
Olathe, KS 66061
—Coordinator: Lynn Stemm
(913) 791-5237

Kentucky

Victim Advocacy / Office of the Attorney General
1049 US 127, South Building
Frankfort, KY 40601
—Director: Marcia Johnson
(502) 564-5904

Victim / Witness Assistance Program
919 College Street
Bowling Green, KY 42101
—Assistant Commonwealth Attorney (DA): John Deeb
(502) 843-5485

Victim / Witness Assistance Program
605 City-County Building
301 Court Street
Covington, KY 41011
—Victim Advocate: Chris Whyle
(606) 292-6580

Victim / Witness Assistance Program
Office of the Commonwealth's Attorney
P.O. Box 581
Eddyville, KY 42038
—Director, Prosecutorial Services: Gloria Stewart
(502) 388-7301

Maine

Cumberland County Victim / Witness Services
142 Federal Street
Portland, ME 04101
—Coordinator: Sandra Dodge
(207) 871-8384

District Attorney's Office Victim / Witness Services
97 Hammond Street
Bangor, ME 04401
—Coordinator: Julie Morse
(207) 942-8552

Somerset County Victim / Witness Advocate
Somerset County Courthouse
Court Street
Skowhegan, ME 04976

—Victim / Witness Advocate: Mary Farrar
(207) 474-2423
or (207) 474-5517

Maryland

Baltimore County Victim / Witness Unit
State Attorney's Office
401 Bosley Avenue, 5th Floor
Towson, MD 21204
—Director: Sandra B. Stolker
(301) 887-6650

Victim / Witness Assistance Center (V-WAC)
101 South Street
Office of the State's Attorney for Anne Archdel County
Annapolis, MD 21401
—Director: Robin Davenport
(301) 224-1160

Victim / Witness Assistance Program
State Attorney's Office
100 W. Patrick
P.O. Box 210
Frederick, MD 21701
—Coordinator: Shelby Lowry
(301) 694-1523

Victim / Witness Assistance Unit
State Attorney's Office for Baltimore City
Clarence Mitchell Courthouse, Room 410
110 N. Clavert Street
Baltimore, MD 21202
—Director: Pam Widgeon
(301) 396-1897

Victim / Witness Assistance Unit
P.G. County State's Attorney's Office

Courthouse 3rd Floor—Marbury Wing
Upper Marlboro, MD 20772
—Contact Person: Sondra Ricks
(301) 952-2703

Massachusetts

Essex County Victim / Witness Assistance
70 Washington Street
Salem, MA 10971
—Director: Michaelene O'Neil McCann
(508) 745-6610

Hampden County District Attorney's Victim / Witness Program
50 State Street
Springfield, MA 01103
—Director: Maria Rodriguez
(413) 781-8100, ext. 2026

Middlesex County District Attorney's Office
Victim / Witness Services Bureau
40 Thorndike Street
Cambridge, MA 02141
—Chief: Jeff Ryan
(617) 494-4604

Michigan

Calhoun County Victim / Witness Assistance Unit
180 E. Michigan Avenue
Battle Creek, MI 49107
—Director: Steven Barver
(616) 966-1265

Kalamazoo County Victim / Witness Assistance Service
227 West Michigan Avenue, #312
Kalamazoo, MI 49007

—Director of Staff Services: Karen M. Hayter
(616) 383-8677

Victim / Witness Services Unit
Room 307, Hall of Justice
Kent County Prosecutor's Office
333 Monroe Avenue, NW
Grand Rapids, MI 49503
—Director: Susan Heartwell
(616) 774-6822

Washtenaw County Prosecuting Attorney—Victim / Witness Unit
P.O. Box 8645
Ann Arbor, MI 48107
—Coordinator: Marsha Bidwell
(313) 996-3026
or (313) 994-2380

Minnesota

Minnesota Citizens' Council Victims Services
822 South Third Street, Suite 100
Minneapolis, MN 55415
—Program Director: Kathleen Alme
(612) 340-5432

St. Louis Victim / Witness Assistance
St. Louis County Attorney's Office
501 Courthouse
Duluth, MN 55802
—Director: Paul A. Gustad
(218) 726-2323

Missouri

Circuit Attorney's Victim Services
1320 Market Street, Room 222
St. Louis, MO 63103

—Project Director: Julie Swanston
(314) 622-4373

Montana

Crime Victims Unit
Box 4659
Helena, MT 59601
—Administrative Officer: Cheryl Bryant
(406) 444-3653

Nebraska

Victim / Witness Unit
Lincoln Police Department
233 South 10th Street
Lincoln, NE 68508
—Administrator: Joan Shlobota
(402) 471-7181

Nevada

Clark County District Attorney's Victim / Witness Services Center
200 S. Third Street
Las Vegas, NV 89155
—Administrative Assistant: Cheryl Gosnell
(702) 455-4204

New Hampshire

Victim / Witness Assistance Program
Hillsborough County Attorney's Office
300 Chestnut Street
Manchester, NH 03101
—Director: Catherine McNaughton
(603) 627-5605

New Jersey

Atlantic County Prosecutor's Office Victim / Witness Unit
19th Avenue at Route 40
Mays Landing, NJ
—Detective Sgt.: Edward Armstrong
(609) 645-7000

Camden County Victim / Witness Service
518 Market Street, 4th Floor
Camden, NJ 08102
—Coordinator: Linda Burkett
(609) 757-8462

Essex County Prosecutor's Victim / Witness Assistance Program
Essex County Courts Building
Essex County Prosecutor's Office
Newark, NJ 07102
—Director: Pamela McCauley-Puchel
(201) 621-4707

Mercer County Prosecutor's Office Victim / Witness Unit
Mercer County Courthouse
P.O. Box 8068
Trenton, NJ 08650
—Coordinator: Mary Effie Raney
(609) 989-6428

Salem County Prosecutor's Office Victim / Witness Unit
87 Market Street
Salem, NJ 08079
—Co-coordinator: Stacey Brainard
(609) 935-7510, ext. 430

Sussex County Prosecutor's Office
Victim / Witness Assistance Program
19-21 High Street
Newton, NJ 07860

—Coordinator: Linda Kuipers
(201) 383-1570

Victim / Witness Assistance Program—Cape May County
Prosecutor's Office
Cape May Courthouse
Cape May, NJ 08210
—County Investigator and Coordinator: Debra Luprette
(609) 465-1135

Victim / Witness Assistance Unit
Bergen County Prosecutor's Office
County Courthouse
Hackensack, NJ 07601
—Coordinator: Arlene Liboser
(201) 646-2057

Victim / Witness Assistance Unit
Middlesex County Prosecutor's Office
P.O. Box 71
New Brunswick, NJ 08903-0071
—Coordinator: Jayne Guarino
(908) 745-3394

Victim / Witness Unit
Gloucester County Prosecutor's Office
Box 623
Woodbury, NJ 08096
—Coordinator: Barbara Carter
(609) 853-3701

New Mexico

Victim / Witness Impact Program
District Attorney's Office
111 Union Square S.E.
Albuquerque, NM 87102

—Contact Person: Sandra Clinton
(505) 841-7100

New York

Crime Victim Assistant Unit
Bronx District Attorney's Office
215 E. 161st Street
Bronx, NY 10451
—Executive Assistant District Attorney: Richard Mangum
(212) 590-2168

Dutchess County Crime Victims Assistance
St. Francis Hospital
North Road
Poughkeepsie, NY 12601
—Director: Jean Craven
(914) 431-8808

Erie County District Attorney's Office
Victim / Witness Assistance Program
City Court Building
50 Delaware Avenue, Suite 350
Buffalo, NY 14202
—Coordinator: Jeffery Ricketts
(716) 855-6860

Monroe County District Attorney's Victim / Witness Center
201 Hall of Justice
Rochester, NY 14614
—Coordinator: Carol Mulhern
(716) 428-5704

Nassau County Crime Victim / Witness Service
320 Old Country Road
Garden City, NJ 11530
—Coordinator: Patricia Chave
(516) 535-3500

Northwest Buffalo Community Center Victim / Witness Program
155 Lawn Avenue
Buffalo, NY 14207
—Director: Martha Dippel
(716) 876-8108

Rockland County Crime Victim / Witness Assistance Bureau
District Attorney's Office
County Office Building
11 Hempstead Road
New City, NY 10956
—Victim / Witness Aide: Susan Edelman
(914) 638-5001

Victim Assistance Services
3 Carhart Avenue
White Plains, NY 10607
—Director: Toni Downes, C.S.W.
(914) 684-6871
Hotline, 24 hrs.: (914) 684-9877

Victim Assistance Unit
Rochester Police
150 South Plymouth Avenue
Rochester, NY 14614
—Senior Victim Service Worker: Patricia Huntington-Siegel
(716) 428-6630

Victim Hotline
Victim Services Agency
2 Lafayette Street
New York, NY 10007
—Executive Director: Dr. Lucy Friedman
(212) 577-7777
Administrative offices: (212) 577-7700

North Carolina

Turning Point: Victim Assistance
1301 N. Elm Street
Greensboro, NC 27401
—Supervisor: Catherine Shaw
(919) 373-1121

Victim Assistance / Rape Crisis Program
825 East 4th Street, #205
Charlotte, NC 28202
—Director: Annette Morrison
(704) 336-2190

Ohio

Victim Services Division
Hamilton County Probation Department
Hamilton County Courthouse, Room 153
1100 Main Street
Cincinnati, OH 45202
—Director: Nancy Rankin
(513) 632-8794

Victim Assistance Program
P.O. Box 962
116 W. North Street
Lima, OH 45801-4311
—Director: David Voth
(419) 222-8666

Victim / Witness Assistance Program
Franklin County Prosecuting Attorney's Office
369 High Street
Columbus, OH 43215
—Victim / Witness Assistants: Connie Scott or Jane Freeman
(614) 462-3555

Victim / Witness Division
Greene County Prosecutor's Office
45 N. Detroit Street
Xenia, OH 45385
—Director: Jeannette M. Adkins
(513) 376-5087

Victim / Witness Division
Montgomery County Prosecutor's Office
41 N. Perry Street, Room 315
Dayton, OH 45402
—Advocate: Rhonda Barner
(513) 225-5623

Victim / Witness Division
Stark County Prosecuting Attorney's Office
P.O. Box 20049
Canton, OH 44701
—Director: Pamela Goddard
(216) 438-0888

Victim / Witness Program—Lucas County Courthouse
Lucas County Prosecutor's Office
3rd Floor
Toledo, OH 43624
—Executive Director: Joanne Coleman
(419) 245-4726

Oklahoma

Cleveland County District Attorney's Office
Victim / Witness Center
210 S. Jones
Norman, OK 73069
—Cordinator: Linda Keener
(405) 321-8268

District Attorney's Victim / Witness Program
P.O. Box 428
Magnum, OK 73554
—Victim / Witness Coordinator: Linda Fletcher
(405) 782-5069

Oregon

Curry County Victim Assistance Program
Box 746
c/o District Attorney
Gold Beach, OR 97444
—Coordinator: Barbara Eells
(503) 247-7921, -7018, -7642

Marion County Victim / Witness Assistance
495 State Street, #201
Salem, OR 97301
—Manager, Rebecca Ewing
(503) 588-5222

Multnomah County Victims Assistance
1021 S.W. 4th Avenue
Room 804
Portland, OR 97204
—Director: Douglass Beloof
(503) 248-3222

Polk County Victim / Witness Assistance Program
Courthouse
Dallas, OR 97338
—Director: Ida Delotell
(503) 623-9268

Victim / Witness Assistance of Yamhill County
County Courthouse
McMinnville, OR 97128

—Coordinator: Mary Ellen Johnson
(503) 472-9371

Victim / Witness Program—District Attorney's Office
County Courthouse
Bend, OR 97701
—Director: Marie Williams
(503) 388-6525

Washington County Victim / Witness Assistance
150 N. First, 3rd Floor
Hillsboro, OR 97124
—Director: Eileen Spencer
(503) 648-8698

Pennsylvania

Center for Victims of Violent Crimes
1520 Penn Avenue
Pittsburgh, PA 15222
—Director: Nancy E. Wells
(412) 392-8582

The Crime Victims Center of Chester County
236 West Market Street
West Chester, PA 19382
—Executive Director: Peggy Gusz
(215) 692-7420

Victims Resource Center
68 S. Franklin Street
Wilkes-Barre, PA 18702
—Director: Carol L. Lavery
(717) 823-0765

Victim / Witness Assistance Program
Office of the District Attorney

Media Courthouse
Front and Orange Street
Media, PA 19063
—Contact Person: John A. Dowd
(215) 891-4227

Women's Services, Inc.
Victim Support Services
P.O. Box 637
Meadville, PA 16335
—Executive Director: Judith A. Griffin
(814) 724-4637

Rhode Island

Rhode Island Department of the Attorney General
Victim / Witness program
72 Pine Street
Providence, RI 02903
—Director: Elaine Rendine
(401) 274-4400

South Carolina

Victim / Witness Assistance
Box 4046
Anderson, SC 29622
—Advocate: Doris Brown
(803) 260-4288

Victim / Witness Assistance Program
Room 318
Greenville County Courthouse
Greenville, SC 29601
—Director: Marsha Barker
(803) 298-8647

Tennessee

Victim / Witness Services
Room 101, Metropolitan Courthouse
Office of the District Attorney General
Nashville, TN 37201
—Director: Jody Schwartz
(615) 862-5549

Victim / Witness Unit of the Attorney General's Office
201 Poplar, Suite 201
Memphis, TN 38103
—Director: Kenneth E. Blackburn
(901) 576-5914

Texas

*Harris County District Attorney's Office Victim /
Witness Assistance Program*
201 Fannin, Suite 200
Houston, TX 77002
—Director: Gail O'Brien
(713) 755-6655

Houston Police Department Crisis Team
61 Riesner
Houston, TX 77066
—Supervisor: Margaret L. Hardman-Muye, M.S.W., C.S.W.-
A.C.P.
(713) 247-1000

Utah

Salt Lake City Attorney's Victim Services
231 East 400 South, 4th Floor
Salt Lake City, UT 84111
—Contact Person: Julie Branch
(801) 363-7900

Victim / Witness
Court Advocates for Abused Children
Weber County Attorney's Office
Municipal Building, 7th Floor
Ogden, UT 84401
—Supervisor: Sherry Venderheide
(801) 399-8762

Virginia

Alexandria Victim / Witness Program
520 King Street, Room 301
Alexandria, VA 22305
—Director: Jenny Cofcia
(703) 838-4100

Fairfax County Victim Assistance Network
8119 Holland Road
Alexandria, VA 22306
—Coordinator: Anne Vanryzin
(703) 360-6910

Victim / Witness Assistance Program
Elderly Victim Assistance Program
P.O. Box 15125
Chesapeake, VA 23320
—Victim / Witness Coordinator: Joyce Walsh
(804) 547-6417

Victim / Witness Assistance Program
Roanoke's Commonwealth Attorney's office
315 W. Church Avenue, S.W.
Roanoke, VA 24016
—Director: Mary Anne Myers
(703) 981-2683

Victim / Witness Program
County of Loudoun

20 E. Market Street
Leesburg, VA 22075
—Director: Irene Wodell
(703) 777-0417

Victim / Witness Program
Commonwealth's Attorney's Office
P.O. Box 1417
Portsmouth, VA 23705
—Victim / Witness Coordinator: Theresa J. Saunders
(804) 393-8581

Washington

Clark County Prosecuting Attorney's Victim / Witness Unit
1101 Harney Street
Vancouver, WA 98660
—Supervisor: Amy Kendis
(206) 699-2008

Lewis County Victim / Witness Program
P.O. Box 918
Courthouse Annex
Chehalis, WA 98532
—Director: John Stoner
(206) 748-9121

Pacific County Victim / Witness Program
P.O. Box 45
Pacific County Courthouse
South Bend, WA 98596
—Coordinator: Beth Kitselman
(206) 268-0891

Victim / Witness Assistance
Prosecuting Attorney's Office
Benton County
7320 West Quinault

Kennewick, WA 99336
—Coordinator: Elaine Osbourne
(509) 735-3591

Victim / Witness Assistance Service
1033 County-City Building
Tacoma, WA 98406
—Director: Eileen O'Brien
(206) 591-7447

Victim / Witness Assistance Unit
Room 329 Courthouse
Yakima, WA 98901
—Administrator: Robyn R. Cyr
(509) 575-4141

Victim / Witness Unit
County-City Public Safety Building
West 1100 Mallon Avenue
Spokane, WA 99260-0270
—Director / Coordinator: Dorothy M. Scott
(509) 456-3646

Wisconsin

Jackson County Victim / Witness Assistance
307 Main Street
Black River Falls, WI 54615
—Coordinator: Hazel Miles
(715) 284-0242

Kenosha County District Attorney's Office
Victim / Witness Services
912 56th Street, Room 312
Kenosha, WI 53410
—Coordinator: Lynn M. Copen
(414) 653-6480

Manitowoc County Victim / Witness Assistance
District Attorney's Office
1010 South 8th Street
Manitowoc, WI 54220
—Victim / Witness Coordinator: Brenda Guse
(414) 683-4074

Marathon County Victim / Witness Assistance Program
Marathon County Courthouse
500 Forest Street
Wausa, WI 54401
—Coordinator: Bill Cerny
(715) 847-5555

Outagamie County Victim / Witness Assistance
401 S. Walnut Street
Appleton, WI 54911
—Director: Katherine Woerishofer
(414) 832-5024

Pierce County Victim / Witness Assistance
Pierce County Courthouse
Ellsworth, WI 54011
—Coordinator: Julie McCain
(715) 273-3531

Portage County Victim / Witness Assistance Program
1516 Church Street
Stevens Point, WI 54481
—Coordinator: Sally Haas
(715) 346-1300

Racine County Victim / Witness Assistance Program
Racine County District Attorney's Office
730 Washington Avenue
Racine, WI 53403
(414) 636-3889
Hotline (WI only): 1-800-924-1506

St. Croix County Victim / Witness Assistance Program
911 4th Street
Hudson, WI 54016
—Coordinator: Ann Gustafson
(715) 386-4666

Victim / Witness Assistance
Fond Du Lac County District Attorney's Office
160 South Macy Street
Fond Du Lac, WI 54935
—Coordinator: Penny Werner
(414) 929-3050

Victim / Witness Assistance Program
125 South Adams Street
Green Bay, WI 54301
—Coordinator: Karen H. Doran
(414) 448-4194

Victim / Witness Assistance Program
P.O. Box 7951
222 State Street
Madison, WI 53707-7951
—Contact Person: Christine Nolan
(608) 266-6470

Victim / Witness Assistance Program
District Attorney's Office
Oconto County Courthouse
Oconto, WI 54153
—District Attorney: Jay Conley
(414) 834-5322

Victim / Witness Assistance Program
Oneida County
P.O. Box 400
Rhinelander, WI 54501

—Director: Bonnie Wilcox
(715) 369-6133

Victim / Witness Assistance Program
District Attorney's Office
615 N. 6th
Sheboygan, WI 53081
—Coordinator: Kathy Huffman
(414) 459-3040

Victim / Witness Assistance Program
1313 Belknap Street
Superior, WI 54880
—Specialist: Darlene Olson
(715) 394-0349

Victim / Witness Services
Room 612 Safety Building
821 West State Street
Milwaukee, WI 53233
—Coordinator: Jo Rolanda
(414) 278-4659

Victim / Witness Unit
Dane County District Attorney
Room 305
210 Monona Avenue
Madison, WI 53709
—Director: Gillian Lawrence
(608) 266-4211

Waukesha County Victim / Witness Assistance Program
Room G-90
515 Moreland Boulevard
Waukesha, WI 53188
—Coordinator: Gerry Wuerslin
(414) 548-7071

Wyoming

Victim / Witness Assistance
200 N. Center Courthouse, Room 300
Casper, WY 82601
—Director: Nancy Johnson
(307) 235-9335

Hotlines for Battered Women and Their Children

Alabama

Domestic Abuse Shelter
Montgomery, AL 36101
(205) 263-0063

Alaska

Abused Women's Aid in Crisis, Inc.
Anchorage, AK 99501
(907) 272-0100

Women in Crisis
Fairbanks, AK 99701
(907) 452-RAPE

Arizona

Sojourner Center
Phoenix, AZ 85002
(602) 258-5344

Arkansas

Advocates for Battered Women
Little Rock, AR 72203
(501) 376-3219

California

Chicano Service Action Center
Los Angeles, CA 90063
(213) 268-7564

A Safe Place
Oakland, CA 94604
(510) 536-7233

Sexual Assault and Domestic Violence Center
Davis, CA 95616
(916) 371-1907

Shelter Services for Women, Inc.
Santa Barbara, CA 93102
(805) 964-5245

Weave, Inc.
Sacramento, CA 95816
(916) 920-2952

YWCA Battered Women's Services
San Diego, CA 92104
(619) 234-3164

YWCA Womenshelter
Long Beach, CA 90813
(213) 437-4663

Colorado

Boulder County Safehouse
Boulder, CO 80302
(303) 449-8623

Safehouse for Battered Women
Denver, CO 80218
(303) 830-8181

Connecticut

Hartford Interval House
Hartford, CT 06106
(203) 527-0550

Susan B. Anthony Project for Women
Torrington, CT 06790
(203) 482-7133

Women's Crisis Center
South Norwalk, CT 06856
(203) 852-1980

Delaware

Child, Inc.
Wilmington, DE 19801
(302) 762-6110, -6111

District of Columbia

Her Sister's Place
Washington, D.C. 20017
(202) 529-5991

House of Ruth—"Herspace"
Washington, D.C. 20002
(202) 347-2777

Florida

Hubbard House
Jacksonville, FL 32202
(904) 354-3114

Refuge House, Inc.
Tallahassee, FL 32315
(904) 681-2111

Safespace—Dade County Advocates for Victims
Miami, FL 33137
(305) 579-2915

Spouse Abuse, Inc.
Orlando, FL 32853
(407) 886-2856

Women in Distress of Broward County, Inc.
Ft. Lauderdale, FL 33302
(305) 761-1133

Georgia

Columbus Alliance for Battered Women
Columbus, GA
(404) 324-3850

Council on Battered Women
Atlanta, GA 30307
(404) 873-1766

S.A.F.E. Shelter, Inc.
Savannah, GA 31403
(912) 234-9999

YWCA Safe Homes Program
Augusta, GA 30903
(404) 826-4500

Hawaii

Child and Family Service Shelter
for Abused Spouses and Children
Honolulu, HI 96817
(808) 841-0822

Military Family Abuse Shelter
Honolulu, HI 96804
(808) 533-7125

Idaho

YWCA Women's Crisis Center
Boise, ID 83707
(208) 343-7025

Illinois

Chicago Abused Woman Coalition / Greenhouse Shelter
Chicago, IL 60647
(312) 278-4586

Dove Domestic Violence Program
Decatur, IL 62523
(217) 423-2238

Evanston Shelter for Battered Women
Evanston, IL 60204
(708) 864-8780

Rainbow House / Arco Iris
Chicago, IL 60629
(312) 521-4865

Sojourn Women's Center
Springfield, IL 62705
(217) 544-2484

Tri-County Women Strength
Peoria, IL 61614
(309) 691-4111
or 1-800-555-SAFE

Indiana

The Salvation Army Family Service Center
Indianapolis, IN 46204
(317) 637-5551

Sojourner / Julian Center
Indianapolis, IN 46208
(317) 251-7575

YWCA Women's Shelters
South Bend, IN 466601
(219) 232-9558

Iowa

Family Violence Center
Des Moines, IA 50309
(515) 243-6147
(Iowa only): 1-800-942-0333

Kansas

Rebeca Vincson Center
Kansas City, KS 66117
(913) 321-0951

YWCA Women's Crisis Center
Wichita, KS 67201
(316) 263-9806

Kentucky

Center for Women and Families
Louisville, KY 40202
(502) 581-7222

Louisiana

YWCA Battered Women's Program
New Orleans, LA 70119
(504) 486-0377

Maryland

Abused Persons Program
Montgomery County DAVMH Services
Bethesda, MD 20814
(301) 654-1881

Family Crisis Shelter
Baltimore, MD 21222
(410) 285-4357

Massachusetts

Battered Women's Hotline
Cambridge, MA 02138
(617) 661-7203

New Bedford Women's Center / Battered Women's Project
New Bedford, MA 02740
(508) 992-4222
Rape crisis: (508) 996-6656

New Beginnings
Westfield, MA 01086
(413) 562-1920

Michigan

Domestic Violence Project / S.A.F.E. House
Ann Arbor, MI 48107
(313) 995-5444

Interim House
Detroit, MI 48107
(313) 861-5300

YWCA Domestic Crisis Center
Grand Rapids, MI 49503
(616) 774-3535

Minnesota

Harriet Tubman Women's Shelter
Minneapolis, MN 55407
(612) 827-2841

Metro Crisis Line
Minneapolis, MN 55404
(612) 646-0994

Women's Advocate
St. Paul, MN 55102
(612) 227-8284

Mississippi

Shelter for Battered Families
Jackson, MS 39205
(601) 366-0222

Missouri

Catholic Charities Dial Help
St. Louis, MO 63108
(314) 371-4357

Rose Brooks Center
Kansas City, MO 64110
(816) 861-6100

Nebraska

Domestic Violence Services
Omaha, NE 68104
(402) 588-5700

Nevada

Temporary Assistance for Domestic Crisis
Domestic Crisis Shelter
Las Vegas, NV 89116
(702) 646-4981

New Hampshire

A Safe Place
Portsmouth, NH 03801
1-800-852-3311
or (603) 436-7924

New Jersey

Jersey Battered Women's Services
Morristown, NJ 07960
(201) 267-4763

The Safe House
Clara Maas Medical Center
Bloomfield, NJ 07003
(201) 759-2154

Shelter Our Sisters
Hackensack, NJ 07602
(201) 944-9600

Womanspace
Lawrenceville, NJ 08648
(609) 394-9000

New Mexico

Women's Community Association
Albuquerque, NM 87103
(505) 247-4219

New York

Alternatives for Battered Women
Rochester, NY 14526
(716) 232-7353

Center for the Elimination of Violence in the Family
Brooklyn, NY 11220
(718) 439-7281

Haven House
Buffalo, NY 14201
(716) 884-6000

Long Island Women's Coalition
Suffolk County, NY
(516) 666-8833

Rockland Family Shelter
Spring Valley, NY 10977
(914) 425-0112

Vera House
Syracuse, NY 13209
(315) 468-3260

Victim Services Hotline
New York, NY 10007
(212) 577-7777

North Carolina

Interact
Raleigh, NC 27604
(919) 828-7740
Hotline, 24 hrs. (rape and sexual assault): (919) 828-3005

North Dakota

Domestic Violence and Rape Crisis Center
Dickinson, ND 58601
(701) 225-4506

Ohio

Battered Women's Shelter
Akron, OH 44305
(216) 374-1111

Choices
Columbus, OH 43206
(614) 224-4663

YWCA—Alice Paul House
Cincinnati, OH 45202
(513) 241-2757

Oklahoma

Women's Resource Center
Norman, OK 73070
(405) 360-0590

YWCA Crisis Intervention Services
Oklahoma City, OK 73102
(405) 947-4506
Rape crisis line: (405) 943-7273

Oregon

Bradley-Angle House, Inc.
Portland, OR 97214
(503) 281-2442

Mid Valley Women's Crisis Service
Salem, OR 97308
(503) 399-7722

Pennsylvania

Domestic Abuse Project of Delaware County, Inc.
Media, PA 19063
(215) 565-4590

Shelter for Abused Women
Lancaster, PA 17603
(717) 299-1249

Women Against Abuse
Philadelphia, PA 19101
(215) 386-7777

Women's Center Shelter of Greater Pittsburgh
Pittsburgh, PA 15224
(412) 687-8005

Rhode Island

Women's Center
Providence, RI 02906
(401) 861-2760

South Carolina

CASA (Citizens Against Spouse Abuse)
Myrtle Beach, SC 29407
(803) 448-6206

South Dakota

Women Against Violence
Rapid City, SD 57709
(605) 341-4808

Tennessee

Family and Children's Services
Chattanooga, TN 37403
(615) 755-2700

YWCA Shelter and Domestic Violence Program
Nashville, TN 37215
(615) 297-8833

Texas

Center for Battered Women
Austin, TX 78760
(512) 385-0620

East Texas Crisis Center
Tyler, TX 75701
(903) 595-5591

Episcopal / Presbyterian Woman's Shelter
Dallas, TX 75208
(214) 942-2998

Shelter for Abused Women and Their Children
Houston, TX 77006
(713) 520-6793

Women's Resource and Crisis Center
Galveston, TX 77550
(409) 763-5605
or (713) 332-HELP

Utah

YWCA of Salt lake City
Salt Lake City, UT 84111
(801) 355-2804

Vermont

Women Helping Battered Women
Burlington, VT 05402
(802) 658-1996

Virginia

Alexandria Women's Shelter
Alexandria, VA 22301
(703) 838-4911

YWCA—Women's Advocacy Program
Chesterfield, VA 23803
(804) 796-3066

YWCA—Women's Advocacy Program
Richmond, VA 23219
(804) 643-0888

Washington

Catherine Booth House
Seattle, WA 98102
(206) 324-7271

Recovery: Aid to Victims of Sexual and Domestic Abuse
Shelton, WA 98584
1-800-562-6025
or (206) 426-5878

YWCA Women's Support Shelter
Tacoma, WA 98402
(206) 383-2593

West Virginia

Rape and Domestic Violence Information Center, Inc.
Morgantown, WV 26505
(304) 292-5100

Wisconsin

Dane County Advocates for Battered Women
Madison, WI 53701
(608) 251-4445

Sojourner Truth House
Milwaukee, WI 53208
(414) 933-2722

Wyoming

Self Help Center
Casper, WY 82601
(307) 235-2814

About the Editor

Albert R. Roberts, D. S. W., is a Professor of Criminal Justice and Social Work at the School of Social Work, Rutgers University, New Brunswick, New Jersey. He previously taught at the Indiana University School of Social Work in Indianapolis, Seton Hall University, the University of New Haven, and Brooklyn College of the City University of New York. He received his doctorate in social work from the University of Maryland School of Social Work with a concentration in social work research and a minor in criminal justice. His M.A. degree is in sociology and criminology and was obtained from Long Island University.

He is a lifetime member of the Academy of Criminal Justice Sciences and an active member of N.A.S.W., C. S. W. E., and the National Council of Juvenile and Family Court Judges. He is a member of the NJ Governor's Juvenile Justice and Delinquency Prevention Commission, as well as the New Jersey Supreme Court's Probation Advisory Board. Dr. Roberts has extensive experience in juvenile and criminal justice research. Over the past two decades, he has served as Project Director or consultant on several research and evaluation projects including: the New Jersey State Law Enforcement Planning Agency's Evaluation Projects, Research for Better Schools, Inc., (Philadelphia) Correctional Education Project, the American Correctional Association's National Study on the Utilization of Instructional Technology in Corrections, and the National Institute of Justice (N.I.J.) funded study on the Effectiveness of Crisis Intervention with Crime Victims at Victim Services Agency in New York City.

He is the founder and current Editor of the 25 volume, *Series on Social Work*, and he serves on the editorial board of *The Justice Professional* and is the Editor-in-Chief of the journal *Crisis Intervention and Time-Limited Treatment*. He has also authored and edited 15 books, including *Helping Crime Victims* (1990), *Crisis Intervention Handbook* (1990), *Critical Issues in Crime and Justice* (1994), *Visions for Change* (with Roslyn Muraskin, 1996), and *Helping Battered Women* (1996). He has more than 90 publications to his credit. In the spring of 1995 he was appointed to the Advisory Board of the newly formed National Victim Assistance Training Academy of the U.S. Department of Justice.

About the Contributors

Ann A. Abbott, Ph.D., Associate Professor and Associate Dean, Rutgers University School of Social Work, Camden Campus, NJ; President, N.A.S.W. (1993-1995).

Grace H. Christ, D.S.W., Assistant Professor, Columbia University School of Social Work, New York, NY; Editor-in-Chief, *Journal of Oncology Social Work.*

Elaine P. Congress, D.S.W., Associate Professor and Director, Doctoral Program, Fordham University at Lincoln Center, Graduate School of Social Services, New York, NY; Associate Editor, *Crisis Intervention and Time-Limited Treatment* Journal.

Sophia F. Dziegielewski, Ph.D., Associate Professor, University of Alabama, School of Social Work, Tuscalosa, AL.

Eric Finn, M.A., Ph.D. Candidate, Department of Clinical Psychology, Teachers College Columbia University, New York, NY.

Les Gallo-Silver, M.S.W., Medical Social Worker, Department of Social Work, Memorial-Sloan Kettering Medical Center, New York, NY.

Anne L. Horton, Ph.D., Associate Professor, Brigham Young University, School of Social Work, Provo, UT.

Bruce S. Liese, Ph.D., Associate Professor, University of Kansas Medical Center, Department of Family Medicine, Kansas City, KS; Director, Kansas City Center for Cognitive Therapy.

Mindy B. Mechanic, Ph.D., Research Psychologist, Department of Psychology, University of Missouri, St. Louis, MO.

Rosemary T. Moynihan, M.S.W., Director, Social Work Department, St. Joseph's Medical Center, Patterson, NJ.

Patricia A. Resick, Ph.D., Professor, Department of Psychology, University of Missouri, ST. Louis, MO.

Albert R. Roberts, D.S.W., Professor, Rutgers, The State University of New Jersey, School of Social Work, Brunswick, NJ; Editor-in-Chief, *Crisis Intervention and Time-Limited Treatment* Journal.

Thomas Strentz, Ph.D., Partner, Academy Associates, Manassis, VA; F.B.I. Training Academy (Retired).

Judith Waters, Ph.D., Professor and Director of M.A. Program in Psychology: Substance Abuse and Addiction Studies, Fairleigh Dickinson University, Madison, NJ.

Marlene A. Young, J.D., Ph.D., Executive Director, National Organization for Victim Assistance, Washington, DC.